(Cooty)

Reminiscing

No. 3. 10 Staves (Medium)

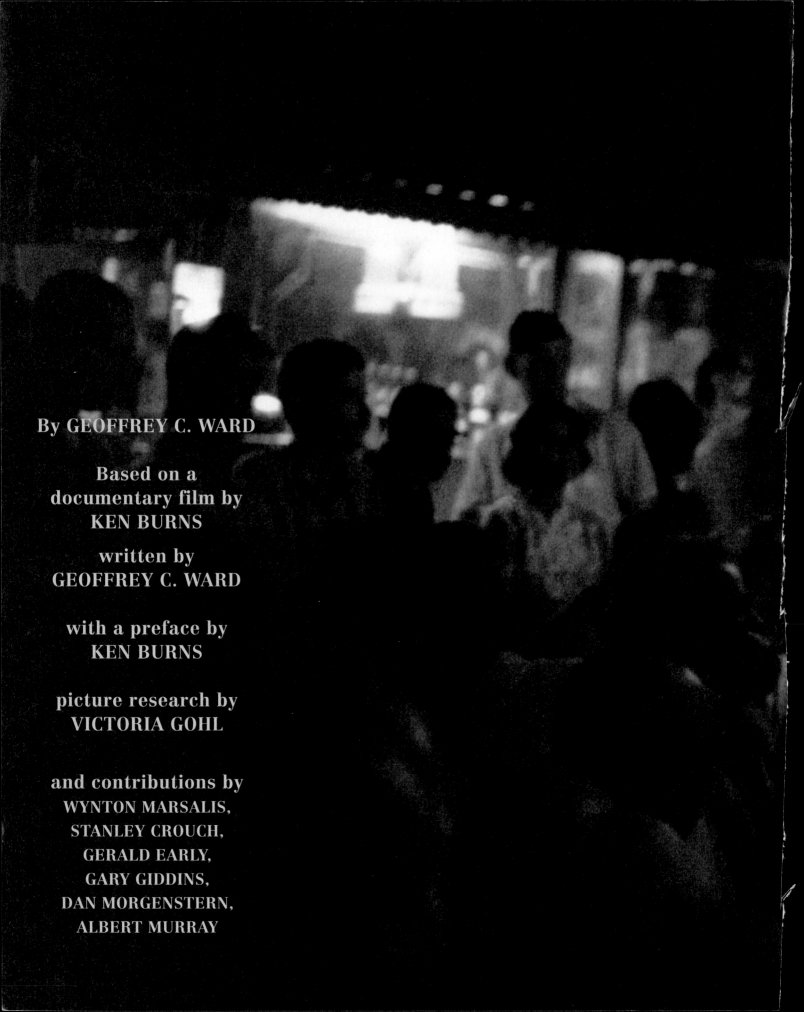

By GEOFFREY C. WARD

Based on a
documentary film by
KEN BURNS

written by
GEOFFREY C. WARD

with a preface by
KEN BURNS

picture research by
VICTORIA GOHL

and contributions by
WYNTON MARSALIS,
STANLEY CROUCH,
GERALD EARLY,
GARY GIDDINS,
DAN MORGENSTERN,
ALBERT MURRAY

JAZZ

A HISTORY OF
AMERICA'S MUSIC

ALFRED A. KNOPF
2000

This Is a Borzoi Book
Published by Alfred A. Knopf

Owing to a limitation of space, all acknowledgments
for permission to reprint previously published
material can be found on pages 487–8.

Library of Congress Cataloging-in-Publication Data
Ward, Geoffrey C.
      Jazz: a history of America's music / by Geoffrey
   C. Ward ; based on a documentary film by Ken
   Burns written by Geoffrey C. Ward ; with a preface
   by Ken Burns.
         p.   cm.
      Includes bibliographical references and
      indexes.
      ISBN 0-679-44551-X
      1. Jazz—History and criticism. 2. Jazz—
   Pictorial works. I. Burns, Ken

ML3506.W37 2000
781.65'09—dc21
                              00-022604

Manufactured in the United States of America

First Edition

Front and back endpapers:
Fifty-second Street

Preceding pages:
Cootie Williams's trumpet part from Duke Ellington's
    "Reminiscing in Tempo," written in the composer's
    hand, 1935
Manhattan jazz club interior, about 1960
The Ornette Coleman Quartet, 1959: Coleman,
    Don Cherry, Billy Higgins (partially obscured),
    Charlie Haden

Following pages:
Louis Armstrong
Apollo Theater marquee, Harlem, about 1934
Frank Trumbauer
Billie Holiday
Duke Ellington
The hands of Art Tatum
Charlie Parker
Miles Davis
Dave Brubeck (foreground) and Paul Desmond
Benny Goodman
Dancers at Harlem's Savoy Ballroom, moving to a ballad
    played by the Lucky Millinder Orchestra, 1942

OUR ART

Put it this way. Jazz is a good barometer of freedom. . . .
In its beginnings, the United States of America spawned
certain ideals of freedom and independence through
which, eventually, jazz was evolved, and the music is so
free that many people say it is the only unhampered,
unhindered expression of complete freedom yet produced
in this country.

—Duke Ellington

In a filmed interview for a documentary history of our national pastime I made several years ago, the writer and essayist Gerald Early said that "when they study our civilization two thousand years from now, there will only be three things that Americans will be known for: the Constitution, baseball and jazz music. They're the three most beautiful things Americans have ever created." Early's words tend to put a smile on the face of the listener, as if he meant them as a joke, a passing comment of little import, but I think he was deadly serious—and absolutely correct. And I realized that my colleagues and I have worked almost unceasingly for nearly seventeen years to honor that truth. Having grappled with constitutional issues in our series on the Civil War (the Constitution's greatest test) and many other films, and having explored our national pastime and its exquisite lessons in our baseball series, we have over the past several years struggled to understand the utterly American art form of jazz, first in a ten-part documentary history for national public television that will be broadcast in January 2001, and now in this companion volume.

What each of the three projects daily reminded us was that the genius of America is improvisation; that our unique experiment is a profound intersection of freedom and creativity, for better and for worse, in nearly every gesture and breath. The Constitution is the greatest improvisational document ever created. Written on four pieces of parchment at the end of the eighteenth century, it is still able to adjudicate the thorniest problems of the fledgling twenty-first. It set us on our improvisatory course, emphasizing that we are a nation in the process of becoming, always striving to create a more perfect union, always, as the Declaration of Independence mysteriously put it, in *pursuit* of happiness. More than anything, it

has helped to ensure our future by making us Americans unusually curious, unsatisfied, experimenting.

In baseball, we have a simple children's stick-and-ball game that offers, in the totality of its experience, not just games won and lost, careers rising and falling, but a unique sense of time, memory, family, and home that has meant something for nearly every generation of this republic. A three-hundred hitter means the same thing to my daughters as it does to me, as it did to my father and my grandfather and my great-grandfather. There's almost nothing else in American life that you can say that about.

And then there is jazz—"our art," the trumpeter Wynton Marsalis calls it—the only art form created by Americans, an enduring and indelible expression of our genius and promise, "a painless way," Marsalis told us, "of understanding ourselves." In an earlier film, the writer Shelby Foote said that the Civil War defined us; it was, in his words, "the crossroads of our being." We searched for a sense of what we had become after that war, and found in baseball a complex and revealing mirror of who we were that went far beyond the box score. In *Jazz,* we complete our trilogy on American life, finding in the music's lines and phrases and riffs not only a meditation on American creativity, but a joyous and sublime celebration of its redemptive future possibilities—at both a collective and an intensely personal and psychological level.

For those of us engaged in trying to understand it for film and book, the history of jazz turns out to be much more than a study of this extraordinary American music. Jazz has been a prism through which so much of American history can be seen—a curious and unusually objective witness to the twentieth century. And so *Jazz* necessarily becomes a story about race and race relations and prejudice, about minstrelsy and Jim Crow, lynchings and civil rights. Instead of suggesting that black history is an inconsequential, politically correct addendum to the American narrative, relegated in the national dialogue to February, the coldest and shortest month, our study of jazz offers the explosive hypothesis that those who have had the peculiar experience of being unfree in a free land might actually be at the center of our history. African-Americans in general, and black jazz musicians in particular, carry a complicated message to the rest of us, a reminder of our great promise and our great failing; and the music they

created and then generously shared with the rest of the world processes the contradictions many of us would rather ignore. Embodied in the music, in its riveting personalities and soaring artistic achievement, is our oft-neglected conscience, a message of hope and transcendence, of affirmation in the face of adversity, unequaled in the unfolding drama we call American history. Jazz seemed to us a template of change in an ever-changing world and yet a repository of carefully conserved verities as old as the American promise of freedom. In clubs and on the concert stage, jazz has kept the American message alive.

But jazz is much more. It is the story of two world wars and a devastating depression, the sound track that helped Americans get through the worst of times. Jazz is about sex, the way men and women talk to each other and conduct the complicated rituals of courtship—a sophisticated and elegant mating call that has all but disappeared from popular music in recent times. It is about drugs and the terrible cost of addiction and the high price of creativity. It is about the growth and explosion of radio and the soul of great American cities—New Orleans, where the music was born, and Chicago, Kansas City, and New York, where it grew up. It is about immigration and assimilation and feeling dispossessed—and the music that came to the rescue. It is about movement and dance and showing your behind. It's about entertainment, the frequently dismissed but sacred communion between artist and audience. It's about solitude and loneliness and the nearly unbearable burden of consciousness. It's about suffering and celebration—it's greatly about celebration—and tapping your feet.

And jazz is the story of the dozens of extraordinary human beings we who have worked on book and film have come to know like family members; protean geniuses—black and white, male and female, addicts and orphans, prostitutes and pimps, sons of privilege and of despair—who, much like the political figures charged with inventing this country, took enormous risks, shouldered unimaginable responsibility, and are able to do what the rest of us can only dream of: create art on the spot.

It has taken us nearly six years to plan, research, write, shoot, edit, and finish this film and this book. We involved the talents of a half-dozen producers and co-producers, nearly two dozen scholars, more than a score of editors and their assistants, and innumerable technicians. We filmed nearly a hundred interviews—from musicians and family members and unabashed fans to writers, critics, and historians—and lost to the merciless passage of time dozens of friends dedicated to jazz. We searched through hundreds of archives and listened to thousands of pieces of music—music that changed our lives—to make this documentary. It represents, we believe, the most comprehensive treatment of jazz ever committed to film. And yet much has had to be left out, dozens of worthy musicians, stories, and moments, so as to honor our aim of making a compelling narrative for a general audience. The true story of jazz, which can never be fully told, is the story of a million nights when, against all odds, men and women of all colors and often astonishing gifts came together and made great art, in each instance recalling centuries of human suffering, cruelty, negotiation, search, and finally joy. It was our decision to follow several remarkable and emblematic stories and try to tell them well, rather than to attempt to be encyclopedic and tell none well. We beg the indulgence of those inside jazz who bridle at these omissions and hope that those new to the music will continue to explore the infinitely rich landscape of "our art."

There are other dangers in the path we have chosen. The very strength of the documentary, it must be said, is also its great weakness. The form is dialectically preoccupied, imprisoned by the need to accentuate opposites, point out good and bad, reveal saints and sinners, expose fraud and exalt heroism, without much recourse to mitigating wisdom and reconciliation. Jazz asked more of us. It is about reconciliation.

Jazz is about peeling away the layers of artifice to get at what is. Jazz looks at a situation and says, "This is." It might be ugly, it might be shameful, it might be beautiful, it might be revelatory, but all those things are true and part of the American experience. Jazz has afforded us the opportunity to explore the sense of our national character and soul at its most profound center. Involved in that is a certain amount of risk and challenge, of tension and attention, a certain presence that suggests how we might become as a people.

Each new project holds out the promise of nearly daily surprise and delight as we seek to discover and then share with a broad national audience the mysteries of whatever subject we're exploring. In the Civil War series, one could not be unaffected by the life and example of Abraham Lincoln, just as the story of Jackie Robinson in *Baseball* stood out in proud and heroic relief. But I was hardly prepared for my response to jazz—and to that "family member" who changed me in ways words will never be able to describe.

When I began the project, I had perhaps two jazz records in my fairly large music collection. Today, I can't find all the others. I listen to jazz all the time—old and new, straight-ahead and avant-garde and fusion, swing and bop and cool. I play it day and night, in the car, as I go to bed, as I write now, its sophisticated rhythms and elegant lines simply medicine for me. But there is one musician whose work I listen to more than any other. The biggest surprise and delight has been getting to know the power, force, and genius of Louis Armstrong.

Even the most cursory study will reveal his centrality to the music we now call jazz. I knew from the outset that Armstrong was important to the history, but he had mostly seemed to me a guy with a smile and a handkerchief, a singer of popular songs like "Hello, Dolly!" and "It's a Wonderful World." I had no inkling of the truth, borne out in interview after interview, record after record: Louis Armstrong is quite simply the most important person in American music. He is to twentieth-century music (I did not say jazz) what Einstein is to physics, Freud is to psychiatry, and the Wright Brothers are to travel. First, Armstrong transformed instrumental playing, liberating jazz, cutting it loose from nearly all constraints, essentially inventing what we call swinging; then he brought an equally great revolution to singing. And he did it all with a heart and a humanity so spiritually encompassing that my own contemplation of mortality is now tempered by the hope that I will get to hear him playing with Gabriel someday (and, as he would say, blowing Gabriel out of the clouds). To make this discovery was startling—and exhilarating.

Each time we did an interview for the film—whether it was with musicians who played with Armstrong years ago or with those struggling today to come to terms with his legacy; whether with critics, writers, historians, friends, hangers-on, or managers—each would in the end shake his head and say that Louis Armstrong was a "gift from God" or "an angel." Near the end of the editing process, I was on the road and happened upon a woman who, for lack of a better word, is a psychic, a medium familiar with things not of this world. When I told her of the interviews and how each person had called Armstrong an angel, she closed her eyes and smiled and said softly, "Biggest wings I've ever seen."

But maybe Wynton Marsalis, a great trumpet player in his own right, said it best when I asked him about Louis. Having already insisted that Armstrong was chosen by God "to bring the feeling and message and the identity of jazz to everybody," he added a final reflection:

> Louis Armstrong's overwhelming message is one of love. When you hear his music, it's of joy. . . . He was just not going to be defeated by the forces of life. And these forces visit all of us. . . . My great-great-grandmother used to say that "life has a board for every behind" and it's a board just fit to yours, so maybe your board is not going to work on someone else's behind. And when it's your turn . . . that paddle is going to be put on your booty and it's going to hurt as bad as it can hurt. And Louis Armstrong is there to tell you after you get that paddling, "It's all right, son."

Ken Burns
Walpole, New Hampshire

Jazz music celebrates life—human life. The range of it. The absurdity of it. The ignorance of it. The greatness of it. The intelligence of it. The sexuality of it. The profundity of it. And it deals with it in all of its . . . it deals with it.
                                                                    —WYNTON MARSALIS

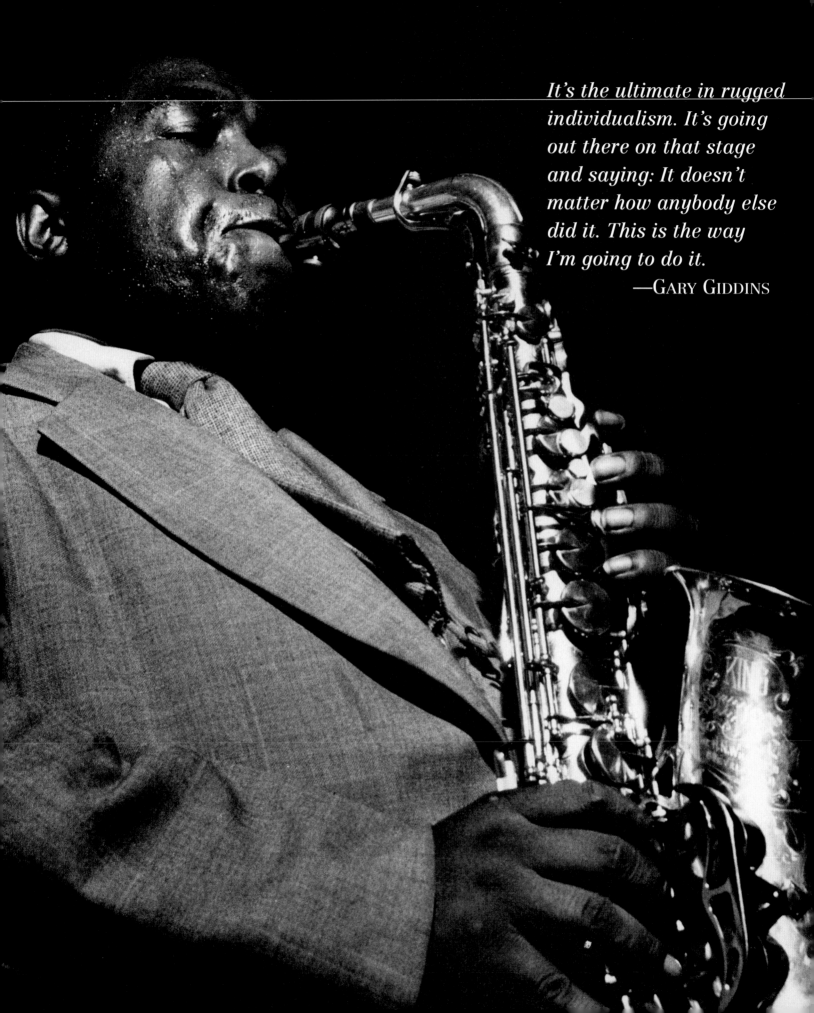

It's the ultimate in rugged individualism. It's going out there on that stage and saying: It doesn't matter how anybody else did it. This is the way I'm going to do it.
—GARY GIDDINS

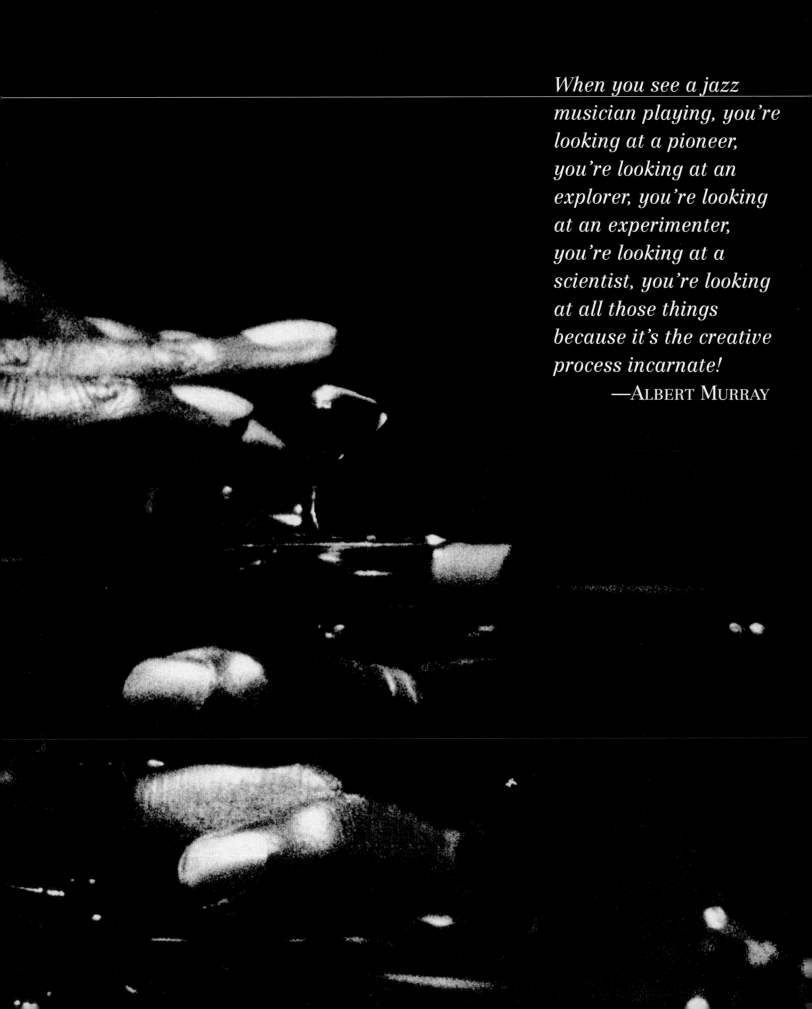

When you see a jazz musician playing, you're looking at a pioneer, you're looking at an explorer, you're looking at an experimenter, you're looking at a scientist, you're looking at all those things because it's the creative process incarnate!
—ALBERT MURRAY

It is America's music—born out of a million American negotiations: between having and not having; between happy and sad, country and city; between black and white and men and women; between the Old Africa and the Old Europe—which could only have happened in an entirely New World.

It is an improvisational art, making itself up as it goes along—just like the country that gave it birth.

It rewards individual expression but demands selfless collaboration.

It is forever changing but nearly always rooted in the blues.

It has a rich tradition and its own rules, but it is brand-new every night.

It is about just making a living and taking terrible risks, losing everything and finding love, making things simple and dressing to the nines.

It has enjoyed huge popularity and survived hard times, but it has always reflected Americans—all Americans—at their best.

"Jazz," the drummer Art Blakey liked to say, "washes away the dust of everyday life."

Above all, it swings.

JAZZ

GUMBO

In September of 1931, brightly colored posters began appearing on walls all over Austin, Texas. They portrayed a beaming young black man holding a golden trumpet and were startling for that place and time in their neutral candor; there was nothing clownish or exaggerated about them; they contained not a trace of the crude minstrelsy with which black Americans were then universally portrayed. "Louis Armstrong, King of the Trumpet, and His Orchestra," the posters said, were to play four dances at the downtown Hotel Driskill beginning on the evening of October 12.

Among those who paid seventy-five cents to get in that night was a freshman at the University of Texas named Charlie Black. The posters had drawn him in. He knew little about jazz music, had never even heard of Armstrong. He just knew there

The Original Superior Orchestra, about 1908. Bunk Johnson is the cornetist; Peter Bocage plays the violin; the clarinetist is Louis "Big Eye" Nelson. This group specialized in variations on ragtime intended for more polite listeners, but Johnson and Bocage also played in the Eagle Band, which played the blues and catered to a far rougher crowd.

were likely to be lots of girls to dance with. Everyone on the dance floor was white; only Armstrong, his musicians, and the waiters were African-American.

Then, Black remembered, Armstrong began to play,

> mostly with his eyes closed, letting flow from that inner space of music things that had never before existed. . . . Steamwhistle power, lyric grace, alternated at will, even blended.

> He was the first genius I had ever seen. . . . It is impossible to overstate the significance of a sixteen-year-old southern boy's seeing genius, for the first time, in a black. We literally never saw a black, then, in any but a servant's capacity. There were of course black professionals and intellectuals in Austin, as one later learned, but they kept to themselves, out back of town, no doubt shunning humiliation. I liked most of the blacks I knew—I loved a few of them—like Old Buck Green, born and raised a slave, who still plays the harmonica through my mouth, having taught me when he was seventy-five and I was ten. Some were honored and venerated, in that paradoxical white southern way—Buck Green again comes to mind. But genius—fine control over total power, all height and depth, forever and ever? It had simply never entered my mind . . . that I would see this for the first time in a black man. You don't get over that. . . . The lies reel, and contradict one another, and simper in silliness and fade into shadow. But the seen truth remains.

Standing next to Black was a boy from Austin High School. "We listened together for a long time," Black remembered. "Then he turned to me, shook his head as if clearing it—as I'm sure he was—of an unacceptable though vague thought, and pronounced the judgment of the time and place: 'After all, he's nothing but a goddamn nigger!' " The boy moved away. But nothing was ever the same for Black again. "Louis opened my eyes wide and put to me a choice. Blacks, the saying went, were 'all right in their place.' [But] what was the 'place' of such a man, and of the people from which he sprung?"

Charlie Black went on to become Professor Charles L. Black Jr., a distinguished teacher of constitutional law. In 1954 he would help provide the answer to the question Louis Armstrong's music had first posed for him: he volunteered for the team of lawyers, black and white, who finally persuaded the U.S. Supreme Court in the case of *Brown v. Board of Education of Topeka* that segregating schoolchildren on the basis of race was unconstitutional, that "separate but equal" no longer could be tolerated under American law.

Genius is ultimately untraceable. No amount of historical or psychological sleuthing can ever fully explain the emergence of artists like Bach or Picasso or Louis Armstrong, who appear as if from nowhere and through the power of their own individual imaginations transform an art. The origins of the kind of music Armstrong played remain elusive, too. Jazz music belongs to all Americans, has come to be seen by the rest of the world as the symbol of all that is best about us, but it was created by people routinely denied the most basic benefits of being American. It grew up in a thousand places but it could only have been born in New Orleans, Louis Armstrong's hometown.

In the early morning hours of January 12, 1819, the brig *Clio* anchored off the levee at New Orleans at the end of a three-week voyage from New York. Among her passengers was the architect Benjamin Henry Latrobe, the father of the Greek Revival style in America, fresh from rebuilding the U.S. Capitol in Washington. He was a worldly, well-traveled man—born in England, he had lived and worked in France, Germany, and Italy—and he was eager for his first glimpse of the South's biggest city and most important port. But when dawn finally came, Latrobe wrote, "so thick a fog enveloped the city that the ear alone could ascertain its existence" and he heard "a sound more strange than any that is heard anywhere else in the world. . . . It is a more incessant, loud, rapid, and various gabble of tongues of all tones than was ever heard at Babel."

The sun eventually warmed away the fog and Latrobe and his fellow passengers could go ashore to discover for themselves the source of this strange cacophony. An open-air market stretched along the levee, Latrobe wrote, "as far as the eye could reach to the West, and to the Market house to the East," two rows of clamoring shopkeepers advertising everything from bananas to tin buckets, fresh fish to rare books:

> some having stalls or tables with a Tilt or awning of canvas . . . but the majority having their wares on the ground . . . on a piece of canvas or a parcel of Palmetto leaves. The articles to be sold were not more various than the Sellers. White men and women, and of all hues of brown, and of all Classes of faces, from round

The old French Market as it looked about 1895. Although this photograph was made seventy-six years after Benjamin Henry Latrobe first saw it, its interior still echoed with many of the disparate voices that so astonished him.

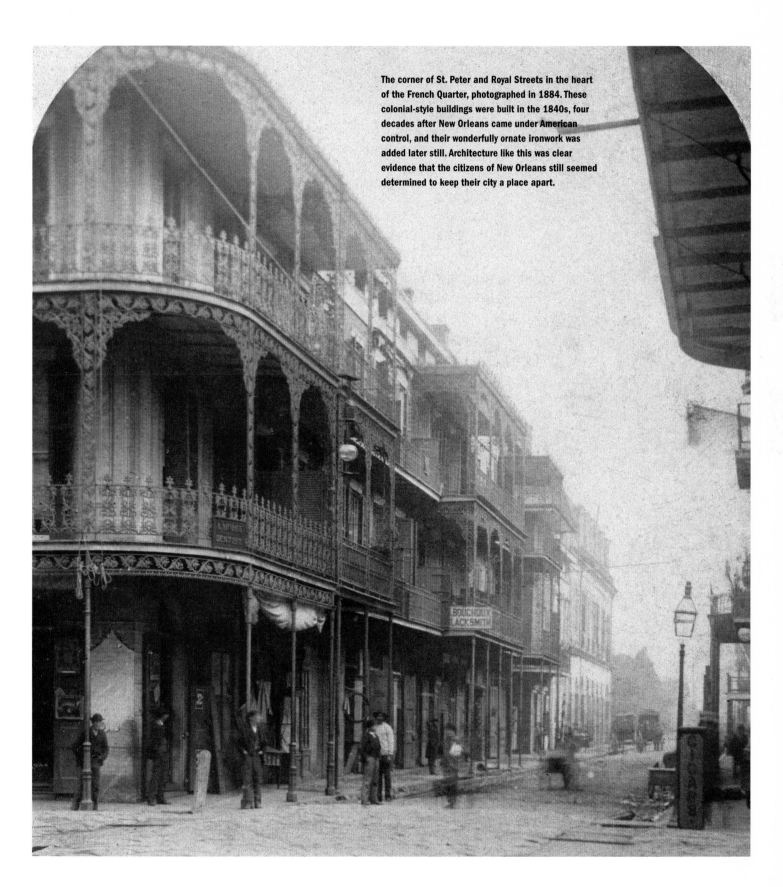

The corner of St. Peter and Royal Streets in the heart of the French Quarter, photographed in 1884. These colonial-style buildings were built in the 1840s, four decades after New Orleans came under American control, and their wonderfully ornate ironwork was added later still. Architecture like this was clear evidence that the citizens of New Orleans still seemed determined to keep their city a place apart.

Yankees, to grisly and lean Spaniards, black Negroes and negresses, filthy Indians half naked, Mulattoes, curly and straight-haired, Quateroons of all shades, long-haired and frizzled, the women dressed in the most flaring yellow and scarlet gowns, the men capped and hatted. . . . I cannot suppose that my eye took in less than 500 sellers and buyers, all of whom appeared to strain their voices, to exceed each other in loudness.

From this unprecedented blend of voices from everywhere on earth would eventually come America's most distinctive music.

"Everything has an *odd* look," Latrobe wrote of New Orleans at the end of his first day in the city; it was "impossible not to stare at a sight wholly new, even to one who has traveled much in Europe and America."

In fact, New Orleans *was* a sight wholly new, the most cosmopolitan city in the country, perhaps the world. Established by France in 1718, in the midst of a mosquito-infested swamp ninety miles north of the Mississippi's mouth, it was briefly ruled by Spain, reclaimed by France, visited by ships from everywhere, then more or less peacefully invaded by American flatboatmen whom the city's French-speaking citizens derided as "Kaintucks," and finally sold to the United States as part of the Louisiana Purchase in 1803.

"There are in fact three societies here," Latrobe noted a few days after he had settled into his hotel overlooking the old French drilling ground that would soon be known as Jackson Square: "1. The French, 2. The American, and 3. The mixed." Latrobe had only begun dimly to understand the city's infinite stratifications. The French themselves were divided. Some were descendants of the city's early settlers; others were refugees from Canada and the French Revolution, from the Napoleonic wars or from the slave rebellions that had only recently overthrown French rule in

When Currier & Ives published this lithographed bird's-eye view in 1885, New Orleans was still the busiest port in the South. The broad thoroughfare (on the opposite page) that runs diagonally from the riverfront to the distant shore of Lake Pontchartrain is Canal Street. It marked the dividing line between "Downtown" (farthest from the observer), the oldest, most fashionable part of the city, where many Creoles of Color made their homes, and "Uptown," or the "American Quarter" occupied by newer arrivals including black immigrants from the countryside.

Gumbo: Beginnings to 1907   5

Daguerreotypes of Creoles of Color, believed to have been made about 1865. The identities of the sitters are unknown but their elegant attire hints at the level of prosperity some nonwhites were able to reach in cosmopolitan New Orleans.

Haiti and Santo Domingo. But all sought to retain their language and Roman Catholic customs, and all proudly differentiated themselves from the Protestant American newcomers now flooding into the town, whose culture, Latrobe noted, seemed antithetical to theirs. The Americans' "business is to make money," he wrote. "They are in an eternal bustle. Their limbs, their heads and their hearts, move to that sole object."

Nor did the city's complexities end there. The "Crescent City"—so called because it was built along a bend in the river—was also home to Choctaw and Natchez Indians. It would soon witness an influx of people from the Balkans: Dalmatians, Serbs, Montenegrins, Greeks, Albanians. Spanish-speaking Filipinos came and stayed, too, alongside Chinese and Malays. After 1850, large numbers of German and Irish and Sicilian immigrants would be added to the mix. By 1860, 40 percent of the people of New Orleans were foreign-born.

New Orleans was a center of the southern slave trade, as well. It would eventually boast two dozen slave auction houses and, several times a year, the spacious ballrooms of its two grandest hotels doubled

as showrooms for human merchandise. But it was also home to the most prosperous community of free people of color in the South. Many were the descendants of French colonists and their African- and Native-American wives and mistresses. They called themselves "Creoles of Color" and spoke French or a distinctive patois that white Americans called "nigger French." A wealthy few sent their children to Paris to school.

Creoles controlled cigarmaking and bricklaying, carpentry and shoemaking in the city. Many lived south of Canal Street in the original, most fashionable section, called "Downtown," and were at best ambivalent about the black servants and slaves and menial workers who crowded together in the "American quarter," called "Uptown."

"See, people down here are very prejudiced," the Creole violinist Paul Dominguez explained. "And your color makes all the difference. . . . [W]e Downtown people, we try to be intelligent. Everybody learn a trade. We try to bar jail. Uptown, across Canal, yonder, they used to jail. There's a vast difference in this town. Uptown folk are all ruffians, cut up in the face, and live

on the river. All cotton—be longshoremen, screwmen. And me, I ain't never been on the river a *day in my life*"

Some years after Latrobe's arrival a visitor named James R. Creecy captured something of the city's heterogeneous character in doggerel:

Have you ever been in New Orleans?
    If not, you'd better go.
It's a nation of a queer place; day and
    night a show!
Frenchmen, Spaniards, West Indians,
    Creoles, Mustees,
Yankees, Kentuckians, Tennesseeans,
    lawyers and trustees,
Clergymen, priests, friars, nuns,
    women of all stains;
Negroes in purple and fine linen, and
    slaves in rags and chains.
Ships, arks, steamboats, robbers,
    pirates, alligators,
Assassins, gamblers, drunkards and
    cotton speculators;
Sailors, soldiers, pretty girls, and ugly
    fortune-tellers;
Pimps, imps, shrimps, and all sorts of
    dirty fellows;
White men with black wives, *et vice-
    versa,* too.
A progeny of all colors—an infernal
    motley crew.

Each element in this progeny of all colors, this infernal motley crew, would bring a unique brand of music to the New Orleans mix and in so doing prepare the ground for jazz.

AURORA BOREALIS

"A bunch of us kids, playing, would suddenly hear sounds," the New Orleans guitarist Danny Barker remembered. "It was like a phenomenon, like the *Aurora Borealis.* The sounds of men playing would be so clear, but we wouldn't be sure where they were coming from. So we'd start running—'It's this way!' 'It's that way!'—and,

New Orleans sugar mill workers of every kind and color line up together to get their weekly pay in this turn-of-the-century photograph by Georges François Mugnier.

sometimes, after running for a while, you'd find you'd be nowhere near that music. But that music could come on any time like that. The city was full of the sounds of music."

Barker was remembering his own early-twentieth-century New Orleans boyhood, but the muddy streets of his hometown had always been alive with music. Long before Latrobe's visit, dancing had been central to the lives of New Orleans citizens: "In the winter," said an early French visitor, "they dance to keep warm, and in the summer they dance to keep cool." And the city's Latin-Catholic tradition, which held that there was nothing sinful about dancing, that Sundays were for celebration as well as worship, proved stubbornly resistant to efforts by Protestant American newcomers to change New Orleans ways. When a band of clergymen called upon the city at least to

limit the dancing season in 1831, the New Orleans *Bee* denounced them as "men who were ordered by God to preach to the world that the dance is a Satanic invention . . . that the Creator gave us the instinct of pleasure only so that we might procure the glory of resisting it." In any case, they had no impact on New Orleans. Ten years later, more than eighty public ballrooms were flourishing in the city, which had become, one visitor wrote, "one vast waltzing and gallopading hall."

Creole musicians—sometimes whole orchestras, more often a string trio or quartet—supplied most of the music for the city's dancers, both white and Creole: waltzes, polkas, schottisches, quadrilles, and sensual, syncopated contredanses, including habaneras, filled with Spanish rhythms carried to New Orleans from Haiti and Cuba.

They played for the celebrated—or notorious—"quadroon balls," too, at which white men sought out Creole women to be their mistresses. Nonwhite males were officially barred, though, since men and women alike often wore masks, it was sometimes hard to tell just who was asking whom to dance. As Danny Barker remarked, in New Orleans there has always been "a whole lot of integrating going on."

Well before the Civil War, the city also exhibited what the New Orleans *Picayune* called "a real mania for horn and trumpet playing," and dance musicians often doubled in the marching bands that seemed always to be playing somewhere in town—entertaining picnickers in the parks or along the southern shore of Lake Pontchartrain, waging what one observer called "a windy war" by blaring different airs from

The sensation Thomas Dartmouth "Daddy" Rice set off when he first performed "Jump Jim Crow" at the American Theater on New York's Bowery on November 25, 1833—an event important enough to be commemorated in this painting by an unidentified artist—would resonate for decades. Minstrel shows brought a lively if distorted form of African-American song and dance to white Americans who couldn't seem to get enough of it. The 1867 collection of so-called Negro melodies (below) was just one of thousands of attempts to cash in on the craze Daddy Rice began.

the decks of steamboats anchored side by side, escorting mourners to and from the cemetery "preceded, followed and hemmed in on every side by a . . . collection of all colors, sexes and conditions."

The New Orleans funeral parade—accompanied by a slow and stately hymn on the way to the graveyard, a stirring light-hearted anthem on the way back—was remarked upon by nearly every early visitor to the city in part because there were so many of them. New Orleans's incessant gaiety could not disguise the fact that the city—surrounded by swamps, subject to annual flooding, lacking in the most basic sanitation—was a breeding ground for disease. Yellow fever scythed its way through the population twenty-three times between 1817 and 1860. Thousands died. Cholera and malaria killed thousands more; as late as 1880, nearly half the nonwhite babies born in New Orleans did not live to see their

first birthday and the average life expectancy of a black citizen was just thirty-six (the average white citizen lived only a decade longer).

Music provided New Orleans with solace, then, as well as high spirits. Theaters featured the bizarre mongrel music of the minstrel show—so-called plantation melodies, often derived from authentic black songs and spirituals but turned into formal compositions by white and black songwriters, performed by whites blacked-up as blacks (and often in later years by blacks blacked-up as whites *playing* blacks). For almost a century, the minstrel show would be the most popular form of entertainment in America, a ritualized blend of lively music, knockabout comedy, sophisticated elegance, the reinforcement of ugly and persistent stereotypes—and simultaneous unabashed enthusiasm for the music and dance of the country's most

despised minority. The first big minstrel hit was written down and performed by a white man in blackface named Thomas Dartmouth "Daddy" Rice—who said *he'd* first heard it being sung by a black stable hand cleaning out a horse's stall. Rice named the tune after the stable hand—Jim Crow—and performed it several times in New Orleans to great applause.

At least once, the Crescent City put its own characteristic spin on minstrelsy. When the well-known blackface entertainer Mick Saunders came to town in 1840 to offer his version of two stock minstrel characters, the sharpster and the shuffling simpleton, he found himself sharing the stage with a real black street vendor, remembered only as "Old Corn Meal," who performed songs he'd been singing on the city streets for years—"My Long Tail Blue," "Old Rosin the Bow," and a series of variations on "The Star-Spangled Banner" that brought down the house.

By 1850, the city supported two symphony orchestras, one white and one Creole, as well as three opera houses, each offering separate tiers of seats for whites, Creoles, and slaves—who were officially supposed to bring with them notes signed by their masters granting permission to

Minstrel star Lew Dockstader—the big man wearing a top hat at center stage—leads his fifty-man company in *The Possum Hunt Club*, a timely 1910 show in which Dockstader played a waiter chosen to accompany former President Theodore Roosevelt to Africa. Al Jolson was among the graduates of Dockstader's well-known company.

attend before they were issued tickets. Visitors from the North were sometimes startled to hear among the cries of street vendors the sound of slaves singing arias; New Orleanians thought nothing of it.

Slaves made their own kind of music, as well. Out for a Sunday afternoon stroll along St. Peter Street not long after he arrived in the city, Benjamin Latrobe heard what he remembered as a "most extraordinary noise, which I supposed to proceed from . . . horses tramping on a wooden floor." Hurrying up the street, he discovered that "it proceeded from a crowd of five or six hundred persons, assembled in . . . a public square. . . . All those who were engaged in the business seemed to be blacks."

He had happened upon Congo Square, a grassy plain on the northwestern edge of the city where the city fathers permitted slaves to dance and sing for a few hours on Sundays. The dancers, Latrobe noted, were formed into two circular groups "in the midst of which were . . . two women dancing. They held each a coarse handkerchief . . . & set to each other in a miserably dull & slow figure, hardly moving their feet or bodies."

The music consisted of two drums and a stringed instrument . . . [one of which was] a cylindrical drum, about one foot in diameter. . . . They made an incredible noise. The most curious instrument, however, was a stringed instrument, which no doubt was imported from Africa. On the top of the finger board was the rude figure of a man in a sitting posture, and two pegs behind him to which the strings were fastened. The body was a calabash. It was played upon by a very little old man, apparently eighty or ninety years old. . . . A Man sang an uncouth song to the dancing which I suppose was in some African language for it was not French, and the Women screamed a detestable burthen on one single note. The allowed amusements of Sundays, have, it seems, perpetuated here those of Africa among its inhabitants.

To Latrobe and the other curious whites who turned out to see and hear them over the years, the slave dances at Congo Square and the music that accompanied them, filled with complex polyrhythms, seemed to provide an authentic glimpse of Africa. And some of those who danced there in the early years really had been brought from West Africa in chains. To these people, for whom music and dancing had always been an integral part of everyday life, Congo Square must have offered a precious opportunity to recover at least a little of what they had lost when they were taken from their homes.

But adversity demanded improvisation. To survive in America, slaves needed to be able to incorporate everything they saw and heard around them, had to find ways to make it all their own. At the time of Latrobe's visit in 1819, the importation of slaves from overseas had been illegal for more than a decade; within a few years of it, most of those who continued to gather in Congo Square had no firsthand memories of Africa at all. They were immigrants or the children of immigrants from the West Indies, their music already heavily alloyed with the infectious Latin-tinged pulse of the Caribbean, their religion a blend of Catholicism and West African spirit worship they called *vodoun*—"voodoo" to the whites who both feared and were fascinated by it.

Others had filtered into the city from the interior of the South, where the music of their ancestors had long since merged with that of their masters. European instruments—fiddles and fifes, Jew's harps, triangles, and tambourines—now appeared alongside drums and rattles and banjos, while the musicians played French and Spanish melodies and dances—along with wholly American songs like "Old Virginia Never Tire" and "Hey Jim Along Josey"—to which the dancers performed jigs and fandangos and Virginia reels that would have mystified their African forebears.

Nor was Congo Square the slaves' only dancing place. Despite a battery of ordinances meant to keep them quiescent and confined at home, New Orleans slaves drank and danced nightly in so many illicit taverns, the editor of the *Bee* complained in 1833, that "Not a street, nor a corner can be passed without encountering [them]. The noise and disturbance is very disagreeable to the neighbors, though it may be profitable to the proprietor."

The New Orleans good-time tradition, the city's near-universal fondness for music and dancing, combined with the surprisingly porous nature of its racial walls, made every kind of music available to every resident. All of them would find their way into jazz.

When Confederate guns opened up on Fort Sumter in Charleston harbor in the early morning hours of April 12, 1861, beginning the Civil War, it was General Pierre Gustave Toutant Beauregard, a favorite son of New Orleans, who gave the first order to fire. His state—and his native city—had already been out of the Union for more than two months. But New Orleans would not be part of the Confederacy for long. Just over a year later, on April 24, 1862, a Union fleet steamed up the river and forced the city's surrender. Federal occupation seemed to signal a new birth of freedom for the thousands of runaway slaves who soon crowded into the city from the southern interior.

"We wish," said the black-owned New Orleans *Tribune* shortly after the war ended, "to be respected and treated as men—not as Africans or Negroes, or colored people, but as Americans and American citizens." Under Reconstruction and in the face of sporadic and sometimes violent

THE FUTURE MUSIC OF THIS COUNTRY

In 1892, the Czech composer Antonín Dvořák arrived in America to become director of the brand-new National Conservatory of Music of America in New York. He was already celebrated for the skill with which he incorporated themes based upon the native songs and dances of his native Bohemia into his symphonic music, and it was the hope of the conservatory's wealthy founder, Mrs. Jeanette Thurber, that he would be able to show young would-be American composers how to do the same thing in the United States. It was a hope Dvořák fully shared: "I did not come to America to interpret Wagner for the public," he said not long after his arrival. "I came to discover what young Americans had in them and to help them express it." He traveled as far west as Iowa during his three years in the United States and grew to admire the chants and rhythms of Native American music, but it was African-American music that moved him most. "I am now satisfied that the future music of this country must be founded upon what are called the negro melodies," he said. "In the negro melodies of America I discovered all that is needed for a great and noble school of music. They are pathetic, tender, passionate, melancholy, solemn, religious, bold, merry. gay, or what you will."

Dvořák's own best-known American-inspired work, Symphony no. 9 in E Minor (*From the New World*) may or may not have drawn upon Negro spirituals—scholars still differ—but it was otherwise indistinguishable from the work of other European composers working in the Romantic idiom. Nonetheless, Dvořák's emphasis on the importance of native forms had a lasting, if indirect, effect on American music. Both Aaron Copland and George Gershwin would study with former students of Dvořák. So, informally, would Duke Ellington, who would demonstrate to the world a whole new way to incorporate the facts of American life into a "serious and original . . . great and noble" wholly American kind of music.

white resistance, real progress would be made toward that goal: public facilities and public schools were integrated, at least on paper, and some black and Creole students peaceably attended classes alongside whites. Citizens of color sued for—and won—the right to sit wherever they liked at the French Opera House. Backed by federal bayonets, they also forced the city to end the system of separate streetcars. Black and white baseball teams played one another, black and white longshoremen went out on strike together, and each year elderly white and black veterans of the 1815 Battle of New Orleans dined amicably together on its anniversary. In 1874, the editor of another newspaper saw evidence of New Orleans's "catholicity of spirit" in the fact that "in our midst the civil and public rights of the colored race [are] more fully realized than has been the case in any other southern city."

It was all too good to last. Three years later, in 1877, the last federal troops were withdrawn from the former Confederacy as white rule and strict segregation were again brutally being reimposed upon the whole region. But for a time, at least, cosmopolitan New Orleans would escape the worst of it.

Meanwhile, the city's rich musical heritage grew steadily richer. Brass bands captivated the whole country after the Civil War—virtually every small town in America boasted at least one—and the New Orleans "mania" for them that had been noted before the war seems only to have intensified afterwards. Citizens of every color and nationality continued to march to German bands, French bands, Irish bands, Italian bands (that highlighted a lyrical, ornamented clarinet style born in Sicily), and the regimental bands of the occupying forces, both black and white. When Patrick Sarsfield Gilmore, the master cornetist and bandleader, who was as celebrated as John Philip Sousa in his day, presented a Grand National Concert at Lafayette Square, five hundred New Orleans brass players turned out to play with him. Every summer during

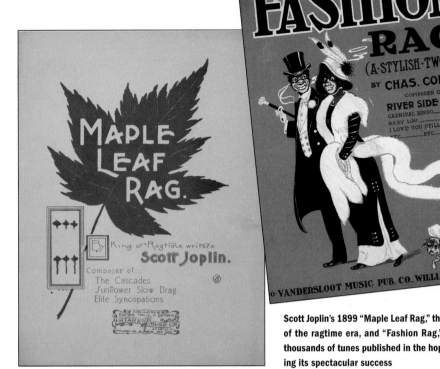

Scott Joplin's 1899 "Maple Leaf Rag," the biggest hit of the ragtime era, and "Fashion Rag," one of the thousands of tunes published in the hope of matching its spectacular success

the 1880s, a summer resort called West End, on Lake Pontchartrain just north of the city, played host to bands from all over the country with concerts day and night at which were played every kind of music from plantation ditties to operatic overtures, waltzes to so-called "coon songs."

Big-time black bands came to town, too, often as part of minstrel companies, among them the "Louisiana Slave Troupe and Brass Band," "Smallwood's Great Contraband Minstrels Brass Band," and Billy Kersand's minstrel band that marched at the head of the Mardi Gras Finale one year with such precision that its leader's standard offer of one thousand dollars to any group that could beat them in "drilling or parading" found no takers.

Black and Creole fraternal and social organizations, as well as the musicians themselves, organized bands. When a memorial parade for the assassinated Republican President James Garfield moved slowly through the city in 1881, several black outfits played dirges alongside white ones. Some musicians—like those in the Eclipse Band, outfitted and trained on for-

mer governor Henry Clay Warmouth's Magnolia plantation in Plaquemine Parish—prided themselves on their ability to read as well as play and were openly scornful of the untutored players who dared compete with them: "fakers," they called them, "ear-men," "routiners," who relied on guesswork and momentary inspiration, not written notes.

By the mid-1890s, three new kinds of music had begun to filter into the city—three strains without which there would have been no jazz.

The first was ragtime, the formal outgrowth of the decades-old African-American improvisational practice of "ragging" tunes—syncopating and rearranging them to provide livelier, more danceable versions. Created by black musicians in the cities of the Midwest, who had found a way to recreate something like the percussive sound of the banjo on the piano, ragtime drew upon everything that had gone before—spirituals and minstrel tunes, European folk melodies, operatic arias and military marches—all filled with broken

The Mathews and Lockport Brass Band, 1904. The name painted on the drum refers not to the musicians—their identities have long since been lost—but to the two small neighboring towns southwest of New Orleans from which they came. At Mardi Gras time, rural brass bands like theirs often made their way to the big city, adding their rough-hewn sound to the joyous celebration.

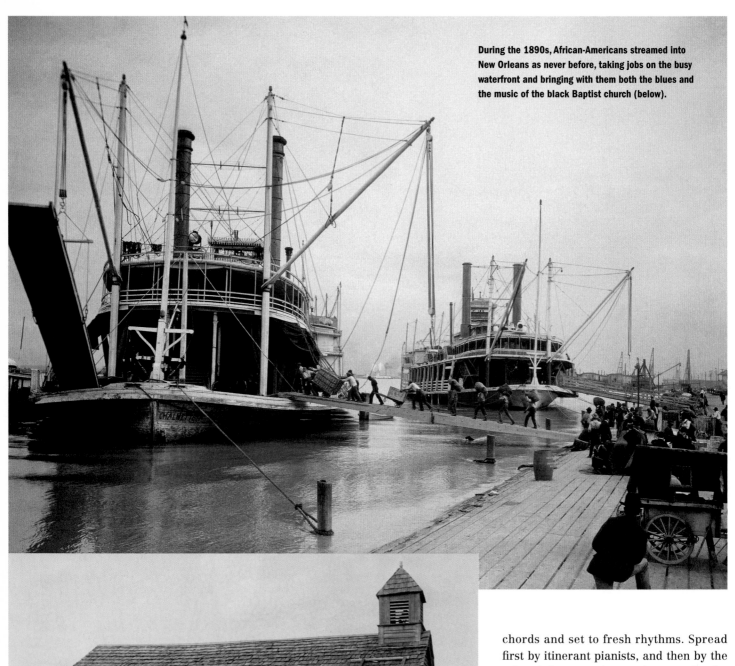

During the 1890s, African-Americans streamed into New Orleans as never before, taking jobs on the busy waterfront and bringing with them both the blues and the music of the black Baptist church (below).

chords and set to fresh rhythms. Spread first by itinerant pianists, and then by the sale of sheet music, ragtime caught the fancy of young dancers all over the country who loved it all the more because—since it encouraged young men and women to dance close together as couples rather than in groups—their parents did not. "Ragtime is syncopation gone mad," the editor of *Etude* magazine would write, "and its victims, in my opinion, can be treated successfully only like the dog with rabies, with

"Each one of my blues is based on some old Negro song of the South," William Christopher Handy wrote in his autobiography. "Something that sticks in my mind, that I hum to myself when I'm not thinking about it. Some old song that is a part of the memories of my childhood and of my race. I can tell you the exact song I used as a basis for any one of my blues." Handy was from Alabama, the son and grandson of Baptist ministers who took a grim view of the kind of secular music he helped spread around the world. He taught music at A & M College in Huntsville and played cornet in a traveling minstrel troupe. In 1902, while leading his own orchestra for white dancers in Cleveland, Mississippi, he learned a lesson about music he would never forget.

"Someone sent up an odd request. Would we play some of 'our native music'? This baffled me. The men in the group could not 'fake' and 'sell' it like minstrel men. They were all musicians who bowed strictly to the authority of printed notes."

The audience then asked Handy's band to take a break and allow a "local" outfit to play a few tunes of their own.

We eased out gracefully as the newcomers entered. They were led by a long-legged chocolate boy, and their band consisted of just three pieces, a battered guitar, a mandolin, and a worn-out bass. . . . They struck up one of those over-and-over strains that seem to have no very clear beginning and certainly no ending at all. The strumming attained a disturbing monotony, but on and on it went, a kind of stuff that has long been associated with cane rows and levee camps. It was not really annoying or unpleasant, but I commenced to wonder if anybody besides small-town rounders and their running mates could go for it.

The answer was not long in coming. A rain of silver dollars began to fall around the outlandish, stomping feet. The dancers went wild. Dollars, quarters, halves— the shower grew heavier and continued so long I strained my neck to get a better look. There before the boys lay more money than my nine musicians were being paid for the entire engagement. Then I saw the beauty of primitive music. They had the stuff the people wanted. It touched the spot. Their music wanted polishing, but it contained the essence. . . . That night, a composer was born, an *American* composer.

Handy began writing down the blues he heard. In 1909, living and working now in Memphis, he orchestrated a tune being sung there about the monumentally corrupt Boss Ed Crump, then running for mayor. The lyrics were not especially flattering to the candidate:

Mr. Crump doan allow no easy riders here.
We doan care what Mr. Crump don't
    allow;
We gonna Barrel-house anyhow.
Mr. Crump can go and catch some air.

But Crump didn't seem to mind. He liked the tune and so did the black and white voters who came out to his rallies to hear Handy's band play it. In 1912, Handy published it with brand-new lyrics as "The Memphis Blues." It was not the first blues ever published—it was delayed just long enough for two other songwriters to get there first—but it launched Handy on the career that earned him the title "Father of the Blues," helped make the blues into an industry, and whetted the public's appetite for jazz.

W. C. Handy's "Aunt Hagar's Blues," a musical portrait of a churchly woman who, despite the stern admonitions of her preacher, finds the blues impossible to resist

a dose of lead. Whether it is simply a passing phase of our decadent art culture or an infectious disease which has come to stay, like leprosy, time alone can tell."

Despite that kind of criticism—and in part perhaps because of it—ragtime had come to stay; jaunty, propulsive, irresistible, it would be America's best-loved music for a quarter of a century. Nowhere was ragtime more popular or more ubiquitous than in New Orleans; by the turn of the century, Crescent City musicians, in dance halls as well as street parades, were routinely giving every kind of music the ragtime treatment.

Meanwhile, a steady stream of black refugees from the Mississippi Delta was pouring into the city, people for whom even hard labor on the levee promised a better life than any they could hope to have back home, chopping cotton or cutting cane. They brought with them as part of their baggage two interrelated forms essential to the development of jazz—the sacred music of the Baptist church and that music's profane twin, the blues.

No one knows where or when the blues were born: "Ain't no first blues," the New Orleans clarinetist Louis "Big Eye" Nelson remembered: "The blues always been." Blues lyrics could be about anything— empty pockets, a mean boss, the devil himself—but most were about the relationship between men and women and each performer was expected to tell a story and to make the listener feel better, not worse:

I'm goin' to lay my head on some
    lonesome railroad track,
I'm goin' to lay my head on some
    lonesome railroad track—
and when the train come along, I'll
    snatch my damn head back.

The earliest blues singers—wandering guitarists who played for pennies along the southern roads—followed no strict musical form. But as first New Orleans musicians and then others around the country began to try to play the blues on their instruments and songwriters started to see commercial possibilities in them, an agreed-upon form was developed: stripped to the essentials, blues came to be built on just three chords most often arranged in twelve-bar sequences that somehow allowed for an infinite number of variations and were capable of expressing an infinite number of emotions.

The blues were good-time music, which was why, to many churchgoers, they were anathema, the work of the devil, forbidden to the saved. But musically, the blues and the hymns black Baptists sang and played in church had always been virtually interchangeable—filled with identical bent notes, moans, and cries. And in the 1890s, the distinction would blur still further as the new Holiness churches that had begun to spring up in the black neighborhoods of big cities all over the country started employing tambourines, drums, pianos, cornets, even trombones in order to make their noise still more joyful to the Lord. "Those Baptist rhythms were similar to the jazz rhythms," said the New Orleans banjoist Johnny St. Cyr, "and the singing was very much on the blues side." "You heard the pastors in the Baptist churches," echoed the drummer Paul Barbarin, "they were singing rhythm. More so than a jazz band."

"In the [church]," the New Orleans clarinet master Sidney Bechet would remember, "the people clapped their hands—that was their rhythm. In the blues it was further down; they didn't need the clapping but they remembered it. . . . And both of them, the spirituals and the blues, they was a prayer. One was praying to God and the other was praying to what's human. It's like one was saying, 'Oh God, let me go,' and the other was saying, 'Oh, Mister, let me be.' "

Jazz music would eventually embody both kinds of invocation, the sacred and the secular, and New Orleans musicians would be the first to deepen the infinitely expressive sound of the blues by bringing it to their horns, the first to echo the collective "moan" of the congregation, the first to reproduce the call-and-response patterns of the religious exhorter and his transported flock.

SEPARATE BUT EQUAL

In the spring of 1885, the New England novelist and critic Charles Dudley Warner had visited the International Cotton Exposition at New Orleans and been astonished by what he saw: "white and colored people mingled freely" at the fairgrounds, he wrote home in wonder, "talking and looking at what was of common interest," still seeming to associate "in unconscious equality of privileges."

But by the 1890s, Jim Crow laws that strictly segregated the rest of the South had begun to delimit life in New Orleans as well. "There are differences between the colored man and the white man which neither education nor law can abrogate," said the New Orleans *Picayune*. "To sit by a negro's side at a hotel table or a concert hall [is], in the opinion of the white people, to ignore the truth." New statutes now barred blacks entirely from theaters where they had once at least been permitted a separate section of their own. "Negroes were not allowed in the places where [classical music] was played," the drummer Baby Dodds remembered, "so I heard it by standing on the outside . . . in the hallway of the Tulane theater. . . . One side was an opera house and the other was this theater and we'd stand in between to hear the music."

In 1890, a bill requiring that blacks and whites occupy different cars on trains traveling within the state easily passed the legislature despite the protest of sixteen black and Creole legislators that the bill was "unconstitutional, unamerican, unjust." Two years later, a New Orleans Creole named Homer Adolph Plessy set out to test the new law by boarding an excursion train and insisting on sitting in the "whites only" car. He was, he said, of "seven-eighths Caucasian and one-eighth African blood . . . [and] the admixture of colored blood is not discernible." He was arrested anyway (the police had been tipped off), tried and con-

victed, and in 1896, in the case of *Plessy v. Ferguson,* the Supreme Court of the United States upheld his conviction. "Separate but equal facilities," it said, were constitutional. That decision would govern life in the American South—and in New Orleans—for nearly sixty years.

Black children were removed from the public schools—though, New Orleans being New Orleans, a considerable number who were especially light-skinned continued to attend them undetected. Black and white boxers and bicycle racers and ball teams were now forbidden to compete against one another. The Louisiana legislature rewrote the state constitution to bar all would-be voters whose grandfathers had been slaves. Ninety-five percent of the city's black men had been entitled to vote in 1897; just 1 percent would be welcome at the polls in 1901. Seating on city streetcars was once again strictly segregated, despite an exasperated warning from the president of the transportation company that "the greatest ethnologist the world has ever seen would be at a loss to classify streetcar passengers in this city."

Overnight, the rarefied world of the Creoles of Color was turned upside down. A little white blood had formerly carried with it certain privileges in New Orleans. Now, a single drop of black blood—any "traceable amount," according to state statute—was enough to rank a person as a second-class citizen.

Creole musicians were especially dislocated by the changes all around them. John Robichaux had been perhaps the city's favorite Creole musician, a well-schooled violinist with a waxed moustache whose elegantly dressed "society"—or "sit-down" —orchestra played sweet dance music for white patrons at two of the most prestigious venues in the city, the Grunewald Hotel and Antoine's Restaurant. "He had the rich people's jobs all sewed up," the bassist George "Pops" Foster remembered. But now, even Robichaux often found himself displaced by white musicians, forced to join a separate

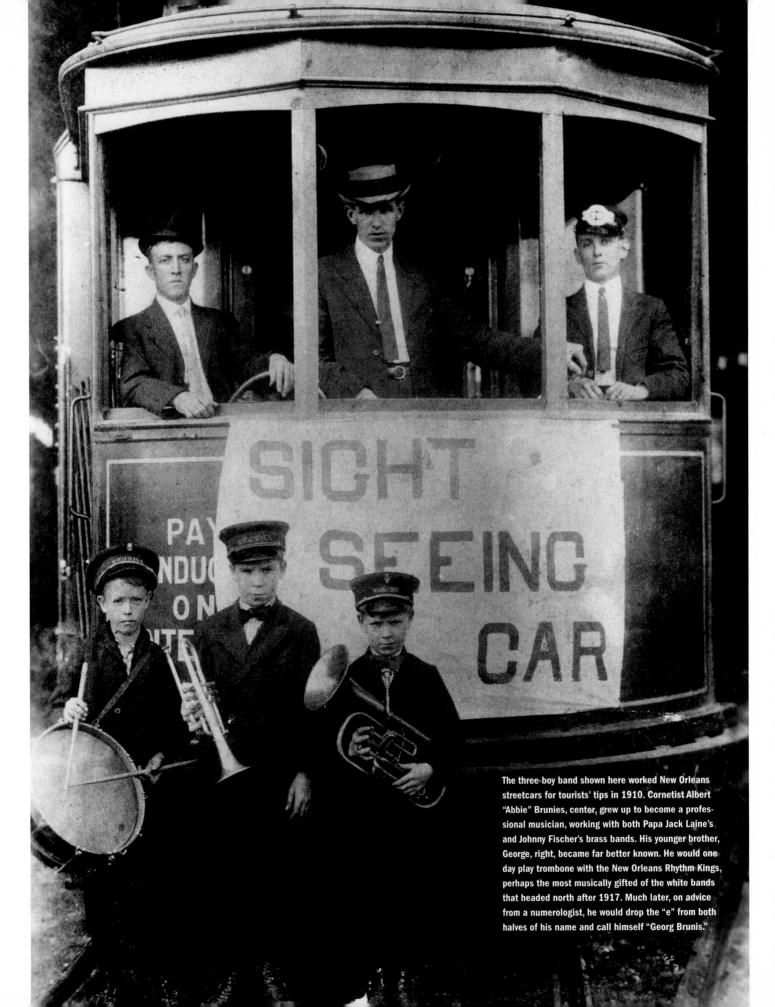

The three-boy band shown here worked New Orleans streetcars for tourists' tips in 1910. Cornetist Albert "Abbie" Brunies, center, grew up to become a professional musician, working with both Papa Jack Laine's and Johnny Fischer's brass bands. His younger brother, George, right, became far better known. He would one day play trombone with the New Orleans Rhythm Kings, perhaps the most musically gifted of the white bands that headed north after 1917. Much later, on advice from a numerologist, he would drop the "e" from both halves of his name and call himself "Georg Brunis."

musician's union and for the first time compete on an equal footing with blacks.

"You know what happened to us [Creole] musicians," Paul Dominguez said.

We were all educated in music and knew our instruments—[but now] we had to change. See us Downtown people, we didn't think so much of this rough Uptown [music] until we couldn't make a living otherwise. . . .

Say, for instance, I was working with the Olympia Band, working one or two nights a week for two dollars and a half a night. The [gambling den called The] 25's here in [the vice district] pay you a dollar and a quarter and tips, but you working seven nights. Naturally, wouldn't I quit the Olympia and go to this tonk? Wouldn't I? . . . Well . . . that's how they make a fiddler out of a violinist . . . a fiddler is *not* a violinist, but a violinist can be a fiddler. If I wanted to make a living, I had to be rowdy like the other group. I had to jazz it or rag it or any other damn thing. . . . [Buddy] Bolden caused all that.

THE *FEELING* OF THE MAN

In the summer of 1898, the Crescent City shared fully in the fevered patriotism that gripped the country as it went to war with Spain. "New Orleans was very enthusiastic," noted Colonel Leonard Wood, commander of the Rough Riders, as he passed through town on the way to the front, "Streets full of people and best of all the American flag in the hands of all. The cost of this war is amply repaid by seeing the old flag as one sees it today in the South. We are indeed once more a united country."

The city's brass bands vied with one another to see which could provide the most impressive send-off from the levee as American troops boarded troopships for Tampa,

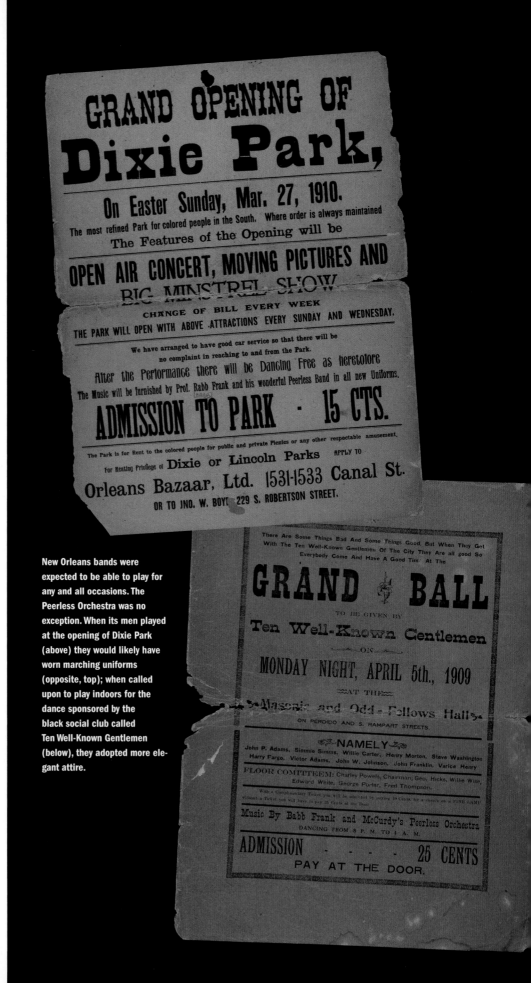

New Orleans bands were expected to be able to play for any and all occasions. The Peerless Orchestra was no exception. When its men played at the opening of Dixie Park (above) they would likely have worn marching uniforms (opposite, top); when called upon to play indoors for the dance sponsored by the black social club called Ten Well-Known Gentlemen (below), they adopted more elegant attire.

The only known photograph of Buddy Bolden and his orchestra, made in 1905. Standing, left to right, William Warner, Willie Cornish, Buddy Bolden, and James Johnson; seated are Frank Lewis and Jefferson Mumford.

the jumping-off point for the assault on Cuba. When it came time to bid farewell to the men of the all-black tenth cavalry, the best-loved black band in town did the honors, and its leader, the cornetist Buddy Bolden, played "Home, Sweet Home" with such tenderness and conviction that some of the men jumped overboard and swam for shore—or so old New Orleans musicians liked to remember.

Like a good many of the stories that would swirl around Buddy Bolden, it clearly never happened. Army officers were rarely impressed by homesickness or sentimental music, no matter how beautifully played; and any soldier, black or white, who had tried to desert by jumping ship would have been recaptured immediately—or shot in the water. But the fact that Bolden's contemporaries found the legend wholly plausible is vivid evidence of the special power his playing must have had.

If the memories of those who heard him are to be trusted, he seems from the first to have been solidly in the American brass band tradition of master cornetists but also somehow different from other New Orleans musicians—louder, bolder, more innovative.

People sought him out not just to hear his band but to hear *him* and what he personally could do with the tunes he played. Marching bands had long since begun to "rag" their music, adding syncopation and embellishments to familiar strains as they moved through the city streets. But Buddy Bolden may have been the *very* first—and was certainly one of the first—to bring that sound inside the dance hall and blend it with the blues.

He remains something of a mystery. Tales tell of a big, flamboyant man who liked to wear his collar open on parade days so that the adoring women who carried his hat and coat could admire his broad chest and red flannel undershirt, but in the single battered photograph that survives he seems sure of himself but otherwise unprepossessing and of normal size. He was never recorded, so that no one now can be sure just how his music sounded. And madness would cut short his career before jazz—the distinctive blend of blues and church music, ragtime and military marches, and all the other elements of the New Orleans mix he helped to pioneer—was known much beyond the confines of his city.

It took the jazz historian Donald M. Marquis more than a decade to hunt down even a handful of indisputable facts about his life. Charles Joseph Bolden was born in New Orleans in 1877, the year Reconstruction ended. The grandson of a slave and the son of a drayman who died when the boy was only seven, Bolden grew up and lived for most of his life on First Street, in an integrated workingman's neighborhood where every kind of music was his for the hearing. Most of the neighbors were Irish and German immigrants: the white jazz clarinetist Larry Shields was born just two doors up the street. Brass bands, both black and white, paraded often through the neighborhood.

Bolden is thought to have attended the Fisk School for Boys, where the rudiments of music were part of the curriculum, and he is known regularly to have worshipped at the St. John Baptist Church, celebrated for the special fervor with which its congregation sang spirituals and jubilees. The trombonist Kid Ory alleged that Bolden also often attended a Holiness church at Jackson and Franklin "but not for religion, he went there to get ideas on music. He'd hear those songs and he would change them a little. In those . . . churches they sometimes had drums and a piano while the people sang and clapped their hands. Sometimes they'd have guests and invite a trumpet player or a trombone player to come over

and play with them. . . . That's where Buddy got it from and that's how it all started." In any case, Bolden's listeners would later routinely compare the response Baptist preachers elicited from the faithful to the shouts of approval that greeted his playing on the bandstand.

He mastered the plasterer's trade—few New Orleans musicians expected to support themselves as musicians in those days—but about 1894 he also took cornet lessons from a neighbor who happened to be keeping company with his widowed mother. Soon, he was playing with a string band for dancing, then leading his own brass band and billing himself as "Professor" Bolden. He and his men performed everything demanding New Orleans audiences could want—waltzes, mazurkas, schottisches, polkas, rags, spirituals, blues. And they performed them all over town: in street parades and at tea dances, at picnic grounds and balloon ascensions, and for black dancers at Masonic Hall, Globe Hall, Jackson Hall, Perseverance Hall, and Union Sons Hall—better known to the patrons who savored its ripe humid atmosphere as Funky Butt Hall.

His more decorous appearances ended with a honeyed version of "Home, Sweet Home" to signal to the dancers that it was time to leave. But around midnight, at places where more was expected of him, he would roar into a signature tune called "Don't Go Away Nobody" and the crowd knew it was in for slow-dancing till sunup. "[O]n those old . . . low-down blues," a fellow musician recalled, "that boy could make the women jump out the window. . . . [H]e had a moan in his cornet that just went through you, just like you were in church or something."

Bolden was an entertainer as well as a musician. His best-known number was variously known as "Funky Butt" and "Buddy Bolden's Blues," with changeable lyrics made up for the occasion. Most were simply raunchy but one version ridiculed a local judge named J. J. Fogarty, who seemed to have it in for members of Bolden's band. "The police put you in jail if they heard you singing that song," one musician remembered, and once, when Bolden launched into it during a street parade, "the people started singing, [and] policemen began whipping heads."

By the time this photograph was taken during the 1930s, Funky Butt Hall, right, where Buddy Bolden often played the blues till dawn, had been transformed into the Greater St. Matthews Baptist Church.

At first, Creole musicians were openly scornful of Bolden and what they called his "ratty" music. Pops Foster recalled that Bolden "played very good for the style of stuff he was doing. He played nothing but the blues and all that stink music, and he played it loud." The cornetist Peter Bocage was only slightly more generous: "He had a good tone, but . . . [h]e played everything in B-flat. He played a lot of blues, slow drag. . . . Blues was their standby."

But the raw power of his music—and its obvious impact on the crowds that turned out to hear him—began to win the grudging respect of some Creoles. The clarinetist George Baquet remembered first hearing Bolden and his band at an after-midnight dance at Odd Fellow's Hall.

Nobody took their hats off. It was plenty rough. You paid fifteen cents and walked in. The band, six of them, was sitting on a low stand. They had their hats on and were resting, pretty sleepy. All of a sudden, Buddy stomps, knocks on the floor with his trumpet to give the beat and they all sit up straight. They played "Make Me a Pallet." Everybody rose and yelled out, "Oh, Mr. Bolden, play it for us, Buddy, play it!" I'd never heard anything like that before. I'd played "legitimate" stuff. But this, it was something that pulled me in. They got me up on the stand and I played with them. After that I didn't play legitimate so much.

John Robichaux was Bolden's greatest rival. On weekend afternoons he and his well-turned-out Creole orchestra presided over the music pavilion in the center of Lincoln Park. Bolden reigned supreme just across Short Street in Johnson Park, and nothing pleased him more than to point his cornet at Robichaux's listeners and blow something so loud, so hot, that they could not resist rushing over to hear what else he had in store for them. He was, he said, "calling my children home."

Soon, younger Creole musicians, too, were answering his call, seeking a way to incorporate into their own playing his driving beat, his affinity for the blues, his eagerness to improvise. Bolden and his men "made their own music and they played it their own way, you understand?" Peter Bocage said. "So that's the way jazz started—just through the *feeling* of the man . . . his improvisations."

There was, as yet, no name for the music Buddy Bolden and other New Orleans musicians—black, Creole, and white—began to play at the dawn of the new century, and some older musicians would call what they played "ragtime" to the end of their lives. But the eventual result would be a brand-new form—"not spirituals or the blues or ragtime" or any of the other kinds of music heard in the streets of New Orleans, one musician remembered, "but everything all at once, each one putting something over on the other." Like the city that gave it birth, like the country that would soon embrace it, this new music would always be more than the sum of its parts.

HELLISH DREAMS

On the evening of Monday, July 23, 1900, three New Orleans policemen spotted two black men sitting on the back steps of a white family's house near the corner of Dryade and Washington Streets. They asked the men what they were doing there.

One gave his name as Robert Charles. He had come to New Orleans from Mississippi six years earlier, after a shootout with a white railroad employee who had dared try to take from him a gun Charles claimed was his. He had become convinced that there was no future for blacks in America, and between odd jobs he handed out pamphlets on the street, calling for wholesale emigration to Africa.

Charles told the policemen he was waiting for a friend. An officer ordered him to

move on and when Charles refused, swung his nightstick, then drew his revolver. Charles pulled his own pistol. The policeman fell, wounded. Charles was hit, too, but made it to his rooming house and picked up a rifle. When the police came after him, he shot and killed two of them before getting away again. The news spread across the city. The following evening hundreds of angry whites gathered at the city's monument to Robert E. Lee. The crowd's self-appointed leader was the mayor of nearby Kenner. "The only way you can teach these niggers a lesson and put them in their place," he shouted, "is to go out and lynch a few of them."

At about that time, Big Eye Nelson remembered, Buddy Bolden was getting ready to play with a string band at The 25's, at the corner of Iberville and Franklin in the black section of the red-light district. Nelson was playing bass that evening and had just slipped his instrument out of its case when a woman ran in off the street and urged the musicians to "knock off"—a white mob was on its way.

Bolden paid no attention: "We never had nothing like that in New Orleans yet," one of his men told her, "and it won't happen tonight." The band began to play. Then, suddenly, the street outside was filled with the sound of running, shouting men. There were shots, curses, screams.

"Me, I was sitting at the inside end of the bandstand playing bass," Nelson recalled. "All them boys flung themselves on me in getting away from the door and out toward the back. The bass was bust to kindling. . . . We made it out the window . . . and into the alley but, man, that alley was already loaded with folks." Nelson, Bolden, and their companions eventually found sanctuary in a friend's house, but the cornetist's gold watch was left behind, hanging on the wall above the bandstand, and when the three-day riot finally ended, the body of Big Eye Nelson's father was found among the dead.

For four days after that, no one could find Robert Charles. Then, a black informer told

The most miserable feeling a youngster in New Orleans can experience is to be in the classroom studying when he hears a brass band approaching, swinging like crazy past the school and then fading off into the distance. You will witness a lot of sad expressions in that room. Now, if it happens to be lunch-hour recess—12 to 1— when the bell rings at 1 p.m. a lot of seats will be vacant. . . . The music would excite and move you to such an extent that when you would realize it, you had second-lined maybe ten or twenty blocks from school.

—Danny Barker

Papa Jack Laine, seated, and his Reliance Marching Band in 1910. Laine was an entrepreneur as well as a musician. He paid two thousand dollars for a languishing tent show that year, grandly renamed it Laine's Greater Majestic Minstrels, and set it up near the streetcar barns at Canal and White Streets, expecting big profits. Instead, a summer hurricane blew away the tent and most of his savings. Laine was a mentor to scores of white musicians: six years after this photograph was taken, clarinetist Alcide "Yellow" Nuñez, second from left, would be working in Chicago with a group called Stein's Band from Dixie, the precursor of the Original Dixieland Jazz Band.

the police he was hiding in a house on Saratoga Street. Hundreds of armed whites joined the police who surrounded it. In the gun battle that followed Charles managed to kill five more attackers and wound another twenty before they finally killed him, then poured so many bullets into his corpse that he became unrecognizable—inspiring the false story that he had somehow escaped.

Whites blamed all the trouble on outside agitators from the North. "Under the dark, seething mass of humanity that surrounds us . . . all appears peaceful and delightful," the New Orleans *Daily State* warned its readers, "we know not, it seems what hellish dreams are arising underneath. . . . We are . . . under the regime of the free negro in the midst of a dangerous element of servile uprising, not for any real cause, but

from the native race hatred of the negro, inflamed continually by our Northern philanthropists."

Robert Charles became a folk hero to a good many black people in New Orleans. Someone wrote a song about him, too; but even years later, it was thought unwise to sing it in the presence of whites.

Race relations in the city never recovered —even when it came to music. For years, black and white bands had played for picnickers along the shores of Lake Pontchartrain, the drummer Paul Barbarin recalled:

On Mondays at Lucian's Pavilion there was always an attraction. You would find a picnic plus the Imperial, the Superior or the Olympia Band. Imag-

AT LAST ON BROADWAY

Will Marion Cook and song sheets for three of his hits

Ragtime, born in the black neighborhoods of the middle west, had already swept New York City by 1898, and the African-American cakewalk was the dance of choice among young people of all races. To men like the classically trained composer Will Marion Cook, a former student of Antonin Dvořák's, and the poet Paul Laurence Dunbar the time seemed ripe to mount an all-black show on Broadway. *Clorindy, or the Origin of the Cakewalk* was the result. An hour-long series of skits filled with so many crude minstrel-style gags that Cook's mother wept with embarrassment when she first heard them, *Clorindy* nonetheless brought twenty-six African-American performers onstage to dazzle Manhattan theater audiences.

Opening night at the Casino Roof Garden was a triumph, Cook remembered: "My chorus sang like Russians, dancing meanwhile like Negroes and cakewalking like angels! When the last note sounded, the audience stood and cheered for at least ten minutes. . . . It was pandemonium but pandemonium was never dearer to my heart. . . . I was so delirious that I drank a glass of water, thought it wine and got gloriously drunk. Negroes were at last on Broadway, and there to stay. . . . Nothing could stop us, and nothing did for a decade."

Other successful shows followed for Will Marion Cook —including *In Dahomey* and *Bandana Land*—and he vowed someday to write one that opened with at least ten minutes of serious music "worthy of his talents" before returning to the light-hearted material white audiences had come to expect from black entertainers. Other black songwriters, including Bob Cole and the Johnson brothers, James Weldon and J. Rosamond, managed to get their work produced on Broadway, as well.

But by 1910, white theatergoers had lost interest in the novelty of seeing black productions. Black casts would not reappear on Broadway until the 1920s, their return brought about in part by the power and popularity of still another African-American creation just being born when Cook and Dunbar put on their first show—jazz music.

ine the summer sunshine, the blue lake, the camps white, green, yellow, every color of paint. The white summer dresses, many colored parasols. The gold lettering on the brewery trucks, the harness shining . . . About five or six bands playing five or six different tunes, and not over 100 yards apart. Laughing men rolling a half keg of beer along the boardwalk to a camp. Hot dogs, oysters, crawfish, green crabs and fat lake trout. Everybody eating, singing and making music. This was a friendly place and a friendly time. Maybe two camps away there would be a white band. Don't think we didn't have many great white jazzmen in those days. We had 'em. And they played great. But there was honest, musical rivalry.

After the Robert Charles riot, that honest rivalry would sometimes turn poisonous. At the turn of the century the best-known leader of a white marching band was Papa Jack Laine, a drummer, blacksmith, and sometime boxer who began organizing his Reliance Brass Bands while still in grade school and kept at it for more than forty years; by 1910 he controlled enough musicians to send ten different outfits into the streets on a single day. Two generations of white New Orleans musicians got their start through him: "I picked them boys up playing . . . when they were in knee-pants," he liked to say.

Laine would contend all his life that non-whites had had nothing whatsoever to do with the music he and his men played; the only reason they ever learned how to syncopate, he claimed, was from listening to him. But two of the musicians he most often hired were actually light-skinned Creoles: clarinetist Achille Baquet and the trombone player Dave Perkins, who routinely stood on the rear platform of New Orleans streetcars rather than have to choose between sitting at the front with whites or in the back with blacks. (They were both "niggers,"

Laine admitted many years later, but "they played so good we couldn't tell what color they was.")

The pointless argument over ownership of America's music started early and, sadly, has never really stopped.

JELLY ROLL

"It is evidently known, beyond contradiction, that New Orleans is the cradle of jazz," Jelly Roll Morton would write in 1938, "and I, myself, happened to be [its] creator in the year 1902." Morton had been only twelve years old in 1902, his kind of music had long been out of fashion when he made his pronouncement, and to many of those who remembered Morton at all it then seemed just the latest in a lifelong series of outrageous boasts. "He claimed he invented a lot of things he didn't," Pops Foster said. "If you'd listen to him talk long enough, he'd claim he invented the piano or anything else that came to his mind."

Jazz had no single creator, of course; it began as a gumbo stirred and seasoned by hundreds of hands. But Morton's claim had more heft than it seemed to have at the time he made it. "He could back up everything he *said*," his friend the clarinetist Omer Simeon once said, "with what he could *do*." Morton was in fact among the first to play jazz, its first theorist and composer and master of form, the first to write it down, and by doing so, among the first to help spread New Orleans music across the country. From the beginning he seems to have wanted, both in his elegant piano playing and in the tunes he began composing about 1905, to produce music that incorporated both blues and ragtime but was clearly different from either one.

The blues were full of passion but too simple, he said; besides, most blues musicians were mere "one-tune piano players." Ragtime players, on the other hand, were too prone to speeding things up, while the principle underlying the music they played

Jelly Roll Morton was just twenty when this portrait was made but already a three-year veteran of the road. "He never stopped running," a friend said, "couldn't seem to rest one place more than a few days."

was just "a certain kind of syncopation, and only certain tunes can be played in that idea."

"Jazz music," on the other hand, he said, is "a *style,* not compositions. Any kind of music may be played in jazz, if one has the knowledge." No one had more style—or more knowledge—than Jelly Roll Morton. "No jazz piano player," he said, "can ever really play jazz unless they try to get the imitation of a band," and, true to that belief, he sought to reproduce something like the polyphony of the New Orleans marching bands at the keyboard: his left hand repro-

Louise Monette, the mother of Jelly Roll Morton

duced the bass line, sometimes interspersed with figures reminiscent of tailgate trombone, while his right hand mirrored the instrumental lead of the cornet and clarinet. He brought to everything he played—ragtime and blues, French and Italian operatic airs, Spanish popular songs and dances—a new, smoother kind of syncopation. Each tune was transformed under his long, supple fingers and to the rhythm of his loudly tapping foot into something altogether new. "You could go by a house where Jelly Roll was playing," the bass player Bill Johnson recalled, "and you'd know it was him because nobody . . . did play just like him."

He was born Ferdinand Joseph Lamothe in New Orleans on October 20, 1890—he eventually changed his last name to Morton for "business reasons," he once explained, "because I didn't want to be called 'Frenchy' "—and he embodied within himself all the racial contradictions of his hometown. He would one day claim that his ancestors "were in the city of New Orleans long before the Louisiana Purchase and all my folks came directly from the shores . . . of France," and he rarely missed an opportunity to contrast his own light skin

and slender features with those of blacks, many of whom, he liked to say, had "lips like bumpers on a boxcar." In fact, the members of his family were relative newcomers to the city, and he was not French at all but the illegitimate son of a Creole mother and father who traced their ancestry back to the island of Haiti.

Nor did his Creole airs keep him from eagerly immersing himself early in the mostly black world of the blues that were everywhere around him. As he himself said about his city, "We had all nations in New Orleans, but with the music we could creep in close to other people," and he never forgot the first blues he heard, played and sung by a neighbor woman named Mamie Desdoumes. She had just three fingers on her right hand, Morton remembered, and only knew one tune, which she played on the piano "all day long after she would first get up in the morning":

I stood on the corner, my feet was
    dripping wet,
I asked every man I met . . .
Can't give me a dollar, give me a lousy
    dime,
Just to feed that hungry man of mine.

Morton would one day make blues like that his own.

His father's wayward ways soon drove his mother to leave him and move in with another man. "We always had some kind of musical instrument in the house," Morton recalled, "including guitar, drums, piano, trombone, . . . harmonica, and jew's harp. We had lots of 'em and everybody played for their pleasure." At the age of seven, he was already good enough at guitar to play for dances in a string trio. A few years later, he was singing in a quartet that specialized in performing spirituals at wakes in exchange for "plenty ham sandwiches, cheese sandwiches, mustard slathered all over the bread." From the first he loved the sound of the piano best, but feared that his friends would call him a "sissy" if he tried it. Then, he was taken to the French Opera

House where, he told an interviewer, "I happened to notice a pianist . . . that didn't wear long hair. That was the first time I decided that the instrument was good for a gentleman same as it was a lady."

When Morton was fourteen, his mother died and he and his two sisters moved in with relatives. The following year—wearing long pants stolen from an uncle's closet to fool the policemen who had orders to chase away youngsters in short ones—he began venturing into Storyville, the wide-open, eighteen-square-block vice district. Named after Joseph Story, the upright alderman who had proposed setting the area aside in 1897 in a futile effort to bring a measure of order to his raucous city, it was a place unlike any other in America, a magnet to men from every state and every stratum of society, all intent on pleasure. Some two thousand prostitutes plied their trade in its 230 brothels, their special talents and racial background—"white," "colored," or "octoroon"—were catalogued annually in an official *Blue Book* sold for a quarter on street corners. No one knows how many more women worked the wooden one-room cribs that lined the nearby streets and alleyways. All the customers were white—or at least able to pass for white—but an unofficial "black Storyville" took up the better part of several more blocks beginning just across Canal Street.

In later years, the legend would grow that Storyville—called "the District" by most musicians—was the birthplace of jazz. It wasn't. Few bands ever played in its crowded bars and brothels, largely because management didn't believe dancers could be counted upon to buy drinks. But parlor pianists were in great demand. They didn't take up much space; helped pull men in off the street; provided music for the "naked dances" and sexual circuses featured at some houses; and created a mood that helped persuade customers to empty their pockets.

One Saturday evening, Morton heard that a Storyville madame was looking for

Tom Anderson's Annex at the corner of Basin and Iberville Streets was the most lavish establishment in Storyville. One hundred electric bulbs in the ceiling of the bar cast a blinding light. The gleaming bar itself was half a block long and manned by a dozen bartenders. There were "Private Rooms for the Fair Sex" upstairs, and Anderson's was one of the few places in the District big enough to employ a full-size dance band. Every single building on the block was a brothel, all of them conveniently located right across Basin Street from the terminus of the Southern Railroad that hauled hundreds of potential customers into town at all hours of the day and night.

a new piano player. By then, he said, he was already one of the best "junior pianists" in the city and easily got the job. To mollify the great-grandmother with whom he and his sisters were then living he explained that he wouldn't be coming home at night any more because he was working the late shift at a barrel factory.

Most whorehouses guaranteed their piano players just a dollar a night; a few went as high as five but, Morton recalled, "very often men would come into the houses and hand you a twenty or . . . a fifty-dollar note. . . . Wine flowed much more than water." Morton claimed that—for him at least—any night he made less than a hundred dollars was "a bad night."

"The piano players waited for their tricks just like the girls did," Pops Foster explained.

If a trick was good for the girls, it was good for the piano player too. Most of the guys who went in the whorehouses were half stewed and the drunker they were, the more money they'd tip. The customer picked out the girl and piano player he wanted, and they'd go off to a room. The customer and the girl would drink and make love while the piano player played some slow blues.

After hours, Morton haunted the back room of a place called The Frenchman's where, he said, "everything in the line of hilarity" was available and all the piano players in the District hung out. "We had Spanish [pianists]," he remembered, "we had colored, we had white, we had Frenchmens, we had Americans. We had 'em from all

parts of the world. New Orleans was the stompin' grounds for all the greatest pianists in the country."

Even Morton never claimed to be the District's best piano player; that honor went to the "man of a thousand songs," a ragtime specialist named Tony Jackson, composer of the perennial favorite "Pretty Baby." But, Pops Foster remembered, "Jelly was the best *entertaining* piano player by himself. He knew all the dirty songs and . . . [w]hen a customer would come in the door, Jelly would make up a dirty rhyme on your name and play it to his piano playing." Many years later, Morton would record for the Library of Congress some of the spectacularly gamey tunes he wrote during his Storyville days. They constitute the most vivid possible proof that when it comes to sex and sin, the citizens of the new millennium know nothing their forefathers hadn't already worked out for themselves.

Morton also began to compose more respectable tunes as well as play them, including "The Wolverines" (renamed "Wolverine Blues" by his music publisher, to his fury); "Milneburg Joys," a paean to a Lake Pontchartrain picnic grove; and "Jelly Roll Blues," a paean to himself:

In New Orleans, Louisiana town,
There's the finest boy for miles
    around
Lord, Mister Jelly Roll, your affection
    he has stole. . . .
He's so tall and chancey,
He's the lady's fancy.
Everybody know him,
Certainly do adore him.

When you see him strolling, every-
    body opens up,
He's red hot stuff,
Friends, you can't get enough.
Play it soft—don't abuse.
Play them Jelly Roll Blues.

Morton's best-known early piece was "King Porter Stomp." Named for his friend, the Florida-born pianist Porter King, he kept it in his arsenal as his secret weapon in contests with other piano players; and in a simplified version it would one day be recorded by more than thirty bands and provide Benny Goodman with one of his biggest hits.

Morton's skill and showmanship eventually landed him jobs with the District's highest-paying "land-ladies"—Hilma Burt, Josie Arlington, Gypsy Schaefer, Lulu White "the Octoroon Queen," Antonia Gonzales, who billed herself as "the only Singer of Opera and Female Cornetist in the Tenderloin," and "Countess" Willie V. Piazza, who once shot and killed a customer who had mistreated one of her girls and then was found blameless by twelve sympathetic New Orleans jurors.

Morton was soon doing well, so well that he could afford a finely tailored suit, a gleaming pair of the fashionable shoes called St. Louis flats, and a Stetson hat. "Those days," he remembered, "I thought I would die unless I had a hat with the emblem in it of the name of Stetson." His high-toned clothes proved his downfall. On her way back from church one Sunday morning, his great-grandmother spotted him coming home from work. How could he afford to look so sharp? she asked, and in an uncharacteristic burst of candor, he told her. She threw him out of the house. "A musician is nothing but a bum and a scalawag," she told him. "I don't want you around your sisters, I reckon you better move."

He continued to send money home for the rest of his life, but from the age of seventeen he was on his own, sometimes working in New Orleans but most often on the road: Biloxi, Jacksonville, Gulfport, Memphis, Chicago, Selma, Houston, Oklahoma City, St. Louis, Indianapolis, Philadelphia, Detroit—and in 1917 all the way west to Los Angeles.

Music was always his "first line of business," he said, but when gigs proved hard to find, he had other ways of making a living. He sometimes blacked-up and performed as one half of a vaudeville duo with a comic named Sammy Russell, and it was during one of their early ad-lib routines, he said, that he gave himself his celebrated nickname.

Sam said to me, "You don't know who you talkin' to." I told him I didn't care and we had a little argument. I finally asked him who was he, and he stated to me he was "Sweet Papa Cream Puff, right outa the bakery shop." That seemed to produce a great big laugh. While I was standin' there muggin', . . . a thought came to me that I better say somethin' about the bakery shop, [so I said] I was "Sweet Papa Jelly Roll, with stove pipes in my hips—and all the women in town was dyin' to turn my damper down."

Between engagements, Morton also gambled at cards, pimped, hustled pool, and peddled door-to-door a sticky elixir made up of salt and Coca-Cola that he claimed would cure tuberculosis. Showmanship was always central to his style. The pianist James P. Johnson remembered seeing him work in California:

He would take his overcoat off. It had a special lining that would catch everybody's eye, so he would turn it inside out and, instead of folding it, he would lay it lengthwise along the top of the upright piano. He would do this very slowly, very carefully and very solemnly as if the coat was worth a fortune and had to be handled very tenderly. Then he'd take a big silk handkerchief, shake it out to show it off properly, and dust off the stool. He'd sit down then, hit his special chord—every tickler had his special trademark chord, like a signal—and he'd be gone! The first rag he'd always play was always a spirited one to astound the audience.

Everywhere Jelly Roll Morton went, New Orleans music went, too, even though he often found himself forced to play with musicians who knew little or nothing about it. "When it was a New Orleans man, that wasn't so much trouble," he remembered, "because those boys knew a lot of my breaks, but in traveling from place to place I found other musicians had to be taught. So . . . I began writing down this peculiar form of mathematics and harmonics that was strange to all the world."

In the process of "writing down" New Orleans polyphony in order that uninitiated musicians could play it, Morton also broke the music down as no one ever had before and few have done since. One by one, he set forth its basic elements:

How to play *breaks*—brief solos played while the band unexpectedly falls silent, meant to add excitement: "A break . . . is like a musical surprise," Morton said.

The "Mirror Ballroom" of Hilma Burt's whorehouse, located next door to Anderson's Annex. Jelly Roll Morton played piano here for the women and their customers but since he was only twelve years old in 1902 when this photograph is said to have been taken, the man at the piano is most likely one of his predecessors.

"Without breaks and without clean breaks and without beautiful ideas in breaks, you . . . haven't got a jazz band and you can't play jazz. Even if a tune hasn't got a break in it, it's always necessary to arrange some kind of a spot to make a break."

How to add *riffs*—unison phrases repeated at regular intervals, meant both to spur on a soloist and to reassure listeners that the band is still working together: "Now the riff is what we call a foundation," he said, "like something that you walk on."

How to mix in what he called the "Spanish tinge"—the languorous bass rhythm of the tango and the earlier Spanish and Caribbean dances New Orleans had always loved—without which Morton believed jazz lacked the proper "seasoning." "You leave the left hand just the same [i.e., playing a tango rhythm]. The difference comes in the right hand—in the syncopation which gives it an entirely different color that really changes from red to blue."

How to set the proper tempo—"A lot of people have the wrong conception of jazz," he said. "Jazz music is to be played sweet. Soft, plenty rhythm."

When you have your plenty rhythm with your plenty swing, it becomes beautiful. . . . You can't make crescendos and diminuendos when one is playing triple forte. You've got to be able to come down in order to go up. If a glass of water is full you can't fill it any more, but if you have half a glass you have an opportunity to put more water in it, and jazz music is based on the same principles.

Despite Morton's efforts, New Orleans music would remain "strange to all the world" for another decade. The Victrola had been introduced in 1901, but no one had yet thought to record New Orleans musicians or the new music they were creating. Jazz was moving across the country, one musician at a time.

A SKY FULL
OF NEW MOONS

Late one April afternoon in 1907, not long after Jelly Roll Morton started composing his own music, a band led by the eighteen-year-old Creole cornetist Freddie Keppard was scheduled to play for a lawn party at the home of Mr. and Mrs. Omar Bechet at 414 Girod Street in New Orleans. Their son Leonard, a promising student of dentistry, was turning twenty-one. There was to be music and dancing on the lawn and plenty of Creole food.

The clarinetist, George Baquet, was late for the engagement and, since the guests had begun to arrive, Keppard and the rest of the band set up in the kitchen and started to play as best they could without him. Then, from somewhere inside the house, a clarinet joined in. "Who the hell is that?" Keppard asked, and went looking for the source of the sound. Eventually, he found the Bechets' youngest son, Sidney, perched in his brother's dentist chair in a darkened room and playing as loudly as he could. The sturdy, round-faced boy was just nine years old and entirely self-taught.

Keppard asked him to come out into the kitchen. "I'll never forget that feeling I had," Bechet remembered, "playing with those men. . . . They were masters. . . . They really gave me the feeling of being discontented until I'd be able to work regular with them. Oh, it was grand!" George Baquet eventually turned up—he'd been playing in a parade. He took out his clarinet, Bechet recalled, "and he ran his hand over my head and . . . just laughed. And he kept me there all evening, playing right along beside of him. That night, I guess I was the richest kid in New Orleans. You couldn't have bought me for a sky full of new moons."

Baquet offered to give the prodigy lessons in exchange for pouches of Bull Durham chewing tobacco. Other clarinetists tried to help him, too. Classically trained Luis "Papa" Tio sought to persuade

Sidney Bechet, already on the road at nineteen. He had, he said, a lifelong "need to be moving."

The Eagle Band which, the bassist George "Pops" Foster said, "played hot all the time." As with a good many New Orleans outfits, its personnel often changed. In this 1916 version, Frankie Dusen is the trombonist and leader and Louis "Big Eye" Nelson plays the clarinet. The cornetist was Buddy Petit who, Danny Barker recalled, played with such power that during parades admirers "would be ten deep around [him] as he walked along."

him to avoid the raw new kind of music now being heard in the streets of his city. "No! No! No!" he told the boy. "We do not like to bark like a dog or meow like a cat!" But Bechet preferred the big "ratty" sound of Big Eye Nelson to Tio's "legitimate" tone: "Some musicians played . . . prettily," he said, "but I like the playing that makes me want to dance." From the first he was too impatient to take instruction from anyone for long. Nor could anyone make him study theory. "He wouldn't learn notes," Nelson remembered, "but he was my best scholar."

The boy's parents had hoped music would be a hobby not a profession—as it was in many Creole families, as it had been with all four of his older brothers. They sug-

gested he become a bricklayer or perhaps a hairdresser, instead of a musician. "We didn't want to jeopardize our family by mixing with the rough element," Leonard Bechet remembered. "We worried a lot about Sidney when he'd be out playing."

The boy didn't care. All he wanted to do was play—and hang around the musicians decades older than he whom he already considered his peers. Still wearing short pants, Bechet was soon sitting in with some of the best bands in New Orleans. At fourteen, he joined forces with another Creole prodigy, cornetist Buddy Petit, and formed a seven-piece band called the Young Olympians, marching in parades, performing at picnics, and cutting a wide swath

among the girls who came out to see them. "We could never keep our hands on that Sidney," Big Eye Nelson once admitted. "Regular little devil running off down the alley after them little women."

The Bechets did everything they could to dissuade their boy from pursuing music. They got a municipal magistrate to order him to stay in school—he paid no attention—and when they locked up his clarinet he either borrowed someone else's or talked whoever had hired him for the evening into putting up enough money to get one out of pawn.

At fifteen or so, he signed on with the hardest-driving outfit in town, the Eagle Band, led by the cornetist Willie "Bunk"

Johnson. Creole musicians, Bechet said, were "damn fine . . . some of the best for ragtime; but when it came to the blues you couldn't beat Bunk or the Eagle Orchestra." This was a "gut-bucket band," Bechet remembered, "a low-down band" and virtually unbeatable in a street contest. When a downtown Creole band strayed across Canal Street into uptown territory, one Creole musician remembered, the only thing to do was "get out of that neighborhood if you see the Eagle Band coming."

Bechet loved it, loved playing at rough joints including Funky Butt Hall, where Buddy Bolden had once held sway, and also loved the worldly ways of its leader, whose heroic drinking and constant womanizing Bechet eagerly learned to emulate. He soon left home to devote himself full-time to music and the musician's peripatetic life, finding quarters where he could—"Tonight he might be here," a friend remembered, "and tomorrow night there"—and playing three and four engagements a day, so many that he sometimes fell asleep on the streetcars that took him from one to the next.

Later, members of Bechet's family would be philosophical about the life he had chosen to lead. "A person has to go through all that rough stuff like Sidney went through to play music like him," Leonard Bechet once told an interviewer. "You have to play with all varieties of people. You have to play real *hard* when you play for Negroes. You got to *go* some to avoid their criticism. . . . If you do, you get that drive. Bolden had it. Bunk Johnson had it."

Sidney Bechet had it, too, and he expressed it with such passion and volume that it sometimes seemed about to tear his instrument apart. "He was always fiery," said Peter Bocage. "It's his makeup. He don't sit still one minute. There's always something he's got to be doing. And when he plays he's the same way. He's fired up all the time."

Bechet quickly earned two reputations. As a difficult personality—"powerful mean," he once admitted, and unwilling to work in any band in which anyone was paid a penny more than he was; and as a clarinet player unlike any other, in New Orleans or anywhere else, who saw music as something like perpetual combat in which he was determined always to come out on top. New Orleans brass band music was an ensemble art, but the cornetist had generally been the first among equals. It was he who played the lead, stating the theme around which the clarinet was expected to weave obbligato embellishments. But second best was never enough for Sidney Bechet. He tried playing lead cornet himself for a time—and was said by those who heard him to have been as loud and forceful as anyone in town. But even on clarinet he performed with such power that he routinely overshadowed cornetists accustomed to the hero's role. "When Sidney was playing . . . around 1914 to 1916," his fellow clarinetist Albert Nicholas said, "he outplayed them all."

Soon, being the most admired clarinetist in his hometown didn't satisfy him, either. "There was so many fine musicianers around New Orleans then, so much a man could learn from," he remembered. "But I was getting restless. I'd been hearing so much about up North, about this place and that place. I was having an itch to go." An enterprising young New Orleans pianist and songwriter named Clarence Williams gave him his first chance to see the wider world. Williams thought big. By traveling from town to town with a quartet that performed comedy acts as well as playing his music, he was sure he could boost the sales of his song sheets at the five-and-dime stores that peddled them. Things didn't work out that way. He had neglected to ensure enough bookings to keep his little troupe in business. "We'd heard all about how the North was freer, and we were wanting to go real bad," Bechet said. "But my God, where do we end up but in Texas. . . . We played dances, shows and one-night stands. . . . For a while there it was nothing but one dime store after another." The quartet

Edward "Kid" Ory, playing trombone, second from left, and his Woodland Band, 1905. Ory grew up on the Woodland Plantation in La Place, Louisiana, less than thirty miles from New Orleans. As a boy, he fashioned homemade instruments from cigar boxes and fishing line for a band of playmates. At thirteen, he organized fish fries and played at baseball games to raise money for factory-made instruments. His Creole family, like Jelly Roll Morton's and Sidney Bechet's, initially took a dim view of his becoming a musician but he paid no attention: "I couldn't see anything but music. . . . The girls was worrying me. . . . I was sure if I learned music, I can get a girl, you know."

eventually fell apart. Bechet joined a carnival, which got him only as far as a little redneck town near Beaumont where black strangers were warned to move on by nightfall and black citizens were forbidden to leave their homes after dark. There, after playing a dance in someone's house, Bechet somehow found himself walking along the railroad tracks after midnight with what he called "an interfering white man . . . who won't stay with his own and won't let you be." Words were exchanged. Bechet felled the man with a piece of wood, then jumped a freight to Galveston, where one of his brothers was living. There, he befriended a Mexican guitarist, with whom he was picked up late one night for being drunk and disorderly. Bechet escaped being brutalized in jail only because his captors wore themselves out beating and kicking his companion senseless. Then, he sat listening in the darkness as his fellow prisoners sang a blues:

> Tied in a hundred feet of chain,
> Every link of the chain was initial to
>   his name
> Warden come early that morning for
>   him to be hung
> On account of something he hadn't
>   done.

"Oh my God, that was a blues," Bechet remembered. "The way they sang it there, it was something you would send down to earth if it had been given to you to be God. What you'd send to your son in trouble if he was on earth and you was in Heaven."

Bechet's brother bailed him out the next morning and he made his way back to New Orleans as fast as he could. But as soon as he got the chance, Sidney Bechet would be on his way again. He would remain restless and dissatisfied all his life. No musician in the whole history of jazz had a more powerful personality, and none would be able to express it more powerfully on his horn. But that same personality would trip him up again and again. "Somehow, there's just no need to go looking for trouble," he wrote.

"The way it is, trouble comes looking for you." Over the coming years, it would come often looking for Sidney Bechet.

BETTER THAN THE REST

By 1906, Buddy Bolden was the best-known black musician in New Orleans, hailed as *King* Bolden by the children who gathered in front of his home on First Street each morning, just to hear him practice. "He blew his horn so loud," one of them recalled, "he'd blow everyone out of the house." But there were other, younger claimants to his crown, most notably young Freddie Keppard whose ability to play loud may even have exceeded Bolden's. Bolden had always been a heavy drinker: "[He] drank all the whiskey he could find or anybody else could find," Jelly Roll Morton remembered. Soon, he started to develop headaches, began to talk to himself, quarreled with the members of his band, seemed increasingly agitated and frightened of everything. His mother did what she could to calm his fears but nothing seemed to help.

On March 2 of that year, his name appeared in the newspapers for the first and only time in his life.

> Thinking that he was being drugged by his mother, Charles Bolden, a negro, living at 2302 First street, jumped out of bed yesterday afternoon while in a state of dementia and struck her over the head with a water pitcher. Bolden, who is a musician, has been sick for some time. His mother was by his bedside yesterday afternoon giving what succor she could when suddenly his mind was carried away with the belief that she was administering some deadly drug to him. Grabbing the water pitcher, he broke it over his mother's head, inflicting a scalp wound, which was pronounced not serious.

He spent a day or two in detention and seemed all right again after his release. But he soon proved so quarrelsome, so unreliable, so suspicious, one musician remembered, that his band fell apart and "all his good friends left him." Challenged to a contest at Globe Hall with a mostly Creole band led by cornetist Manuel Perez and his old friend Big Eye Nelson, he failed to turn up at the appointed time. On Labor Day, he set out to play in the big annual parade, just as he had for years. But somewhere along the line of march he abruptly walked away from the other musicians and went home. He would never play his horn in public again.

On March 13, 1907, a little over a year after his first arrest, his mother again had to call the police. She was afraid her son would hurt her—or himself. In April, he was locked up in the State Insane Asylum at Jackson. He was just twenty-nine years old and would never leave the institution. One of the doctors in charge later described his condition:

> Accessible and answers fairly well. Paranoid delusions, also grandiose. Auditory hallucinations and visual. Talks to self. Much reaction. Picks things off wall. Tears his clothes. Insight and judgment lacking. . . . [L]ooks deteriorated, but memory is good. Has a string of talk that is incoherent. Hears the voices of people that bothered him before he came here. . . . DIAGNOSIS: *Dementia praecox,* paranoid type.

No longer able to recognize his own mother when she came to visit, too disturbed even to play in the Colored Patient's Band, Bolden would live on for twenty-five years, oblivious to what happened to the music he had been among the first to play. Sometimes, though, the chaplain remembered, he would ask to borrow a cornet and blow a chorus or two—enough so that "you could tell he was better than the rest."

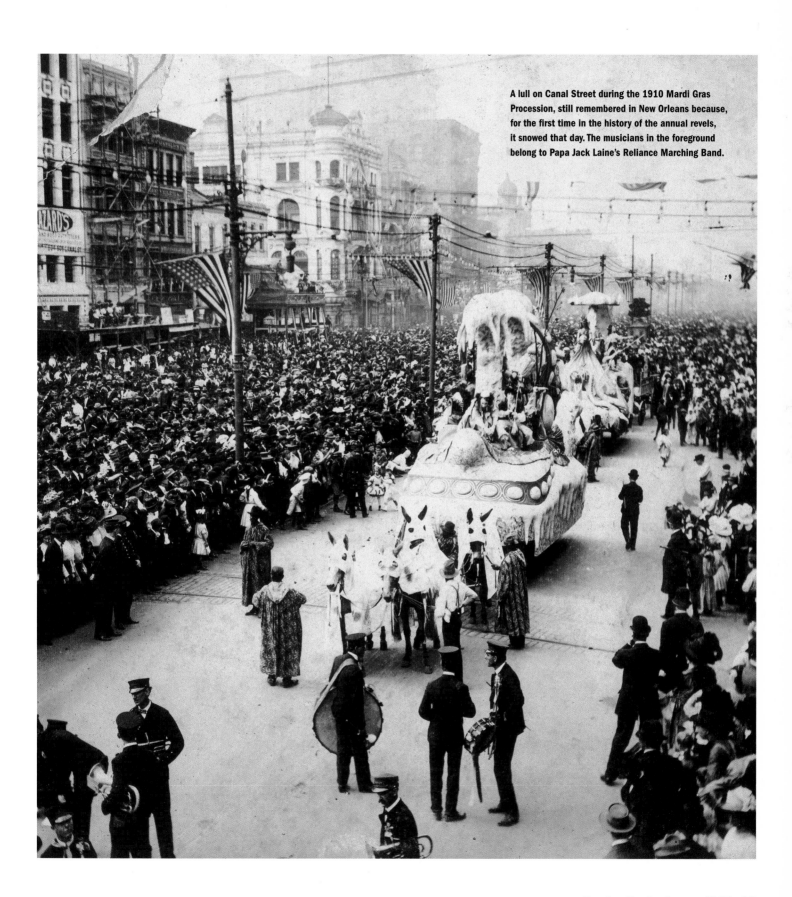

A lull on Canal Street during the 1910 Mardi Gras Procession, still remembered in New Orleans because, for the first time in the history of the annual revels, it snowed that day. The musicians in the foreground belong to Papa Jack Laine's Reliance Marching Band.

THE GIFT

One day in late 1912, before Sidney Bechet had left his parents' home to fend for himself, Bunk Johnson had turned up at the Bechets's door, asking for him. He'd heard a boys' quartet singing for pennies on a street corner in black Storyville, Johnson said: Sidney had to come and hear "how they sing and harmonize." Bechet agreed to go with him. The boys were "real good," he remembered, so good he asked them to come home with him for dinner. He wanted his family to hear them sing.

The bright-eyed eleven-year-old who sang tenor said he would love to come—the prospect of a good Creole meal was very pleasing—but the soles of his shoes were so full of holes that it would be painful for him to walk all the way across town to get there. Bechet, only fifteen himself but already earning a grown-up's wages, grandly tossed the

The Original Tuxedo Jazz Band played for white picnickers—and every other kind of audience in New Orleans. Oscar "Papa" Celestin, the cornetist, and trombonist William "Bébé" Ridgley shared its leadership until 1925, when Celestin formed his own Tuxedo Jazz Orchestra that specialized in playing for dances. He was a mentor to a host of fine musicians, including Louis Armstrong, who recalled the Tuxedo Band as "the hottest in town."

boy a fifty-cent piece to get his shoes re-soled, then hurried home again to tell his mother there'd be guests for dinner.

The eleven-year-old pocketed the coin. Neither he nor his friends ever bothered to turn up at the Bechets. "I remember running around with a lot of bad boys," the boy wrote many years later, "which did a lot of crazy things." He was known by the pimps and prostitutes who were his closest neighbors as "Little Louis," but his full name was Louis Armstrong, and the story of his rise is as astonishing, as American—and ultimately as inexplicable—as Abraham Lincoln's.

"My whole life has been happiness," he wrote toward the end of it. "Through all the misfortunes . . . I did not plan anything. Life was there for me, and I accepted it." Raised mostly on the turbulent streets of black Storyville, and surrounded from birth by enough vice and violence to fill a sociologist's file cabinet, he took part in some of it, observed all of it, made no easy judgments about any of it, and managed miraculously to incorporate it all into his art—the good and the bad, the ugly as well as the beautiful. In the process, his unrivaled genius, his "gift," he called it, helped turn jazz into a soloist's art—influenced every singer, every instrumentalist, every *artist,* who

came after him. For more than five decades, he would make everyone who heard him feel that no matter how bad things got, everything was bound to turn out all right, after all.

He was born on August 4, 1901—not, as he himself always believed, on July 4, 1900—at 723 Jane Alley in a section of New Orleans so violent it was called "The Battlefield." His father, William Armstrong, who stoked boilers at a turpentine factory when he could find work, abandoned his children early and only rarely saw them afterward. "We had no father," Armstrong remembered.

His mother—Mary Albert, known as Mayann—was just fifteen, a refugee from the sugarcane fields. She sometimes worked as a prostitute to support herself and left her son in her own mother's charge for the first five years of his life. But after she took him back again and moved him and his younger sister Beatrice (later known as Mama Lucy) into her single rented room at Liberty and Perdido Streets in the heart of black Storyville, she regularly took her children to church every Sunday and taught them independence and self-respect. "[S]he held her head up at all

times," Armstrong recalled. "She never envied no one, or anything they have. I guess I inherited that . . . from Mayann."

That would remain Armstrong's attitude all his life: "I say, never worry what the other fella have, as long as you're having a nice time in your way," he would tell an interviewer when his was one of the most famous faces on earth. "Things ain't never going to get that bad where I can't enjoy a good meal at least once a day and if I have to take a bath in that tin tub again, I'm *still* gonna wash my ass."

As a small boy he was left pretty much on his own to tumble through the muddy streets, dodging wagons and horses, playing and squabbling with other boys, chasing after the music that would become his life. Brass bands often blared their way through the neighborhood, and Funky Butt Hall was just a few steps from his mother's room. There, on Saturday nights, the musicians played on the sidewalk out front for half an hour or so to help draw a crowd for the dance that began inside at sundown. Louis would stand alongside the other children then, listening and dancing, and after the musicians and the grown-up dancers had filed inside—"It was a real rough place," Armstrong remembered. "You'd have to take your razor with you, 'cause you might have to scratch somebody before you leave"—he peered through the cracks in the hall's weathered wall and watched all that went on inside: the blues-drenched music, the sweating dancers who "got down to the floor and wiggled" when they weren't clinging closely to one another in the sensual slow drag, and the fights that sometimes sent everybody spilling out into the street again.

> All of 'em was huggin' their chick you know with their hat on their arm. That's the only time they take their hat off, and they put it on their arm and dance with the chick. . . . they ain't gonna drop it. And nobody better touch it, cause there'll be the

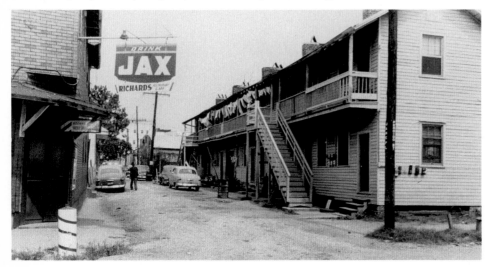

Louis Armstrong was born in this battered house at the corner of Jane Alley and Perdido Street in 1901. The photograph was taken sixty-two years later, shortly before the heedless city tore the building down.

Nineteen-year-old Louis Armstrong, his mother Mayann, and his sister Beatrice pose for a New Orleans photographer in 1920.

The Morris Karnofsky family that treated the young Louis Armstrong with unexpected kindness, photographed in 1917

damndest fight you ever had in your life . . . if you touch that Stetson. They'd wait till the dance is over and the guy would walk up and say, "Did you touch my hat, partner?" and he'd say, "Yeah." "Wop!" he'd hit him right in the chops. And the battle royal's on.

The heroes of his neighborhood were pimps and gamblers. "I was brought up around them people," he said. "They lived happily and they didn't have a whole lot of money, but they . . . always had a little pad and a clean shirt on, collar and tie and that blue suit'd been pressed so much it looked like a mirror, but it's sharp just the same." Armstrong sometimes speculated on what he might have become if he hadn't resolved early on to be a musician: a small-time gambler, he finally decided, who wouldn't "steal too much."

Mayann sent her boy to the Fisk School for Boys on Franklin Street, the same school Buddy Bolden had attended twenty years earlier, but before and after school, start-

ing at the age of seven and continuing for four years, he worked for a Russian Jewish immigrant named Morris Karnofsky, who collected rags and bones and old bottles and delivered coal to the prostitutes of Storyville. Louis rode in the wagon, blowing a long tin horn to let clients know the Karnofskys were coming. He especially enjoyed carrying buckets of coal into the cribs, he recalled, because he could hear music from the nearby honky-tonks and also get "my little peek" at the women waiting for customers in their underwear.

He liked the Karnofskys, too. "Every night we would come in late . . . from buying old rags and bones," he remembered. "When they would have their supper they would fix a plate for me, saying, 'You've worked—might as well eat here with us . . . by the time you get home it will be way too late for your supper.' " After dinner, as Mrs. Karnofsky sang lullabies to her infant son and the family joined in, "so soft and sweet," Louis would be given a part to sing, too. In a world in which most of

the whites he encountered were at best contemptuous, the hospitality of the Karnofskys was a revelation. "They were always warm and kind to me, which was very noticeable to me—just a kid who could use a little word of kindness, . . . just starting out in the world." Because of that kindness, Louis Armstrong would always retain a special affection for Jews—they had "wonderful souls," he said; all his life he would wear a Star of David, and when he finally settled down he saw to it that his breadbox was perpetually stocked with matzohs.

At about the age of ten and "after blowing my tin horn so long," Armstrong wrote, "I wondered how I would do blowing a real horn." When he spotted a battered cornet in a pawnshop window he asked his employer if he would advance him five dollars to buy it. He did, and Armstrong paid him back from his earnings at fifty cents a week.

The little cornet was real dirty and had turned real black. Morris (one of the Karnofsky boys) cleaned [it] with some brass polish and poured some oil all through it. . . . He requested me to play a tune on it. Although I could not play a good tune, Morris applauded me just the same which made me feel very good. As a young boy coming up, the people whom I worked for were very much concerned about my future in music. They could see that I had music in my soul. They really wanted me to be something in life. And music was it. Appreciating my every effort.

When Armstrong was eleven, and despite the kindness of the Karnofskys, he left his job, dropped out of school in the middle of the third grade, and began to drift into trouble. "You must realize it was very shaky . . . during my days growing up in New Orleans," he wrote. "You had to fight and do a lot of ungodly things to keep from being trampled on," enough ungodly things evi-

The Colored Waif's Home Brass Band, 1913. Twelve-year-old Louis Armstrong sits proudly just behind the band's manager, Peter Davis. After Davis allowed him to join the band, Armstrong recalled, "I was in seventh heaven. My ambition had been realized."

dently so that his name became familiar to the police of the Third Ward.

Music still fascinated him, though, and he soon organized the street-corner quartet that had so impressed Sidney Bechet, singing and dancing for tips while keeping a sharp eye out for truant officers and policemen. "A drunk [would] come along and maybe give us a dollar," Armstrong said. "The grown folks were working for a dollar a day." In the early hours of New Year's Day, 1913, at the corner of Rampart and Perdido, his sharp eye failed him. Years later, he offered his own version of what happened. Earlier that winter he had noticed that the latest in the long series of "stepfathers" who moved in with Mayann over the years owned a .38 revolver, which he kept in a trunk beneath her bed. On New Year's Eve—when Louis and the members of his quartet planned to stay out late, hoping for especially big tips from cheer-ful revelers—it struck Louis as a fine idea to spirit the weapon out of the house so that at the stroke of midnight he could pull it out of his shirt and make his own contribution to the spectacular din with which the city customarily hailed the coming of the New Year:

Everybody shot their pistols, shotguns, firecrackers, roman candles. . . . And we went up Rampart Street singing

Johnny Fischer's Marching Band swings into action along North Rampart Street in New Orleans, about 1910. The two small boys hurrying to keep up at the right are the first sign of the cheering, dancing second line that will soon engulf the musicians as they move through the streets. "For the least significant occasion, there would be some music," the guitarist Danny Barker remembered. "That's why so many kids in New Orleans took up music. They heard it all the time."

"My Brazilian Beauty," that was our theme . . . "My Brazilian beauty, down on the Amazon, that's where my love has gone, gone, gone. . . ." And just then a little old cat across the street pulls out a pistol . . . a kid's pistol [and fires]. The cats in my quarter said, "Get him Dipper," and I said, "OK"—"Voom! Voom! Voom!" Aww, it was fun. And then all of a sudden two arms hugged me, and I looked up and there was a big tall detective. Boy, I thought the world was coming to an end . . . and I cried, "Oh Mister, . . . let me alone, just take the pistol."

The policeman took the pistol—and the boy. He spent a cold, frightened night in jail and the next morning, because the juvenile

judge considered him "an old offender," he found himself sentenced to an indeterminate term in the Colored Waif's Home.

It seemed a grim place, at least at first, run along strict military lines: runaways received more than one hundred lashes, administered while the other boys held the fugitive down. For the first two weeks, Louis was so anxious and homesick he barely ate. But even in the Waif's Home, New Orleans music was inescapable, Armstrong remembered, and as he lay in his dormitory bed on Saturday nights the sounds of Freddie Keppard's cornet sometimes drifted in through the open window from one nearby lawn party or another. "Them cats was playing so fine," he recalled. "Just relaxed music."

He wanted to play that relaxed music, too. The pride of the school was its uni-

formed marching band, which raised funds by playing engagements all around the city. (One reason for the band's popularity was that, unlike the members of grown-up bands, its musicians were so happy to be out on the streets again even if only for an afternoon that they never complained when asked to march long distances; a veteran remembered once walking twenty-five miles in the blazing sun.)

Armstrong desperately wanted to join, but the music director, Peter Davis, barred him for weeks, convinced that no boy from the "Battlefield" could ever amount to anything. "I had a bad stamp," Armstrong recalled. "I was a bad boy running around with bad kids in a bad neighborhood." He did everything he could think of to persuade Davis to take a chance on him, tapping out rhythms with a pair of chair rungs, break-ing into "comedy dances" whenever the band began to play.

Finally, the director relented, allowing Armstrong first to try the tambourine, then the alto horn and bugle, finally the cornet. He swiftly mastered all the best-loved marching tunes—"Home, Sweet Home," "Maryland, My Maryland," and "Ole Miss" —and soon developed what an older musi-cian called a "good solid tone" remarkable for one so young. In June, Davis took him aside to tell him he was now the leader of the band. "I jumped straight in the air," Armstrong remembered, "and ran to the mess room to tell the boys the good news."

Soon, the drummer Zutty Singleton re-membered, Armstrong's reputation began to build beyond the Waif's Home.

> Some of the fellows that were sent there would come back and say how fine this Louis Armstrong was play-ing. Then I saw Louis playing in a band at a picnic. He was marching along with the band, so we got up real close to him to see if he was actually playing those notes. We didn't believe he could learn to play in that short time. I can still remember he was playing "Maryland, My Maryland." And he sure was swingin' out that melody.

When Armstrong led the band through his old neighborhood for the first time that summer, he remembered, "all the whores, gamblers, thieves and beggars were wait-ing for the band because they knew that Mayann's son would be in it." But, he said, "they had never dreamed that I would be playing the cornet, blowing it as good as I could. They ran to wake up Mama . . . so she could see me go by." The onlookers— Armstrong called them "the *sporting* crowd"—were so proud to see that "Little Louis," someone from their neighborhood, was doing so well, he remembered, that they filled his hat and those of the other boys with enough nickels and dimes and

Freddie Keppard—known as "King" Keppard to his fans—in the uniform of his own Olympia Orchestra, photographed before circumstances forced his exit from New Orleans. In addition to being a gifted and powerful cornet player, an admiring Sidney Bechet remembered, Keppard "was a hell of a go-round man."

quarters to buy uniforms and brand-new instruments for the band.

As Armstrong played and practiced within the walls of the Waif's Home, times out-side were getting hard. Ships now shunned New Orleans in favor of ports further east, Biloxi and Miami. There were fewer and fewer jobs for musicians, black or white.

Then, in the early morning hours of Easter Sunday, 1913, the proprietors of the Tuxedo dance hall and the rival 102 Ranch just across Franklin Street in Storyville got into a shootout that left both of them dead and several hapless witnesses wounded. The city closed all the dance halls for sev-eral months. Some musicians abandoned music altogether.

New Orleans music on the move: Papa Jack Laine's Reliance Marching Band, left, provides the music for the smartly turned-out members of the West End fire department at the 1912 Firemen's Parade in Biloxi, Mississippi. The West End district of New Orleans was adjacent to a resort of that name on the south shore of Lake Pontchartrain celebrated for weekend band concerts. They would be immortalized sixteen years later in Louis Armstrong's recording of King Oliver's "West End Blues."

By the summer of 1914, Freddie Keppard and George Baquet—who had been playing at the Tuxedo when the shooting began—had made it all the way to Los Angeles. There, with five other New Orleans refugees, they formed the Original Creole Orchestra and were happy to get a night's work playing between boxing matches at Doyle's Arena. The fight crowd's reaction to their music that night was decidedly mixed. A local sportswriter declared it a "disgusting exhibition. . . . While waiting for [the fighters] someone connected with the management had an unhappy inspiration to allow a company of negroes, perpetrating a vile imitation of music, to enter the ring and insult the audience by very obviously begging for coins."

But George Baquet remembered that when they broke into a New Orleans version of a Broadway tune called "In Far-off Mandalay" from ringside and Keppard stepped up onto a bench to blow his cornet, using his derby as a mute, the whole crowd began to sway in time with the music. The band was made to climb into the ring and perform another number; a fighter named Battling Brant, waiting for his introduction, was so excited by their playing he broke into a dance; and afterwards a representative of the vaudeville impresario Alec Pantages who had happened to be in the crowd offered the group a contract. He didn't care what kind of an act they put on, he said, as long as he had that music.

Keppard and the Original Creole Orchestra would tour vaudeville theaters for the next four years. Traveling from Winnipeg to Brooklyn, Boston to Salt Lake City, they put on the kind of show white audiences then expected from black entertainers, corked-up, cracking jokes, dressed as countrified field hands. But everywhere they went, like Jelly Roll Morton, played the big-city music of New Orleans.

By the time Freddie Keppard and his band began touring in vaudeville in the summer of 1914, thirteen-year-old Louis Armstrong

was back on the street. His good behavior and startling musicianship had something to do with it. But so had the intervention of two white strangers. For a poor, wayward black boy to get a second chance in that place and time, influential whites had to be persuaded to take an interest in him. Powerless to do anything to free her boy on her own, his mother had asked the family whose washing she did to vouch for him, while his absentee father persuaded the man who ran the turpentine plant in which he sometimes worked to intercede with the judge on Louis's behalf.

It was a lesson Louis Armstrong never forgot. Much later in his life, when people asked him to explain his stubborn loyalty to his white manager Joe Glaser, whose crude ways at one time or another alienated a good many of the people with whom he came in contact, Armstrong liked to recall advice given to him by a black bouncer back in Storyville: "Always keep a white man behind you that'll put his hand on your shoulder and say, 'That's *my* nigger.' " To some, that smacked of subservience; to Armstrong, it was simple realism. The bouncer's clear-eyed counsel had only served to reaffirm what life in New Orleans had taught him. In a world run by whites, a black man, no matter how gifted he might be, would always need protection to get ahead.

Armstrong was still scuffling to support his mother and sister. Over the next few years he would work at any number of jobs to put food on the table: he sold newspapers—and sometimes fought white boys who considered such sales their exclusive territory; he unloaded banana boats and downed so many bananas on the sly that in later years he could not abide even the smell of one; he bought up broken lumps of coal for resale at a nickel a bucket; he rifled through barrels of food discarded by produce houses, looking for unspoiled fruit and vegetables to sell to restaurants—even dipped his face in flour, entered an amateur con-

The Square Deal Boys gather a steadily growing crowd as they make their way down Dumaine Street toward a funeral home, 1946.

More than three decades after Louis Armstrong marched in his first funeral parades, New Orleans musicians still followed the same time-honored form. They played a mournful hymn on the way to the cemetery, the drummer Baby Dodds recalled, "to put a weeping in their hearts." They had no duties during the actual burial and on hot afternoons, as the minister spoke at the graveside, some of the men would scatter for refreshments. It was up to the drummer, Dodds remembered, to get them back in line when the time came.

> When they put the body in the ground and say, "ashes to ashes"—well, that's the drummer's cue right there. . . . And the snare drummer alone goes out into the middle of the street and he'd start to roll and he rolled loud. . . . And you could see guys jumpin' over graves and comin' out of people's houses and out of bar rooms and, oh, just flyin'. And it just gave me so much pleasure to see those guys that had overstayed themselves & come out runnin'. Some of them with a sandwich in their hand or a jelly roll stickin' out where they're tryin' to chew fast and get it down. Some guys with some whiskey in their hands. And some guys kiss their woman and say, "I'll see you, so long, goodbye" and the door slam, BAM! See 'em runnin' down the steps, some guys with no [uniform] cap, that had left their cap, had to go back & get it. . . .

Then, reunited, the men would march away from the cemetery playing something joyous, like "Oh, Didn't He Ramble," in celebration of the departed's entry into heaven.

test at the Iroquois Theater, and took his prize money home to his mother.

And all the while, he looked for opportunities to play the music that now meant everything to him. "I remember once when Louis came out to Lincoln Park in New Orleans to listen to the Kid Ory Band," the cornetist Mutt Carey said. "I was playing trumpet with the Kid then and I let Louis sit in on my chair. Now, at that time, I was the 'Blues King' of New Orleans, and when Louis played that day he played more blues than I ever heard in my life. It never did strike my mind that blues could be interpreted so many different ways."

It was Armstrong's soulful blues playing that got him his first real jobs, working in three-piece bands, first at a honky-tonk owned by a Frenchman named Henry Ponce, and then at the Sicilian Henry Matranga's, both in black Storyville. Every night there was rough, Armstrong recalled, but Saturday night was special. The streets were crowded with men in overalls, in from the sawmills and levees and cane and cotton fields, with a week's pay in their pockets and looking for a good time. Some carried .45's; most carried knives or razors. The sporting crowd that profited from their

visits was rough and often violent, too— "a notorious group," Armstrong remembered—that included Cheeky Black, Funky Stella and Cross-Eyed Louise, Long Head Willie Logan, Roughhouse Camel, Cocaine Buddy, Mary Meat Market, and Black Benny Williams, a six-foot-six sometime parade drummer who acted as the boy's protector for a time. Armstrong now had neighborhood nicknames of his own, among them "Hammock Face," "Rhythm Jaws," "Dippermouth," and "Satchelmouth."

Each of the tonks in which he played had three rooms, Armstrong remembered: a bar, a room given over to a card game called cotch, and another "for dancing—doing that slow drag, close together, humping up one shoulder—maybe throw a little wiggle into it." Pine benches lined the walls. Armstrong and his companions played from a bandstand so small they could not turn around. "Drinks were cheap—and strong. Used to get beer in tin lard buckets and it was *cold*— liked to see that sweat on the outside."

The men were expected to play all night. After four in the morning, Armstrong remembered, the whores, powdered with pink chalk they had scented with fifteen-cent perfume, would begin to trickle in,

"big stockings full of dollars—and give us a tip to pay the blues. . . . [T]hey was attractive and very encouraging to look at." They were also not to be trifled with. He once watched as a celebrated prostitute named Mary Jack the Bear and a younger rival remembered only as Deborah battled one another in the middle of Gravier Street, slashing each other with knives until the faces of both women were masks of blood.

Early one Sunday morning, Armstrong himself came close to a violent end. As he and Henry Ponce lounged in the doorway of Ponce's tonk talking about the blues he'd just finished playing, several men appeared across the street, all of them employees of Ponce's archrival, a Sicilian club owner named Joe Segretta. Suddenly, one of them pulled a pistol and opened fire. Bullets whistled past Armstrong's head. Ponce drew his gun and fired back. His attackers ran and Ponce ran after them, firing as he went. When the smoke cleared, three of his would-be assassins lay writhing in the street. As friends rushed to Armstrong's side, asking if he'd been hit, he fainted. "I continued to work in tonks" after that, he wrote, but "I was always on the alert."

———

Armstrong's growing reputation as a musician did nothing to shield him from the indignities of daily life for black citizens of New Orleans. One evening he was having a beer with friends in Henry Matranga's place, he remembered, "when Captain Jackson, the meanest guy on the police force," burst in with several other officers. Someone had just been robbed on Rampart Street, he said, so everybody in the tonk was going to jail. Protesting their innocence, Armstrong and the others were marched to the Parish Prison, just a couple of blocks away.

There, he found himself surrounded by convicted criminals with names like Dirty Dog and Steel Arm Johnny who were awaiting transfer to state prison. Sore Dick, the black "captain of the yard," made him sweep the prison yard with a broom over and over again. "All newcomers, I later found out, had to sweep out the yard whether it needed it or not. That is the way they get you in the groove before you start serving a term." Armstrong spent several days behind bars fearing the worst before Henry Matranga's lawyers arranged for his release. "It was part of a system that always worked in those days," he said. "Nevertheless, I'll never forget that experience as a stay-a-whiler with those long-termers."

He never forgot what happened the next day, either. It happened to be Mardi Gras, and members of the Zulu Social Aid and Pleasure Club, the oldest black krewe in the city, were marching through the Uptown streets in blackface just as they did every year. The club had been formed by men from Armstrong's own neighborhood in 1909 to parody the white krewes that otherwise dominated the festivities. It was made up, he wrote, of "coal-cart drivers, bar tenders, waiters, hustlers, etc. But they loved each other . . . and put their best foot forward." They were the boisterous escorts of a mule-drawn float that carried the gaudy King of the Zulus, also in blackface, who was meant to be a grotesque caricature of "Rex," Carnival's white king. The

Joe "King" Oliver, about 1905

King's costume varied every year—a woman's evening gown instead of Rex's flowing robes, a hambone in place of a jeweled scepter—but it was "the dream of every boy in the neighborhood," Armstrong said, to be chosen King and he had been especially proud as a small boy when one of his several stepfathers had been picked for the honor.

White onlookers thought the marchers hilarious. Some members of the city's black establishment already thought them a grotesque embarrassment. But to Armstrong and his friends and neighbors from the poorest part of town, parading in blackface provided a rare sanctioned opportunity to lampoon white stereotyping and parody white society all at the same time. Best of all from Armstrong's point of view this particular year, a local character named Garfield Carter—known in black Storyville as "Papa Gar"—dared to parade alongside the Zulu King's float disguised as the notorious Captain Jackson himself, strutting along in open blackfaced mockery of the man who had put Armstrong and so many of his friends in jail. At the sight of him, Armstrong remembered, the crowds

in black Storyville went wild with laughter: "It's a funny thing," he wrote, "how life can be such a drag one minute and a solid sender the next."

Armstrong was still working in tonks when he came to the attention of the man who would become his mentor, Joe "King" Oliver—"the top cornet in New Orleans, the first big musician in my life and still . . . the best I ever met." Oliver was then playing with the trombonist Kid Ory at Pete Lala's in Storyville and when it closed at midnight it became his habit to come and listen to the youthful Armstrong.

"I loved Joe Oliver," Armstrong said., "He did more for young musicians . . . than anyone I know of." That was not his reputation. He was "rough as pig-iron," Ory said. Short and barrel-chested, he weighed well over two hundred pounds and because he had lost the sight in one eye and, inside or out, always wore a derby hat cocked at an angle to hide it, he was known as "ol' Cocky"—but few dared use his nickname in his presence. He kept a brick near him on the bandstand to bang on the floor if his men didn't heed the stomping foot with which he started and stopped each number, and to keep would-be rivals from seeing just what he was doing on the bandstand he sometimes covered his fingers with a handkerchief. A musician who played with him a few years later remembered that rehearsals were sometimes accompanied by a certain tension.

> The King would walk in with the music on his arm and his gun in the bosom of his coat. He would throw everything down on the table and look around to see if everybody was there. Then he would pick up his gun and ask, "Is everybody here?" Everybody reported yes, we were there, then he would put his gun back on the table, and the rehearsal would go on.

According to the pianist Richard M. Jones, who claimed to have been an eyewitness,

Oliver had been appearing at a cabaret called the Abadie at Marais and Bienville, when he snatched the crown as the city's finest cornetist from Buddy Bolden's heir, Freddie Keppard. For days, Oliver had been irritated that Keppard was drawing big crowds to another club just down the street. Finally, he could stand it no longer. "Get in B-flat," the pianist remembered being told. "He didn't even mention a tune." Then, Oliver stalked outside, "lifted his horn to his lips and blew the most beautiful stuff I have ever heard. People started pouring out of the other spots along the street to see who was blowing all that horn. Before long our place was full and Joe came in, smiling, and said, 'Now, that ——— won't bother me no more.' "

To ballyhoo their upcoming appearances, Oliver and Kid Ory and their band often performed from the back of a mule-drawn furniture wagon as it moved through the streets. Louis Armstrong described the contests that frequently followed:

> The wagon would pull up in the neighborhood and start playing. They was always catchy tunes. . . . People came out the doors from all over the neighborhood. . . . Now Kid Ory and Joe Oliver's band liable to be playing for one dance, and here come the Imperial Band, playing for another dance, so they'd pull up together, and that's where that bucking contest used to come. . . . They chained the wheels to these furniture wagons so they couldn't move. Just stay there and blow, and the crowd would applaud. . . . Different tunes, trying to outplay each other. King Oliver and Ory used to cut them all. And after they'd pull off, Ory used to play a little thing . . . on the trombone, people would just roll [on the ground laughing], 'cause, they know what he's sayin,' you know . . . "Kiss my fucking ass."

But in the end, it was neither Joe Oliver's volume nor his competitiveness that pulled in the crowds; it was his craft. Oliver was a master of mood. He could play roughly enough to suit the whores and pimps of Storyville and sweetly enough to please white dancers at Tulane University. And he was a showman, besides; the finest manipulator of mutes in the business, he employed a whole arsenal of objects—water glasses, buckets, kazoos that fit into the bell of his horn—anything to make his cornet growl or groan, crow like a rooster or cry like a baby. "Joe could make his horn sound like a holy roller meeting," Mutt Carey said. "God, what that man could do with his horn!"

Armstrong looked for opportunities just to be close to his idol. "He was the nearest thing to Buddy Bolden to me," he said. "When he went into a bar to yackety with the guys—he didn't drink—or when he'd be parading and not blowing, I'd hold his horn so all he had to do was wipe his brow and walk." Armstrong ran errands for Oliver's wife, too—and got to eat delicious meals of red beans and rice in return—and whenever he could he asked Oliver for tips on how to improve his playing.

The younger man already had begun to develop the astonishing facility that would one day dazzle the musical world and he loved to play what he called "figurations"—ornate improvisations on the chord changes, he remembered, "just like a clarinet player." Sidney Bechet himself had once been astonished to hear Armstrong race effortlessly through a clarinet solo on "High Society" made famous by Alphonse Picou. Virtuosic displays like that left Joe Oliver cold. With him, melody always came first. "Play some lead on that horn, boy," he told Armstrong over and over again. "Play the lead so people can know what you're doing."

The older man admired the boy's big warm tone, liked his eagerness and willingness to learn, began to let him substitute for him in the band he led with Kid Ory,

and one day passed on to him a battered cornet. Armstrong was overwhelmed: "I prized that horn and guarded it with my life," he recalled. "I blew on it for a long, long time before I was fortunate to get another one."

BLESSED

During the summer of 1914—the same summer thirteen-year-old Louis Armstrong was released from the Colored Waif's Home in New Orleans—a fifteen-year-old boy from Washington, D.C., on vacation with his mother in the resort town of Asbury Park, New Jersey, took a temporary job washing dishes at the Plaza Hotel. He hated the hot steamy work "with a perfect hatred," he would admit many years later, but while he was at it the headwaiter talked him into going to hear a Philadelphia ragtime pianist named Harvey Brooks during his off-hours. It changed his life. "I cannot tell you what that music did to me," he would one day tell an interviewer. "It was different from the average piano selection. The individuality of the man showed itself in the composition as he played it. I said right then, 'That's how I would like to play a piano, so without being told, everybody would know I was playing.' "

Everything Edward Kennedy Ellington would do during his long career as pianist, bandleader, composer, and arranger would be built upon that conception. No one remotely familiar with his touch on the piano or the sound of the orchestra he led for fifty years could ever mistake it for anyone else's. And at the same time, he would find ways to encompass within his astonishing outpouring of music everything he saw and heard around him, would manage to make it representative not only of what he himself called "Negro feeling put to rhythm and tune," but of the rhythm and feeling of his whole country. "At its best," his friend the novelist and critic Albert Murray wrote, "an Ellington performance

Daisy Ellington, Duke Ellington's mother

Edward Kennedy Ellington himself, already regal at the age of four

J. E. Ellington and the son who admired him, photographed sometime during the 1920s

sounds as if it knows the truth about all the other music in the world and is looking for something better. Not even the Constitution represents a more intrinsically American statement and achievement than that."

Ellington would remain a major figure in American music for more than half a century, yet almost no one claimed to have known him well. His younger sister, Ruth, remembered that "there was just veil after veil after veil." His private feelings were kept private, expressed only through his music. He is largely missing from his own autobiography, *Music Is My Mistress,* a compilation of shrewd but benign jottings about people he'd known, places he'd been. Reading it, one would think he'd never had to struggle, never made an enemy or suffered a slight. The Ellington papers deposited at the Smithsonian Institution document his methods of composition but offer precious few clues to the personality of the man who moved the pen. Offstage as well as on, he seems almost always to have

been the Duke, glittering but opaque, his languid, courtly manner part put-on and part put off, designed both to delight the public he professed to love madly—and to keep it at a proper, respectful distance.

Ellington's snug, cosseted boyhood could not have been more different from Louis Armstrong's. He was born in the home of his maternal grandparents on Twentieth Street in northwest Washington on April 22, 1899, and spent his earliest years in a big comfortable house on Ward's Place, just a few blocks from the White House.

The nation's capital then had the largest black population of any city in the United States—nearly one hundred thousand souls—and as the cornetist Rex Stewart, who would one day become one of Ellington's brightest stars, remembered, Northwest Washington was the home of "the lighter complexioned people with better-type jobs, such as schoolteachers, . . . clerks, or in government service."

Ellington's father, James Edward Ellington—known as "J.E." to outsiders and "Uncle Ed" to his own children because being called "father" made him feel old—was a man of modest means but lofty aspirations, a "Chesterfieldian gentleman," according to his daughter, Ruth, "who wore gloves and spats." A former coachman and chauffeur, he was butler to a prominent Washington physician, sometimes served as a caterer at the White House, and eventually became a blueprint maker at the Washington Navy Yard. But his son remembered that "he raised his family as if he were a millionaire" and was given to gallant flattery of the sort for which Ellington himself would one day be celebrated. When it snowed, he liked to say, "the millions of beautiful snowflakes" were a tribute to the beauty of his wife, Daisy.

She was the daughter of a police captain and so devoutly religious, her daughter remembered, that she wore no lipstick "because she thought that a woman should not be attracting another man." She had lost one child in infancy and so focused special attention on the son who seemed to represent the second chance for which she'd prayed. Nothing was too good for him: "I was pampered and spoiled rotten, by all the women in the family," Ellington remembered; "my feet were not allowed to touch the ground until the age of six." His mother took him to church twice each Sunday, once to the Nineteenth Street Baptist Church to which her family had always gone, and again to the John Wesley African Methodist Church favored by her husband; she saw to it that not one but *two* doctors were in attendance when her boy fell ill with pneumonia; played light classics on the piano for him so beautifully that he sometimes wept; and made certain when he was old enough to reach the piano keys himself that he faithfully practiced following each lesson with the neighborhood teacher, Marietta Clinkscales.

"As though I were some very, very special child," Ellington wrote, "my mother would say, 'Edward, you are blessed!' " But being blessed was not enough. He must allow nothing to stop him, she said. Unpleasant facts and potential barriers were simply to be ignored. In *his* life there were to be "no boxes"; he "could do anything anyone else could do." In part because she believed that, he would believe it, too, and his mother would always remain the most important person in the world to him.

His mother's enthusiasm for her boy was evidently contagious. "Everything Edward did was wonderful," his sister remembered. "Everybody in the whole family, aunts, uncles, cousins—everybody adored Edward. So whatever he did was marvelous, whatever he played was wonderful." One of his cousins remembered that she and her sister had been expected to curtsy to the bright-eyed little boy whom an admiring schoolmate would soon nickname "Duke."

Ellington's own memories of his boyhood were understandably idyllic: eating grapes

The Nineteenth Street Baptist Church, one of the two churches to which Daisy Ellington took her son each Sunday; and (opposite page) the Gayety Burlesque, where the boy began his secular schooling at the age of twelve

from the arbor in his grandmother's shady backyard; dining on steak and terrapin brought home for the family from one or another of the elegant affairs his father catered; playing baseball with neighborhood boys on Sixteenth Street while President Theodore Roosevelt, out for his afternoon ride, watched from horseback.

The Ellington children, Ruth Ellington recalled, were raised in a household "full of love, where people [did] not talk of hostile incidents. . . . I guess that was their way of protecting us." As the years went by, that determined reticence must sometimes have been hard to maintain. In Washington as elsewhere, the federal government had long since beaten a dispiriting retreat from Reconstruction. Black Washingtonians had once played a real part in the running of their city; now, they were largely powerless and Jim Crow laws and southern custom had combined to segregate housing and public facilities.

Still, the poet Paul Laurence Dunbar wrote in 1900 that Washington had "a higher standard of culture among people of color than obtains in any other city." It was the home of Howard University. There were independent black churches, schools, theaters, orchestras, choral societies, a conservatory of music. A tightly knit group of some sixty families reigned over Washington's colored world, the descendants of free blacks and mostly of "doe-nut or ginger-cake color," according to the black-owned Washington *Bee.* Just below them were businessmen, professionals, and government workers like the J. E. Ellingtons. At the bottom of the ladder were those whom the *Bee* called the "masses," mostly dark-skinned descendants of slaves who lived largely out of sight in the fetid alleys behind some of the city's most elegant dwellings. "I don't know how many castes of Negroes there were in the city at that time," Duke Ellington remembered, "but I do know that if you decided to mix carelessly with another you would be told that one just did not do that sort of thing. It might be wonderful for somebody, but not for me and my cousins."

Ellington's reticence about his private life started early. He remained close to his mother but determined also to be his own man, which meant learning early how to keep some things from her. Like Jelly Roll Morton before him, he was unwilling to bend to his family's strictures and soon got to know other worlds, out from under his mother's watchful eye. At twelve, he and his friends began slipping into the Gayety Burlesque Theater, where—when he could tear his eyes away from the "rather gorgeous girls"—he got his first taste of the show-business glamour of which he would one day be a master; "I am a man of the theater," he liked to say. Soon, he was also a regular at Frank Holliday's pool room next to the Howard Theater at Seventh and T Streets, a meeting place for men from

every segment of the city's black population: gamblers and pool hustlers as well as college graduates and Pullman porters with colorful stories of all the places they had been. "You would hear them say," Ellington recalled, " 'I just left Chicago, or last night I was in Cleveland.' " There was always something worth hearing being said in that poolroom, where it "always sounded as if the prime authorities on every subject had been assembled. . . . Baseball, football, basketball, boxing, wrestling, racing, medicine, law, politics, everything was discussed with authority." It was the beginning of a lifetime of careful listening by Ellington. And it was at Holliday's pool hall, he remembered, that he saw for the first time how "all levels could and should mix."

In 1913, some black Washingtonians had thought they saw encouraging signs of political change. On March 4, Woodrow Wilson, the former Democratic governor of New

Jersey, was sworn in as President of the United States. During the presidential campaign he had declared it his "warmest wish to see justice done to the colored people in every matter, and not mere grudging justice, but justice executed with liberality and cordial good feeling." No Democratic presidential candidate had ever seemed so sympathetic to African-American aspirations, and many of the city's black citizens attended the ceremony at the Capitol to hear what the future might hold for them.

Among them had been Jane Thompson Stewart of Georgetown and her five-year-old son, Rex. It was a bitterly cold day, he recalled, and his mother decided to get some coffee from an outdoor vendor. But when she courteously asked him for two cups he looked right through her. She tried again, only to be ignored again, Rex Stewart remembered.

At last Mother said, "I want two cups of coffee," in a loud voice which seemed to shock the attendant into answering, "How's that auntie?" It was the first time I had seen my mother angry. She seemed to start swelling up like a giant, as she replied, "I'm not your auntie and I am not here to be insulted. This is a very cold day and I demand a hot beverage for my son and myself, in the name of common decency."

The vendor told her he wasn't selling "nigger coffee" and if he had been he still wouldn't sell it to her because he didn't like "smart niggers." A white stranger intervened and intimidated the man into pouring two nickel cups of coffee. The vendor demanded a dollar, and when the boy and his mother finished their coffies, contemptuously smashed the cups they'd used.

It might as well have been an omen. The new President had had no intention of honoring his pledge. Within three months he issued an executive order that imposed Jim Crow on the federal government itself. Restrooms in all federal buildings were segregated. Black clerks were separated from white colleagues alongside whom they'd worked for years. The whole city fell in line: The National Theater hired a black doorman because the managers thought he would be best able to detect light-skinned would-be ticket-buyers trying to pass for white. At the dedication of the Lincoln Memorial armed Marines would make sure black invitees—including the president of Tuskegee Institute, one of the speakers—did not stray from their separate roped-off seats across a dirt road from the Great Emancipator.

Black Washingtonians redoubled their efforts at building self-reliance. Community newspapers exhorted their readers to forget the differences that had divided them; patronize black businesses and boycott white ones that discriminated against them; support black charities and take pride in black achievements. Meanwhile, the assistant superintendent of the Colored Schools urged that the children in his charge be "taught about the great men of our race" so that they might "escape being overwhelmed by white prestige and avoid impairment of colored initiative." Ellington was in eighth grade at William Lloyd Garrison Junior High when the Wilson administration began, and remembered all his life the lessons its principal, Miss Boston, had sought to inculcate in all her students:

When we went out into the world, we would have the grave responsibility of being practically always on stage, for every time they would see a Negro they would go into a reappraisal of the race. She taught us that proper speech and good manners were our first obligations, because as representatives of the Negro race we were to command respect for our people. This being an all-colored school, Negro history was crammed into the curriculum, so that we would know our people all the way back. They had pride there, the greatest race pride.

After returning from his dishwashing sojourn in Asbury Park in 1914, Ellington entered Samuel H. Armstrong Technical High School. He was now determined to become a piano player—in part, he liked to say, because he had noticed that girls were attracted to piano players and he was attracted to girls. In fact, it was because of the instant excitement he had felt at hearing Harvey Brooks play, the conviction that music would be his way to express himself.

An able but alcoholic pianist named Lester Dishman gave him lessons for a time, in exchange for the boy's help in navigating from one engagement to the next. Soon, Rex Stewart remembered, Ellington was playing piano for teenage dances at True Reformers Hall on U Street for seventy-five cents a night, "and fixing that famous hypnotic grin on the nearest pretty girl." And he had begun to work up his own tunes, including "Soda Fountain Rag" and "What You Gonna Do When the Bed Breaks Down?" which he remembered as "a pretty good 'hug-and-rubbin' crawl." Its title alone must have appalled his mother, but it made him very popular among his classmates.

THE ORIGINATORS OF JAZZ

On May 13, 1915, a five-piece white group from New Orleans arrived in Chicago for a six-week engagement at a basement restaurant at Randolph and Clark called Lamb's Café. They billed themselves as "Brown's Band from Dixieland," after their trombonist, Tom Brown, a veteran of Papa Jack Laine's marching bands. The kind of music they played was already growing familiar in black neighborhoods of the city, but most white Chicagoans had never heard anything like it, and at first they were anything but enthusiastic. The cashier covered her ears whenever the men began to play, and a string orchestra quit rather than perform on the same bandstand with anyone making such crude noises.

Vaudeville dancer and comedian Joe Frisco, arms outstretched, poses for a publicity photograph on a Chicago street during the summer of 1915. Behind him, fresh from New Orleans and not at all sure how their music will go over in the Windy City, are the five members of Brown's Band from Dixieland, including trombonist Tom Brown (over Frisco's left shoulder) and clarinetist Larry Shields.

"[O]ur debut was pitiful," the cornetist Ray Lopez later admitted. "Those Yankees wouldn't listen or dance. They just walked out on us. We took turns talking to the customers. 'Folks, this is New Orleans music. Hot music. People down South dance. You've got to dance. Come on and try. Have fun!' For six nights we pleaded. No dice." Then, a touring vaudeville company reserved the café for a party and word got out that they had had a good time; after that, Lopez remembered, their music "caught on like magic"—until the restaurant closed for renovations. Brown's Band from Dixieland broke up soon afterward, and most of its members went back home to New Orleans.

Meanwhile, out on the road, Freddie Keppard's playing was winning him an enthusiastic following at least among those musicians who managed to hear him. "He hit the highest and the lowest notes on a trumpet that anybody outside of Gabriel ever did," his friend and fellow Creole Jelly Roll Morton remembered. "[He] had all degrees of power, great imagination and more tone than anybody." It was said he played so loudly that people who sat in the front rows sometimes asked to move back when he began to blow, and the saxophonist Garvin Bushell remembered that when Keppard played in a cabaret he "could make the glasses on the bar move—they'd bet on that." But for all his artistry and power, Keppard was also suspicious and self-protective, so fearful other cornetists would copy his fingering that, like Joe Oliver, he was said sometimes to use a handkerchief to hide his right hand when he played.

In December of 1915, Keppard and his Original Creole Orchestra were playing a New York theater when a spokesman for the Victor Talking Machine company is said to have offered to record them. But first, he explained, they would have to hold a try-out to see if the firm's primitive recording device could pick up the sound of the band's bass player. Keppard turned Victor down. His clarinetist George Baquet said it was

The barnstorming Creole Orchestra with Freddie Keppard and George Bacquet advertises its wares in Los Angeles, 1914.

because Keppard had felt insulted at being asked to audition without pay; others remembered him saying, "Nothing doing, boys. We won't put our stuff on records for everybody to steal"; still others heard he'd asked for as much money as was paid to the operatic tenor Enrico Caruso, the best-selling recording artist in the world, and was turned down flat. Keppard's friend Sidney Bechet declared there was only one real reason for his reluctance to record: "Freddie just didn't care to, that's all." In any case, he passed up the opportunity to become the first jazz musician to make a recording.

Tom Brown's success at Lamb's Café had inspired other Chicago club owners to look for more white bands from "Dixie." One of them was a hastily put-together quintet from New Orleans led by the drummer Johnny Stein that included the pianist Henry Ragas and three more veterans of Papa Jack Laine's marching bands—clarinetist Alcide "Yellow" Nuñez, trombonist Eddie "Daddy" Edwards, and cornetist Dominick James "Nick" LaRocca.

In April of 1916, their band was booked into a cheap cabaret called the New Schiller Café, on Thirty-first Street, which was fortunate enough to be visited one Saturday night by a phalanx of some sixty determined women from the Anti-Saloon League, intent on exposing the evils of alcohol. With them came a reporter from the Chicago *Herald*. The story that appeared the next day under the headline "Sixty Women Rip Mask off Vice" turned out to be a publicist's dream.

A line of taxicabs radiated from the Schiller to the east, west, north and south. In front of the doors a crowd of people fought for admission. A perspiring doorman held them back. "Can't come in," he shouted. "We're crowded to capacity." . . . [Once inside] it was impossible for anyone to be heard. The shriek of women's drunken laughter rivaled the blatant scream of the imported New Orleans

Jass Band, which never seemed to stop playing. Men and women sat, arms about each other, singing, shouting, making the night hideous, while their unfortunate brethren and sisters fought in vain to join them.

The newspaper reporter may have hoped readers would be horrified by the vice he and the crusaders had uncovered, but a good many were simply intrigued, wanted to see and hear for themselves what all the fuss was about. Crowds at the café doubled overnight. "The impact we had on the people of Chicago was terrific," LaRocca remembered. "Women stood up on the dance floor, doing wild dances. They had to pull them off. . . . The more they would carry on, the better we could play. . . . The crowd would start yelling, 'Give us some more jass.' I can still see these women who would try and put on a show . . . raise their dresses above their knees and carry on, men shrieking and everybody having a good time."

LaRocca had never been one of New Orleans's best-known cornetists—he had been hired for the Chicago job mostly because he had happened to be able to come up with the $125 needed to pay the group's railfare north from New Orleans—but he burned with ambition, was determined not to return to New Orleans a failure. Raised in the tough "Irish Channel" section of New Orleans, he was the son of a shoemaker from Sicily, and therefore a member of one of his polyglot hometown's most disdained minorities. The city's celebrated spirit of tolerance had never extended to Italian-Americans. There were thought to be some eighteen thousand of them living in New Orleans by the turn of the century, and in the minds of a good many of their fellow citizens they were all tarred with the Mafia brush. Warfare between rival Italian gangs had led to a police crackdown in 1890, the year after LaRocca's birth, and when someone shotgunned the police chief to death on Basin

Street the following year, nineteen Sicilians were indicted for the crime. Nine were tried. When six were found not guilty and the jury could not agree on a verdict for the other three, a mob of indignant whites and blacks stormed into the Orleans Parish Prison and butchered all nine of the accused, plus two others who had not yet come to trial. The mayor commended the mob for its swift work: "The Italians had taken the law into their own hands," he said, "and we had no choice but to do the same."

No one was ever indicted for the lynching but its memory remained raw for decades. As LaRocca was growing up, he and other Italian-Americans in New Orleans were routinely taunted with cries of "Who Killa da Chief?" As a Sicilian, he always felt himself something of an outsider in his own hometown—"a poor dago boy from the wrong side of the track," he said—a fact which may help account both for his enormous drive to succeed and for his unwillingness to acknowledge that African-Americans—members of the only minority he felt that he himself could look down upon—could have had anything whatsoever to do with creating the music he would later claim to have come up with all on his own.

Had LaRocca's father had his way, he would never have been a jazz musician at all. The old man had himself once played the cornet for dancers in his off-hours, but he believed professional musicians were "bums," and insisted that his son study to become a doctor so that he could demonstrate to the world that Italians were as good as anyone else. When Nick proudly performed his first tune for his parents at about the age of nine, his father waited until the boy was finished awkwardly fingering the valves on his own old cornet, then tore the horn from his son's hands and smashed it with an ax. When the boy stubbornly bought himself another cornet and began practicing it in secret in the outhouse, his father crushed that one, too.

Then, his father died. LaRocca immediately abandoned all thought of a medical career. He worked as a stagehand at the French opera house, learned electrical contracting work, and played music whenever he could, just for "eats" at first and then for pay. Never able to read music, he was an aggressive but unconventional player; like his idol, Ray Lopez, he held his horn in his right hand and fingered the valves with his left.

By the time he got to Chicago to join Johnny Stein at the New Schiller Café, in 1916, he had worked in at least fifteen New Orleans bands. Stein's group, too, broke up after the café's management refused them a raise and the trombonist punched the drummer in the nose. LaRocca then talked three of the men—Edwards, Ragas, and Nuñez—into joining him in a new cooperative group called the Original Dixieland Jass Band. They added a drummer, Tony Sbarbaro, and eventually replaced Nuñez with clarinetist Larry Shields, who had been born in a shotgun house just two doors up the street from Buddy Bolden's family home.

The ODJB spent the next six months at a gangster hangout called the Casino Gardens that billed itself as "The Theatrical Profession's Most Popular Rendezvous." The vaudeville star Al Jolson heard them there and would later claim that he was largely responsible for getting them the New York engagement that would finally make all of LaRocca's dreams come true—in the Paradise Ballroom, part of the new Reisenweber Restaurant complex on Columbus Circle.

They opened there on January 17, 1917. At first, Manhattan dancers fled the dance floor when the band began to play, just as Chicagoans had initially fled from Tom Brown's outfit. LaRocca remembered drunken patrons shouting, "Tell those farmers to go home!" But after the master of ceremonies carefully explained, "This music's meant for dancing," a few venturesome couples tried it. More joined them. "This 'jaz' thing sounds like . . . musicians trying to draw business into a sideshow," *Variety* reported. "It's what would be called 'stewed music' for you have to be that way to like it." But its impact on dancers was undeniable.

[O]ne thing is certain. . . . the melodies as played by the Jazz organization at Reisenweber's are quite conducive to making the dancers on the floor loosen up and go to the limit in their stepping. Gingery, swinging music is what the dancers want. . . . Late in the morning, the jazzers go to work and the dancers hit the floor, to remain there till they topple over. . . . If the dancers see someone they know at the tables, it's common to hear, "Oh, Boy!" as they roll their eyes while floating past. And the "Oh, Boy!" expression probably describes the Jazz Band better than anything else could.

Reisenweber's ran newspaper advertisements hailing jazz as "An Overnight Furore —the Fad of the Hour," and put up a neon sign: THE ORIGINAL DIXIELAND JAZZ BAND—THE CREATORS OF JAZZ. (The spelling had been hastily changed from "Jass," LaRocca remembered, because small boys had been spotted scurrying along nearby streets scratching the letter "J" off their posters.)

Within a week of the opening at Reisenweber's, Columbia Records decided to try and record the music that was making such a stir. On January 30, 1917, the ODJB assembled in a tiny studio and nervously

The same air of cheerful anarchy that put off the first New Yorkers who heard the Original Dixieland Jazz Band in 1917 had become a selling point by the time this cartoon was drawn for the Victor Talking Machine Company three years later.

In the spring of 1914, the dance team of Vernon and Irene Castle embarked on what they called their "Whirlwind Tour" of the United States—thirty cities in twenty-eight days. Vernon Castle was an English entertainer whose real name was Vernon Blyth; his wife was a doctor's daughter from Westchester County. They were so slender, one reporter noted, that "standing side by side [they] are about as wide as one rather slim human being." But they were elegant dancers, refined and reassuring to parents worried about the morals of their children.

Ragtime had spawned a host of provocative dances, all of them born in African-American dance halls but eagerly embraced by young dancers of all races. The New York *Herald* spoke for a good many older white people in deploring ragtime as "symbolic of the primitive morality and perceptible moral limitations of the Negro type." Some black Americans were worried, as well, but for different reasons. "The Negro Race is dancing itself to death," warned the Reverend Adam Clayton Powell Sr., pastor of Harlem's Abyssinian Baptist Church. "Our people are too frivolous because they feed on too much trash. You can see the effects of the Tango, the Chicago, the Turkey Trot, the Texas Tommy and ragtime music not only in their conversations but in the movement of their bodies about the home."

"We were clean-cut," Irene Castle remembered, "we were married, and when we danced there was nothing suggestive about it. We made dancing look like the fun it was and so gradually we became a middle ground both sides could accept." The couple grew so popular that when Irene Castle bobbed her hair, 250,000 American women were said to have followed suit.

The Castles danced beautifully but they owed a great deal to the blend of rhythmic drive and musical polish provided by the ten-piece black orchestra that traveled with them everywhere—and to its remarkable conductor, James Reese Europe. Born in Alabama and raised in Washington, where he studied violin and piano, he had acted as musical director for all-black revues on Broadway and saw it as his duty to reveal to the world "the musical proficiency of the African race." The New York local of the American Federation of Musicians barred blacks, and so, in 1910, Europe

Vernon and Irene Castle offer lessons in suitably decorous dancing to the readers of *The Ladies Home Journal*, December 1914.

helped establish a rival organization, the Clef Club, to defend their interests and act as a clearinghouse for jobs. Two years later, he organized and led a pioneering concert of African-American music at Carnegie Hall. His 105-piece Clef Club Symphony Orchestra performed ragtime, spirituals, plantation songs, choral works, show tunes—and

instrumental numbers featuring ten grand pianos all playing at once. It was a triumph. "The Negroes," said the New York *Evening-Journal,* "have given us the only music of our own that is American—national, original and real."

Europe tried always to present black music with dignity, though even he sometimes had to cater to the curious

expectations of white audiences." [The] Europe gang were absolute reading sharks," remembered his pianist, Eubie Blake. "They could read a moving snake and if a fly lit on that paper he got played . . . but the people wanted to believe that Negroes couldn't learn to read music but had a natural talent for it. So we never played with no music. . . .

I'd get all the latest Broadway music from the publisher, and we'd learn the tunes and rehearse 'em until we had 'em all down pat. Never made no mistakes. . . . All the high-tone, big-time folks would say, 'Isn't it wonderful how these untrained, primitive musicians can pick up all the latest songs instantly without being able to read music?' "

"During breath-catching intermissions" on the Castle tour, W. C. Handy wrote, "Jim would sit at the piano and play slowly the 'Memphis Blues.' He did this so often that the Castles became intrigued by its rhythm, and Jim asked why they didn't originate a slow dance adaptable to it." The result was the fox-trot, the Castles' longest-lasting

legacy and the basis for scores of dances and thousands of songs over the coming years.

Europe's was the first black orchestra ever to record, and the smaller bands he supplied for New York society dances were so popular that one white bandleader complained to a newspaper that it "will not be long before the poor white musician will be obliged to blacken his face to make a livelihood or starve." Europe was unrepentant. There was now a new kind of Negro musician at work, he said, who combined "serious study" with "a natural talent" and who was contributing to American music "whatever distinctive quality it possesses." When the New York local of the musician's union became the first in the country to integrate its ranks, Europe signed right up but he was still not satisfied. Black performers were doing better now, he told a reporter, but black composers were still paid far less than their white counterparts. That, too, would change, he said: "Some day it will be different and justice will prevail."

Europe's "Castle House Rag" was named for a short-lived institution organized by Manhattan society matrons so that young people could dance safely to his orchestra without being exposed to what they called "discredited elements."

James Reese Europe and roughly two-thirds of the Clef Club Symphony Orchestra he led at the Manhattan Casino in Harlem in 1911. His "Monster Melange and Dancefest" included new music by black composers, a minstrel show, and orchestral versions of Negro spirituals.

THE
JAZZ AGE

On February 26, 1917, President Woodrow Wilson appeared before a joint session of Congress to ask for the power to arm American merchant ships against unrestricted attacks by German submarines in the Atlantic. Wilson had struggled hard to keep the country out of the European war that had now been raging for nearly three years—his new policy was still called "armed neutrality"—and much of the country remained opposed to taking sides. But it looked more and more likely now that German belligerence would draw America into the conflict anyway.

That same day, the members of the Original Dixieland Jazz Band tried again to record their version of New Orleans music. They were at the New York studios of the Victor Talking Machine Company this time, and they were going to play

Bennie Krueger's Brunswick Orchestra and the singer Dorothy Jardon garner some publicity for their appearance at Brooklyn's Brighton Beach Pavilion in the summer of 1922. The bandleader is at the left, playing C-melody saxophone. "Jazz maniacs were being born," remembered the songwriter Hoagy Carmichael, "and I was one of them."

two tunes they played often—"Dixieland Jass Band One-Step" and "Livery Stable Blues." The Victor engineer worked hard to balance the instruments properly. The emphasis was on comedy: Nick LaRocca made his cornet whinny like a horse; Larry Shields crowed like a rooster with his clarinet; Daddy Edwards made his trombone moo. No one improvised; every note had been carefully worked out in advance.

But the music was hotter and livelier than anything that had ever been recorded before—the engineer had insisted the men play especially fast to fit the whole tune on a record—and most Americans still had never heard anything remotely like it. Released on March 7, the record cut that day would sell more than a million copies at seventy-five cents each—more than any single record by Caruso or John Phillip Sousa had ever sold—and before long the ODJB was back in the studio recording more tunes: "At the Jazz Band Ball," "Fidgety Feet," "Sensation Rag," "Tiger Rag," "Clarinet Marmalade Blues."

"One moment jazz was unknown, obscure—a low noise in a low dive," the bandleader Paul Whiteman remembered (with some help from his silent writing partner Mary Margaret McBride). "The next it had become a serious pastime of a hundred million people, the diversion of princes and millionaires. . . . The time was ripe. . . . The war spirit was on the loose. The whole tempo of the country was speeded up. Wheels turned like mad. Every factory was manned by night shifts. Americans . . . lived harder, faster than ever before. They could not go without some new outlet. Work was not enough and America had not yet found out how to play. . . . Meanwhile was brewing in New Orleans a restorative for the national nerve complaint . . . [t]he great American noise, jazz."

The ODJB's version of that noise was rowdy, irreverent, assertive, and utterly American. "An Englishman entered a place as if he were its master," the New York

Times critic Olin Downes wrote, "whereas an American entered as if he didn't care who in blazes the master might be. Something like that [is] in this music." Young people loved it, and Victor couldn't believe its luck—though it wasn't entirely sure just what it was its engineers had recorded. Jazz was "organized disorganization," the Victor advertising copywriters said.

Spell it Jass, Jaz, or Jazz—nothing can spoil a Jass band. A Jass Band is the newest thing in cabarets, adding greatly to the hilarity thereof. You never know what it's going to do next, but you can always tell what those who hear it are going to do—they're going to "shake a leg."

The Jass Band is the very latest thing in the development of music. It has sufficient power and penetration to inject new life into a mummy, and will keep ordinary human dancers on their feet till breakfast time.

LaRocca and his men cheerfully played along with the publicity department, pretending everything they did had been made up on the spot, declaring themselves "musi-

The record that started it all, "Livery Stable Blues," by the Original Dixieland "Jass" Band

cal anarchists," allowing Daddy Edwards to claim, "None of us know music," when he himself read it perfectly well.

Back in New Orleans, musicians were swept up in the excitement engendered by the Original Dixieland Jazz Band's success. Dance-band violinists all over town lost their jobs because the ODJB did not happen to have one; Kid Ory fired one of the members of the sextet in which he and Joe Oliver played just to match its five-man line-up; and Oliver himself soon joined an exodus of musicians, both black and white, hurrying north to Chicago, where club owners were now frantically looking for people to bring Crescent City music to their clientele.

Louis Armstrong listened to the ODJB's records along with the rest of the country. He had somehow managed to save up enough money to buy a wind-up Victrola—on which he had been listening to operatic arias by Caruso and the Irish tenor John McCormack, whose "beautiful phrasing" he especially admired—when the first jazz sides appeared. "We thought they were great," he remembered. "Everybody was blowing a whole lot of jazz in New Orleans but [the Original Dixieland Jazz Band's] the one that put it over." He liked the sound of Nick LaRocca's cornet well enough, but he loved Larry Shields's clarinet solo on "Clarinet Marmalade" and was soon intimidating other cornetists by the ease with which he could reproduce it flawlessly on his horn.

Sidney Bechet, on the other hand, was scornful of the ODJB and its claim to have written tunes like "Livery Stable Blues." "Those were all numbers they had learned from playing opposite us back in New Orleans," he said later. "All these Dixieland musicians could do was play what they learned from us, and after that there wasn't anything more for them to do." But the jazz mania sparked by the ODJB provided fresh opportunities even for Bechet. In July, a vaudeville impresario turned up in New Orleans and persuaded him and four other

JASS, JASZ, JAZZ

"Jazz," wrote the bandleader Paul Whiteman in 1926, was originally a "slang phrase of the underworld with a meaning unmentionable in polite society. . . . It reached the drawing room finally on the strength of its terse expressive virility. On the way up, it was variously a verb and a noun, generally denoting speed or quick action of some kind. It appears now to be firmly established as a member of that long list of American words in good social standing." The New Orleans music spreading fast across the country had first been called "ratty music," "gut-bucket music," "hot music." But now, people began to call it "jass," "jasz," and "jazz," though no one has ever been entirely sure why. As early as 1906, a San Francisco sportswriter was using the word to denote pep and enthusiasm on the baseball field, and there were those who thought it might have originally come from a West African word for speeding things up. But most authorities believe that the term, like the music, came from New Orleans—from the jasmine perfume allegedly favored by the city's prostitutes, or from "jezebel," a common nineteenth-century term for a prostitute, or as a synonym for sexual intercourse in Storyville, where some brothels were said to have been called "jays'n houses." "The original meaning of jazz was procreation," says the trumpet player Wynton Marsalis, "you can't get deeper or more profound than that unless you're contemplating the Creator."

The Original Dixieland Jass Band changed the spelling of its name soon after the RCA Victor catalogue at right was published in March 1917, but five years later, the singer Sarah Martin (below) was still calling her group the "Jass Fools."

New Victor Records Jass Band and other Dance Selections

The Original Dixieland Jass Band

SPELL it Jass, Jas, Jaz or Jazz—nothing can spoil a Jass band. Some say the Jass band originated in Chicago. Chicago says it comes from San Francisco—San Francisco being away off across the continent. Anyway, a Jass band is the newest thing in the cabarets, adding greatly to the hilarity thereof.

They say the first instrument of the first Jass band was an empty lard can, by humming into which, sounds were produced resembling those of a saxophone with the croup. Since then the Jass band has grown in size and ferocity, and only musicians to join her touring stock company, playing the band's biggest hits: "They are all red hot," the Indianapolis *Freeman* said about Bechet and his companions, "and the tremendous crowds howl and rave to hear them play the 'Livery Stable Blues.' "

THE HELLFIGHTERS

America had entered the Great War on April 6, 1917—just thirty-one days after the release of the ODJB's first record—and on New Year's Day of the following year, the two thousand men of the Fifteenth New York Regiment landed at Brest on the coast of Brittany. The French soldiers and sailors and civilians who turned out to greet them had never seen or heard anything like these Americans. The officers were white, as had been all of the American combat soldiers who had trooped ashore in France since the previous June. But these enlisted men were all black. So were all the members of the big regimental band, and as it swung into its distinctive version of the "Marseillaise," the onlookers on shore were still more puzzled. These Americans played with such spirit and rhythmic drive that it took the French eight or ten bars to recognize their own national anthem. Then, one of the musicians in the band remembered, "there came over their faces an astonished look" followed instantly by "alert snap-to-it attention and [a] salute by every French soldier or sailor present."

Marching at the head of the band was its director, Lieutenant James Reese Europe, who had been the most eagerly sought-after society dance bandleader in New York before America entered the war, the man who, as musical director for the dancers Vernon and Irene Castle, had introduced the country to the fox-trot. He had joined up two years earlier, he told a friend, not out of any special sense of patriotism or because he was especially fond of martial music, but because he thought a National Guard unit for Harlem would "bring

Lieutenant James Reese Europe in France, 1918

together all classes of men who stand for something in the community" and he would have felt remiss if he were not a part of it.

The regiment had first been sent south for training, to Spartanburg, South Carolina, over the strenuous objections of the city's mayor. "I was sorry to learn that the Fifteenth Regiment has been ordered here," he told the press, "for, with their northern ideas about race equality, they will probably expect to be treated like white men. I can say right here that they will not be treated as anything except negroes. . . . This thing is like waving a red flag in the face of a bull, something that can't be done without trouble."

On the first Saturday after the regiment's arrival, Europe's band played a concert in downtown Spartanburg. A big muttering crowd of local whites gathered, Major Arthur W. Little remembered, and

the talk which some of us overheard through that crowd during the early stages of the concert was by no means reassuring. . . . But there must be something in the time-honored line about music and its charms; for, gradually, . . . the noises of the crowd grew less and less, until finally, in that great public square of converging city streets, silence reigned. Lieutenant Europe conducted, as was his custom, with but a few seconds between numbers, and the program appeared to be short. When the final piece had been played and the forty or fifty bandsmen had filed out of the stand in perfect order with the "Hep—Hep—Hep—" of the sergeants as the only sound from their ranks, the flower of Spartanburg's citizenry looked at each other foolishly, and one could be heard to say: —"Is that all?" while another would say: — "When do they play again?"

The next day, members of the Spartanburg chamber of commerce came calling upon Major Little. Would the band be available to play for dancing the following Saturday at the country club?

Europe's music may have mollified some white citizens of Spartanburg, but others continued to be angered by the presence of black troops. In the interest of keeping the peace, the men pledged to follow Jim Crow practice whenever they went into town and to do their best to look the other way when insulted. But white troops from other New York units training nearby had made no such promises. They berated shop owners who wouldn't serve their fellow soldiers, whatever their color, and when a black doughboy was assaulted for failing to leave the sidewalk fast enough to suit several

Members of Europe's Hellfighter's Band

James Europe and his men outside a Paris hospital, serenading wounded troops. "When they played the 'Memphis Blues,'" wrote the Kentucky-born war correspondent Irvin S. Cobb, "the men did not march, the music poured in at their ears and ran down to their heels, and instead of marching they literally danced their way along. I think surely this must be the best regimental band in our army. Certainly it is the best one I have heard in Europe during this war."

ning new friends among the French. The songwriter Noble Sissle, who served as the band's vocalist, remembered its first appearance before French civilians, a Lincoln's Birthday concert at the Nantes opera house. The men played French marches, "The Stars and Stripes Forever," plantation melodies, and ragtime pieces, which the French had never heard before. Then came "the fireworks," Sissle wrote, W. C. Handy's "Memphis Blues": it began with a "soul-rousing crash" of cymbals by the drummers, their shoulders shaking in time, then "both director and musicians seemed to forget their surroundings. . . . Cornet and clarinet players began to manipulate notes in that typical rhythm which no artist has ever put down on paper. The audience could stand it no longer, the 'jazz germ' hit them and it seemed to find the vital spot, loosening all muscles and causing what is known in American as an 'eagle rocking it.' "

The music Europe's men played was still orchestrated ragtime meant for marching, not jazz, and no one was allowed to improvise. But it was filled with jazz elements —breaks, riffs, trombone smears, and rhythmic excitement no other marching band could come close to matching. "Everywhere we gave a concert it was a riot," Europe told a reporter, "but the supreme moment came in the Tuileries Gardens when we gave a concert in conjunction with the greatest bands in the world—the British Grenadier's Band, the Band of the *Garde Republicain* and the Royal Italian Band. My band, of course, could not compare with any of these, yet the crowd, and it was such a crowd as I never saw anywhere else in the world, deserted them for us. We played to 50,000 people, at least, and had we wished it, we might be playing yet."

The British and French and Italian bandmasters were impressed, too, and asked to examine the instruments Europe's men had used; they couldn't believe that such sounds could be made through ordinary horns. It was not the instruments his men played, Europe patiently explained, but the

lounging whites, white New Yorkers beat his attackers to the ground. Then, when the proprietor of a downtown hotel knocked a black private down for having failed to doff his hat before buying a newspaper in the lobby, officers had to restrain angry white troops from burning the place down. Finally, it had been thought best to have the

regiment's training completed in France, where, their commander assured his men, there was "no color line."

Not long after the Europe band came ashore in France, Army brass saw that its brand of martial ragtime would be good for morale, providing "the feel of home" for bored or battered doughboys, while win-

The Hellfighters Band leads the 369th Infantry up Fifth Avenue past the New York Public Library, February 17, 1919.

way they played them that made the difference. "We play the music as it is written," but play it in a syncopated manner that is "a racial musical characteristic. I have to call a daily rehearsal of my band to prevent the musicians from adding to their music more than I wish them to. Whenever possible they all embroider their parts in order to produce new, peculiar sounds. Some of these effects are excellent and some are not, and I have to be continually

on the lookout to cut out the results of the musicians' originality."

On the night of April 20, 1918, Europe became the first African-American officer to face combat during the war, accompanying a French night patrol across no-man's-land under heavy enemy fire. Six weeks later, he survived a German poison gas attack that left his lungs too weak for further fighting but failed to dim his creativity. Lying on a hospital cot he wrote a

new song, "On Patrol in No Man's Land," then arranged it for the regimental band with special effects—sirens and alarm bells, artillery explosions, and rattling bursts of machine-gun fire, all to be produced by the band's two drummers.

Meanwhile, the men of the Fifteenth New York—its name now changed to the 369th Infantry Regiment, U.S. Army—endured 191 unbroken days of combat, won 171 decorations for bravery, more than any

We return from the slavery of uniform which the world's madness demanded [of] us to don the freedom of civil garb. We stand again to look America squarely in the face . . . : This country of ours, despite all its better souls have done and dreamed, is yet a shameful land.

It lynches. . . . It disfranchises its own citizens. . . . It encourages ignorance. . . . It steals from us. . . . It insults us. . . .

We return from fighting. We return fighting.

Make way for Democracy! We saved it in France, and by the Great Jehovah, we will save it in the U.S.A. Or know the reason why.

Everywhere, African-Americans redoubled their efforts to build their own institutions—banks, businesses, baseball teams—while men like Alain Locke and James Weldon Johnson began to prophesy that a "race genius" was bound to come along soon, someone who could take black folk music—spirituals, blues, ragtime—and transform it into something altogether new, altogether American. Somehow, they failed to see that

jazz would be that music; that point would first have to be made overseas, by someone who had never set foot in the United States.

On the Fourth of July, 1919, just five days after the ODJB's triumph at the Savoy ball in London, the Southern Syncopated Orchestra, a troupe of some forty black musicians and singers, opened a five-month run at the Royal Philharmonic Hall. Their musical director, Will Marion Cook, was a proud, irascible man. A product of the same middle-class Washington world from which Duke Ellington came, he had studied violin at Oberlin College, in Berlin, and with Antonín Dvořák during the Czech composer's brief sojourn in New York, only to abandon the concert stage at thirty because he had come to see that there was no future on it for a black artist. According to Ellington, who knew him well, the catalyst had been a patronizing review that called him "the world's greatest Negro violinist." Cook called upon the critic, smashed his violin across his desk, saying, "I am the greatest violinist in the *world!*" then stormed out, vowing never to play in public again. He had turned his attention first to bringing the most authentically African-American

music the traffic would bear to turn-of-the-century Broadway, writing the score for the poet Paul Lawrence Dunbar's revue *Clorindy, or the Origin of the Cakewalk,* as well as three hit shows for the comedy team of Bert Williams and George Walker—*In Dahomey, In Abyssinia,* and *Bandana Land.*

Cook continued to believe it his mission to "place the musical art of the Negro—truly American, distinctive, characteristic, sublime—in the sphere it properly belongs . . . for in the democracy of art, the prejudices of race must disappear." The "musical art of the Negro," according to Cook's definition, included everything "from the old spirituals to the standard works of the modern Negro composers"—everything, that is, except jazz. He had deplored Jim Europe's brassier arrangements for being "undignified," loathed the Original Dixieland Jazz Band and its white imitators, whose crude novelty music he saw as just the latest manifestation of the old minstrelsy he detested, and insisted that all of his musicians play his orchestrations precisely as written—with a single exception. Twenty-one-year-old Sidney Bechet, whom Cook had found playing in Chicago, was allowed to improvise his own solo just

Sidney Bechet, at far right, and the Jazz Kings, the group he often played for in and around London after the Southern Syncopated Orchestra fell apart, 1921

Mug shots of Sidney Bechet made by the London police, 1922

before the finale each night on a tune called "Characteristic Blues." It brought down the house. "I don't know which took the more exercise, the audience or the performers," wrote the reviewer for the London *Daily Herald.* "As the music grew raggier and raggier they swayed and we swayed . . . they snapped their fingers and clapped their hands, as we clapped more, and were all quite excited."

The Swiss conductor Ernest Ansermet came several times to hear Bechet that summer and later wrote about him and his music in a prophetic article for the *Revue Romande.*

There is in the Southern Syncopated Orchestra an extraordinary clarinet virtuoso who is, so it seems, the first of his race to have composed perfectly formed blues on the clarinet. I've heard two of them which he had elaborated at great length, then played to his companions so that they could make up an accompaniment. Extremely difficult, they are equally admirable for their richness of invention, force of accent, and daring novelty and the unexpected. . . .

I wish to set down the name of this artist of genius; as for myself, I shall never forget it, it is Sidney Bechet. When one has tried so hard so often in the past to discover one of the figures to whom we owe the advent of an art . . . what a moving thing it is to meet this very black, fat boy with white teeth and that narrow forehead, who is very glad one likes what he does, but who can say nothing of his art, save that he follows his "own way," and then one thinks that his "own way" is perhaps the highway the whole world will swing along tomorrow.

Sidney Bechet would follow his own way all his life. He was a "good friend and a fine fellow," a fellow member of the orchestra remembered, "but he just couldn't trust himself. He was so impetuous. . . . when the time came nothing on earth would stop him from doing what he wanted to do." One evening, as Cook's wife, the soprano Abbie Mitchell, began her big number, an aria from *Madame Butterfly,* Bechet jumped up from his chair in the orchestra, strode into her spotlight and began blowing a complex, keening obbligato. Cook, who detested onstage surprises of any kind, wanted to fire Bechet on the spot until his wife told him how much she'd liked it.

After the Southern Syncopated Orchestra split up, Bechet would stay on in London, playing with a shifting cast of former band members who called themselves the Jazz Kings. It was the kind of outfit he liked—there was no cornet or trumpet player to compete with him for the lead— and they were eventually booked to follow the Original Dixieland Jazz Band into the vast Palais de Danse at Hammersmith, sometimes performing for five thousand dancers an evening. When the Palais closed at midnight, Bechet moved on to play until dawn at a small club called Rector's where, a regular remembered, he liked to sit down in the middle of the dance floor, "legs crossed, tailor-fashion, and proceed to give us solos, . . . usually starting off with the Prologue from *Pagliacci.*"

Bechet was often playing a new instrument now—the soprano saxophone, preferring it to the clarinet, he said, because it was so loud. No brass player would ever again be able to drown him out. Musicians derided it as "Sidney's fish horn" at first, and made fun of the distinctive tremolo with which he played it, but that same huge impassioned sound would soon overwhelm nearly everyone who tried to play alongside him. It was unlike anything anyone had ever heard before and has never been duplicated since.

Bechet's private life remained as turbulent as his music. He drank too much, lost jobs for failing to turn up on time and didn't seem to care. He gambled, too, once betting and losing his horn to a fellow musician who charitably gave it back because without it Bechet couldn't earn a living. And he pursued—and was pursued by—British women. He was "as attractive as a panther," the smitten shipping-company heiress Nancy Cunard remembered, "and rather like one—young with a beautiful, light-brown skin, rippling blue-black hair. He had innate courtesy and beautiful clothes." Then, in a murky incident never fully explained, he was arrested, accused of assaulting a London prostitute. It was just "a silly man-woman kind of dispute," Bechet claimed, but he was found guilty and sentenced to two weeks in Brixton Prison, followed by deportation. "Oh, I can be mean," Bechet admitted many years later. "I know that. But not to the music. That's the thing you gotta trust. You gotta mean it, and you got to treat it gentle."

FAST FINGERS

Louis Armstrong had been sad to see Joe Oliver head north for Chicago in 1918, but he was thrilled when he was asked to take his mentor's place as lead cornetist at Pete Lala's cabaret in the band Oliver and Kid Ory had led. He did his best to master its repertoire, even wrote a tune of his own which Clarence Williams bought from him for fifty dollars. (As "I Wish I Could Shimmy Like My Sister Kate," it would eventually become a big hit up north.) He competed in bucking contests, too, facing off against other cornetists, including Sam Morgan, Chris Kelly, Ernest "Punch" Miller, and Buddy Petit.

But his chief rival was Henry "Kid" Rena, a Creole fellow graduate of the Colored Waif's Home band, who shared his delight in high notes and elaborate embellishment. "Kid Rena and I used to have some awful battles," Armstrong remembered. "Rena could all but whistle through that cornet of his, but then my chops were pretty strong, too." Sidney Bechet had earlier defied New Orleans tradition by trying to capture the lead from the cornet. Now, Armstrong and Rena sought somehow both

to retain the lead and to take over the clarinet's embellishing role as well. Armstrong continued to play clarinetlike "figurations . . . fast fingers and everything," and when he marched in Oscar "Papa" Celestin's elite Tuxedo Brass Band, the best—and most handsomely uniformed—marching outfit in town, he sometimes mystified his fellow musicians. "I didn't never understand Louis Armstrong," the trombonist Sunny Henry admitted, "because that son-of-a-gun he . . . didn't care what you played. . . . He would play an obbligato all the time; be off [the melody], you understand; he wouldn't never once play straight with you. But everything he put in there, by Ned, it worked."

Soon, Armstrong remembered, "I was beginning to get very popular around that good old town of mine." His responsibilities were increasing along with his reputation. At eighteen, he married a hot-tempered prostitute named Daisy Parker, who ate up his earnings and variously attacked him with a razor, a bread knife, and bricks, which, he remembered, she could hurl as fast and as accurately as Satchel Paige would later throw a baseball. And when a cousin gave birth to a baby named Clarence and then died, and then the infant suffered brain damage, he took on his care, as well.

Out-of-town musicians offered him work from time to time, but he still had little thought of moving away from his hometown. "I used to see so many kids leave," Armstrong said, "and then you look around and they have to hobo their way back home. Wasn't nobody going to get me to leave New Orleans but Papa Joe [Oliver]."

He had to wait four years before Papa Joe finally sent him the telegram he was waiting for, but he put the time to good use. He spent three summers playing for dancers aboard steamboats owned by four brothers named Streckfus, whose fleet of floating ballrooms plowed up and down the Mississippi—from New Orleans all the way north to St. Paul, Minnesota, and back again. The bandleader and pianist, Fate

Fate Marable's band aboard the S.S. *Sidney*, 1919. Young Louis Armstrong is second from left; the bassist is George "Pops" Foster; Baby Dodds sits behind the drums. The big dance floor was filled most evenings with white dancers from small river towns, many of whom had never before encountered black musicians. "We had to listen to plenty of nasty remarks," Armstrong recalled. "We were used to that kind of jive, and we would just keep on swinging as though nothing had happened. Before the evening was over they *loved* us. We couldn't turn [around] for them singing our praises and begging us to hurry back."

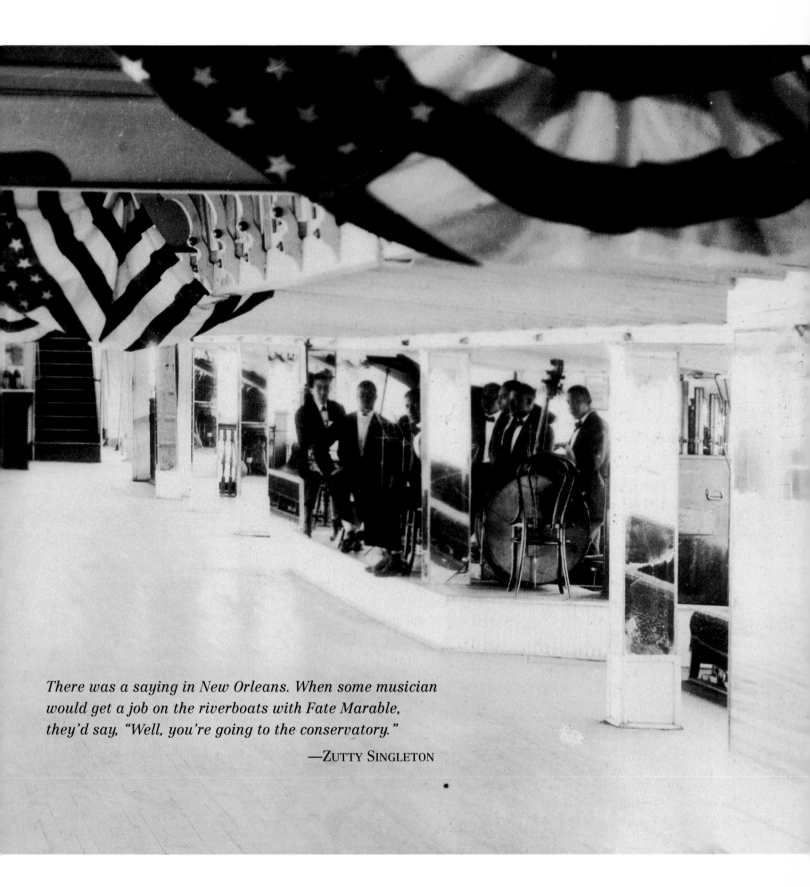

*There was a saying in New Orleans. When some musician
would get a job on the riverboats with Fate Marable,
they'd say, "Well, you're going to the conservatory."*

—Zutty Singleton

Marable, who doubled on calliope, was a disciplinarian who insisted that his young cornetist learn to read music as well as play it. The nine men in his band were expected to play waltzes, light classics, and the latest songs, while a cashier with sharp ears for music tallied up the wrong notes played each evening and dunned errant musicians accordingly. A man who failed to live up to Marable's rules was literally given the ax; when he got to work the next day he would find a hatchet on his chair signaling that he was through. But Armstrong got paid fifty dollars a week plus a five-dollar bonus, more money than he had ever seen, and he got to play alongside some of the best young musicians in New Orleans including Pops Foster, the clarinetist Johnny Dodds and his drummer brother, Warren, known as "Baby."

According to Baby Dodds, the band had included white musicians until they began grumbling about working for a colored man—even one so light-skinned and red-haired as Fate Marable—and the Streckfus brothers were trying their all-black outfit only as an experiment. "They'd advertise before we got there that we were colored," Dodds said, "so people wouldn't be disappointed," and he remembered once docking at Hannibal, Missouri, where whites had filed aboard, then just stared, refusing to dance. "They saw Negro roustabouts but had never seen a Negro with a tie and collar on, a white shirt, playing music. They just didn't know what to make of it." But they listened and the next time they docked at Hannibal, Dodds said, "My God, you couldn't get them off the boat. . . . They were the dancingest people I ever found."

At St. Louis, there were Monday-evening cruises for black dancers only. Pops Foster remembered that the musicians called Monday "Getaway Night" because "they could get away with anything." They drank, smoked, got to talk to the customers and to put on a livelier show. Baby Dodds drew special attention to himself by shimmying while playing drums: "The colored people

had never seen anything like that," he said. "Used to have a bunch around me packed five or six deep; and Louis Armstrong would have a bunch five or six deep. It was a wonderful thing, and we were the two sensational men on the boat, Louis and I."

When their boat tied up at Davenport, Iowa, in the summer of 1920, a seventeen-year-old high school student named Leon "Bix" Beiderbecke heard Armstrong play—and never forgot it. Neither did a young trombonist from Texas named Jack Teagarden, who happened to be standing on the New Orleans levee one moonlit evening when he heard the distant sound of a cornet from somewhere across the water. He couldn't see anything at first except the vague form of an excursion boat gliding toward him through the mist. But the sound, growing louder as the boat neared shore, was unlike anything he had ever heard before. It was Louis Armstrong, he remembered, "descending from the sky like a god."

On July 4, 1919, Louis Armstrong, Johnny Dodds, and Pops Foster went ashore together at St. Louis and stopped in a bar owned by a man named Boots to buy themselves a half pint of whiskey each. They planned to celebrate that night—Armstrong believed he had been born on Independence Day and that he was turning nineteen—but they also had heard that Prohibition was soon to begin, Foster remembered, and wanted to have something to tide them over until sanity returned. It would not return for thirteen years. The Fifteenth Amendment went into effect on January 20, 1920. Intended to close down the corner saloon traditionally frequented only by men, it spawned tens of thousands of speakeasies and roadhouses instead, to which both men and women flocked. Alcohol never went away; it just went underground. Prohibition encouraged organized crime, corrupted American politics. But for jazz music —which had started out in the saloons as well as the streets of New Orleans—and for

jazz musicians, it would prove a godsend. Theirs would become the music of choice in cabarets and speakeasies and road-houses, would provide the accompaniment for the period F. Scott Fitzgerald would soon call the Jazz Age.

I'D GO TO HELL TO HEAR A GOOD BAND

By the time the Original Dixieland Jazz Band got back to New York in July of 1920, they found the city filled with noisy imitators: the Louisiana Five, Georgia Five, Alabama Five, St. Louis Five, Domino Five, Original Indiana Five, the Frisco Jass Band, and the Original New Orleans Jazz Band, which featured four authentic New Orleans musicians but was actually the creation of a Brooklyn-born ragtime piano player named Jimmy Durante. "In some of those bands in those days the cornet player played the melody," Durante remembered, "in some others the clarinet played the melody. In our band, *nobody* played the melody."

For most of these groups melody—and music—were less important than noise and novelty. The message they seemed to want to convey, Ralph Berton, the younger brother of the drummer Vic Berton, remembered was, "Let's all get loaded and see how nutty we can sound." The Louisiana Five's biggest hit was "Yelping Hound Blues," on which Tom Brown's one-time clarinetist Yellow Nuñez imitated a dog baying at the moon. One of the most popular jazz groups in town, Earl Fuller's Famous Jazz Band at Rector's restaurant, played almost entirely for laughs: as its leader played piano, drummer John Lucas banged away at what was advertised as "64 square feet" of bells, cymbals, woodblocks, and "pieces of . . . apparatus [that] are electrically worked," the trombonist used his foot to manipulate his slide, and Ted Lewis juggled a top hat with one hand while playing clarinet with the wobbliest comic tone he could muster.

Nut jazz. The Frisco Syncopators (top) and a clownish outfit led by the dummer Albert "Doc" Wrixon (bottom) who sometimes worked aboard the same Streckfus boats on which Louis Armstrong had played.

The ODJB continued to do well for a time, even attempting a somewhat smoother style that included a saxophone. But nothing Nick LaRocca or his publicists could think of could restore the band's preeminence, not even an elaborately staged appearance at the Bronx Zoo, where their music allegedly inspired a polar bear to shimmy with pleasure but drove a female hippopotamus to take cover underwater. Too much drinking and too many one-nighters eventually wore its members down; one by one they would leave the road until Nick LaRocca himself suffered a nervous breakdown in 1925, abandoned music, and returned to the construction business in New Orleans as if he'd never left it.

Later on, as the first jazz histories were published, filled with praise for Creole and black musicians from New Orleans like Sidney Bechet, Joe Oliver, and Louis Armstrong, LaRocca would react violently, convinced conspirators were out to strip him of the credit for creating jazz that he was sure belonged to him alone. Like his mentor, Papa Jack Laine, LaRocca would always insist that his music—and *all* jazz music—had nothing at all to do with black people. "Our music is strictly white man's music. We patterned our earlier efforts after military marches, which we heard in park concerts in our youth. Many writers have attributed this rhythm that we introduced as something coming from the African jungles and crediting the Negro race with it. My contention is that the Negroes learned to play this rhythm and music from the whites. . . . The Negro did not play any kind of music equal to white men at any time."

The postwar decade would one day be caricatured as "the Roaring Twenties," and it was a time of unprecedented prosperity—the nation's total wealth nearly doubled between 1920 and 1929, manufactures rose by 60 percent, for the first time most people lived in urban areas—and in homes lit by electricity. They made more money than

Vassar's Scale Steppers at the Lincoln Gardens on Chicago's South Side, 1921. Violinist Milton Vassar, second from left, was the leader; Tommy Ladnier from New Orleans, kneeling, played trumpet. The following year, this same bandstand would be occupied by King Oliver and Louis Armstrong.

they ever had before and, spurred on by the giant new advertising industry, spent it faster, too—on washing machines and refrigerators and vacuum cleaners, twelve million radios, thirty million automobiles, and untold millions of tickets to the movies, that ushered them into a new, fast-living world of luxury and glamour their grandparents could never have imagined. Meanwhile, at the polls and in the workplace as well as on the dance floor, women had begun to assert a new independence.

For many of the millions of people for whom the twenties never roared at all, fearful of such rapid change and nostalgic for the small-town America of the turn of the century, jazz music came to seem not merely an annoyance but a threat, one more cause of loosening morals and frightening dislocation. Ragtime had been bad enough, with its insinuating rhythms and daring couple-dancing, but the jumpy, raucous version of New Orleans polyphony projected by the ODJB and many of its imitators seemed much worse. "As I understand it," said Professor Henry Van Dyck of Princeton University, "it is not music at all. It is merely an irritation of the nerves of hearing, a sensual teasing of the strings of physical passion. Its fault lies not in syncopation, for that is a legitimate device when sparingly used. But 'jazz' is an unmitigated cacophony, a combination of disagreeable sounds in complicated discords, a willful ugliness and a deliberate vulgarity." The editor of *Musical Courier* reported on a poll of academically trained musicians: most found "the 'ad libbing' or 'jazzing' of a piece . . . thoroughly objectionable," he said, "and several of them advanced the opinion that this Bolshevistic smashing of the rules and tenets of decorous music" spelled disaster for American music.

For some, jazz simply became synonymous with noise. Thomas Edison, whose invention of the phonograph had made its sudden rapid spread possible, claimed that he played jazz records backwards because "they sound better that way." When the *New York Times* reported that the citizens of one Siberian village had driven hungry polar bears from its streets by banging pots and pans, the headline read "Jazz Frightens Bears," and when a celebrated British conductor collapsed with a fatal heart attack while visiting Coney Island, the same paper blamed the jazz bands now loudly competing with one another along the boardwalk for his demise.

Jazz—and the dancing it inspired—was also said to be having a catastrophic impact on the national character. "Moral disaster is coming to hundreds of young American girls," reported the New York *American,* "through the pathological, nerve-irritating, sex-exciting music of jazz orchestras." In just two years in Chicago alone, the Illinois Vigilance Association reported in 1923, the downfall of one thousand girls could be traced directly to the pernicious influence of jazz music. In Cincinnati, the Salvation Army obtained a court injunction to stop construction of a theater next to a home for expectant mothers on the grounds that "the enforced proximity of a theater and jazz palace" would implant dangerous "jazz emotions" in helpless infants. A social worker reported on the "unwholesome excitement" she now encountered even at small-town dances in the Midwest. "Boy-and-girl couples leave the hall in a state of dangerous disturbance. Any worker who has gone into the night to gather the facts of activities outside the dance hall is appalled . . . by the blatant disregard of even the elementary rules of civilization. . . . We must expect a few casualties in social intercourse, but the modern dance is producing little short of holocaust."

Beyond its disturbing sounds, its fast pace, and its supposed impact on morals, jazz was also condemned because of its origins. Many white older Americans were appalled to see their children dancing to music that was believed to have emerged from what the music critic of the New York *Herald Tribune* called "the Negro brothels of the South." "Jazz," said the editor of *Etude,* "is often associated with vile surroundings, filthy words, unmentionable dances." It was originally "the accompaniment of the voodoo dancer," declared Mrs. Max Obendorfer, national music chairman of the General Federation of Women's Clubs, "stimulating the half-crazed barbarian to the vilest deeds. . . . [It] has also been employed by other barbaric people to stimulate brutality and sensuality." (Blacks were not the sole sources of the jazz contagion. The critic Carl Engel also worried about the effects on Anglo-Saxon youth of what he called "Semitic purveyors of Broadway melodies," while Henry Ford's *Dearborn Independent* blamed what it called "the abandoned sensuousness of sliding notes" on sinister Jews.)

There was nothing new in these attitudes. Twenty years earlier, many whites had deplored ragtime in part because it was based on black songs and dances, just as their descendants would one day denounce rock 'n' roll because of its links to the African-American blues tradition. But something altogether new really was happening here and there across the country. A few white youths—living in small towns and comfortable suburbs as well as big-city slums—started to see more than mere novelty and excitement in this new primarily black music, began actually to hear their own feelings mirrored in the playing of African-Americans, and to look for ways they might participate in it themselves. In a country in which by law and custom blacks and whites were forbidden to compete on anything like an equal basis in any arena—even boxing: the heavyweight title was then off-limits to black challengers—these young men were willing to brave a brand new world created by black Americans and in which black musicians remained the most admired figures.

Nothing quite like it had ever happened before in America.

In late 1921, eight white musicians who called themselves the New Orleans Rhythm Kings had begun what would turn into a seventeen-month run at a little cellar cabaret called the Friar's Inn, at 343 South Wabash on Chicago's Near North Side. The club advertised itself as the "Land of Bohemia Where Good Fellows Get Together." It "smelled just right," one visitor remembered, "funky, run-down, sinister and dusty" and the good fellows who sometimes got together there included the gangster Dion O'Banion, nicknamed "the Florist" because he provided the flowers for gangland funerals (and sometimes the corpses, as well), and young Al Capone, who would soon order O'Banion murdered and then take over his post as boss of the North Side.

The most celebrated members of the New Orleans Rhythm Kings—cornetist Paul Mares, trombonist George Brunies, and clarinetist Leon Roppolo—were all really from New Orleans. Mares, who had put the band together, was becomingly modest about its attainments. "We had only two tempos, slow drag and the two-four one-step," he recalled. "We did our best to copy the colored music we'd heard at home. We did the best we could, but naturally we couldn't play real colored style."

For whatever reason, the Rhythm Kings sounded very different from the Original

The New Orleans Rhythm Kings at the Friar's Inn in 1922. George Brunies plays trombone, Paul Mares is on cornet, Leon Ropollo plays clarinet.

Dixieland Jazz Band and its host of white imitators—less ragtimey and agitated, more relaxed and flowing. They had relatively little interest in comedy, and in part because the Friar's Inn was a small place with a low ceiling, they had also learned to modulate their sound. Mares stayed carefully in the middle range of his cornet and modeled his blues-based style after King Oliver's, while Brunies was solidly in the New Orleans tailgate trombone tradition. But Leon Ropollo's lyrical clarinet had its own unmistakable sound, suffused with an eerie melancholy even on the most apparently cheerful tunes. (Like Buddy Bolden, Ropollo would eventually go mad and be confined to a Louisiana asylum.) Ralph Berton summed up the band's impact on young white jazz enthusiasts in Chicago. "They played not in the zany, tongue-in-cheek spirit of the white bands . . . but *seriously*—mean and low

down, pretty or funky, driving or lyrical, but always *for real.* As we said in those days— there was no higher praise—*they played like niggers.*"

Most of the New Orleans Rhythm Kings themselves were under twenty-one and therefore forbidden to drink on the Friar's Inn bandstand, and underage fans were barred from the club altogether, one remembered, "so the only way we could hear them was to go down and stand in the doorway and listen. It was great when someone opened the door and we could hear it louder."

But some exceptions were evidently made and in the spring of 1922, one of the Friar's Inn's frequent patrons was a jug-eared nineteen-year-old prep school boy from Iowa named Leon Bix Beiderbecke. "Bix would come in and quietly sit and have

dinner," the Rhythm Kings' banjo player, Lou Black, remembered. "Our rhythm section played for the dinner crowd, starting at 6 p.m., and the full band came on about 10 p.m. Bix would stay to hear the music. Our headwaiter . . . didn't think a high school student should be in the club so late. He often made a menacing move towards Bix to throw him out. When he tried, the whole band would stand up and say, 'If he goes, so do we.' This was a great band, make no mistake about it. When we got to cooking, Jemima, our hat-check girl, would come out and start dancing right in front of her counter."

Beiderbecke wasn't interested in dancing. He had with him a battered cornet in a paper bag and lived for the moments when his heroes allowed him to sit in. His favorite tune was "Angry," Paul Mares remembered. "It sometimes seemed like that was the only tune he knew."

For Beiderbecke, just being there was an act of rebellion. His parents had sent him to the highly disciplined Lake Forest Academy in the Chicago suburb of Lake Forest the previous September precisely to keep his mind off jazz, yet night after night since his arrival he had been leaving his dormitory room, with or without permission from the headmaster, and traveling thirty-five miles into the city to seek out the music that already seemed to be all that mattered to him. Twice, he had been officially censured by the school and there had been talk of expelling him if he did not mend his ways. He paid no attention. It was as if he could not help himself.

Bix Beiderbecke was a shy, deeply self-doubting product of the Iowa corn country, who never learned more than the rudiments of written music and rarely spoke unless someone spoke to him first. His favorite phrase was "What the hell?" He was never a virtuoso in the sense in which that term applied to Louis Armstrong or Sidney Bechet; he can be heard on some 250 recordings but never won any serious

Bismarck and Agatha Beiderbecke of Davenport, Iowa, and their children in 1904. Bix sits on his father's lap, flanked by his brother Charles and sister Mary Louise.

derisively called "the Number One jazz saint," and to inflate his genuine gifts until he came somehow to seem a white counterpart to Louis Armstrong. None of this was fair to him or to his music.

For Armstrong's mother and the people among whom they lived in black Storyville, jazz music had been a step up, a way out for "Little Louis"; for Bix Beiderbecke's parents and their neighbors in Davenport, Iowa, his decision to become a jazz musician would come to seem like a plunge into the netherworld. He was born at 1934 Grand Avenue in Davenport, Iowa, on March 10, 1903. His father, Bismarck Beiderbecke, was a well-to-do coal-and-lumber merchant named after the Iron Chancellor of his family's native Germany. His mother, Agatha, was a steamboat captain's daughter. Both loved music—he had performed in his father's choral group; she was a gifted amateur pianist and played organ in the Presbyterian church—and they encouraged their younger son's early interest in the piano. He could play a one-fingered version of one of his mother's favorites, "Oh, Mr. Dooley," before he was three, and at seven was the subject of an admiring article in the Davenport *Daily Democrat* that began, "Little Bickie Beiderbecke plays any selection he hears!"

"He was a dreamy little fellow," his kindergarten teacher remembered, "and was happy finding his own niche rather than joining the larger group." Bix would always be dreamy, always remain a little apart from everyone else. At ten, his older brother, Charles, remembered, "he stopped coming home for supper," hurrying down to the riverfront instead, and slipping aboard one or another of the excursion boats to play the calliope. "Mother understood how distracted he was by his music. . . . I can remember having supper without Bix and hearing tunes played as only he could play them. . . . It was reassuring to know where he was." The plots of the silent films Bix and his friends paid a nickel to see on Saturday afternoons didn't interest him

celebrity outside the circle of his fellow musicians; and he drank himself to death before he was twenty-nine. But the understated eloquence of his solos and the silvery brilliance of his tone—"every note went through you like a shaft of light," a friend remembered, "making you feel all clear and clean and open"—would bring a kind of quiet lyricism to jazz and provide a whole generation of young white musicians with the proof they badly needed that they, too, might make a lasting contribution to this new American music.

"Bix was a mystery to us," one of his most ardent disciples remembered. "We knew him, admired him, thought he was a great guy. But in a way we didn't know him at all. He wasn't really *like* us." And, because he seemed unknowable even by those with whom he shared the bandstand, and because he died so soon, some romantic writers—who understood him even less well than his friends had—sought posthumously to transform him into a kind of selfless martyr to his art, to make him what the British saxophonist and writer Benny Green

The S.S. *Capitol*, the Streckfus steamboat on which both
Louis Armstrong and Bix Beiderbecke played during their
early years

much, but the minute the lights went on again, a friend remembered, he'd rush home to see if he could duplicate the melodies the accompanist had played during the action. He would always remain interested in the piano, struggling to work out fresh harmonies whenever he could get to a keyboard. But perhaps because his ear had been so accurate as a boy he never fully mastered music theory, a failing that would only add to the lack of self-confidence that seemed always to plague him.

In January of 1919, his brother returned from the army with a wind-up Victrola and an armful of records, including the Original Dixieland Jazz Band's frantic version of "Tiger Rag." Bix was fifteen—and transfixed. He listened to it over and over again, his brother remembered, "his head almost in the bell," then borrowed a neighbor's cornet and began to teach himself to play it, slowing down the turntable to hear each separate note, transposing it for the piano, then trying to reproduce it on his horn. "At first it was hard on the rest of us, his playing consisted of short blasting notes, until he got a mute. The mute was a godsend and we were able to go on with our lives."

Beiderbecke never had any formal instruction on his instrument, but two other young cornetists, both from New Orleans, deeply influenced him. The first was Louis Armstrong, just two years older than he, whom he heard playing aboard a Streckfus boat that spent a month based at Davenport in the late spring of 1920. "Bix would come aboard," Armstrong recalled, "listen, then go home and practice what he heard. He was never satisfied." The following winter, Beiderbecke heard a youthful white musician named Emmet Hardy, who played accompaniment for a shimmy dancer at a downtown Davenport theater with such beauty and drive that after Hardy's early death Beiderbecke would write his mother that her son had been "the greatest musician I have ever heard."

Bix couldn't get into the local musician's union because he couldn't read music well enough, but he found plenty of nonunion pickup jobs with small-time bands in and around his hometown: Billy Greer's Melody Jazz Band, Buckley's Novelty Orchestra, the Ralph Miedke Society Orchestra, the Ten Capitol Harmony Syncopaters, and the grandly named Plantation Jazz Orchestra with which he sailed for a time aboard the Streckfus steamer *Majestic* in the summer of 1921. That July, he heard Louis Armstrong again when his boat and the *St. Paul* both docked at the little town of Louisiana, Missouri; Armstrong and the Fate Marable band were "the talk of the River," Bix wrote home.

By the age of eighteen, Bix was good enough to play alongside older musicians—and to join them behind the bandstand between sets to sip corn whiskey and bootleg gin. At nineteen, he was arrested for what the Davenport police blotter called a "lewd and lascivious act with a child"—apparently just a fellow teenager, a girl from down the street. The case never reached court but the scandal must have been humiliating to him and to his family.

Bix's parents were appalled. Classical music was one thing. Jazz—and the sordid life it seemed to encourage—was quite another. It represented everything they detested, constituted a serious threat to the peace and stability of life in respectable communities like theirs. They had always wanted their boy to go on to Princeton, and in the autumn of 1921, evidently hoping to force him to focus on his studies and wean him away from jazz and the bad habits they believed went with it, they packed him off to Lake Forest.

It didn't work. Within a week of his arrival at school in September, he was writing home to tell his brother that he had already managed to make it to the South Side and talk his way into three different black clubs on Thirty-fifth Street in eager search of what he called "real jazz niggers." "Don't think I'm getting hard Burnie," he wrote, "but I'd go to hell to hear a good band."

Bix Beiderbecke as a student at Lake Forest Academy. "If you don't mind," he wrote home soon after reaching the school, "please send me all those Dixieland Jazz records I ordered. My room-mate has a victrola."

Bix Beiderbecke was a musician before he was anything else, eager to hear and learn from the best, whatever their color. At Thanksgiving, he slipped into the Hotel Sherman to hear Louis Panico, the cornetist with Isham Jones's white dance band. Panico was a mute specialist and an admirer of Joe Oliver, celebrated for his comedy effects and skilled enough to publish a book on cornet technique called *The Novelty Cornetist.* "When I told him I lived on the old Mississippi & played on the *Capitol*," Bix proudly reported home, "he told me he would show me how to laugh [on his horn] which he doesn't often do."

Bix helped organize a band on campus and almost immediately got in trouble with the headmaster for performing indecorously at a school dance. He had also already begun to develop the spare cornet style for which he would one day be remembered. When a schoolmate who prided himself on playing saxophone with a lot of flash accused him of being too restrained—"a note miser"—Beiderbecke shot back, "The trouble with you is you play so many notes, but they mean so little." From the beginning, Bix wanted every note to mean as much as possible.

He began regularly leaving the campus to play at downtown Chicago hotels. Once, when he appeared at an exclusive girls' school, the headmistress took the bandleader aside to complain: "That *nice boy* of yours is exciting my girls!" she said. "Make him stop." In May of 1922 alone, he slipped out of his room at different times to play in Gary, Indiana, at the Edgewater Beach Hotel, and at Northwestern University, and also found time to hear the New Orleans Rhythm Kings at the Friar's Inn as well as Joe Oliver, now appearing at a South Side café called the Lincoln Gardens. His grades understandably went from bad to worse.

Then, in the early morning hours of May 20, he was caught on the fire escape, trying to climb back into his dormitory room. The faculty voted to expel him the next day. His disappointed father came to take him home, but the boy somehow talked him into letting him spend the rest of the year seeing if he couldn't earn a living as a musician. He worked excursion boats and dance bands in Michigan and Wisconsin, then returned to Chicago and joined a youthful septet, the Royal Harmonists of Indiana, for an engagement in Syracuse, New York.

Its banjo player was Eddie Condon, an Indiana saloon-keeper's son who was just seventeen but already a fast talker—his nickname was "Slick." Beiderbecke didn't impress him much at their first meeting. Bix was wearing a battered cap and a threadbare green overcoat, Condon remembered, and "had a round face and eyes that had no desire to focus on what was in

front of him." They boarded the train for Syracuse and went to sleep. The next morning, bored by the flat Ohio landscape sliding past the window, Condon began idly to play his banjo. The saxophone player unpacked his horn. "Finally," Condon recalled, "Beiderbecke took out a silver cornet . . . put it to his lips and blew a phrase. The sound came out like a girl saying yes. . . . 'All right,' Beiderbecke said, '*Panama.*' At last I was playing music; so far as I was concerned it could go on forever. We disrupted the train. People crowded in from the other coaches; they stood in the aisles and on the seats. We couldn't wait to get to Syracuse; I hoped I would be stuck forever with Beiderbecke."

HYPNOSIS AT FIRST HEARING

Louis Armstrong had also been traveling that summer. On July 8, 1922, he boarded a train at New Orleans, bound for Chicago. He was twenty-one years old and finally going to join his idol, King Oliver. He had been making $1.50 an evening in New Orleans; in Chicago he could look forward to $52.50 a week, plus roughly the same amount in tips from enthralled customers. "There was plenty of work [in Chicago]," Armstrong remembered, "lots of *Dough* flying around, all kinds of beautiful women at your service. A musician in Chicago in the early twenties [was] treated and respected just like—some kind of a god."

He carried only his cornet case and an old valise that held his patched, threadbare tuxedo. His mother, Mayann, had packed him a trout sandwich to eat aboard the train and made sure he was wearing long underwear; she had heard that where he was going it was cold even in midsummer.

In setting out for Chicago, Armstrong was joining what came to be called the "Great Migration," a northern exodus that since 1917 had sent more than half a million African-Americans northward—and

Above, the Chicago *Defender* advertises just some of the entertainment available to black residents of the city's South Side on June 17, 1922. King Oliver is already starring at the Lincoln Gardens and about to send for Louis Armstrong to come north and join him. (Opposite) Armstrong and Oliver in Chicago, 1922. Oliver, said the younger man, was "always my inspiration and my idol. No trumpet player ever had the fire that Oliver had. Man, he really could *punch* a number."

that would propel a million more to follow before the end of the 1920s. As Alain Locke explained in the introduction to his 1925 compendium of black art and literature called *The New Negro,* there was no single reason for this exodus.

The tide of Negro migration, northward and cityward, is not to be fully explained as a blind flood started by the demands of war industry coupled with the shutting off of foreign immigration, or by the pressure of poor crops coupled with increased social terrorism in certain sections of the South and Southwest. Neither labor demand, the boll weevil, nor the Ku Klux Klan is a basic factor, however contributory any or all of them may have been. The wash and rush of this human tide on the beach line of the northern city centers is to be explained primarily in terms of a new vision of opportunity, of social and economic freedom, of a spirit to seize, even in the face of an extortionate and heavy toll, a chance for the improvement of conditions. With each successive wave of it, the movement toward the larger and the more democratic chance—in the Negro's case a deliberate flight not only from countryside to city, but from medieval America to modern.

Most immigrants from the deep South ended up at the end of the Illinois Central line, in Chicago. It was considered "the safest place near New Orleans," Danny Barker recalled. "All other places between those two points were looked upon as just visiting points. . . . I recall relatives returning to New Orleans telling humorous tales of looking out the windows of the train at such places as Memphis, Bowling Green, Kankakee, Natchez. They would say, 'I just can't figure how colored folks can live in them places that close to Chicago and not *go* there.' " Well over one hundred thousand black Americans now called Chicago

Michigan Avenue in downtown Chicago, 1924. The city's tallest buildings and most fashionable neighborhoods were a long way from the crowded South Side where most black refugees from Jim Crow settled. But they kept coming anyway. In Chicago, one explained, colored people were not "required to say, 'yes, ma'am' or 'yes, sir' to white people whether you desired to or not." "You can go anywhere you want," another said, and "don't have to look up to the white man, get off the street for him, and go to the buzzard roost [segregated balcony] at shows."

home, most of them clustered together on the South Side, and not even the vicious race riots that had gripped the city during the summer of 1919 could shake their belief that life in the North was preferable to returning to the Jim Crow South. The "Stroll"—the black bright-light district that shifted slowly down South State Street during the decade as more and more migrants poured into South Side tenements—was "the Bohemia of the Colored Folks," according to the black-owned Chicago *Whip,* a "Mecca for Pleasure," celebrated in black communities all over the country. There were clubs that limited their clientele to blacks only, and others, called black-and-tans, that welcomed patrons of both races. Shops and restaurants never closed their doors. "Excitement from noon to noon," the poet Langston Hughes recalled. "Midnight was like day. The street was full of workers and gamblers, prostitutes and pimps, church folk and sinners." And the police largely looked the other way, under orders from Big Bill Thompson, the red-faced, spectacularly corrupt Democratic mayor of the city who took a dim view of Prohibition—"I'm as wet as the middle of the Atlantic Ocean," he said—and, as he moved from club to club with his entourage, liked to bellow: "Get a horn and blow loud for Chicago. Let the jazz band play! Let's show 'em, we're all live ones!"

Louis Armstrong had never been so far from home before, and when he stepped down at Chicago's Twelfth Street Station and Joe Oliver was not there to meet him, he asked himself if he had made a mistake leaving New Orleans.

> I saw a million people, but not Mister Joe, and I didn't give a damn who else was there. I never seen a city that big. All those tall buildings, I thought they were universities. I said, no, this is the wrong city. I was just fixing to go back home—standing there in my box-back suit, padded shoulders,

King Oliver's Creole Jazz Band, 1923. Left to right, Baby Dodds, trombonist Honoré Dutrey, Joe Oliver, bassist Bill Johnson, Louis Armstrong, clarinetist Johnny Dodds, and pianist Lil Hardin

wide-legged pants—when a redcap Joe left word with came up to me.

The redcap put him in a taxi and sent him along to the Lincoln Gardens Café, an enormous and ornate dance hall at Thirty-first and Cottage Grove, just a few blocks from the Stroll, in the heart of the South Side. When he got there and heard the music drifting out through the door, Armstrong remembered, he said to himself, "No, I ain't supposed to be in *this* band, they're too good." But then Oliver spotted him: "You little fool," he said. "Come on in here."

Once Armstrong was inside, everything seemed familiar. The sound of Oliver's foot could be heard stomping off the tempo just as it had back in New Orleans; the musicians were free to shed their coats if things got too hot; and a bucket of water with a dipper and a big block of ice floating in it occupied a corner of the bandstand in case

anybody got thirsty. Oliver invited him to play. "That was heaven," Armstrong wrote. "Papa Joe was so elated that he played half an hour overtime. I was so happy I did not know what to do. I had hit the big time. I was up North with the Greats. I was playing with my idol, The King, Joe Oliver. All of my boyhood dreams had come true at last. . . . I was home."

Joe Oliver's Creole Jazz Band would remain Armstrong's home for the next two years. It was an all-round orchestra and sounded good at any speed. "We played so soft," said the drummer, Baby Dodds, "that you could . . . hear the people's feet dancing. The music was so soothing and then when we put a little jump into it, the patrons just had to dance." And its members were all expected to be showmen: Oliver was a master of what Northerners called "New Orleans hokum"—comedy vocal effects built around his profusion of mutes. Baby Dodds shimmied at the drums. The bassist Bill Johnson sometimes played while lying down. Louis Armstrong danced, too, he remembered, and slid and fell "like I was going to hurt myself."

But it was the music that he and Oliver played together that now began to draw big crowds to the Lincoln Gardens. Oliver and Armstrong perfected a style of playing duet breaks by which Armstrong seemed instinctively to know just what his boss was about to play and was always ready with the perfect complement to it. Different every night, but in perfect harmony, their breaks mystified the musicians who began crowding around the bandstand to hear them. It was not magic, of course, but craft. "While the rest of the band was playing," Armstrong explained, "Oliver'd lean over to me and move the valves on his cornet in the notes he would play in the next break. . . . Whatever Mister Joe played I just tried to make it sound as pretty as I could. I never blew my horn over Joe Oliver at no time unless he said, 'Take it!' "

Among those who regularly turned out to hear Oliver and Armstrong at the Lincoln Gardens was a band of eager white high school boys, some of them in knee pants. "Night after night we made the trip" to the South Side, one remembered, and neither the fact that the club was "by and for Negroes," nor the presence of the 350-pound bouncer who razzed them genially every evening about coming to the South Side for their "music lessons," could keep them away.

They were a rough-hewn bunch, rebellious and headstrong. Some were streetwise products of the city slums; others came from comfortable suburban homes or were refugees from the rural heartland, captivated by what one musician called "the bursting feeling of life in the city." But all of them felt alienated from the worlds in which they had been brought up, and each came to see jazz both as an outlet for emotions they otherwise could not express and

Members of the Austin High Gang. Left to right, would-be clarinetist Frank Teschemacher; cornetist Jimmy McPartland and his guitar- and banjo-playing brother, Richard; tenor saxophonist Lawrence "Bud" Freeman and his brother, Arny, who became an actor instead of a musician. "For my money," Bud Freeman remembered, "Chicago was the greatest place for a young jazz musician to be born."

as a symbol of personal defiance, what one of them would call "a collectively improvised nose-thumbing at all pillars of all communities, [a] syncopated Bronx cheer for the righteous squares everywhere."

Among the first were a handful of high school students who got together in the autumn of 1922 in a manicured West Side neighborhood called Austin and therefore became known to jazz history as the Austin High Gang—though none of them was ever actually graduated from that school. They included fifteen-year-old Jimmy McPartland, already a veteran street fighter from the roughest part of the Near West Side, who thought he might like to play cornet; his guitarist brother, Richard; a shy, bespectacled violin student named Frank Teschemacher, who would soon shift his allegiance to jazz clarinet; and Bud Freeman, another product of a tough part of town and already interested in the saxophone. They would soon be joined by Dave

Tough, a reticent bookish would-be drummer from the prosperous suburb of Oak Park. All of them felt themselves to be outsiders; at fifteen, both Tough and Jimmy McPartland were already drinking hard.

Their journey into jazz had begun with white bands. "Every day after school," McPartland remembered, "we used to go to a little place called the Spoon and Straw. It was just an ice cream parlor. But they had a Victrola there, and we used to sit around listening to records. One day we put on some new records by the New Orleans Rhythm Kings. Boy, when we heard that, I'll tell you, we were out of our minds. Everybody flipped. It was wonderful. We stayed there from about three in the afternoon until eight at night, just listening to those records . . . and we decided we would get a band and try to play like these guys."

Just as Bix Beiderbecke had done a few years earlier, they doggedly learned their first tunes from records: "We'd have to tune our instruments up to the record machine, to the pitch, and go ahead with a few notes. Then stop!" McPartland said. "A few more bars of the record, each guy would pick out his notes and boom! . . . Each guy'd pick his notes, so we got the right harmonies and everything. We developed ourselves. Because you were allowed to copy anything from the record of the ensembles, but you had to play your own solo. Each guy had to play his own solo his own way, not the way the guy did it on the record. . . . We just said, 'That's not fair, you can't copy a guy's music.' "

They began hanging around the door of the Friar's Inn to hear their heroes in person, formed a group of their own called the Blue Friars in homage to them, and started getting pickup jobs around town. Then, after playing a fraternity party at the University of Chicago, on the South Side, a college student took several of them along with him to hear Oliver and Armstrong at the Lincoln Gardens. "After that," Bud Freeman remembered, "we never went back to the New Orleans Rhythm Kings because

THE EMPRESS OF THE BLUES

In the spring of 1927, the train carrying the blues singer Bessie Smith and her band was halted outside a southern Ohio town. Floodwaters covered the track. The troupe had to be ferried to the theater in which they were to perform by rowboat. When the audience called upon Smith to sing a blues about the flood she said she was sorry she didn't know any, but as soon as she got home she wrote one out. She was first and foremost a spectacular entertainer, but her public—overwhelmingly black, mostly poor—also looked to her to say what they could not. "When I was a little girl," the gospel singer Mahalia Jackson remembered, "I felt she was having troubles like me. That's why it was such a comfort for the people of the South to hear her. She expressed something they couldn't put into words."

Bessie Smith was not the first woman to record the blues. Mamie Smith beat her to it in 1920—and sold seventy-five thousand copies for Okeh records in one week in Harlem alone. And there were other singers with big followings, including Ma Rainey, the "Mother of the Blues"; Ida Cox, "Queen of the Blues"; Clara Smith, "The World's Champion Moaner"; Chippie Hill; Sippie Wallace; and Alberta Hunter. But almost from the moment she recorded "Down-Hearted Blues" for Columbia in 1923, Bessie Smith was the unchallenged "Empress of the Blues," celebrated both for her majestic voice and for the utter lack of sentimentality or self-pity in her songs.

Born in Chattanooga in 1894, she began singing for pennies on streetcorners at nine and, while still a child, traveled the South in a tent show with Ma Rainey. Then she moved up to become a star on the black vaudeville circuit officially known as the "Theater Owners Booking Association," or T.O.B.A.—but remembered by black performers as "Tough on Black Asses." "She was new," the trumpet player Adolphus "Doc" Cheatham remembered, "and people had begun to listen to the blues. Some liked it and some didn't. Some people—the schoolteachers—came to hear Bessie Smith, but they didn't want to be seen in there. So they would hide their faces."

The records Bessie Smith and her rivals made were a sensation in black communities all over the country. Newsboys sold blues records. So did door-to-door salesmen. Pullman porters carried copies south to peddle at whistlestops. The Chicago *Defender* urged "lovers of music everywhere and those who desire to help in any advance of the Race" to buy the work of black singers and musicians. Soon, Okeh, Paramount, Vocalion, and Columbia had all developed specialty labels meant for black audiences—race records—just as they had already created special ethnic catalogues for other minorites. And W. C. Handy's song-publishing partner, Harry Pace, had established the first black-owned recording company, Black Swan, with the slogan, "The Only Genuine Colored Records—Others Are Only Passing for Colored." Soon, race records were selling more than 5 million copies a year.

Bessie Smith lived the life she sang about in her songs. Her first agents, the songwriter Clarence Williams and Frank Walker, supervisor of race records for Columbia, did her out of her royalties. In 1923, she married Jack Gee, a nightwatchman who liked to pretend he'd once been a policeman but proved more interested in collecting her earnings than in making her happy. The two fought—with words and fists—for six tumultuous years, during which she also took a host of lovers, both men and women. Once, she chased her husband down the railroad track, firing a revolver. Drinking only made her meaner. If she didn't like the way things were going onstage she was known to tear the curtains down around her. She could not abide rivals and sometimes refused to appear on the bill with other singers if they were more slender or lighter-skinned than she. "She would tell *anybody* to kiss her ass," a niece remembered. "Nobody messed with Bessie, black or white, it didn't make any difference."

One hot July night in 1927, she and her troupe were performing under canvas in Concord, North Carolina. A member of the band stepped out to have a smoke and spotted half a dozen hooded men who were about to collapse the tent on Smith and her audience. He urged her to flee. Smith wouldn't hear of it. Instead, she ran toward the Klansmen, shaking her fist and cursing. "I'll get the whole damn tent out here," she shouted. "You just pick up them sheets and run." The Klansmen, faced with the prospect of a confrontation with scores of her angry fans, took off instead. Smith returned to the bandstand, told her band they were "nothin' but a bunch of sissies," and began again to sing.

Above) Bessie Smith in repose and (below) in action on a Philadelphia stage, billed as "the Greatest and Highest Salaried Race Star in the World"

"There's fourteen million Negroes in our great country," said the pioneer black record producer Perry Bradford in 1920, "and they will buy records if recorded by one of their own, because we are the only folks that can sing and interpret hot jazz songs just off the griddle correctly." Race records would eventually include recorded sermons, gospel music, spirituals, and comedy routines—anything the manufacturers thought might interest African-American audiences. Okeh (right), a subsidiary of the General Phonograph Corporation, was the first in the field, but they were soon joined by Victor, Brunswick, and others. By 1927, some five hundred new sides were being issued every year.

Jack and Irving Mills, whose first offices were at Forty-seventh Street and Eighth Avenue (left), built their music-publishing business on vaudeville tunes—"Mr. Gallagher and Mr. Shean" was their first big hit—but when the blues excitement broke in 1920 they began buying up blues songs as fast as they could find them. Before long, Irving Mills would have some of New York's most gifted African-American songwriters working for him, and then he would form a fateful partnership with the young Duke Ellington.

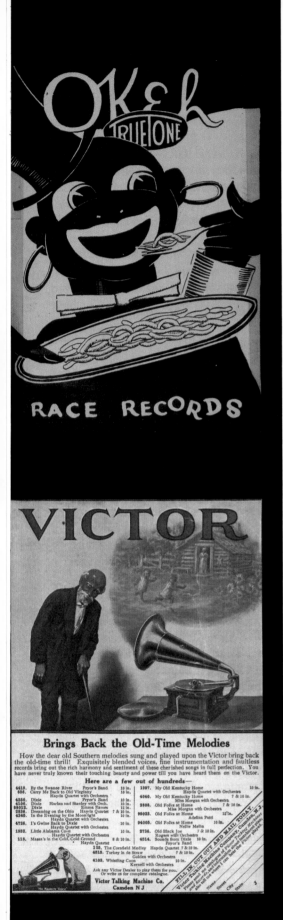

when we heard . . . King Oliver . . . we knew that we were hearing the real thing for the first time. . . . *We had to hear that music as one had to eat.*"

Other young white musicians who had also rejected the commercial dance music—by turns sentimental and frenetic—that still meant jazz to their family and friends in favor of the more exciting sounds of the South Side soon found themselves following Armstrong and Oliver all over town, just as the Austin High Gang did.

Eddie Condon first heard them play for a private fraternity party at a North Side Club called the Chez Paree. It was "hypnosis at first hearing," he remembered. "The two wove around each other, like suspicious women talking about the same man." Soon he, too, was a regular at the Lincoln Gardens.

In the cubicle outside where we paid admission, the sound was loud: it came like a muscle flexing regularly, four to the bar. As the door opened the [cornets], King and Louis, one or both, soared above everything else. The whole joint was rocking. Tables, chairs, walls, people, moved with the rhythm. It was dark, smoky, gin-smelling. People in the balcony leaned over and their drinks spilled on the customers below. There was a false ceiling made of chicken wire covered with phony maple leaves, the real roof was twenty-five feet up. A round, glass bowl hung from the middle of the chicken wire; when the blues were played it turned slowly and a baby spotlight worked over it. There was a floor show and a master of ceremonies named King Jones. He would stand in front of Oliver and shout, "Oh! One more chorus, King!" Oliver and Louis would roll on and on, piling up choruses, with the rhythm section building the beat until the whole thing got inside your head and blew your

brains out. There was a place near the band reserved for musicians who came to listen and to learn; we sat there, stiff with education, joy and a licorice-tasting gin purchased from the waiters for two dollars a pint. You could bring your own but it didn't matter much; in the end the effect was the same—the band playing . . . and everything and everybody moving, sliding, tapping out the rhythm, inhaling the smoke, swallowing the gin.

Bud Freeman learned more than music from his visits to the South Side. The dancing fascinated him, too: "I never saw people enjoy it so much," he wrote. "Their bodies seemed to be glued together, as though they were trying to go through each other. . . . They did not have the money to go to a club or dance hall more than once a week, but they had a wonderful freedom of spirit when they felt this music. I didn't know a white man with money who had that spirit."

"In those days," Freeman continued, "we were brainwashed into believing that blacks were inferior to us, . . . to look down on any race that wasn't white. . . . Now here were these black people who were allowed no privileges. They were not allowed to come into our shops and cinemas, but we whites were allowed to go out to their community, where they treated us beautifully. I found their way of life equally as important as their music. It was not just their music that moved me but the whole picture of an oppressed people who appeared to be much happier than we whites who had everything. It was on the strength of this that I developed a love for them and became a jazz musician."

On April 5, 1923, King Oliver, Louis Armstrong, and the rest of the Creole Jazz Band took the train from Chicago to Richmond, Indiana, home of the Gennett Record Company. It was not especially friendly territory for jazz—or for black Americans. Gennett

The Washingtonians at the Hollywood Club just off Times Square, 1924. Left to right, Sonny Greer, Charlie Irvis, Bubber Miley, Elmer Snowden, Otto Hardwick, and Duke Ellington, who would soon take over as leader. "The Hollywood Club was a good place for us to be," Ellington wrote, "because it stayed open all night."

Garvin Bushell happened to be with him when it happened. "Bubber and I sat there with our mouths open," he remembered. "The trumpets . . . in the East had a better 'legitimate' quality, but the sound of Oliver touched you more. It was less cultivated but more expressive of how the people felt. He played things that hit you inside."

Back in New York, Miley made it his business to master the art of hitting people inside, too, and eventually brought to the Black Sox orchestra a repertoire of

muted churchly moans and cries more startling even than King Oliver's. Miley "used to growl all night long," Ellington said, "playing gut-bucket on his horn. It was then that our music acquired new colors and characteristics." Miley's sound also brought the men their first serious notice. "This colored band . . . includes a trumpet player who never need doff his chapeau to any cornetist in the business," wrote Abel Green of the New York *Clipper*. "He exacts the eeriest sort of modulations and 'singing' notes

heard. . . . The boys look neat in dress suits and labor hard, but not in vain at their music. They disclose painstaking rehearsal, playing without music."

"That was when we decided to forget all about the sweet music," Ellington said. In fact, he never forgot about anything. Nothing would ever be alien to the music he was about to begin composing; it would always represent the most delicate possible balance between sweet and hot. He was in charge now. The men in the band had chosen him to be their leader after they found Elmer Snowden helping himself to more than his share of their pay. "There was some sort of magnetism to [Ellington] you wouldn't understand," Sonny Greer explained to an interviewer many years later. "In my whole life, I've never seen another man like him. When he walks into a strange room, the whole place lights up."

Ellington changed the band's name to the Washingtonians and started writing songs and making the rounds of music publishers on Broadway, sometimes selling hastily written-out blues for fifteen dollars outright and yearning for something more. He eventually sought out Will Marion Cook, white-haired now and called "Dad" by young songwriters who hoped to match his record of success. Cook remained as touchy as ever, but was willing to offer counsel to a suitably deferential newcomer from his native Washington like the young Ellington. One summer day, as they rode home together through Central Park in a taxi with an open top, Cook urged Ellington to get formal training at a conservatory.

"Dad, I don't want to go to the conservatory," Ellington answered, "because they're not teaching what I want to learn."

In that case, Cook told him, "First . . . find the logical way, and when you find it, avoid it, and let your inner self break through and guide you. Don't try to be anybody else but yourself."

Duke Ellington would follow that advice all his life.

THE KING OF JAZZ

On the snowy afternoon of February 12, 1924, jazz, which had been born in the streets and the dance halls of New Orleans, and nurtured in big-city saloons and speakeasies and vaudeville theaters, found itself for the first time on the concert stage. It was a distinctive kind of jazz, to be sure —so-called *symphonic* jazz—and it was to be presented at Manhattan's exalted

Paul Whiteman. "He trembles, wobbles, quivers," wrote the *New York Times* critic, "a piece of jazz jelly, conducting his orchestra with the back of the trousers of the right leg, and the face of a mandarin the while."

Aeolian Hall by the best-known dance bandleader in America.

Paul Whiteman was a formally trained musician from Colorado who had first heard jazz being played by New Orleans musicians in San Francisco in 1915. "We first met— Jazz and I—at a dance hall dive on the Barbary Coast," he remembered. "It screeched and bellowed at me from a trick platform in the middle of a smoke-hazed, beer-fumed room." Everything had seemed to go wrong for him that day, he remembered: he was bored with his job playing viola with the San Francisco Symphony, he had been soaked with rain going to and from a dismal rehearsal, had cracked his shaving mirror, even overcooked his breakfast eggs. A

friend had had to drag him to the club. All of that was forgotten the moment the musicians began to play. "My whole body began to sit up and take notice. It was like coming out of blackness into bright lights. My blues faded when treated to the Georgia blues that some trombonist was wailing about. My head was dizzy, but my feet seemed to understand that tune. I wanted to whoop. I wanted to dance. I wanted to sing. I did them all. Raucous? Yes. Crude— undoubtedly. Unmusical—as sure as you live! But rhythmic, catching as the small pox, and spirit-lifting."

Three years later, he abandoned his symphonic career and joined a dance band—only to be fired two days later for being unable to improvise on the spot. "You can't *jazz*," his boss said, when asked for an explanation, "that's all." Humiliated but still drawn to the music, Whiteman determined to find a way to orchestrate jazz, to retain its rhythm and color and harmony while rendering it as precise and predictable as symphonic music. His father— superintendent of music for the Denver public schools—was scornful of jazz and deeply disappointed by his son's decision to abandon classical music, which may account in part for Whiteman's self-appointed mission to "remove the stigma of barbaric strains and jungle cacophony," and "make a lady of jazz."

In any case, with arrangements by the pianist Ferde Grofé—who would eventually go on to compose semiclassical pieces like the "Grand Canyon Suite"—Whiteman turned his orchestra into what he called "an efficient arrangement. Every member knows exactly what he is to play every minute of the time. Even the smears are indicated in the music." He brought his men east to Atlantic City in 1918, made a recording of "Whispering" in 1920, which would sell more than 2.5 million copies, played for the *Ziegfeld Follies,* and eventually settled into a long successful run playing for wealthy dancers at the Palais Royal nightclub on Broadway. Other orchestra leaders had experimented with arranged jazz, including Paul Specht, Vincent Lopez, and Art Hickman—whose California dance band may have been the first to use a whole section of saxophones. But none could match either the smooth polish of Whiteman's music or the tireless energy with which he promoted it. A big man—he stood well over six feet tall, sometimes weighed more than three hundred pounds, and bore a startling resemblance to the corpulent movie comic Oliver Hardy—Whiteman was a master of public relations, willing to go along with almost any publicity stunt so long as it drew attention to his band.

The Aeolian Hall concert was his idea, meant to lend artistic legitimacy to his music—and to head off the challenge of Vincent Lopez, who had announced plans for a Manhattan concert of his own. To ensure that serious attention would be paid, Whiteman let it be known that he had sent complimentary tickets to the most eminent figures in music whether or not they actually were able to attend—Igor Stravinsky, Leopold Stokowski, Sergei Rachmaninoff, John McCormack, Amelita Galli-Curci, as well as every music critic in the Northeast. "Mr. Whiteman," the program promised, "intends to point out the tremendous strides which have been made in popular music from the day of discordant popular music which sprang into existence about ten years ago, to the melodious music of today, which—for no good reason—is still called Jazz."

To show how far Whiteman thought American music had come, the program opened with a raucous five-man lampoon of "Livery Stable Blues," the recording by the Original Dixieland Jass Band that had started the national mania for the music seven years earlier. (Whiteman was said to have been momentarily unnerved by the unexpected enthusiasm with which the audience received what was meant to be a burlesque.) Everything that followed over the next four hours was elegant and orchestral, without a hint of improvisation. White-

PAUL WHITEMAN
AND HIS
Palais Royal Orchestra
WILL OFFER
An Experiment in Modern Music

Zez Confrey
and
George Gershwin

New Typically American Compositions by Victor Herbert, George Gershwin and Zez Confrey will be played for the first time.

AEOLIAN CONCERT HALL
Tuesday, Feb. 12th (LINCOLN'S BIRTHDAY) at 3 P.M.

Tickets now on Sale, 55c. to $2.20

Victor Records   Chickering Pianos   Buescher Instruments

Poster for Paul Whiteman's concert at New York's Aeolian Hall, 1924

man's twenty-three men—including eight violinists—performed syncopated versions of light classics and old favorites such as "A Pretty Girl Is Like a Melody," "To a Wild Rose," and "Song of the Volga Boatmen." The climax was a brand-new specially commissioned work by George Gershwin, an immigrants' son, who, like Duke Ellington, had spent hours listening to the masters of Harlem stride. Gershwin's piece, "Rhapsody in Blue," was something new—a classical piece suffused with jazz feeling—and would become one of the best-loved compositions in all of American music.

The New York *Herald* called the concert "an uproarious success." The orchestra was made to play five encores. Whiteman, said *Variety*, "had proven conclusively that the dance orchestra or the band or the jazz craze, or any of the other names it has been identified with, will never die. It is part of

American culture and an absolute necessity." And though his men had actually played precious little jazz that afternoon, Whiteman was now billed everywhere as "The King of Jazz."

Later, some would accuse him of diluting jazz, and he himself evidently shared something of their concern. "The demoniac energy, the fantastic riot of accents and the humorous moods have all had to be toned down," he once said. "I hope in toning it down we shall not, as some critics have predicted, take the life out of our music." Others charged him with misappropriating the music of African-Americans. He himself was always unpretentious about his achievements—"I know as much about *real* jazz," he would confide to one interviewer, "as F. Scott Fitzgerald knew about the Jazz Age"—and he was perfectly clear about the artistic debt he owed to black musicians, as the very first paragraph of his autobiography makes clear: "Jazz came to America three hundred years ago in chains. The psalm-singing Dutch traders, sailing a man of war across the ocean, described their cargo as 'fourteen black African slaves for sale in His Majesty's Colonies'. . . . [P]riceless freight destined three centuries later to set a whole nation dancing. . . . Jazz . . . was to be their gift to . . . posterity." He regularly gave work to black arrangers, too, and in 1923, a year before his Aeolian Hall concert, he had stunned his own managers by offering jobs in his orchestra to two members of Armand Piron's black New Orleans ensemble at the Roseland Ballroom. They didn't accept, one of them explained many years later, only because they were tired of New York and wanted to "get home."

Black musicians may have resented the celebrity and riches Whiteman had gained playing music they had pioneered, but few seem to have harbored personal grudges against him. No one could deny the quality of his musicianship, and if his efforts to "elevate" jazz sometimes seemed naïve and even patronizing in retrospect, those same efforts also redounded to the benefit of all jazz musicians of whatever color. "Paul Whiteman was known as the King of Jazz," wrote Duke Ellington, who admired Whiteman's lofty ambitions for his music, his eye for first-rate musicians, and the managerial skill with which he built and ran his band, "and no one as yet has come near carrying that title with more certainty and dignity. . . . I used to hear Whiteman records taking the snobbishness out of . . . music and opening the doors."

THE ONE THING

Not even the reassuring sounds of Paul Whiteman and his genteel competitors could win over people like Bix Beiderbecke's parents. They still detested jazz in all its forms, still hoped their son could be persuaded to abandon the music—and the musician's life—that had brought an abrupt end to his education and destroyed their dream of having him go on to college and a career in business. In February of 1923, he had dutifully returned to Davenport and gone to work for his father, weighing coal, collecting payment from customers, standing in line at the bank to deposit checks. It was tedious and demeaning work but he kept at it for five months, living for the evenings when he could get out of the house and sit in with local bands.

By July, he could stand it no more and left for Chicago. During the days he played aboard a Lake Michigan excursion boat in a band that included an often-seasick fourteen-year-old clarinetist named Benny Goodman, and he spent as many evenings as he could at the Lincoln Gardens listening to Oliver and Armstrong. Sometimes, a friend recalled, he was even allowed to sit in for a chorus or two and was rewarded with "friendly nods of approval" from the band. It was from listening to Armstrong, Beiderbecke's friend Esten Spurrier said, that Bix learned how to construct a coherent solo. He called it "the correlated chorus, play two measures, then two related,

and you had four measures upon which you played another four measures related to the first four, and so on, *ad infinitum,* to the end of the chorus."

In the autumn, Bix found himself in Ohio, part of a brand-new septet at the Stockton Club, a seedy roadhouse just outside the town of Hamilton. It was run by gangsters—illegal gambling went on upstairs—and at first the group had little more than enthusiasm to recommend it. They played Jelly Roll Morton's "Wolverine Blues" so often that when someone suggested they call themselves the "Wolverines," the name stuck. The engagement came to an abrupt end on New Year's Eve when two rival groups of small-time hoodlums turned up for the festivities. The manager tried to segregate them, seating the boys from Cincinnati and their girlfriends on one side of the dance floor and those from Hamilton on the other. But as the band played and bootleg liquor flowed, words led to punches, and the air was soon filled with bottles and furniture. Stories differ as to what happened next. One musician recalled playing "Chinatown, My Chinatown" for what seemed like an hour while the gangs battled back and forth, but another remembered that he and the rest of the band had all hidden behind chairs and tables for fear of injuring their lips or fingers. The Stockton Club was padlocked the next day in any case—too many citizens had turned up in bandages for the authorities to ignore its illegal existence any longer—and the Wolverines were out of a job.

They moved on to Cincinnati, where they played in a dingy third-floor ballroom called Doyle's Dancing Academy. Older dancers stayed away—the Wolverines had no sweet arrangements or slow dances to please them—but young working girls and high school students and a scattering of local musicians crowded the floor for the hot numbers. Students on nearby campuses liked them, too. And in February, buoyed by these first tentative signs of success, the Wolverines hired the same Gennett studio

at which King Oliver and Louis Armstrong had first recorded almost a year earlier, and cut four sides.

It was Beiderbecke, just twenty-one, who set the Wolverines apart—now soaring above his friends, now spurring them on to greater effort. Ralph Berton remembered the impact on him of first hearing Beiderbecke on record:

> It was tantalizing; somehow simultaneously excitingly hot and quietly cool and detached; a controlled ardor, a passion veiled in reticence. It had a chaste *understatement* never heard before in jazz, flowing yet so naturally from an open horn, staying modestly and casually within the middle register. The *attack* was like nothing I'd heard on any brass instrument in classical music or jazz—each note not as though blown, but struck.

Then, Bix got a letter from a friend, a laconic would-be songwriter named Hoagy Carmichael, who was leading a dance band at Indiana State University while studying law. If the group could get to Indianapolis on its own, Carmichael suggested, he might be able to arrange a full season of weekend dances for them on and around the campus. It sounded good to the Wolverines, but the manager of Doyle's Dance Academy refused to let them go. They had signed a contract that still had weeks to run, and as insurance against their skipping out on him, he locked their instruments in his ballroom. The next night, Bix and his friends somehow slipped into the building and, using a length of clothesline, carefully lowered from the third-floor window into a waiting car their tuba, string bass, and brightly painted bass drum, then set out for Indianapolis.

There, they were a sensation. They cut more records, performed for nearly all the university's fraternities and sororities, and played dances all over Indiana and Michigan. The leader of a band that had the bad luck to precede them on one bandstand recalled their impact.

Jazz is the product of a restless age: an age in which the fever of war is only now beginning to abate its fury; when men and women, after their efforts in the great struggle, are still too much disturbed to be content with a tranquil existence; when freaks and stunts and sensations are the order—or disorder— of the day; when painters delight in portraying that which is not, and sculptors in twisting the human limbs into strange, fantastic shapes; when America is turning out her merchandise [at] an unprecedented speed and motor cars are racing along the roads; when aeroplanes are beating successive records and ladies are in so great a hurry that they wear short skirts which enable them to move fast and cut off their hair to save a few precious moments of the day; when the extremes of Bolshevism and Fascismo are pursuing their own ways simultaneously, and the whole world is rushing helter-skelter in unknown directions.

Amid this seething, bubbling turmoil, jazz hurried along its course riding exultantly on the eddying stream. Nevertheless, the end of civilization is not yet, and jazz will either be trained and turned to artistic uses or else vanish utterly from our midst as a living force. But even if it disappears altogether it will not have existed in vain. For its record will remain as an interesting human document— the spirit of the age written in the music of the people.

—R. W. S. MENDL, 1926

MOONLIGHT DA
TO NIGHT
ON STEAMER
CAPITO
NINE
WONDERFUL
MUSICIANS
TONY'S IOWANS
ADMISSION 10¢ DANCI

TONIGHT

A truck ballyhoos an appearance by trumpeter Tony Catalano's
Iowans, another of the scores of bands that played up and down
the Mississippi during the late teens and early twenties.

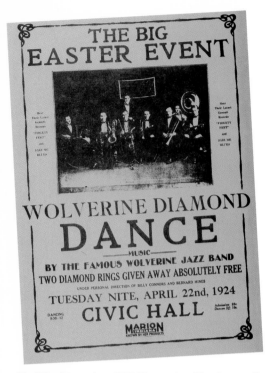

We played a set or two kind of soft and sweet. Our band's turn ended with a few polite hand-claps. Then the Wolverines started! Bix and the boys crushed into their tune, and the place was kind of stunned. Then the place started to rock. . . . The kids forgot about poise and delicacy and were jiving like at a football rally. Soon, the dancers gathered around Bix, Jimmy [Hartwell] and George [Johnson], listening with their ears practically in their horns. . . . Following every hot lick . . . laughing at every hot break and roaring into king-size appreciation at every hot chorus. This was a spectacle.

Everywhere, people warmed to Beiderbecke's sound but Bix himself remained stubbornly elusive. Even the stories his friends told and retold about him don't reveal much. He always had a jug of corn whiskey nearby and cared little for food, fueling himself with chili and oyster crackers (and if the restaurant kitchen ran out of chili, making do with more crackers spattered with catsup). He washed less often than some of his friends liked, rarely bothered to clean his horn because he said it sounded "hard" when he did, followed the fortunes of his favorite baseball player, Rogers Hornsby of the St. Louis Cardinals, disliked Mozart and Beethoven, and enjoyed both the absurdity of surrealist

The Wolverines on tour, 1924. The promise of jewelry as well as hot music was meant to pull crowds into the Madison, Indiana, Easter dance advertised above. In Indianapolis a few weeks later, the band found itself dwarfed by the spectacular art nouveau backdrop at the Palace Theater. Bix Beiderbecke is second from the right.

The Wolverines in the Gennett recording studio in Richmond, Indiana, February 18, 1924. Left to right, Min Leibrook (tuba), Jimmy Hartwell (clarinet), George Johnson (tenor saxophone), Bob Gillette (banjo), Vic Moore (drums), Dick Voynow (piano), Bix Beiderbecke (cornet), Al Gandee (trombone)

poetry and P. G. Wodehouse's whimsical fiction about the British upper classes.

Mostly, he kept to himself. He "had an air of cynicism and boredom about most things, just sitting around, lazy-like with his legs crossed and his body drooping," wrote the Chicago-born clarinetist Milton "Mezz" Mezzrow, who first got to know him that summer, "but it wasn't an act with him. . . . His shying away from things showed that what got most people worked up left him completely cold. . . . Music was the one thing that really brought him to life. Not even whiskey could do it, and he gave it every chance." Mezzrow identified with black musicians so deeply that he rarely even listened to anyone else. But Bix, he said, was different. "Despite the whiskey fumes that blew out of his battered cornet, I had never heard a tone like he got before or since. He played mostly open horn, every note full, big, rich and round, standing out like a pearl, . . . with a powerful drive that few white musicians had in those days. . . . Powerful and energetic, every note packing a solid punch, with his head always in full control over his heart." Playing with him, Mezzrow remembered, had been "like slipping into a suit made to order for you by a fine tailor, silk-lined all through."

In late summer the Wolverines got the kind of offer they'd been waiting for: a thirty-day New York City engagement at the Cinderella Ballroom, on Broadway. They left Indiana on Labor Day in two ancient touring cars. It would take them three days to get there but they were finally headed for the Big Time.

HERE COMES
TROUBLE ITSELF

Twenty-five-year-old Sidney Bechet was already a legend among musicians when he finally got back to New York after three years abroad, both for the power and passion of his playing and for the combative personality that threatened always to plunge him into difficulty. But he still had not been heard on records.

Then, on June 30, 1923, almost three months after Oliver and Armstrong made their first recordings, Bechet finally got to cut two sides—"Wild Cat Blues" and "Kansas City Blues"—with Clarence Williams's Blue Five. From the opening note, he is fully in charge. As he wails and weaves and roars his extravagant way through the tunes, the cornetist sensibly retreats to a subordinate role. No previous jazz record had ever given so much time to a soloist; and no soloist on records had come anywhere near matching the emotional power of his playing. He went on to record with a whole series of blues singers, some good, some bad, but all immeasurably bolstered by his presence—though his sheer volume sometimes got him in trouble. "When it got to my chorus," he remembered, "the needle would jump. I couldn't play the way I wanted to. The engineers would almost go crazy when they saw me coming into the studios. They'd say, 'Here comes trouble itself.'"

Bechet's sound was a revelation to young musicians. In Boston, Harry Carney and Johnny Hodges, both future stars of the Duke Ellington orchestra, wore out Bechet's first records. If it hadn't been for him, Hodges would remember, "I'd probably just be playing for a hobby." In Bechet's hometown of New Orleans, the clarinetist Barney Bigard, another future Ellingtonian, recalled "every time you would pass someone's house that had the . . . windows open they would be playing [Sidney] on their Victrola."

Bechet delighted in the sensation he was causing and kept a sharp eye out for competition. When the Missouri-born tenor saxophonist Coleman Hawkins was overheard to say that New Orleans musicians couldn't play, Bechet hurried down to the Band Box club to challenge him. The two men battled all night, and when at six the following morning Hawkins finally packed up his horn and fled the stand, Bechet was said to have followed him up the street, still playing.

But Bechet's explosive personality, his inherent inability ever to take orders from anybody, continued to undercut him. He got a job with James P. Johnson only to find that "Johnson wanted to make . . . orchestrational Jazz, and I was playing New Orleans, playing foundations in the numbers, but ad-libbing and giving my improvisation to it. . . . If you know in advance every note you're going to play and just the way you're going to play there's no need to have feelings." Johnson told him to stick to the arrangements. Bechet wouldn't, and Johnson let him go.

Then, in 1924, he took a summer job playing dances in New England with Duke Ellington, who was himself temporarily without a bandstand; the gangsters who owned the Hollywood Inn had deliberately set the club on fire in April in order to collect insurance money rather than settle for the lean profits they would have made during the hot summer months.

Bechet "fitted our band like a glove," Ellington remembered, and Ellington loved the competitive spirit Bechet brought to the group. He was "like a gladiator," Ellington said. "He'd go out and blow and the next guy to follow him had to beat what he did." His main challenger was Bubber Miley. "They would growl at each other something awful, Bechet would go out and play ten choruses and Bubber would play ten choruses, and while one was playing the other was back there taking nips!"

Over the years, Ellington would earn a well-deserved reputation for putting up with unreasonable behavior by his musi-cians—provided they could play. But Ellington was only twenty-five years old in 1924, and older and more experienced men than he had found Bechet impossible to control. Bechet insisted on bringing to work a massive German shepherd named Goola; he somehow convinced himself that Bubber Miley and trombonist Charlie Irvis, another master of the muted growl, were conspiring against him; and he once ran up a two-hundred-dollar "transportation" bill by hiring a New York taxi to take him to a dance date outside Boston, then paying for a night in the local whorehouse for the cabbie so that he wouldn't have to look for a ride back to the city again the next day.

Finally, after Bechet arrived three days late for an engagement and claimed it wasn't his fault—his taxi driver had gotten lost, he said—Ellington sadly let him go. "Bechet was always a rover," he said, "who wanted to see over the other side of the hill." But Ellington remained determined to find men who would bring more of the New Orleans sound that Bechet epitomized into his own music.

READY FOR
THE NEW DAY

During the first two weeks of October of 1924, a prescient jazz enthusiast visiting the West Side of Manhattan could, within one evening and without walking more than four blocks, have seen and heard three of the music's best-remembered figures at the dawn of their careers, could have witnessed the first stirrings of the transformation that would turn what had mostly been a novelty music into an art.

Duke Ellington and his Washingtonians were now back in residence at their cellar club at Forty-ninth Street and Broadway. It had been renamed the Hollywood Club and refurbished by its owners after the convenient seasonal fire—there would be a second blaze the following January, this one

Despite the publisher's claim that this version was the original, the Charleston was an African-American dance long before it was published, in 1923. "Jimmy Johnson" was the pianist and composer James P. Johnson, and the song was the hit of his Broadway show, *Runnin' Wild*.

Jazz, which took its name from music—Negro music—has spread itself revealingly over the American temperament and become the expression medium for it, a sign and symbol of the American pace, of its moving spirit. . . . What an immense, even if unconscious, irony the Negroes have devised! They, who of all Americans are . . . least considered and most denied, have forged the key to the interpretation of the American spirit.

—CHARLES S. JOHNSON, *Opportunity, 1925*

signaled by a helpful hint from the manager to Sonny Greer that it might be wise for him to take his drums home after work—but it remained an unprepossessing spot: Greer had standing orders to step up the volume of his playing whenever the rats that sometimes scuttled among the tables began to squeak. The band still had just six pieces, and Ellington was mostly arranging other people's tunes rather than writing his own. But the fresh colors and textures he had already begun to develop in his arrangements and the startling growls of Bubber Miley and Charlie Irvis were drawing so much attention that the club had begun to advertise itself as the place "Where the Professional Musician Makes His Rendezvous." Paul Whiteman was a frequent early-morning visitor after finishing up at the Palais Royal around the corner, Ellington remembered, and he usually left a fifty-dollar tip.

Just a block down Broadway at Forty-eighth Street, Bix Beiderbecke and the Wolverines—their name changed to "The Personality Kids" for their New York debut—were playing at the Cinderella Ballroom. Word of their consistently hot music had preceded them—it was then still rare for any white band to play serious jazz and nothing but jazz, especially in New York—and on opening night in September at least fifty musicians had climbed the stairs to the second-floor ballroom, eager to hear the Wolverines in person. Paul Whiteman and Beiderbecke's first hero, Nick LaRocca, were there, and so was a young jazz fan from Yale, Richardson Turner. "No one was dancing," he recalled. "The Wolverines were playing. It's impossible to put into words the electrical thrill that bunch produced. . . . Bix played in an unorthodox way. He shook the horn with all his fingers up and played leaning over at the floor at about a 45 degree angle. . . . They took about ten 'last' choruses—standing up around the drums—playing at the drummer. It was fantastic!"

Abel Green, now working for *Variety,* agreed, pronouncing the Wolverine Orchestra "a torrid unit." "Their sense of rhythm and tempo is ultra for this type of dance music and their unquestionable favor with the dance fan speaks for itself." But in the end, the Wolverines would prove altogether too ultra for the Cinderella Ballroom. The frantic dance called the Charleston had caught on with young New Yorkers, and the Wolverines were the ideal band to spur them on, but, as their saxophone player George Johnson remembered, "Those who did not dance it, and some of those who did, found a crowded floor a disadvantage, objecting to the danger to life and limb in the shape of flying feet. . . . [Soon,] the Charleston dancers came to the Cinderella and the rest of the dancers who liked less violence went elsewhere."

Bix, as always, seemed unconcerned, turning up to play each evening, drinking and fooling with the piano through the day. "In the morning," a musician who roomed with him in New York remembered, "Bix would sit on the edge of the bed, swing his legs a few times. Then he would reach for a barrel-shaped glass that he had in his suitcase. He'd pour four healthy ounces of gin, drink it 'as is,' and say that he had drunk his daily 'orange juice.' He'd splash some water on his face, comb his hair, and was ready for the new day."

The Wolverines' contract was not renewed, and in October, Bix would accept an offer to bring his bright sound to one of the Detroit-based orchestras run by one of Paul Whiteman's chief rivals, Jean Goldkette. Before he left, he sent to Chicago for seventeen-year-old Jimmy McPartland to replace him. "I like you, kid," Bix told his young admirer. "You sound like me. But you don't copy me." To a young admirer like McPartland, still searching for a way to bring something of his own to the music, there could have been no higher praise.

Many of the dancers who found the floor at the Cinderella too crowded hurried back

Fletcher Henderson, back row, second from right, was graduated with his class from Atlanta University, 1920, intending to pursue a career in science. Instead, within a few years he found himself producing records with titles like "Shake It and Break It."

bia, His savings had run out before he could get started, and to support himself, he took a job as a song-plugger with W. C. Handy, then joined the Black Swan record company as an accompanist. He preferred the label's more genteel offerings—spirituals, popular songs, and excerpts from operas—to jazz or blues and was uncomfortable when asked to accompany Ethel Waters on tour. "[H]e wasn't sure it would be dignified enough for him, a college student . . . to be the piano player for a girl who sang blues in a cellar," she remembered. "Before he would go . . . Fletcher had his whole family come up from Georgia to look me over and see if it would be all right," and to get him to play the kind of "damn-it-to-hell" bass line she insisted upon, she made him listen again and again to piano rolls by James P. Johnson.

In 1923, Henderson found himself leading a band of his own at the Club Alabam, on Forty-fourth Street, just off Broadway. (The men elected him their leader because of his good looks and elegant manners.) The band already included at least three musicians who would become important jazz soloists—Coleman Hawkins, cornetist Joe Smith, and trombonist Big Charlie Green—and Henderson was sometimes billed as "the Colored King of Jazz." But, like the or-

down the stairs and up Broadway to the Roseland Ballroom, on Fifty-first Street. It was the biggest and most opulent dance hall in New York, with two orchestras alternating every evening. At one end of the vast dance floor was Sam Lanin's white orchestra; at the other was the most admired black band in the city, led by Fletcher Henderson. And sitting in its brass section was a brand-new cornetist, Louis Armstrong.

It had taken Lil Hardin more than a year to get Armstrong to marry her and then to leave Joe Oliver. He owed "Mr. Joe" everything, he said, and he wasn't sure he could make it on his own. But his bride persisted: "I don't want to be married to a second trumpet–player," she told him. "I want you to play first!" He finally, reluctantly, left the Creole Jazz Band in June of 1924, only to be turned down flat by Sammy Stewart, leader of Chicago's most elegant black dance band. "I wasn't 'dicty' enough," Armstrong remembered, "regardless of how

good I played, I wasn't up to his society." He took a job at the Dreamland Café instead, backing a journeyman singer named Ollie Powers. Then, he got a telegram from Fletcher Henderson offering him fifty-five dollars a week to come to New York.

Even though he was no longer in Joe Oliver's band, he could not bring himself to say yes until the older man gave him permission to go: "When I explained to the King that it was my one big chance to New York, where the people *really do things,* he dug me (I knew he would) and released me."

Fletcher Henderson was one of the biggest names in dance music, though he had never planned to be a musician at all. Born in Cuthbert, Georgia, the son of a piano teacher and the principal of an industrial training school, he was an Atlanta University graduate and had initially come north to New York to pursue an advanced degree in chemistry at Colum-

THE MOTHER OF US ALL

"God," Ethel Waters wrote, "made me tough, headstrong and resilient." She was born in 1896 in the red-light district of Chester, Pennsylvania, the unwanted outcome of a rape. Her mother was only twelve. Her grandmother tried to raise her right, but by the age of ten, she was the leader of a gang of children, who stole food to survive and acted as lookouts for the pimps and prostitutes in their neighborhood.

She began her career as a shimmy dancer and singer. "I sure knew how to roll and quiver," she remembered, and soon found herself appearing in black theaters and tent shows for ten dollars a week, billed as "Sweet Mama Stringbean." Some of her records were in the bawdiest blues tradition—"Organ Grinder Blues," "Do What You Did Last Night," "Handyman." But unlike Bessie Smith and the other blues stars of her time she had a light, clear voice, specialized in sly insinuation, and did not indulge in what she called "unladylike shouts and growls."

In 1925, her manager insisted she try what he called "white time"—the all-white vaudeville circuit—and brought her new, Tin Pan Alley songs to perform, including "My Man" and "He's Funny That Way." She was certain she would fail. "I thought white people wouldn't understand my type of work," she recalled, "and I wasn't going to change it." But white people loved it. One New York critic hailed her as "the greatest artist of her race and generation." She became the first black woman to headline at the Palace Theater in New York, starred at the Plantation and Cotton Clubs, and went to Hollywood in 1929 to appear in a film in which she introduced her best-remembered song, "Am I Blue." For a time the best-paid woman in show business, black or white, Ethel Waters demonstrated that black performers were not necessarily limited to the blues, that they could successfully perform every kind of material and appeal to every kind of audience. Lena Horne once paid her the highest possible compliment: Ethel Waters, she said, was "the Mother of us all."

Ethel Waters as the star of her first Broadway show, the 1927 revue *Africana*. "It was a good, fast show," she remembered, "and gave the theater-going ofays of Broadway their first long look at me."

ganization led by Paul Whiteman, his was not primarily a jazz band at all; it was a popular dance orchestra specializing in cheerful light music with only a judicious jazz seasoning, still very much in the East Coast tradition best described by Garvin Bushell. New Yorkers "played foxtrot rhythm and still adhered to the two-beat rhythmic feel . . . nearer the ragtime style and . . . less blues. There wasn't an eastern performer who could really play the blues. . . . We didn't put that quarter tone pitch in the music the way the Southerners did. Up North we leaned to the ragtime conception—a lot of notes." Henderson's arrangements were written by the young alto saxophonist Don Redman and consciously patterned at first after those of the Whiteman band, syncopated but stiff, filled with brief staccato solos and call-and-response figures scored for the reed and brass sections. The result was "soft, sweet and perfect," said a writer for the Chicago *Defender,* "not the sloppy New Orleans hokum, but peppy blue syncopation in dance rhythm, . . . not at all like the average Negro orchestra, but in a class with the good white orchestras such as Paul Whiteman."

Praise like that had helped win Henderson his invitation to play at Roseland in the summer of 1924. Then, just days after the engagement began, Joe Smith abruptly left for a better-paying job in a Broadway pit band. Recordings by Joe Oliver and other New Orleans masters had begun to sell well in the city, and the black band from New Orleans that Henderson was replacing at Roseland, led by the violinist Armand J. Piron, had been popular with its clientele. And so, casting around for a replacement, Henderson resolved to find someone who could bring some Crescent City fire to his band. While on the road with Ethel Waters in 1921 he had heard Louis Armstrong in New Orleans, had even offered him a job which Armstrong had turned down. "Knowing the way that horn sounded," he said, "I had to try to get him for my band. . . . Truthfully, I didn't expect him to accept the

Times Square in the midtwenties. The Roseland Ballroom, home base for Fletcher Henderson's orchestra for many years, is at the left.

offer and I was very surprised when he came to New York and joined us."

Armstrong's arrival in New York on September 30 had not been auspicious, Don Redman remembered: "[The drummer] Kaiser Marshall had a car and brought us downtown to meet Louis. He was big and fat, and wore high top shoes with hooks in them, and long underwear down to his socks. When I got a load of that, I said to myself, Who in the hell is this guy? It *can't* be Louis Armstrong." And his arrival at the first rehearsal with the band was no more promising. The Henderson men prided themselves on always looking sharp—"English walking suits that cost a hundred-ten dollars," Marshall remembered, "seven-dollar spats and eighteen-dollar shoes." Armstrong turned up wearing the kind of big thick-soled footwear policemen wore, "and came walking across the floor, clump-clump-clump, and grinned and said hello to the boys."

No one was impressed. "The band was . . . inclined to be a little bit reserved toward the new arrival," Henderson said, "and there seemed to be a little tension in the air." Armstrong had learned to read in Fate Marable's band but still preferred to play mostly by ear, and the first sheet music Henderson handed him—"a medley of beautiful Irish waltzes"—seemed especially intimidating to the newcomer. He was "perplexed by the trumpet part I gave him," Henderson said, "marked with a *diminuendo* down to *pp* [pianissimo—very soft]. The band followed these notations and was playing very softly, while Louis still played . . . at full volume. I asked him about that *pp*, and Louis broke us all up by replying, 'Oh, I thought that meant pound plenty.' There was no tension after that."

Armstrong still felt out of place among Henderson's musicians, he said, until at a rehearsal a few days later, Charlie Green and the tuba player got into a shoving match. "Oh, I'm gonna *like* this band," he said. It liked him, too, and so did the

dancers at Roseland, once he got over his initial nervousness. His section-mate Howard Scott remembered his debut: "He was scared at first. He said, 'How am I doing, Scottie?' I said, 'Listen, just close your eyes and play what you feel. . . . Just let it go, Louis. Be yourself. . . . Forget about all the people.' So he did. People stopped dancing to come around and listen to him . . . and we were told that there were some people passing by [in the street] that stopped, listening to him. He was so loud. The next night you couldn't get into the place."

"You got to remember that all along I was just a young kid coming up," Armstrong later explained. "I couldn't read music like a lot of them cats, but I never was embarrassed in music with bands 'cause I'd state my case. I'd say, 'Now I can *blow*—and you give me elbow room, you going to have a nice time. But don't put me to no tests.' "

Because Armstrong's innovations would soon be so universal, not only in jazz but throughout all of American popular music, and because he was given so little solo space on the records he began making that fall with Fletcher Henderson, it is hard now to hear him freshly, as the dancers at Roseland and scores of awestruck New York musicians did in 1924. The Henderson sides feature the kind of jaunty choruses, carefully arranged breaks, and stiff agitated solos that were being played by men in half a dozen other bands. Then, suddenly, Louis Armstrong bursts forth, as if from another universe, boldly pointing the way to the future. He is simultaneously hotter than anyone else and more relaxed, pushing or retarding the beat whenever it suits his purposes, sustaining end-of-phrase tones instead of biting them off as the New Yorkers did, soaring above the sometimes plodding ensemble, always unmistakably himself and always related to the blues, no matter the tune or tempo.

Armstrong's presence transformed the Henderson orchestra. At his suggestion, the

clarinetist Buster Bailey, another veteran of the King Oliver band, was added to deepen the orchestra's down-home flavor. Don Redman began to work on a new kind of arrangement—less self-consciously "symphonic," simultaneously more supple and more driving—in which the sections played figures intended to sound like improvisations. Coleman Hawkins remembered a night at Roseland when the crowd wouldn't let Armstrong stop after soloing on a pseudo-Oriental novelty called "Shanghai Shuffle." "I think they made him play ten choruses. After that . . . a dancer lifted Armstrong onto his shoulders. Fletcher Henderson kept beating out the rhythm on the piano and I stood silent, feeling almost bashful, asking myself if I would ever be able to attain a small part of Armstrong's greatness." Until that moment, Hawkins had been best known as a master of comedy effects on his instrument—clucking and slap-tonguing in the vaudeville tradition—but afterward he devoted himself to finding a way to incorporate Armstrong's ideas into his own playing, and in the process transformed the role of the tenor saxophone in jazz.

Whenever they could get away from the Hollywood Club, Duke Ellington and his men came to Roseland to hear Armstrong, too. "There weren't the words coined for describing that kick," Ellington remembered. "Everybody on the street was talking about the guy." And, like Hawkins, Ellington himself would soon be searching for ways to adapt Armstrong's ideas to his own music.

Armstrong dazzled the musicians of New York, but he was also broadening his own horizons by listening closely to the dance bands of Sam Lanin and Vincent Lopez that sometimes appeared opposite the Henderson Orchestra. Each boasted an able lead cornetist who played in ways with which Armstrong was still largely unfamiliar. When he heard Vic D'Ippolito playing for Lanin, Armstrong recalled, "I commenced

The Fletcher Henderson Orchestra, 1924. Left to right, Howard Scott (trumpet), Coleman Hawkins (tenor saxophone), Louis Armstrong (cornet), Charlie Dixon (banjo), Fletcher Henderson (piano and leader), Kaiser Marshall (drums), Buster Bailey (clarinet and saxophones), Elmer Chambers (trumpet), Charlie Green (trombone), Bob Escudero (tuba), and Don Redman (arranger and alto saxophonist). "For years," the writer Wilder Hobson recalled, "virtually every musician in New York . . . listened to Fletcher Henderson."

to notice how valuable a first chair man is. Vic had tone and he had punch." B. A. Rolfe, who played with Lopez, was still more impressive: a European-born cornetist—he had toured the Continent as "The Boy Trumpet Wonder"—he was fond of acrobatic effects, a master of his instrument's upper register. After hearing Rolfe win applause night after night during a week-long engagement in Pittsburgh for soaring through "Shadowland" an octave higher than it was written, Armstrong resolved to "go after that high range."

Soon, he would be unmatchable. In that time, cornetists and trumpet players rarely played higher than high C. Armstrong would come to routinely finish up his choruses on F, and he did so with a big, robust tone very different from the thin, almost falsetto one that even Rolfe required to reach such dizzying heights. Other trumpet players would eventually play higher than Armstrong had, but no one has ever gone so high with such a consistent blend of power and warmth.

The cornetist Rex Stewart, then playing with a long-forgotten band called Leon Abbey's Bluesicians, remembered going with two other brass players to hear Armstrong play with the Henderson band one evening at the Savoy Ballroom in Harlem. "We decided that the only proper way to enjoy Armstrong was to help the mood along with liquid refreshments. So we all filled Coca-Cola bottles with our favorite refreshments. I chose gin, which was a mistake. . . . Every time he'd end on a soaring F, I tossed a Coke bottle, and you couldn't

Alberta Hunter, 1923. "Louis Armstrong played with all the love he had," she remembered. "Everybody loved him."

even hear the crash over the applause. But the bouncers didn't understand." Stewart's enthusiasm for Louis Armstrong got him barred from the Savoy for several years.

Within days of Armstrong's arrival in New York, his New Orleans acquaintance Clarence Williams had begun clamoring to get him into the recording studio. During the next fourteen months he would accompany fifteen different blues and novelty singers, including Ma Rainey, Alberta Hunter, Clara Smith, and the formidable Empress of the Blues herself, Bessie Smith, whom he remembered as a "very quiet woman—didn't bother nobody. But God, don't mess with her." On records like "Cold in Hand Blues," his spare, poignant phrasing perfectly complimented Smith's magisterial voice and sometimes added a fresh countermelody all his own. He was not always happy about the singers with whom he found himself working, he said later, but "Everything I did with her I *like*." Smith was less generous. Armstrong played too loudly, she said, by which she meant that he some-

times dared compete with her voice for the listener's attention; she preferred Joe Smith, who was careful always to keep discreetly in the background.

Armstrong also found himself sometimes recording with Sidney Bechet, a fact which did not always please his fellow New Orleanian. From the moment Bechet started making records, he had been the star of every instrumental session on which he had played; even when asked to accompany vocalists his presence often left a more lasting impression than did their singing. Then, Armstrong came to town. Bechet had been present, playing as a guest with the pit band at the Lafayette Theater, when the younger man made his Harlem debut, playing several choruses of "Whatcha-Call-'Em Blues" onstage with the Henderson Orchestra. Bechet heard the crowd cheer the newcomer; worse, he found that his fellow musicians couldn't seem to stop talking about him.

He and Armstrong were always cordial enough with one another, but had never

really been friends. The old New Orleans antipathy between Creoles and blacks may have had something to do with it. So might the fact that at their first meeting, eleven-year-old Armstrong had made off with the older boy's half dollar. But beyond all that, each saw the other as his only real rival. Something of their competitiveness can be heard on two recordings of a tune called "Cake-Walking Babies" they made that winter. The first version was cut three days before Christmas for Gennet, and from the opening chorus it seems almost like an ambush. Bechet hurls himself to the forefront, as if determined to demonstrate once and for all that all the fuss being made about Armstrong is misguided, that he remains unrivaled as the hottest soloist in jazz. Armstrong, his cornet muted and his efforts further hampered by poorly balanced recording that pushes him into the background, does his best to hold on to the lead and has no trouble keeping up with Bechet's headlong rush, but there is no question as to who is in charge.

Gertrude "Ma" Rainey and her Georgia Minstrels in Chicago in 1925. Her piano player, Thomas A. Dorsey, then celebrated for his risqué tunes, would soon leave all that behind, and become the father of modern gospel music. "I'm not ashamed of my blues," he said later. "A beat is a beat."

Less than three weeks later, the two men faced off again, this time in the studios of the Okeh Record Company. If Armstrong had been caught off-stride by Bechet's ferocity the first time they'd tackled this tune, he was more than ready for him now. The record remains mostly an ensemble piece, but each man plays a furious solo and each takes a swooping break so dramatic it still takes the listener's breath away. The contest seems more or less a draw up to that point. Then, Armstrong suddenly launches into a series of ripping, tearing, rhythmically complicated runs that no other musician of the day, not even Sidney Bechet, could match.

Many years later, Armstrong's greater celebrity still rankled with Bechet. Bud Freeman once made the mistake of praising him too extravagantly in Bechet's presence. "Well, I don't know, man," Bechet responded. "I might have some things I want to say myself."

"The band gained a lot from Louis and he gained a lot from us," Fletcher Henderson recalled. "[H]e *really* learned to read in my band, and to read in just about every key. [And] he made the men really swing-conscious with that New Orleans style of his." Before Armstrong's arrival, most New York bands were still playing "oompah and ricky-tick," the trumpeter Max Kaminsky remembered, "breaking up the rhythm into choppy syncopation." Armstrong changed all that, moving the music away from the two-beat feel made famous by the Original Dixieland Jazz Band toward the flowing, evenly distributed 4/4 that would one day become the pulsing heart of big band swing. It was only the first of his many gifts to American music.

"Above all," Kaminsky wrote, "above . . . the electrifying tone, the magnificence of his ideas and the rightness of his harmonic sense, his superb technique, his power and ease, his hotness and intensity, his complete mastery of his horn—above all this he had the swing. No one knew what

Louis Armstrong in New York, 1925

swing was till Louis came along. It's more than just the beat, it's conceiving the phrases in the very feeling of the beat, molding and building them so that they're an integral, indivisible part of the tempo.

The others had the idea of it, but Louis could do it; he was the heir of all that had gone before and the father of all that was to come."

OUR LANGUAGE

Jazz had been born in New Orleans and nurtured in Chicago and New York and on the West Coast, but by the mid-1920s, versions of it were being played in dance halls and roadhouses and speakeasies all over the country. The blues, which had once been the product of itinerant black musicians, the poorest of the southern poor, had become an industry, and dancing consumed a country that seemed convinced prosperity would never end. There were "all-girl" orchestras on the road now—including Babe Egan's Hollywood Redheads, a band billed as the Twelve Vampires, and the Parisian Redheads, all of whom actually came from Indiana. More than one hundred dance bands regularly crisscrossed the wide-open spaces between St. Louis and Denver, Texas and Nebraska, playing one-nighters. They were called

Pianist Ben Smith, center, and his Blue Syncopaters, 1928. Based in El Paso, Texas, Smith's outfit never recorded but, like scores of other so-called territory bands, they traveled thousands of miles every year bringing music—and more than a dash of elegance—to communities all across the plains and prairie states.

The Parisian Red Heads, who billed themselves as "America's Greatest Girl Band" and later changed their name to The Bricktops, 1929

BEAN

"I made the tenor sax," Coleman Hawkins said once. "There's nobody plays like me and I don't play like anybody else." All of it was true. More than anyone else, Hawkins was responsible for turning what had been a raucous novelty instrument into one of the central solo voices in jazz, by turns exhilarating and seductive, aggressive and infinitely tender.

He was born in St. Joseph, Missouri, in 1904—though in later years he liked to pretend he'd been born later for fear of scaring off younger women. Hawkins was a thoroughly schooled musician. His mother, who played the organ for her church, taught him to read music before he could puzzle out words. He studied cello, too—his father, a factory worker, worked two jobs to pay for his lessons—and he was a lifelong admirer of Pablo Casals. Then, his parents gave him a C-melody saxophone on his ninth birthday. It was used in vaudeville shows and marching bands then. "The funnier the noise," Hawkins remembered, "the better the playing." But he took to it right away. By the age of twelve he was playing at dances. In 1921, he joined Mamie Smith's Jazz Hounds in a touring tent show and soon thereafter shifted to the tenor saxophone. He was already supremely self-confident, and eager to challenge any musician willing to take him on. "When some young kid would come along," Hawkins remembered, "I'd have to go down and cut this boy. That's how Fletcher Henderson . . . happened to find me." Henderson offered him a job with his band in 1924. He stayed with it for more than a decade—and, inspired by what Louis Armstrong and Art Tatum were doing on their instruments, forever altered the way the saxophone was played.

He was given the nickname "Bean" because of the richness of the musical ideas that tumbled from his fertile brain. His sound was surging, virile, impassioned, filled with vibrato—and *loud*. As one of his disciples, Nick "Big Nick" Nicholas, said, "*All* of [Hawkins's] notes were big." Hawkins was of only moderate height but because of that huge sound and the self-assured way he carried himself he seemed far taller. The alto saxophonist Julian "Cannonball" Adderley, taken to see the Henderson band when he was a small boy, remembered Hawkins as "the most impressive looking jazz musician I've seen in my life. He just looked so authoritative. I kept looking at him. I never did look at Fletcher. I said, 'Well, that's what I want to do when I grow up.' "

Hawkins was a loner all his life; "a sometimes guy," the bassist Pops Foster said. "Sometimes he'd look right at you and didn't know you and sometimes he did." He loved fine clothes and good cognac and fast cars. During his years with Henderson, he speeded from engagement to engagement in his own Chrysler Imperial at better than one hundred miles an hour. He distrusted banks and some-

times carried thousands of dollars in cash. He was a prodigious eater. Johnny Williams, a fellow saxophone player in the Henderson band with a hearty appetite of his own, remembered dining with him: "We used to go in a restaurant together, and each of us would order two meals. The waitress would start setting up for four and Hawkins would say, 'No, Miss, it's just two of us.' " But otherwise, he kept largely to himself. His first wife left him when he seemed never to come home, and took with her almost all the furniture in his New York apartment. He didn't bother to replace it. He wasn't planning to be home much, anyway.

He lived for musical combat. "When we used to finish playing with the band," he remembered, "I'd make all the clubs. They all had little bands playing in them. So I'd hear something that sounded good. I'd come back to New York and have some new riffs."

In the 1920s the Hoofer's Club in Harlem sent out invitations to weekly "suppers," jam sessions meant to test players of a single instrument—pianists, trumpet players, trombonists, as well as saxophonists. No matter what the chosen instrument of the evening was, Coleman Hawkins would be there. "I just happened to stop by and had my horn," he'd say, and join right in. "You knew," a veteran of those sessions said, "he'd come in to carve somebody."

Several generations of saxophone players committed Hawkins's solos to memory, note for note, but he was himself never satisfied with his playing, was always eager to find out what younger musicians were up to and then try to beat them at their own game. He was "ashamed" of most of his earlier records, he once told a friend. Nobody should ever look back. Music, he said, should always be "an adventure."

Coleman Hawkins

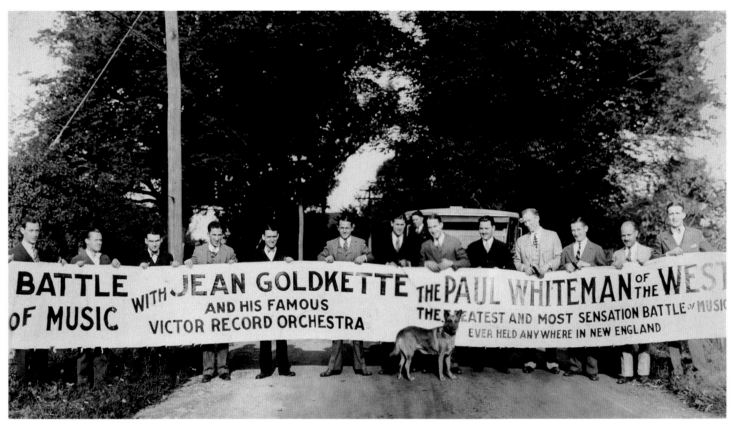

The Jean Goldkette Orchestra advertises its willingness to take on all comers, New England, 1926.

[was] too strong, what with Steve Brown slapping hell out of that bass . . . and Frankie Trumbauer's inspiring leadership as he stood out front wailing on his C-melody." As for Bix, with whom Stewart happily shared a locker during their joint appearance at Roseland, he was a "once-in-a-million artist." Many years later, someone asked Benny Carter if the Goldkette band had been as good as some said it was. "Good, hell!" he said. "They were frightening." The two bands would meet again at Roseland the following January and battle to what Buster Bailey remembered as a hard-fought draw: "We weren't about to be taken twice. . . . You can bet there was a lot of great music that night."

A reporter for *Billboard* predicted on the basis of the Goldkette band's first performance at Roseland that it would soon be making records that "would scorch the wallpaper off the studio walls." But when the men actually got into the Victor studios, Edward King, the executive in charge, had something else in mind. King was unenthusiastic about jazz in general and brass players in particular and insisted on recording only strictly commercial arrangements. "Geez," Bill Challis remembered, "they picked out the *stinking-est* tunes for us. We really didn't get any good tunes to do. They didn't want any improvising. They were trying to make a hit, and in doing that they made us play the melody. . . . Bix used to steal in on the last eight bars of some of the tunes—even though they were real corny. . . . Bix would stand and improvise right over the band." The records sold well enough but failed to capture the excitement that those who heard the band in person never forgot. "I don't really know why [King] hired the band at all," the alto saxophone player Stanley "Doc" Ryker remembered.

"The stuff he *didn't* want . . . that was our style."

The chronic idiocies of race in America had a good deal to do with it. Most of the men who ran the record business thought sweet and sentimental tunes should remain the exclusive purview of white bands, while black orchestras had better stick with the blues and stomp numbers that supposedly came to them "naturally" and which the executives were convinced were all that buyers of race records could possibly want. Thus, white bands like Goldkette's and Ben Pollack's were rarely able to demonstrate on records how hard they could swing, while black bands like Fletcher Henderson's were kept from displaying the full scope of their skills. "Although the Henderson band played a variety of music on tours," Rex Stewart complained, "the record executives characterized [us] as a stomp band. They didn't accept the fact that a Negro band could play sweet, though as a matter of fact, we used to get tremendous applause at Roseland and other places for playing waltzes beautifully."

Meanwhile, a singer named Red McKenzie talked Tommy Rockwell—the same Okeh executive responsible for producing Louis Armstrong's Hot Fives—into recording Bix and Tram in a series of small-group recordings that eventually included "Clarinet Marmalade," "Ostrich Walk," "Riverboat Shuffle," "I'm Coming Virginia," and the closest thing to a genuine hit either man ever had, "Singin' the Blues."

"Singin' the Blues" had long been a favorite of both men and each had polished his playing of it to something like perfection before he reached the studio. Trumbauer's supple, relaxed opening chorus inspired a generation of young imitators, white and black. "*Everybody* memorized it," said the tenor player Budd Johnson; Trumbauer was "the baddest cat around and everybody was trying to play his stuff." And Bix's solo—bright and silvery, poised and carefully crafted—was memorized by brass players, as well. Fletcher Henderson admired "Singin' the Blues" so much that he would later hire Bill Challis to write an arrangement of it for his band in which the saxophones recreated Trumbauer's solo in unison while Rex Stewart played Beiderbecke's, note for note.

"Singin' the Blues" provided a sort of epiphany for the young clarinetist Artie Shaw. He was playing in a dance band then, and dissatisfied.

I was doing things you shouldn't do, but I didn't know who to follow, I didn't know who to copy. And finally I heard Bix and Trumbauer and . . . those were the guys. Being a white guy, I was subjected to white music and I heard Bix and Trumbauer and they were the exemplars. . . . And they played like they knew where they were going, there was a direc-

tion to what they did, there was a definition, a kind of discipline. . . . I knew that was the way to go.

Even "Singin' the Blues" failed to please Bix. For years, he had worked after hours on a dreamy piano piece of his own, a string of improvisational phrases rather than a full-blown composition but filled with pastel tone colors like those used by the French impressionists he admired. Rockwell encouraged him to record it, too. He ran too long on the first take, but Tram was there to give him a fifteen-second warning on the second and he got to the end without any trouble. Characteristically, he had never thought of a title for it and it was left to Trumbauer finally to come up with one. "Well, I thought to myself, Bix was certainly in a fog when he made it. And then it hit me. Fog. Mist. In a Mist. That's it—'In a Mist.' "

Jean Goldkette loved his flagship orchestra but he was also a businessman: the salaries he was paying its stars were outstripping his profits, and he could see no way to turn things around. And so, just nine days after Beiderbecke recorded "In a Mist," on the evening of September 18, 1927, the Goldkette band was back at Roseland for what would be its final performance. The pianist Irving Riskin remembered that all the men had tears in their eyes that night as they systematically played their way through the band's book in tribute to the arrangers who had helped make them sound so good. Every man took a solo on every tune, he said, and when they were finally finished and tried to leave the bandstand, the overflow crowd wouldn't let them go. "We started up again and played to almost frenzied cries from the audience. Many of *them* now had tears streaming down their cheeks. No one wanted this night to end." Finally, the manager of the ballroom called the local precinct and "soon dozens of policemen were pushing their way through, . . . making a lane for us to depart. . . . Even as we scurried through the long line of police offi-

cers, patrons tried to reach through and around the blue barrier just to touch us one more time."

The Goldkette men scattered in search of work. Bix and Tram would soon find it with the best-known, highest-paying bandleader in America, Paul Whiteman.

JUNGLE MUSIC

In New York that same fall, word spread that the gangsters who owned and operated Harlem's most opulent nightspot, the Cotton Club, were looking for a new band. The club had a colorful history. Built as a casino above the Douglas Theater on the northeast corner of 142nd Street near Lenox Avenue in 1918, it was run as the Club Deluxe by former heavyweight champion Jack Johnson before it was bought by a syndicate of mobsters headed by a British-born gangster with a high girlish voice and a long prison record named Owney Madden.

Harlem had become a magnet for wealthy whites eager to experience for themselves something of its supposedly "primitive" excitement, a turn of events that puzzled a good many Harlem residents. "What occasions the focusing of attention on . . . the Negro?" asked the writer Rudolf Fisher in the *American Mercury*.

Granted that white people have long enjoyed the Negro entertainment as a diversion, is it not something different, something more, when they bodily throw themselves into Negro entertainment in cabarets? Now Negroes go to their own cabarets to see how white people act. . . . And what do we see? Why, we see them actually playing Negro games. I watch them in that epidemic Negroism, the Charleston. I look on and envy them. They camel and fish-tail and turkey, they geeche and black-bottom and scrontch, they skate and buzzard and

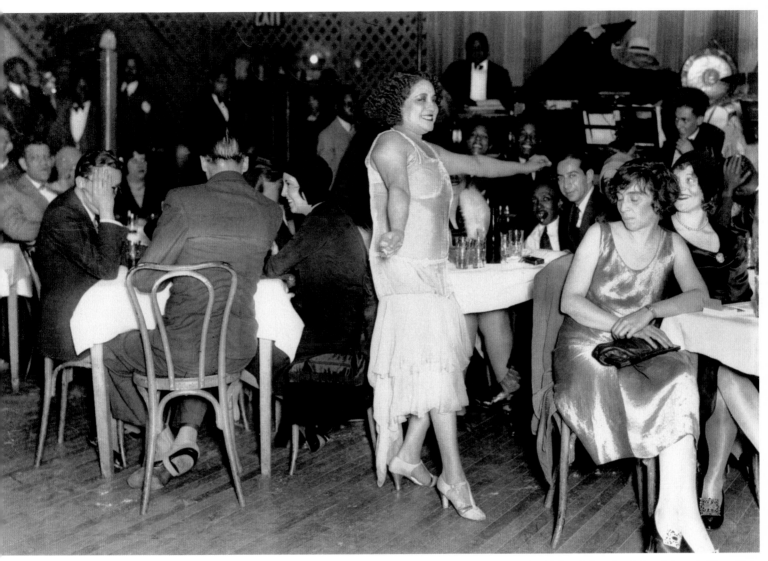

A light-skinned performer dances for black and white customers at Small's Paradise in Harlem—while one anxious patron does his best to keep from being photographed in such surroundings, 1929. "The best of Harlem's black cabarets," wrote Rudolf Fisher, "have turned white."

mess-around—and they do them all better than I!

This interest in the Negro is an active and participating interest. It is almost as if a traveler from the North stood watching an African tribe-dance, then suddenly found himself swept wildly into it, caught in its tribal rhythm. . . . Maybe these Nordics at last have tuned in our wave-length. Maybe they are at last learning to speak our language.

"Harlem's night life now surpasses that of Broadway itself," wrote *Variety*. "From midnight until after dawn it is a seething cauldron of Nubian mirth and hilarity." "At this time Harlem was as white as it was black," the tap dancer Honey Coles remembered. "At night everybody from downtown came up, after everything closed downtown. Diamonds and minks and furs." No one knows how many speakeasies and cellar clubs and other drinking establishments then flourished in Harlem—estimates vary from five hundred to several thousand—but

by the late twenties a considerable number were doing well by catering to white thrill seekers. A card handed out to tourists on Manhattan street corners hinted at the excitement they would encounter uptown if they hired one of the advertiser's "Slumming Hostesses."

Here in the world's greatest city it would amuse and also interest you to see the real inside of the new Negro Race of Harlem. You have heard it discussed, but there are very few who

Seventh Avenue and 135th Street in 1928. The entrance to Small's Paradise—the second club of the same name run by a former elevator operator named Ed Smalls and popular with black and white patrons alike—is at the right. There, conventioneers attending the Elks rally welcomed on the banner hung across the street might have heard Willie the Lion Smith or Fletcher Henderson and would certainly have been served by waiters on roller-skates dancing the Charleston.

really know. . . . I am in a position to carry you through Harlem as you would go slumming through Chinatown. My guides are honest and have been instructed to give the best service. . . . Your season is not completed with thrills until you have visited Harlem.

No nightspot offered more thrills than the Cotton Club. Nostalgia for the antebellum South set the bizarre theme—the big stage was designed to resemble the veranda of a plantation house, complete with tall white columns and a painted backdrop of slave cabins and live oak trees draped with moss—and the main attraction was a lavish floor show in the Florenz Ziegfeld tradition that featured songs, dances, and lots of light-skinned, lightly clad chorus girls billed as "Tall, Tan and Terrific." Celebrities like Ethel Waters and Bill "Bojangles" Robinson were sometimes granted tables, but black patrons were generally barred; W. C. Handy himself, the "father of the blues," was once turned away. "It isn't necessary to mix with colored people if you don't feel like it," the author of a guidebook to Manhattan nightlife reassured his readers. At the Cotton Club "you have your own party and keep to yourself. But it's worth seeing how they step."

A leering reviewer for *Variety* gave a vivid sense of what brought most of the club's white patrons northward. "The almost Caucasian-hued high yaller gals look swell and uncork the meanest kind of cootching ever exhibited to a conglomerate mixed audience," he wrote. "The big attraction, of course, are the gals, 10 of 'em, the majority of whom in white company could pass for Caucasians, possessed of the native jazz heritage, their hotsy-totsy performance if working sans wraps could never be parred by a white gal. The brownskins' shivaree is worth the $2 couvert alone."

Still, despite the omnipresent gangsters, the whites-only seating policy, and the glorified minstrelsy, the Cotton Club also presented black entertainers as good-looking and glamorous. "On Sunday nights," Duke Ellington remembered, "when celebrities filled the joint, [the women in the chorus] would rush out of the dressing room after the show in all their finery. Every time they went by, the stars and the rich people would be saying, 'My, who is *that?*' They were tremendous representatives." And the music and choreography, costumes and stage sets rivaled the best of Broadway. In any case, it was the job every ambitious black bandleader in town wanted, including Duke Ellington.

Ellington was already on the rise. Four years playing just off Times Square at the cellar club first called the Hollywood Inn and then the Kentucky Club; three triumphant summer tours of New England ballrooms; a successful season playing for an all-black revue called *Jazzmania* at Harlem's Lafayette Theater; and a number of recordings that featured the startling, soulful growls of Bubber Miley had all helped see to that.

And he now had the help of a shrewd, tireless manager. Irving Mills was a squat, cigar-chewing Broadway operator, a one-time song plugger and vaudevillian fond of the royal "we": "We were very aggressive and colorful," he told an interviewer toward the end of his long life, "and up-to-the-minute with ideas and new things to do." Born on the Lower East Side in 1894, the son of Jewish immigrants, he had made himself one of the most successful music publishers in the business with a stable of songwriters and arrangers that would include Harold Arlen, Hoagy Carmichael, Dorothy Fields, James P. Johnson, Jimmy McHugh, Will Vodery, and Spencer Williams. When the blues became big business he began collecting them, too, sometimes for as little as fifteen dollars a tune.

At some point—Ellington and Mills themselves differed as to just when it was—Mills began to see that Ellington was somehow different from other bandleaders, that

something more might be made of him, to their mutual profit. "He used to come to the Kentucky Club often," Ellington remembered, "and one night he said he didn't know what we were doing with our music, but he liked it and would like to record some of it with our band. We jumped at the chance and this was really the beginning of a long and wonderful association.... He had the contacts.... We recorded for almost every existing label under different names: Duke Ellington on Victor, the Jungle Band on Brunswick, the Washingtonians on Harmony, the Whoopee Makers on Perfect, Sonny Greer and his Memphis Men on Columbia, the Harlem Footwarmers on Okeh."

Ellington and Mills would eventually form a partnership that in effect gave Mills and his attorney 55 percent of everything the orchestra earned. Some members of the band objected, especially when Mills's name began appearing as the co-composer of songs Ellington alone had written. But Ellington never publicly complained about

The door to the Cotton Club on 142nd Street at Lenox Avenue in Harlem, and a souvenir program that promises lurid goings-on inside

the bargain he had made, for he knew that in exchange, it had become Mills's mission to promote him as no black artist had ever been promoted before, as "a great musician who was making a lasting contribution to American music." The two men would eventually part, but Ellington refused to listen to others speak ill of Mills. "In spite of how much money he made on me," he wrote, Mills had been "the first to see our possibilities," and whatever the complications of their relationship, "I respected the way he operated. He . . . always preserved the dignity of my name . . . and that is the most anybody can do for anybody."

On November 29, 1926—ten weeks after Jelly Roll Morton began recording with his Red Hot Peppers, eleven days before Benny Goodman's recording debut and the death of Goodman's father—Duke Ellington recorded his first important original composition, "East St. Louis Toodle-o." Touring New England by bus the previous summer, the men in the band had passed so many billboards around Boston advertising "Lewando Cleaners" that they began to chant, "Oh, Lee-wan-*do*" whenever they saw another. Bubber Miley took up the phrase on his horn. Ellington shaped that kernel of an idea into a haunting theme, matched it with a second strain, then worked out with his men a carefully structured arrangement of the whole thing, along with a story to go with it. "In those days, . . . practically everything we wrote was supposed to be a picture of something," he said. "We were walking up Broadway one night after playing the Kentucky Club, and we were talking about this old man, after a hard day's work in the field, where he and his broken walk [are] coming up the road. But he's strong, in spite of being so tired because he's headed [home] to get his feet under the table and to get that hot dinner that's waiting for him. And that's the 'East St. Louis Toodle-o.' " (He had intended to call it "East St. Louis *Todalo*"—a todalo being a kind of halting dance—but the person who typed the copy for the record label evidently got the

Irving Mills

name wrong and it stuck.) It would be the band's theme song for the next fifteen years. "People heard it," Sonny Greer remembered, "and said, 'Here they come!' "

Ellington would follow that pattern again and again during his long career: an improvised melody developed by him or one of his men would be transformed under his direction into a full-scale arrangement that somehow also vividly evoked a scene from everyday American life. The difference between his and Fletcher Henderson's bands, Ellington once said, was that while Henderson's was "basically an ensemble group . . . in our band the solos . . . all the various stars we have had . . . always dominated everything." Ellington's boundless self-confidence was generally alloyed with becoming public modesty. His band would indeed always include extraordinary individual voices, each of which he carefully chose for precisely that reason, but it was his own genius, his own restless adventurousness and uncanny sense of form that made his music—and his orchestra—like no one else's.

In the autumn of 1927, Ellington recorded two more important pieces featuring Bubber Miley: "Creole Love Call," in which Miley shared solo space with an unearthly wordless vocal by the singer Adelaide Hall; and "Black and Tan Fantasy," an alluring blues-oriented piece that evokes the steamy atmosphere of places like the Cotton Club and then suggests—in a mournful but sly ending that quotes from Chopin's funeral march—that after all those good times the piper must inevitably be paid. It is filled with disparate elements—blues and spirituals, Chopin and King Oliver, and more than a hint of a New Orleans funeral parade—but it is also unmistakably Duke Ellington's.

It was shortly after recording "Black and Tan Fantasy" that Ellington and Mills got the news that the Cotton Club was looking for a new band. Mills urged the club's managers to hire Ellington. So did the songwriter Jimmy McHugh, who was writing the music for the club's next revue. But the manager insisted on holding auditions and wanted at least ten men, while Ellington, then playing at the Gibson Standard Theater in Philadelphia, still had only eight. Six other bands were scheduled to try out on the appointed day. "The audition was set for noon," Ellington said, "but by the time I had scraped up eleven men it was two or three o'clock. We played for them and got the job. The reason for that was that the boss, Harry Block, didn't get there till late either, and didn't hear the others! That's a classic example of being at the right place at the right time with the right thing before the right people." There was just one more obstacle. Ellington was under contract to finish out his run in Philadelphia. Owney Madden sent a go-between named Yankee Schwartz to see the theater manager there with word that he wanted Ellington for his club and he wanted him now: "Be big," Madden's agent is supposed to have said. "Be big or be dead." The manager wisely chose to be big.

In a still from a 1929 motion picture called *Black and Tan*, Duke Ellington and his orchestra preside over a stage show at the Cotton Club.

Duke Ellington and his orchestra opened at the Cotton Club on December 4, 1927, and stayed for almost four years. "When I began my work," Ellington recalled, "jazz was a stunt, something different. Not everybody cared for jazz and those who did felt that it wasn't the real thing unless they were given a shock sensation of loudness or unpredictability, along with the music." American popular music had always exploited the "exotic"—Oriental-sounding dances, songs with Hawaiian or American-Indian or African-American themes—anything that seemed to add novelty and spice. Cotton Club audiences now thought they heard in Ellington's new music, with its array of growls and moans and cries, its novel voicings and pervasive sensuality, echoes of Africa—which was just what they had trooped up to Harlem to hear.

Ellington fully understood the absurdity of much that went on at the Cotton Club. "That part was degrading and humiliating to both Negroes and whites," he said. "But there was another part of it that was wonderful." The Cotton Club was "a classy spot," he remembered; unruly guests were politely asked to be quiet and if they failed to take the hint were gently but firmly removed. (At the Kentucky Club they'd been given Mickey Finns.) He loved all the elegance, enjoyed meeting celebrities and getting to know the women in the chorus, even came to like playing cards after hours with the mobsters who ran the place. The club provided him with a priceless training ground, taught him how to produce on deadline, how to showcase talented people, even how to disguise the limitations of those less talented. "A lot of people worked as hard as hell to put those shows together," he remembered. "That was the Cotton Club spirit. Work, work, work. Rehearse, rehearse, rehearse. Get it down fine. . . . We knew we had a standard of performance to match every night. We knew we couldn't miss a lick. And we rarely did." In any case, nothing could demean Duke Ellington because he refused ever to be demeaned.

Even in the jittery old film of him enjoying his success at the Cotton Club, surrounded by dancers wearing some white choreographer's ludicrous notion of African costume, he remains somehow set apart at the piano in his white tails, invincibly dignified, in on the joke that is being played on everybody else. In 1929, when he appeared in a short called "Black and Tan," in which two black comedians performed stereotyped roles—stumbling, shiftless, illiterate, overly fond of alcohol—he was portrayed precisely as what he already was, a handsome, elegant, hardworking composer.

And, while the "jungle music" tag would remain with him for a time, neither distant Africa nor the perverse version of it that helped lure whites to Harlem was ever his source of inspiration. For that, he would always draw upon what he called "the everyday life and customs of the Negro," as the titles of the tunes that seemed to pour effortlessly from his pen during his Cotton

Club years attest: "Black Beauty," "Jubilee Stomp," "New Orleans Low Down," "Swampy River," "Stevedore Stomp," "Dicty Glide," "Parlor Social Stomp," "Harlem River Quiver," "Harlem Flat Blues," "Memphis Wail," "Mississippi Moan," "The Breakfast Dance," "Rent Party Blues," "Saturday Night Function." Like his mother and father, like his teachers at William Lloyd Garrison High School in segregated Washington, Duke Ellington continued to manifest what he called "pride . . . the greatest race pride" no matter what else was going on around him. His goal was to write "Negro music," he said, to express "Negro feelings put to rhythm and tune." "I am not playing 'jazz,' " he told one of his first interviewers. "I am trying to play the natural feelings of a people." He was, in the admiring parlance of the time, a Race man.

Ellington's long-term residency at the Cotton Club made him the most celebrated black bandleader in New York, but it took the radio to introduce him to the whole country. The band first broadcast nightly from the Cotton Club on local station WHW. Then, at the urging of one of Ellington's most ardent admirers, the popular announcer Ted Husing, the brand-new Columbia Broadcasting System put him on the air nationwide several times a week, sometimes at midnight, sometimes at suppertime. "The world was *waiting* for that from coast to coast," Sonny Greer remembered. "[T]he people didn't get anything to eat till we came off. Cats working all day *starved* to death until we got off."

"We were very, very fortunate," Ellington said, "because . . . at that particular period all the other bands in the country were trying to imitate Paul Whiteman and naturally they were souped up with a lot of grandiose fanfares and all that sort of thing. But we had a very, very plaintive sort of style, and out of contrast alone we stuck out, and caught on."

In fact, some listeners were already hearing far more than mere "contrast" in

Ellington's music. The writer Ralph Ellison, then a high school student in Oklahoma City, remembered Ellington

first as a strangely familiar timbre of orchestral sounds issuing from phonograph records and radio.

Familiar because beneath the stylized jungle sounds (the like of which no African jungle had ever heard), there sounded the blues, and strange because the mutes, toilet plungers and derby hats with which I was acquainted as a musician had been given a stylized elegance and extension of effect unheard of even in the music of Louis Armstrong. It was as though Ellington had taken the traditional instruments of Negro American music and modified them, extended their range and enriched their tonal possibilities. We were studying the classics then, working at harmony and the forms of symphonic music. While we affirmed the voice of jazz and the blues despite all criticism from our teachers because they spoke to a large extent of what we felt about the life we lived most intimately, it was not until the discovery of Ellington that we had any hint that jazz possessed possibilities of a range of expressiveness comparable to that of classical European music.

At roughly the same time, R. D. Darrell, a New York critic writing for *disques,* a journal normally devoted only to the classics, was frank enough to admit that he had initially misjudged Ellington's music. "Black and Tan Fantasy" was the instrument of his conversion:

With the majority I did not recognize it when it first came to my ears in the form of the "hottest, funniest record you ever heard." . . . I laughed like everyone else over its instrumental wa-waing and garbling and gobbling, the piteous whinnying of a very

Duke Ellington during his Cotton Club days

ancient horse, the lugubrious reminiscence of the Chopin funeral march. But as I continued to play the record for the amusement of my friends I laughed less heartily and with less zest. In my ears the whinnies and wa-was began to resolve into new tone colors, distorted and tortured, but agonizingly expressive. The piece took on a surprising individuality and entity as well as an intensity of feeling that was totally incongruous in popular dance music. Beneath all its oddity and perverseness there was a twisted beauty that grew on me more and more and could not be shaken off.

A work like this was alien to all my notions of jazz. It had nothing of the sprightly gusto of Gershwin, . . . nothing of the polish of the Whiteman school, nothing of the raucous exuberance of the Negro jazz I had known. Nor was it in the heavily worked "spiritual" tradition except in that it sounded an equal depth of poignance. For all its fluidity and rhapsodic freedom it was no improvisation, tossed off by a group of talented virtuosi who would never be able to play it twice in the same way. It bore the indelible stamp of one mind, resourcefully inventive, yet primarily occupied not with the projection of effects or syncopated rhythms, but the concern of great music—tapping the inner world of feeling and experience . . . seizing the human heart.

NEVER SATISFIED

On the afternoon of October 27, 1927, the day after Ellington recorded "Black and Tan Fantasy" in New York and a little over a month before he took his band into the Cotton Club, Bix Beiderbecke and Frankie Trumbauer stepped out of a taxicab in front of the Indiana Theater in Minneapolis and hurried inside. The Paul Whiteman Orchestra was appearing there as part of a forty-week cross-country tour. "The Whiteman band was to the music world what the 1927 New York Yankees were to baseball," its first trumpet player Charles Margulis remembered. "We were giants."

Bix and Tram agreed. "We found the stage door and stopped," Tram remembered. "The stage show was on. Never had we heard music like this before in our lives. We just stood there, like two kids. Oh, we had played with some good bands, that's true, but listening to the King made everything else seem small. . . . 'What music,' cried Bix. 'Aw, Tram, what the hell are we doing here, anyway?' "

In his dressing room at intermission, the huge Whiteman hugged them both—he was dripping with sweat, Trumbauer recalled— then hustled them right onstage, wearing borrowed crimson jackets and without any sheet music. Halfway through the first tune, Jimmy Dorsey poked Trumbauer with his clarinet to signal that Whiteman wanted him to take the next chorus.

Me? Oh, no! How did I get into this? What's the tune? The key? Where the hell's my horn? Oh yes, I'm holding it. . . . A great searing javelin of light from afar, away up somewhere, hit me in the face and I was on my feet and playing. . . . The band yelled! It broke up Paul, too. I felt a little better then and looked around at Bix. He was laughing, but I don't think he meant it because he knew that he was next. I gave him a familiar lead-in on the ending, and he picked up my phrase and carried on with a beautiful chorus. I dropped to my chair, amid the applause of the audience.

Whiteman took them out for dinner afterward, told them how delighted he was to have them in his orchestra, even urged them to record on their own: "If your records go over," he said, "we'll all benefit by them." Neither man could credit his luck.

Bix's father may still have disapproved of what his son was doing, but when the Whiteman orchestra played the Chicago Theater in Chicago that fall Bix got word that his mother was on her way to see him play. "Now he had been out the night before on a tear," Charles Margulis remembered, "and he looked in pretty bad shape, but by the time his mother arrived . . . he looked like Joe College. He was neat as a pin and all spruced up. His mother was very pleased that he had (in her words) made it to the top! She felt her son had reached the height of his career."

There is no reason to think Bix himself did not share that opinion, at least at first. He enjoyed the lush arrangements, the elegant variations on the classics, the cheerful antics of the singing trio called the Rhythm Boys—Harry Barris, Al Rinker, and Harry Lillis Crosby, whom the men in the band called "Bing." And Whiteman even encouraged him to compose—and perform—more of his impressionistic piano pieces. But the pressure of playing night after night took a steady toll. So did the admirers who lay in wait for Bix wherever Whiteman's tours took him. "There were always people in his room," his friend the clarinetist Pee Wee Russell remembered.

They would knock on the door even at six a.m. . . . I remember how, at one hotel, he used to leave word that he wasn't in. So some fellows would check into the hotel, take a room on the floor below Bix's room; then they'd come up and . . . pound on the door. . . . He even had a piano in the room, and when he had a spare moment, he'd try to get a composition started, but with all those people always hanging around he didn't have a chance. In a sense, Bix was killed by his friends. But I think the term is being used loosely. Because they were the kind of people who liked to be able to say, "Last night I was up at Bix's and oh, was he drunk. . . ." And Bix couldn't say no, he couldn't say no to anybody.

Beiderbecke began missing trains, hiding bottles beneath the bandstand, forgetting his cues. Many years later, a cornetist examining copies of Whiteman's sheet music discovered a notation in a section-mate's hand: "Wake up Bix." He could now not bear to hear his own recordings; when an admiring musician borrowed his cornet and played his solo on the Wolverines' 1924 "Riverboat Shuffle," thinking he'd be pleased, Bix was just annoyed. "What on earth did you play *that* for?" he asked. He was merely "a musical degenerate," he had told a friend, still too ignorant about music ever to be able to express himself as he wished, unable to find in the kind of music he was playing the fulfillment he craved.

When the Whiteman orchestra came back to the Chicago Theater the following July, Louis Armstrong bought a ticket for the very first show and took his seat in the balcony. He remembered Bix both as a tow-headed teenager back in Davenport and

as a frequent visitor to the Chicago clubs in which he performed; he had especially admired "Singin' the Blues," and was now eager to hear him play with the best-known band in the country.

By now, the Whiteman orchestra had become a sort of traveling army. There were thirty-three men—and some 125 instruments—onstage for the second number, the *1812 Overture,* Armstrong recalled.

[Whiteman] had those trumpets way up into the air, just blowing like mad, and my man Bix was . . . blowing beautifully, and just before the end, they started to shooting cannons, ringing bells, sirens were howling like mad, but you could still hear Bix. The reason why I saw through all those different effects that were going on at the ending—well, you take a man with a pure tone like Bix's and no matter how loud the other fellows may be blowing, that pure . . . tone will cut through it all.

Armstrong went backstage to see Bix after the concert, he remembered, and "we hugged and kissed something wonderful." That night and for several nights that week, as soon as Whiteman's stage show was over, Beiderbecke would hurry down to the South Side café where Armstrong was playing and sit listening quietly until the last customers left at four a.m. "Then," Armstrong recalled, "we would lock the doors. Now you talking about jam sessions, huh, those were the things, with everyone feeling each other's note or chord, and blending with each other instead of trying to cut each other. We tried to see how good we could make music sound."

No one can ever know precisely what caused Bix Beiderbecke's rapid, steady decline into alcoholism and despair. Most of the reasons for it must lie buried in his boyhood. But some part of his chronic dissatisfaction with his own playing and with the music he was being asked to play may well have grown out of the maddening fact

that the America of his time provided him with so few opportunities to play alongside the "real jazz niggers" who were the heroes of his boyhood, musicians like Louis Armstrong whose strengths might have helped him further develop his own. Many years later, Armstrong was asked what memories of Bix Beiderbecke remained with him: "Quiet," he said. "Never satisfied with his solos, and people raving. Always figured he had one better."

On November 30, Bix checked in to the Palace Hotel in Cleveland with the rest of the Whiteman orchestra for a weeklong run at the new Music Hall. Bix was now having more and more trouble controlling his drinking—and the depression that it seemed only to intensify. Onstage in Cleveland that evening, he passed out in the middle of a tune. His section-mate Charles Margulis managed to keep him from sliding off his chair but then, he recalled, Bix "was uncertain where he was, . . . took a

Sheet music used by the Paul Whiteman orchestra with "Wake up Bix" written in the hand of one of Bix Beiderbecke's long-suffering section-mates

This greeting from Paul Whiteman to the readers of *Variety* appeared on the show business weekly's cover in 1928.

Armstrong among all the musicians in jazz now continued to hold his full interest.

When a reporter for the Davenport *Sunday Democrat* came to interview him as a local celebrity, Beiderbecke was both self-effacing and oddly ambivalent about the music he was playing. He enjoyed all the "traveling about" he got to do with the Whiteman band, he said, but jazz itself was "musical humor," nothing more. Yet, "even in the hands of white composers it involuntarily reflects the half-forgotten suffering of the negro," he continued. "Jazz has both white and black elements and each in some respects has influenced the other. Its recent phase seems to throw the light of the white race's sophistication upon the anguish of the black." Other than the short article the same newspaper had once run describing him as a promising pianist at the age of seven, this would be the only feature piece published about Bix Beiderbecke during his lifetime.

THE MOST DOG

Sidney Bechet remained Louis Armstrong's only serious rival as the most daring soloist in jazz. But, as Armstrong's fame continued to spread, Bechet's career was undercut again and again by the turbulent personality that found its best expression in his music. In the summer of 1925 he had opened his own Harlem cabaret on Seventh Avenue, the Club Basha—so-called because that was the way most New York musicians mispronounced his name—and was doing well, leading a house band that included one of his most avid admirers, nineteen-year-old alto saxophonist Johnny Hodges, until he got into a quarrel with his partner over the affections of a belly dancer and abruptly walked away from the business.

In September, he sailed for France with the all-black cast of a new musical, *La Revue Nègre,* which played Paris, Brussels, and Berlin. Bechet had only a small part: dressed as a peddler in a long duster, he

poke at me and sort of settled back into his haze." Whiteman had seen it all, and at intermission ordered Bix taken back to his hotel room. There, he suffered an attack of *delirium tremens* and smashed up the furniture. Whiteman had no choice but to put him under the care of a male nurse and move on to the band's next engagement.

"Bix still gone," Frankie Trumbauer noted in his diary the next day. "Stayed in Cleveland with DT's. I spent 4 years with him to no avail." He was hospitalized at the Rivercrest Sanitarium on Long Island, where he was found to have been suffering from pneumonia as well as alcoholism. Six weeks later, he left the hospital and checked into a hotel on Forty-fourth Street in New York, planning to rejoin the band when it got back to town the next day. But that night, accompanied by a friend, he visited

a speakeasy where, in an incident never fully explained, someone beat both men bloody and gashed Beiderbecke's thigh so badly with a broken bottle that he was left with a permanent limp.

This time, Whiteman made sure Bix went home to Davenport to recuperate. It was not a happy visit. A friend remembered Bix telling him that not long after he got there, he had discovered in a hall closet all the Paul Whiteman records he'd proudly sent home to his parents; his father had never even unwrapped them. If the story was true—and the family subsequently denied it—Bismarck Beiderbecke's apparent lack of interest in his work can only have served to reconfirm his own self-doubt. He was too good-natured ever publicly to criticize other musicians but, according to Frankie Trumbauer, only Louis

La Revue Nègre introduced Josephine Baker (above)—and the sound of Sidney Bechet—to thousands of Parisians in 1925. Later, Bechet moved on with Frank Withers's orchestra to Moscow, where the photograph on the opposite page was taken. Bechet stands at the center with his arm around a woman's shoulder. He and other members of the Withers and Sam Wooding bands spent a lot of time at the Moscow Artist's Club that winter, the reed player Garvin Bushell remembered, because "that's where the girls were."

pushed a brightly painted cart piled with artificial fruit onstage, then played a long improvised blues. But the show made an international sensation of the American dance the French called "le Charleston"— and an international star of its lead dancer, a long-limbed teenaged chorus girl from St. Louis named Josephine Baker. The French thought all the black performers wonderfully exotic. Critics called Baker "the black venus that haunted Baudelaire" and compared her to a snake, a giraffe, a kangaroo. When she began to parade along the boulevards with a live cheetah, admirers speculated as to which "animal" was more wonderfully "savage," the one at the end of the leash or the one holding it. "The white imagination," Baker admitted privately, "is sure something when it comes to blacks."

After she left the show, the *Revue Nègre* collapsed and Bechet found himself touring the Soviet Union with a band led by the trombonist Frank Withers, an old friend from Will Marion Cook's Southern Syncopators. Then, he rejoined a much-reduced version of the original *Revue Nègre* that traveled to Berlin, Athens, Istanbul, Cairo, Oslo, Madrid, Prague, Rome. At the end, he admitted, the band was mostly made up of "Frenchmen, Germans and Cubans," but he still got star billing as "the Talking Saxophone," and he was bringing jazz to regions so remote that people sometimes wet their fingers and rubbed Bechet's hand or cheek to see if the color came off.

Wherever he went, his competitiveness and quick temper went, too. Somewhere along the way he had picked up a dog, a blend of Doberman and bulldog, whose pugnacity was almost a match for his own. When he got to Berlin in 1926 and learned that the American reedman Garvin Bushell was also in town, playing with Sam Wooding's orchestra, and that Bushell was the proud owner of a Great Dane named Caesar, he lost no time in calling upon him.

About four o'clock one morning, Bushell heard a knock on his door. It was Bechet.

"Sidney what you want? It's four o'clock in the morning."

"Just open the door, I want to tell you something."

I opened the door and he had this squatty dog with him.

"I brought my dog 'round here," Sidney said, "and I really want to let you know just how much dog you don't have, and how much dog I've got. So come on out in the hall and let 'em fight."

By now, Caesar's clawing in the back, trying to get me out of the way to get to this Doberman. I said, "Would you take your dog and get away from here?"

"No, we gonna fight 'em out here this morning in the hall." Bushell closed the door and went back to bed.

Before long, Bechet was back in Paris, playing in a Left Bank nightclub, drinking and gambling with fellow expatriates—and soon in trouble again. "It's like there's somebody else inside a man," Bechet once admitted, "somebody that's not really that man, and when a thing happens, an anger, . . . that other person takes over. That's not to make excuses. I know well enough it's me all the time. . . . I can be mean. It takes an awful lot; someone's got to do a lot to me. But when I do get mean, I can be powerful mean."

Early one morning he got into an altercation at a café just off the rue Fontaine with a banjo player named Gilbert Michael "Little Mike" McKendrick. One eyewitness remembered that the trouble began when McKendrick dared question Bechet's knowledge of the chords of a song they'd just played. A piano player from Chicago named Glover Compton took McKendrick's side—although he would later claim the subject of dispute had actually been Bechet's chronic unwillingness to pay for a round of drinks—and accelerated things further by sneering at Bechet as "Dixie-boy."

Bechet went home, got his revolver, and came back. By now, the morning rush hour had begun and the streets were filled with Parisians on their way to work. "Mike had [a pistol] in his pocket but didn't nobody know it," Compton remembered. "Mike stepped out onto the sidewalk and I stepped out right behind him. That's when the shooting started." Pedestrians scrambled to get out of the way. McKendrick missed Bechet, whose own shots spun past his intended target: one smashed into Compton Glover's leg; others slightly wounded two women.

Bechet and McKendrick were arrested, tried, and sentenced to prison. Bechet got fifteen months but was released after eleven, provided he promised to leave France right away. The two men eventually became friends again. But Bechet never forgave Glover Compton for siding against him, and when rumors reached him that the pianist was thinking of going to court for compensation for his shattered limb, he sent word that if Compton dared try it, he should watch out for the welfare of his other leg. Compton dropped his plans to sue.

THE SUN'S EYE

Louis Armstrong, the man Bechet considered his greatest rival, was a hero now on the South Side of Chicago. "I became quite a figure," he said, "especially with the gals" who flocked to see him at the Vendome. One of them was Alpha Smith, a pretty nineteen-year-old nursemaid who came to the theater twice a week and always made sure she sat in the front row, "where I could get a look at her legs." Armstrong had grown unhappy at home. He didn't much like being a sideman in his wife's band and was embarrassed when his fellow musicians called him "Henny," for henpecked. Lil's mother, who now lived with the Armstrongs and had never approved of jazz, thought Armstrong unworthy of her educated daughter and said so, loudly and often. "[T]here was no happiness there," he said. "We were always fussing and threatening to break up. If I sat on the bed after it was made up, why Lil would almost go into 'fits,' spasms, etc.—and poor Clarence, my adopted son with his nervous self used to almost jump out of his skin when Lil or Lil's mother would holler at him." And he had heard rumors that his wife had been seeing someone else while he was in New York. "Ever since I was a little boy in New Orleans hanging around those ole hustlers and pimps," he wrote, "they used to tell me, 'Never worry over no one woman—no matter how pretty or sweet she may be—Any time she . . . ain't playing the part of a wife, get yourself somebody else, also. And get another woman much better than the last one at all times.' Alpha commenced inviting me to her home." Soon he separated from Lil, took Clarence with him, and moved in with Alpha and her mother in their tiny apartment at Thirty-third and Cottage Grove. Both he and Clarence preferred it there, where no one nagged them, he said. They "didn't have to 'put on airs with a certain spoon for this and a certain fork for that.' . . . Alpha had fallen deeply in love with me by this time, anyway, and I was crazy about her."

In the spring of 1926, Armstrong had left the Dreamland, too, to join a band fronted by the violinist Carroll Dickerson at the Sunset Café, the most successful black-and-tan in town. It was billed as "Chicago's Brightest Pleasure Spot" and stood at the corner of Thirty-fifth and Calumet, just off the brightly lit South Side Stroll. Most of its customers were slumming whites, the pianist Earl Hines remembered. "Even the mixing

Alpha Smith, Louis Armstrong, and an unidentified friend mug for an amusement park photographer.

of white girls and colored pimps seemed to be an attraction." It was a tough place in a tough neighborhood. The owner of record was the mother of Joe Glaser, the crude-talking young man who managed it (and who would one day manage Armstrong himself), but it was really run by the mob and raided so often by the police, Hines said, that he used to run for the paddy wagon as soon as it pulled up in order to get a good seat. Al Capone—Armstrong remembered him as "a nice little cute fat boy"—was a frequent visitor.

Armstrong loved it. "I was young and strong, a flying cat, and God, I blew the people right out of the place. . . . The Sunset was packed every night. All the white people, all the nightlifers, the rich people from Sheridan Road and the big hotels would come out there on the South Side. . . . I'd

sing songs through a megaphone and four of us would close the show doing the Charleston."

Before long, Joe Glaser nudged Carroll Dickerson aside so that the band could be renamed "Louis Armstrong and his Stompers," and made Earl Hines its musical director. Hines was an innovator in his own right and played what came to be called "trumpet-style" piano, confidently spinning out complex, hornlike melodies with his right hand, while setting a looser rhythm with his left that helped push the music far beyond the strict beat of ragtime. He and Armstrong were rivals as well as friends, each spurring the other to greater heights. Together, they made an astonishing series of recordings—"Muggles," "Fireworks," "A Monday Date," "Skip the Gutter," "St. James Infirmary," "Basin Street Blues," "Save it Pretty Mama," "Beau Koo Jack," "Tight Like That," and an unprecedented trumpet-piano duet called "Weather Bird." "Making records we liked to do," Hines remembered. "Ideas used to come to us in the studio. . . . I think the public realized that we were really playing from the heart."

That "public" included the young white musicians who continued to come every night to play and learn. Armstrong called them "my boys." "I don't know how many musicians came to sit and jam with us," Hines said. "Whatever section they wanted to sit in, why a musician would step out from his chair. We all got a kick out of listening to each other, and we all tried to learn. We sat around waiting to see if these guys were actually going to come up with something new or different."

Armstrong was not the only great teacher at work at Thirty-fifth and Calumet. Joe Oliver was playing at the Plantation Café just across the street, and Jimmy Noone was appearing at an upstairs club called the Nest right next door to him. As many early mornings as they could manage, Eddie Condon and his friends headed for the Nest after the Sunset and the Plantation had closed. "We left our golf clubs there, our

The Carroll Dickerson band backs the floor show at Chicago's black-and-tan Sunset Café in 1922. Its leader stands at the center, his violin at his chin. When Louis Armstrong joined the orchestra four years later, Dickerson would be shunted aside in favor of the trumpet star.

instruments, our galoshes," he wrote. "There [we] listened to Jimmie Noone do things with a clarinet which no one had considered even probable. Jimmie was a chubby, congenial, gentle Negro. He had gold keys on his clarinet and almost every morning after one the clarinet was pointed down at [Frank] Teschemacher, who sat smack up against the bandstand, staring up at Jimmie. Benny Goodman was there often, too." One night, a flutist with the Chicago Symphony brought Maurice Ravel to hear Noone spin out chorus after chorus of "Four or Five Times." "Impossible!" Ravel muttered. "Then he tried to write down some of the runs Jimmie was playing, but he quickly gave it up," Condon said. "After that he just sat back like the rest of us, listening and staring at the gold keys."

When Joe Oliver first saw the sign go up outside the Sunset reading "The World's

The Plantation Café, where King Oliver led his Dixie Syncopators in 1926

Greatest Trumpet Player," he is supposed to have sent word to Armstrong to "Close those windows or I'll blow you off Thirty-fifth Street." The windows stayed open, Condon remembered, and, "with Louis and Oliver and Jimmie all playing within a hundred feet of each other . . . unless it happened in New Orleans I don't think so much good jazz was ever concentrated in so small an area. Around midnight you could hold your instrument in the middle of the street and the air would play it. That was music."

Louis Armstrong was walking through his South Side neighborhood with Bud Freeman one afternoon in the spring of 1928, when they stopped to listen to some street musicians play "Struttin' with Some Barbecue," one of the tunes recorded by the Hot Five. The trumpet player was laboring his way through Armstrong's own solo, note for note.

When the man had finished, Armstrong applauded politely, then stepped closer and

murmured, "Man, you're playing that too *slow.*"

"How would *you* know?" asked the trumpet player, indignant.

"I'm Louis Armstrong. That's my chorus you're playing."

When he passed by the next day, the musicians had put out a hand-lettered sign next to their tin cup: "Pupils of Louis Armstrong."

In a sense, all musicians now saw themselves as Armstrong's pupils, even the men who played the sweet, melodic dance music of Guy Lombardo. When Lombardo was working at the Granada Café on the North Side that same year, he made sure that Armstrong was not only admitted to the club—which otherwise had an exclusively white clientele—but that he was welcomed as an honored guest. "Louis said he was never treated any better anywhere in his life [than] he was by this famous orchestral group," a black newspaper reported after he and his friend, the drummer Zutty Singleton, had made a visit. "The Granada is one of the swellest night clubs in the country and is known from coast to coast. The minute the cornet king entered was the signal for the chord from the orchestra. . . . The boys were given a table in juxtaposition to the bandstand. They were wined and dined until the wee hours of the morning."

Armstrong would remain a lifelong admirer of Lombardo's orchestra. "I haven't heard no band that plays more perfect music," he said. No one else could play "that straight lead and make it sound so good."

All of Armstrong's records were now eagerly awaited by musicians, but one recording, made on June 28, 1928, would stand out above the rest. "West End Blues" was written by King Oliver and named for one of the resorts on Lake Pontchartrain that had played host to New Orleans bands like those in which he and his protégé had played back home, but Armstrong's treatment of it was unlike anything ever heard there—or anywhere else on earth.

It begins with an unaccompanied clarion cadenza, twelve seconds of bravura playing so dazzling that no other trumpeter has ever quite succeeded in replicating it, and so thrilling, the conductor and composer Gunther Schuller has written, that it "served notice for the first time that jazz had the potential to compete with the highest order of previously known expression." A reflective ensemble chorus follows; trombonist Fred Robinson has his mournful say. Then clarinetist Jimmy Strong restates the melody in his low register while Armstrong croons a heartfelt, wistful, wordless obbligato, as moving in its way as anything he

Earl Hines, 1928

ever played on the trumpet. Earl Hines adds an elegantly flowing piano chorus before Armstrong takes up his trumpet again and breaks into one of his most magisterial solos, beginning with a single note held without discernible effort for four measures, as if time itself meant nothing to him, and then plunging into the heart of the blues. "West End Blues" is one of the most sublime recordings in the history of music.

It almost didn't get made at all. According to Hines, when he and Armstrong and the other men got to the studio they knew only that Armstrong was going to open with his astonishing introduction and would need a rest soon thereafter to get his breath back. Having him scat a chorus solved that problem, but they still hadn't worked out a satisfactory finish. "We got to the end of it and Louis looked at me and I thought of the first thing I could think of, a little bit of a classical thing . . . and after I finished that I held the chord and Louis gave the downbeat with his head and everybody hit the chord on the end." But then, Zutty Singleton fumbled the final clop cymbal. The take was ruined. The engineers had to heat a new wax disc so that it would accept the imprint of the recording stylus, then start all over again. Singleton failed a second time. On the third take, he dropped his cymbal, which crashed to the floor. "So we spent hours in there with the hot wax," Hines continued, "and then sometimes after the hot wax was complete . . . the needle wasn't working. But it was a lot of fun—afterwards. . . . Louis and I stayed by that recording practically . . . two hours and we just knocked each other out because we had no idea it was going to turn out as good as it did."

"West End Blues" literally changed people's lives. Artie Shaw, then playing in a small-time dance band in Cleveland, heard the record and was so moved that in the summer of 1928 he resolved that he had to hear Armstrong play in person. By then, Arm-

Louis Armstrong's "West End Blues"

strong had moved on to headline at a splendid new South Side dance hall called the Savoy Ballroom. "I made a pilgrimage," Shaw recalled some seventy years later. "I took a week off and went up to Chicago . . . and I found my way to a place called the Savoy. And I sat on a bandstand which was about two feet off the ground . . . and just waited and he came on. And the first thing he played was 'West End Blues.' And I heard this cascade of notes coming out of a trumpet. No one had ever done that before. And so I was obsessed with the idea that this was what you had to do. Something that was your own, that had nothing to do with anybody else. . . . I was influenced by him, not in terms of notes, but in terms of the idea of doing what you are, *who* you are."

Young Max Kaminsky came to Chicago from Boston that same summer for more or less the same reason. He had dropped out of high school, he said, because he was usually too sleepy from playing somewhere the night before to pay attention to his teachers, and because none of his schoolmates—with the exception of his friend Harry Carney, who had now left school to join the Ellington band—"knew or cared

about the one thing I was interested in." He had no guarantee of work in Chicago, but he had heard Armstrong's Hot Fives and Hot Sevens—which, he said, had sounded like "just a lot of clatter" to most of the dance-band musicians with whom he'd been playing in New England—and decided that "if this was the kind of jazz going on in Chicago, then Chicago was the place to be."

A chance meeting with Bud Freeman introduced him to the ragtag crew of jazz-mad young whites whose version of New Orleans music the critics would eventually label "Chicago style." Since 1922, when the old Austin High Gang began haunting first the Friar's Inn and then the Lincoln Gardens, their numbers had grown steadily. The drummer Gene Krupa and cornetist Muggsy Spanier were both Chicagoans, but George Wettling, also a drummer, was from Topeka, Kansas; pianist Jess Stacy came from Bird's Point, Missouri, and had played on boats belonging to the same Streckfus line that had employed Armstrong and Beiderbecke. The cornetist Wingy Manone, who had lost his right arm in a childhood streetcar accident, hailed from New Orleans and remembered first hearing jazz on its "main stem—when the colored bands in trucks advertising a dance, battled it out."

"Though barely in their twenties themselves," Kaminsky wrote, "these men had been deeply immersed in the music for six or seven years, absorbing it firsthand from the New Orleans jazzmen while developing their own style and feeling, whereas I had heard it only in tantalizing dribbles and snatches." He somehow landed a job nonetheless, playing at a Chinese restaurant with Frank Teschemacher and George Wettling, with whom, he said, he "fitted in as naturally as a baseball bat fit into Babe Ruth's hands. . . . It seemed as if every day was the Fourth of July."

One evening, Wettling and Wingy Manone took him to hear Armstrong play

IT BEATS SEX

Arthur Arshawsky as a patriotic little boy in 1914, and (at the far left of the photograph at right) reborn as Artie Shaw, clarinetist in the Joe Cantor orchestra, one of several bands in which he would play before striking out on his own.

Arthur Jacob Arshawsky was born on the Lower East Side of Manhattan in 1910, the only child of immigrant dressmakers who eventually separated. When Arthur was seven, the family moved to New Haven, Connecticut, where the boy found himself an outcast, tormented by schoolmates who called him "sheeny" and "kike" and "Christ-killer." "My father'd left home," he remembered, "and I didn't like my life very much. I didn't like school, I didn't like anything. So it was a choice between getting a machine gun or an instrument. Luckily I found an instrument."

He visited a vaudeville theater and saw a musician in a snappy white-striped blazer kneel down on one knee in the spotlight and play "Dreamy Melody" on a shiny gold saxophone. "That did it," he remembered: music would be his way to fame and fortune. He worked in a grocery store to earn money for a saxophone, practiced so hard the inside of his lower lip bled, played amateur shows, and formed his own four-piece Peter Pan Novelty Orchestra, which earned him two dollars a night playing dances. School was

now only an interruption. "I was determined that I would play this instrument, so I managed to get flunked. I worked it out so that I got flunked two months in a row, and they threw me out. And despite my mother's pleas to the principal of Hillhouse High in New Haven, they wouldn't have me. So that meant I was free to play."

Like Benny Goodman, who would one day be his great rival, he adopted the clarinet, and joined a touring dance band as a full-time professional. Whenever he could, he went to Harlem to study with Duke Ellington's mentor, Willie the Lion Smith—whose fond nickname for him was "Snow White." His first musical models were Bix Beiderbecke and Frankie Trumbauer.

Eager to be accepted by audiences everywhere, and then "ashamed of being a Jew," he said, Arthur Jacob Arshawsky changed his name to Artie Shaw. He became one of the best-known bandleaders of the swing era but it was the challenge of improvisation that kept him fascinated:

You're aiming at something that cannot be done, physically can't be done. So you're trying to play a horn, and here's this clumsy series of keys on a piece of wood and you're trying to manipulate them with the reed and the throat muscles and what they call an embouchure, and you're trying to make something happen that never happened before. You're trying to make a sound that no one ever got before, or a combination of sounds creating an emotion. You're trying to take an inarticulate thing and take notes and make them come out in a way that moves you. If it moves you, it's going to move others. But very rarely does it happen, and when it does you remember it for the rest of your life. What can I say? It's the most exuberant experience you can have. It beats sex. It beats great food. It beats anything.

at the Savoy. As soon as they got inside, Armstrong came over to greet Wettling and Manone. They introduced their new friend, and Kaminsky and Armstrong shook hands. "From listening to his records I already had some inkling of the warmth and power of the man," Kaminsky wrote, "but I was totally unprepared for that remarkable penetrating awareness underneath the genial, easygoing manner. All his senses seem to receive impressions of you; you feel he's not so much sizing you up as opening his mind to you, like a receiver set. You can't fake it with Louis. He can tell."

Kaminsky wasn't prepared for the power of Armstrong's playing, either. The first number was "West End Blues," and when Armstrong began his bravura introduction, Kaminsky was literally stunned. "I sent one quivering look at Wingy and George and took my leave. The sheer loveliness of Bix's tone and feeling had captured me, but the combination of Louis's dazzling virtuosity and sensational brilliance of tone so overwhelmed me that I felt as if I had stared into the sun's eye. All I could think of doing was to run away and hide till the blindness left me."

MAY IT PLEASE YOU

At one-thirty in the morning on February 7, 1928, federal agents swooped down on a dozen of Chicago's leading North Side nightspots, took the names of every one of the hundreds of startled patrons caught with liquor on their tables, and padlocked the doors. A brand-new "hip flask" law now held that even those who provided ice and gingerale for patrons to mix with their own alcohol were liable to prosecution. Vice raids, launched by William Dever, Big Bill Thompson's Republican successor as mayor, had already closed several black-and-tans on the South Side. "Chicago was once the hottest café town in the United States," *Variety* reported, "famous for siz-

zling music, torrid night life, a great little spot for the great little guys. But that's history now. Night by night it gets tougher for the cabarets."

It got tougher for Chicago musicians, too. Some two hundred of them would lose their jobs by May. One hundred and fifty more were already out of work—or about to be—as popular enthusiasm for *The Jazz Singer* convinced theater owners to install equipment for talking pictures and dispense with the expensive orchestras that had accompanied the silents. Other musicians now felt themselves in actual physical danger. The music business in Chicago had often involved a certain amount of personal risk: a few years earlier, Bud Freeman had not been wholly reassured when the mobster who owned the club in which he was working took him aside and said, "Buddy, don't you ever worry about anybody in this here joint because nobody in this here joint will hurt you unless he gets paid for it." But now, as business slumped, Al Capone and his rivals began to war openly over the shrinking profits. Bombs gutted the Café de Paris and the Plantation Club, where Joe Oliver had been playing. An exodus of musicians began. Most headed for New York—Joe Oliver, Eddie Condon, Dave Tough, Gene Krupa, and Max Kaminsky among them.

The Ben Pollack Orchestra had led the way in February. Now billed as "The Big Band with the Little Leader," it played at a place called the Little Club at first, then at the Million Dollar Pier in Atlantic City, finally at the elegant Park Central Hotel, where the refugees from mob-run Chicago were made to feel more at home than they may have liked when the big-time gambler Arnold Rothstein, shot by persons unknown, staggered downstairs to die underneath the balcony on which they were playing.

Benny Goodman was still in the band, now playing alongside his old friends Jimmy McPartland and Bud Freeman as well as his brother, Harry. And Glenn Miller had been replaced by a big, bearlike, hard-

Jack Teagarden, 1924

drinking, hard-living young trombone player who was changing the way his instrument was played—Jack Teagarden.

Born and brought up in Texas cattle country, Teagarden began playing the trombone at the age of eight. His arm was then too short to manipulate the slide much beyond the bell, so he taught himself to reach low notes by developing a versatile embouchure that was the envy of every brass player who ever watched him on the bandstand. Once, when a pianist asked him "how come he never seemed to knock himself out going for low notes in fast passages," Teagarden answered, "Man, I don't like workin' that hard—I just use my lip." He had also still been just a boy when he learned to love the shouts and moans and bent notes that were the heart of blues music by listening night after night to Negro tent revivals held in a vacant lot just across the street from his family home. "The music seemed just as natural to me as anything. I could hum along with 'em with no trouble

HARD, HARD TIMES

In 1928, the year before the Great Crash, Bessie Smith had recorded "Poor Man's Blues."

> *Mister rich man, rich man, open up your*
>   *heart and mind*
> *Mister rich man, rich man, open up your*
>   *heart and mind*
> *Give the poor man a chance, help stop*
>   *these hard, hard times.*
> *Please listen to my pleadin', 'cause*
>   *I can't stand these hard times long,*
> *Aw listen to my pleadin', 'cause I can't*
>   *stand these hard times long,*
> *They'll make an honest man do things*
>   *that you know is wrong. . . .*

She had been singing then about the plight of the people left behind by the prosperity of the

Andy Kirk's Clouds of Joy take time out along the road at Fort Smith, Arkansas, in 1929. Violinist Claude Williams kneels at the far left. Andy Kirk, second from the right, then still playing tuba, had only recently become leader. No band would work harder or travel more during the lean Depression years.

twenties. Now that the whole country was hurting, not even the blues seemed able to ease its pain. "Nobody wants to hear blues no more," Bessie Smith said. "Times is hard."

No crisis since the Civil War affected Americans more seriously than did the Great Depression. As the 1930s began, one out of every four wage-earners was without work, more than 15 million men and women. In Mississippi, on a single day in 1932, one quarter of the entire state went under the auctioneer's hammer. Thousands of jobless men wandered the landscape. Dust storms born in Texas and the Dakotas would soon begin to darken skies all the way east to Washington. Prices of wheat and corn and cotton fell so low that crops were left to rot in the fields. In Boston, children with cardboard soles in their shoes walked to school past silent shoe factories with padlocks on the doors. In New York, a jobless couple moved into a cave in Central Park and stayed there for a year. They could find nowhere else to live.

The music business came close to collapsing. Membership in the American Federation of Musicians fell by one third—even after their dues were cut in half, many musicians could no longer pay them. More than one hundred New York dance halls closed their doors and nearly half the theaters on Broadway were shut down or turned into movie houses. In Chicago, shivering jobless men burned old phonograph records to keep warm. American record companies, which had sold more than 100 million discs a year in the midtwenties, were soon selling just 6 million. Okeh, Gennett, and Paramount records all went out of business. The RCA Victor Talking Machine Company stopped making record players altogether for a time, and sold radios instead. Even Paul Whiteman had to lay off ten members of his thirty-man orchestra and ask the rest to take a 15 percent cut in pay.

"We . . . didn't realize how little chance we had in New York," Eddie Condon wrote. "The only place we could play was in our rooms, at our own request." He and Max Kaminsky were eventually locked out of their hotel in midwinter for failing to pay their rent. "We gnawed at each other's wrists," Condon recalled. "We bled to death in those years." When Kaminsky was finally lucky enough to land a job, he found himself running his own breadline every evening, passing out fifty-cent pieces to musicians less fortunate than he.

Hard times hit black Americans hardest. In some northern cities, six out of ten African-American workers lost their jobs. Poor southern migrants continued to come north, crowding into neighborhoods already packed with people, competing for the fast-dwindling number of jobs. Black businesses failed, crushing the entrepreneurial spirit that had been an essential element of the Negro Renaissance. The collapse of a black-owned bank in Chicago took with it all the savings of the musician's union's black local.

Harlem would never recover, but its speakeasies and dance halls, nightclubs and ballrooms continued to flourish for a time, as black residents and white visitors alike sought ways to forget their troubles, at least for an evening. The Cotton Club remained Harlem's most glamorous nightclub. But the community's biggest and most beautiful ballroom was the Savoy. It covered a whole city block on Lenox Avenue between 140th and 141st Streets, employed two bands at once so that the music need never stop, and was so popular with dancers that its maple-and-mahogany floor had to be replaced every three years. Just fifty cents on weeknights—seventy-five cents on Sundays—the Savoy billed itself as "the Home of Happy Feet." All the best bands appeared there. So did Harlem's most admired dancers. George "Shorty" Snowden was on the floor nearly every night. It was he who in 1928 had come up with the new dance filled with improvised "breakaways"—flinging his partner out and improvising solo steps before bringing her back again—which came to be called the lindy hop after the hero of the hour, Charles Lindbergh. Snowden's friendly rival, George "Twist Mouth" Ganaway, was also a constant presence; his long legs, spectacular dancing, and distinctive ensemble—blinding white from his shoes to the broad-brimmed hat he never took off—all helped distract lookers-on from the disfigurement that had prompted his

Music helped lift the spirits of a sharecropper's family in rural Louisiana during the Depression.

Chick Webb at work. "This man," the great drummer Jo Jones said of him, "taught me something that I had almost forgotten. He taught me how important the drum was."

would not dance, because as much as these particular people in this idiom love to dance, and as obvious as it is that this is dance-oriented music from the beginning—the whole conception is based on percussive dance-oriented statements—these people were so impressed with what Ellington was doing to the music that they'd dress up and just sit, and Duke wanted them to dance too. But people would say, "Yes, well I'll buy the record and dance to that at home but he's *present.*" So, people anticipated him coming to town. It was like a sacred event.

As Ellington's fame grew, so did his popularity with women. He regarded them all as "flowers," his sister Ruth recalled, and they "fell on their faces in front of him." All of which angered his wife, Edna, and, when she discovered he was having an affair with a dancer at the Cotton Club, she slashed his cheek. He would carry the scar for the rest of his life, and deflected everyone who dared asked him about it. "Oh this?" he replied to one brash television interviewer much later in his life. "I have three stories. Taxi accident. What's the other one? Oh, Heidelberg. Heidelberg, you know—old Heidelberg. And sabers. You know, you stand toe-to-toe and the first one to move back loses? So, if you don't move back, you get the scar. . . . Then there's another one, too. I can't think of it at the moment. More personal."

Ellington and his wife never divorced, but they would never live together again, either. In 1931, he sent for his father and mother and sister to join him, his son, and his new love, a Cotton Club dancer named Mildred Dixon, in a big new apartment at 381 Edgecombe Avenue, in Harlem's best neighborhood, Sugar Hill. His father was reluctant at first—like Benny Goodman's father, he did not like the idea of living off his son—but his mother came right away. In Daisy Ellington's eyes, her son could do no wrong. Soon, she was happily cleaning

and cooking for him again, and longing for the moment each evening when he walked in the door and announced, "Mother, I'm home to dine." Ellington showered her with gifts and refused to listen to her protests at his extravagance: "Mother," he said, "if you don't take these things, I won't work." She received ropes of pearls, a fur coat, and a chauffeur-driven Pierce-Arrow so that she could follow her son from engagement to engagement. "After a couple of thousand people had stopped applauding," his sister remembered, "my mother was still applauding."

AIN'T THAT SOMETHING?

"Chicago's own Louis Armstrong and his orchestra are the current rage in New York," the columnist Dave Peyton assured the readers of the Chicago *Defender* early in 1929. "They have taken the city by storm." Armstrong was headlining in Harlem *and* playing on Broadway now, and his recordings were bringing him a still-broader audience. The breakthrough had been his version of a Jimmy McHugh–Dorothy Fields love song, "I Can't Give You Anything But Love." He had been playing such tunes in person for years—Art Hodes remembered having heard him improvise for thirty minutes on Noel Coward's "Poor Little Rich Girl" back at the Chicago Savoy—but black performers were only rarely given standard pop songs to sing on records. Soon, Louis Armstrong would record scores of such tunes—"Ain't Misbehavin'," "Stardust," "Some of These Days," "When You're Smiling," "Rockin' Chair," "Body and Soul" —transforming each into something altogether new, altogether his. In the process, he would revolutionize American singing, just as he had revolutionized instrumental jazz. He brought scatting into mainstream music; altered melodies and shifted rhythms to suit his own purposes; infused the most inane lyrics with honest feeling; and

brought to singing the same irrepressible sense of swing that had already changed forever the way instrumentalists approached their music. "Louis Armstrong," said Bing Crosby, "is the beginning—and the end—of American music."

He was a single act now. He had lost his job at Connie's Inn after his men failed once too often to turn up on time, and had then decided, under Tommy Rockwell's prodding, finally to break up the band and move out on his own.

Among the first Broadway tunes he had recorded was Fats Waller's "Black and Blue," originally written for *Hot Chocolates* as a complaint by a dark-skinned woman about her man's preference for lighter-skinned rivals. Armstrong transformed it, without a hint of self-pity, into a song about being black in a world run by whites. "In those days if one black man called another man 'black' that was fighting words," Arvell Shaw, Armstrong's bassist later in life, remembered. "But Louis was the first man I heard to say, 'You're black, be proud of it. You're black, you're not white, you're not yellow, you're black—be *proud* of it.' He was saying that when it was so very unpopular."

Armstrong was proud of his race, but unblinking about the reality of race relations in America. When a friend in California suggested that he come west on his own and try his luck in Los Angeles, he was initially apprehensive: "Naturally in those days," he wrote much later, "the minute a colored man gets off a train anywhere west or south he would have his head whipped worse than a kettle drum." But Armstrong went anyway and quickly found himself a hero in Los Angeles, just as he had been in Chicago and New York. He spent nearly a year there, fronting Les Hite's band at Frank Sebastian's New Cotton Club in Culver City, getting to know the movie stars who dropped in every night from the MGM studio lot right next door, and impressing West Coast musicians precisely as he had thrilled

Before the fall: Louis Armstrong in Culver City, 1930. Armstrong stands next to the owner of the New Cotton Club, Frank Sebastian, and the director of the band that backed him there, Les Hite. Lionel Hampton, then Hite's drummer, is third from the left.

their eastern counterparts. "Aspirants for Louis' coveted title" of trumpet king, reported a correspondent for the Pittsburgh *Courier,* "have sat around the Cotton Club night after night trying to figure out how the dark boys do it. Some of them are getting pretty good, but every time they think they have stolen his thunder Louis comes up with a brand-new lead." The trombonist Lawrence Brown remembered that "People used to come from way up around Seattle to hear him. Every trumpet player at that time tried

to play *one* of his choruses." There were more memorable recordings, too—including "Sweethearts on Parade," "I'm a Ding-Dong Daddy," "I'm Confessin'," "If I Could Be with You," "Shine," "Memories of You," "Just a Gigolo," and "Blue Yodel No. 9," on which he played obbligatos behind and around the vocal by the "singing brakeman," Jimmie Rodgers, demonstrating how closely allied are the blues and country-and-western traditions—a fact largely ignored by enthusiasts for both musics until Ray

Charles revealed the truth of it again more than three decades later.

Then, potential disaster struck. *Variety* reported the bare facts in March 1931.

Vic Berton, drummer with Abe Lyman's Band, and Louis Armstrong, colored trumpet artist in Sebastian's Cotton Club in Culver City, were arrested at the Cotton Club by narcotics officers and arraigned on charges of possessing marijuana, a dopeweed

In the lobby of the Royal Theater in Baltimore, Louis Armstrong distributes free coal to an unidentified woman, 1931. His manager, Johnny Collins, on the right, made sure his star got plenty of publicity out of his largesse, but Armstrong's generosity was genuine. "I came up through life the hard way just like those folks," he said. "And they made it their business to come backstage and thank me—of course, it caused me to stick out my chest with pride." The inscription on this copy of the photograph was written to the clarinetist Milton "Mezz" Mezrow, who supplied Armstrong and a good many other musicians with marijuana.

used in cigarettes. . . . Charge against them is a felony punishable by not less than six months and no more than six years in the penitentiary.

Armstrong had been an enthusiastic "viper" —marijuana-user—since returning to Chicago from New York in 1925. To him, pot was "an assistant, a friend, [and] a nice cheap drunk," safer than alcohol and akin to the natural herbs and grasses with which his mother had fed and cured him as a boy. Vic Berton had been sitting in with Armstrong's band at the New Cotton Club that evening—the former drummer with Bix Beiderbecke's Wolverines, he was so good that the band's young drummer, Lionel Hampton, had turned over his sticks to him the minute he walked in—and at intermission the two old friends had walked out into the parking lot to light up.

At that point, two policemen closed in, confiscated the evidence, and took them both into custody. Armstrong, with vivid memories of his own boyhood encounters with the New Orleans police, worried he would be beaten on the way to the station house and asked the officers not to "hit me in the 'chops.' " They turned out to be fans, and one told him that they would never even have been arrested had an envious bandleader playing nearby not turned them in.

Armstrong faced six months in jail and a thousand-dollar fine. As soon as Tommy Rockwell got word of his star's arrest, he dispatched a thug named Johnny Collins to see what he could do to get Armstrong out of jail. No one is sure what happened next. Some claimed that Collins used underworld connections to influence the judge. Vic Berton's brother, Ralph, suggested that it

was actually his brother's boss, Abe Lyman, who exercised political pull. In any case, Armstrong and Berton were given suspended sentences and released. "I went to work that night," Armstrong recalled, and "wailed—just like nothing happened. . . . I laughed real loud when several movie stars came up to the bandstand while we played a dance set and told me they thought 'marijuana' was a chick . . . that really fractured me!"

Armstrong left California for Chicago a few days later. Collins traveled with him and at some point evidently told Armstrong that Tommy Rockwell was no longer interested in acting as his manager. Armstrong signed on with Collins, instead. Nothing seemed to have changed since his release from the Waif's Home or the New Orleans Parish Prison. "If you didn't have a white captain to back you in the old days—to put his hand on your shoulder—you was just a damn sad nigger," he explained many years later. "If a Negro had the proper white man to reach the law and say, 'What the hell do you mean locking up MY nigger?' Then—quite naturally—the law would walk him free. Get in that jail *without* your white boss, and yonder comes the chain gang!"

Armstrong played a triumphant homecoming engagement at the Regal Theater, then took a ten-man band made up mostly of New Orleans musicians into a new West Side black-and-tan called the Showboat. There, new trouble started. Collins had lied to Armstrong: Rockwell had never intended to drop him; he still believed himself Armstrong's manager and in fact had signed him up for a return engagement at Connie's Inn in Harlem. Armstrong wasn't interested. He had not forgotten that Connie Immerman had fired him and his band the year before. "I did not want any part of those people ever again," he wrote. "I am just that way. If you kick my ass once you can bet I won't come back if I can help it so you can kick it again. . . . Connie's Inn was going down by degrees and at that time I was the Rage of the Nation."

But neither Rockwell—nor Connie Immerman's silent partner, Dutch Schultz—liked to be disappointed. First, two thugs tried and failed to shake Armstrong down. "We were just trying to get him to change managers," one of them told the policeman who arrested him. Then, someone started a fight in front of the bandstand. A woman was knocked senseless with a chair. Armstrong just kept playing. "Things like that never frighten me," he said. "I've seen so much of that bullshit during my days of playing music." Finally, a man with a revolver turned up in his dressing room. Armstrong was going to play Connie's Inn, the man insisted, and he was going to leave for New York the next day. Then, he marched Armstrong to a phone booth, where the voice of someone in New York—Armstrong later said he recognized it but would never tell anyone who it was—warned him not to fail to be on the morning train.

To get the menacing voice off the phone—and the gunman out of his dressing room—Armstrong said he'd be on it. He didn't mean it: "I ain't goin' to New York," he told Collins. "But get this straight—I ain't staying in Chicago neither. I'd rather take a walk through the cemetery at midnight." Instead, he and his band boarded a bus headed south the next morning. Behavior like that—open defiance of mobsters—at first seems out of character for the infinitely agreeable Louis Armstrong whom audiences thought they knew for nearly half a century. Max Kaminsky saw deeper, to the steel within.

This roly, rotund brown-skinned man with his marvelously expressive face, the comfortable broad-nostriled snub nose, the lips scarred from all that blowing, the wise, knowing, and innocent eyes, radiates warmth and energy like a cozy fireplace. But unaffected and unphony as he is, Louis has always been King. The white people didn't know about him for a long while, but he always had an enor-

On Armstrong's 1931 tour of the Deep South white patrons were welcome at the dance heralded in the newspaper notice at the top—but only to watch. In Memphis, Tennessee (above), whites alone were allowed on the floor.

mous following among the colored people right from the start. He was always regal; from the very beginning, the musicians, colored and white, always came to *him,* and he'd hold court wherever he happened to be—

backstage at a theater or night club, between takes at a recording studio, or soaking in a steaming tub in his hotel bathroom. . . . Louis knows who he is. Not only that, he knows who you are, and though he is the most approachable, most genuine person in the world, and though his charity is legendary, you can't mess with Louis. . . . [His] trumpet comes first—that's Louis's first law. To him his playing is a gift, and he'll just sit there and think about the horn before he gets ready to play—accepting his gift he calls it. . . . Louis has never forgotten what he wants to do—just play that music—and in doing that he has done everything.

In June of 1931, Collins booked Armstrong into New Orleans. He hadn't been back to his hometown for nine years and wasn't sure what kind of reception he would get, but when his train pulled into the same station from which he had left to join Joe Oliver in Chicago, a huge cheering crowd and eight marching bands, led by his old neighborhood friends from the Zulu Social Aid and Pleasure Club, were waiting on the platform. "All in all," Armstrong recalled years later, "I think that day was the happiest day in my life."

He visited the Colored Waif's Home, where he had learned to play the cornet as a boy, delighted in a "Louis Armstrong Special" cigar specially manufactured in his honor, and outfitted a baseball team, Louis Armstrong's Secret Nine.

He had a three-month contract to play at the Suburban Gardens, a big restaurant on the edge of town with its own live radio program. Only whites were allowed inside, and several who had played with Armstrong as boys greeted him warmly. But some ten thousand blacks gathered along the riverbank in the darkness to hear their hero play through the open windows. And when the broadcaster who was supposed to act as master of ceremonies muttered

HOMECOMING

"The last of the magnolias were still on the trees, the smell of them on the air," Louis Armstrong remembered, when he returned to New Orleans in the spring of 1931. But it had been nine years since he'd gone north to join King Oliver and he wondered if people "had forgotten me in all the time I'd been away. But I soon found they had not. . . . As soon as I got off the train the crowd went crazy. They picked me up and put me on their shoulders and started a parade down the center of Canal Street. . . . My, my it is a wonderful feeling to go back to your home town and find that while you were away you have become a big man."

(Top, left) Louis Armstrong, mobbed by old friends and new fans in front of the Astoria Hotel at Rampart and Gravier Streets in the heart of the neighborhood in which he'd spent his boyhood. Armstrong is the blurred but grinning figure in the open collar standing at the left. (Bottom, left) Captain Peter Jones, the man who ran the Colored Waif's Home, welcomes back his institution's most celebrated inmate. (Below) A special five-cent cigar rushed onto the market in New Orleans just in time for its namesake's arrival

(Opposite, top left) Armstrong and the pianist in his band, Charlie Alexander, clowning at the WSMB microphone during their three-month engagement at the Suburban Gardens. (Opposite, right) Armstrong's Secret Nine, and its proud sponsor. Most of the players were fellow members of the Zulu Social Aid and Pleasure Club and their win/loss record was said to have been damaged by their reluctance to dirty their splendid white uniforms by sliding. (Opposite, bottom) Armstrong, center, and the members of his orchestra sit in with the latest version of the outfit that gave him his start—now renamed the Municipal Boys Home Band. Peter Davis, the band manager who had once thought Armstrong unfit to join its ranks, stands at the far right.

So many people clamored for tickets to see them at the Salle Playel in Paris that two additional concerts had to be added to the schedule.

Best of all, according to Greer, Mills saw to it that an American flag flew above every hotel in which the orchestra stayed.

> In honor of us. Just like they flew the flag if a diplomat come and stay in the hotel. . . . We carried the flag and the prestige of my people. I am an American Negro. You hear the cats say, 'Black this . . .' I'm an *American Negro,* pal. We carried the flag for the American Negro . . . everywhere. We carried the flag for the dignity of the American Negro all over the world. We were treated with the utmost respect.

"The main thing I got in Europe was *spirit,*" Ellington told a reporter after he and the band got home that fall. "That kind of thing gives you the courage to go on. If they think I'm *that* important, then maybe . . . our music does mean something." Americans may still have seen him mostly as a bandleader, but some Europeans considered him a serious composer. "A musician," he said, "should have both Europe *and* America."

A twelve-week tour of the South followed the band's return. Even for men accustomed to the American road, the contrast was startling: "Of course all the places we played down there," Harry Carney said, "they were happy to hear the band. The drag was they'd be screaming and applauding and afterward you'd have to go back across the tracks. . . . In Europe we were royalty; in Texas we were back in the colored section. It was some adjustment, but we were young and could take it." The music critic of the Dallas *News* called Ellington "something of an African Stravinsky" who had "erased the color line" between jazz and classical music. But black fans in the South had to hear him from the balcony of the theaters he played; white hotels and restaurants excluded him and his band.

Daisy Ellington had taught her son from childhood simply to rise above all unpleasantness; after his southern tour, rather than again suffer the indignity of being turned away from hotels and restaurants, he and Mills arranged for the orchestra to travel in its own private Pullman cars so that the men could eat and sleep in the railroad yards, and saw to it that a fleet of taxicabs was waiting to ferry them to and from their appearances.

"They never *seen* nobody like us," Sonny Greer said.

> They had heard different colored aggregations that come through on a little raggedy-ass bus, but we had our own Pullman car, our own baggage car, . . . full possession of the diner, nobody could come in our Pullman car because the door stayed locked, because people autographing annoy you. . . . We had our own lighting equipment, own stage, one of the first bands to use a roll-down stage, . . . one of the first bands with all them overhead pinpoint lights, electrician. They never seen that. That's the way Irving Mills made us travel. . . . We didn't have to go through that junk— colored over this side, white over this.

"The natives would come by and they would say. 'What on earth is that?' " Ellington remembered. "And we would say, 'That's the way the President travels.' You do the very best with what you've got."

Ellington and his orchestra would always represent the very best, as the young Ralph Ellison remembered seeing for himself when the band turned up in Oklahoma City that year.

> Then Ellington and his great orchestra came to town—came with their uniforms, their sophistication, their skills; their golden horns, their flights of controlled and disciplined fantasy; came with their art, their special sound; came with Ivie Anderson and

Ethel Waters singing and dazzling the eye with their high-brown beauty and with the richness and bright feminine flair of their costumes and promising manners. They were news from the great wide world, an example and a goal, and I wish that all those who write so knowledgeably about Negro boys having no masculine figures with whom to identify would consider the long national and international career of Ellington and his band, and the thousands of one-night stands played in the black communities of this nation. Where in the white community, in any white community, could there have been found examples such as these? Who were so worldly, who so elegant, who so mockingly creative? Who were so skilled at their given trade and who treated the social limitations placed in their paths with greater disdain?

SOMETHING MUST BE DONE

In July of 1933, a month after Ellington's overseas tour began, John Hammond himself set sail for England, aboard the steamer *Homeric.* When he found that among his fellow passengers were Louis Armstrong and his companion, Alpha Smith, traveling abroad for a second time, he eagerly sought them out. One evening in Armstrong's stateroom Hammond was witness to a violent argument between him and his drunken manager, Johnny Collins, who was telling his star what he should and should not play onstage. Armstrong was resisting.

Collins became abusive. "Called me a nigger in the middle of the ocean," Armstrong remembered, "he's my manager and he's never done it before. But, you can see that 'nigger' brings out your fucking thoughts sometimes. I said, 'You know, Mr. Collins, I have been in show business for a long time. I'm an old hustler [from] way

Thomas "Fats" Waller ate more food, drank more liquor, played as much piano—and seemed to be having more fun than any other musician of his time. He was a big man, nearly six feet tall, sometimes weighed more than three hundred pounds, and wore size fifteen shoes. He routinely downed three steaks for lunch, drank a quart or more of gin or whiskey at every recording session, and called the liquor he drank upon awakening each morning, his "liquid ham-and-eggs."

The stride piano master, James P. Johnson, was his friend and teacher, and he never lost the mighty, rumbling left hand Johnson had taught him. But the touch of his right hand was light, melodic, irrepressible. "Concentrate on the melody," he told one interviewer. "You got to hang on to the melody and never let it get boresome." He was never boresome. He sold some four hundred songs to publishers for as little as fifty dollars—and he sometimes sold them several times. "You had to buy them," said the music publisher Irving Mills, "even though you knew [he] probably had sold it elsewhere down the street or even across the hall." Waller's tunes included "Ain't Misbehavin'," "Honeysuckle Rose," "Squeeze Me," "I'm Gonna Sit Right Down and Write Myself a Letter," "Blue Turning Grey Over You,"

"The Joint Is Jumpin'. " Waller also made almost seven hundred records, and appeared on countless radio programs, kidding his own music and everybody else's, too. No song was too dreary for him to make memorable.

But there was another side to Fats Waller, hidden from his fans. He was the favorite child of a mother whose early death he never quite got over and the son of a grim clergyman whom he permanently alienated when at the age of fifteen he chose to play what the old man called "the Devil's music." A white tough stabbed him when he was a boy; another shot and badly wounded his brother, standing right next to him; and a cross was burned on his lawn when he moved his family to Queens long after he became a recording star. His first marriage went bad and he twice did time for failing to pay alimony. A second liaison was

happier, but he spent little time with the two sons that were the products of it. He grew bitter at having sold away his songs for so little money, and could only rarely persuade record executives to let him play on the instrument that was his first love—the pipe organ. He held a solo recital at Carnegie Hall in 1942, but too many congratulatory toasts before the performance undercut his skills that night, and reviewers were unforgiving. His relentless high living caught up with him the following year. He developed pneumonia while appearing at a club in California and died in his sleep aboard the train that was carrying him home to New York. When Louis Armstrong heard the news he cried all night. "Some little people has music in them," James P. Johnson remembered. "But Fats, he was all music—and you know how big he was."

Fats Waller and the camera had a symbiotic relationship. (Top, left) He goes for a stroll in London with his English bulldog as a prop; (above) he cheerfully mugs for the camera forty-four times.

THE MUSIC OF THE DEGENERATE

Jazz music, built upon the principle of free expression, has always made dictators uncomfortable. The Soviet regime was ambivalent about jazz, at first. Ragtime had been popular under the last czar and touring American musicians like Sidney Bechet were still warmly received in the years following the Revolution. Things changed when Josef Stalin took power. In a 1928 article for *Pravda* entitled "The Music of the Gross," the novelist Maxim Gorky laid out the party's new position. Jazz was capitalist poison being deliberately spread among black Americans to keep them from dwelling on their status as slaves of the System.

> [T]here are rumblings, wails and howls like the smarting of a metal pig, the shriek of a donkey, or the amorous croaking of a monstrous frog. This insulting chaos of insanity pulses to a throbbing rhythm. Listening for a few minutes to these wails, one involuntarily imagines an orchestra of sexually driven madmen conducted by a man-stallion brandishing a huge genital member. The monstrous bass belches out English words; a wild horn wails piercingly, calling to mind the cries of a raving camel; a drum pounds monotonously; a nasty little pipe tears at one's ears; a saxophone emits its quacking nasal sound. Fleshy hips sway, and thousands of heavy feet tread and shuffle. The music of

the degenerate ends finally with a deafening thud, as though a case of pottery had been flung down to earth from the skies.

Jazz and jazz dancing were now seen as anti-Soviet. Schoolchildren who confessed to liking jazz were made to confess their errors in front of their classmates. Anyone caught playing American jazz records was subject to six months in jail.

Then, in 1933, Adolf Hitler came to power in Germany. Within weeks, the Nazis banned what they called "Nigger-Jew" music from the radio. Brownshirts broke up jazz concerts. National contests were organized to find a suitably Aryan substitute for jazz—Neue Deutsche Tanzmusik—"New German Dance Music." The result was leaden and cloying, without a hint of improvisation. Jews were eventually driven from the musician's union. Records made by artists identified as black or Jewish were dropped from some German record catalogues. Benny Goodman's records were formally banned when the Nazis learned that he was Jewish in 1937, but Artie Shaw went right on selling because the propaganda ministry had somehow become convinced that he was the son of the Irish writer George Bernard Shaw.

As the Nazis railed against the jazz "baccilus," the Soviet Comintern radically altered its attitude toward the music, even organized its own unwieldy forty-three–man State Jazz Orchestra of the Soviet Union. American Communists fell into line. For a time, the American party called for a Black Republic of the South, stretching from Virginia to Texas. African-Americans were henceforth to be seen as a *colonized* people, and jazz was officially declared a worthy folk music, expressive of their victimization. "Jazz has its roots in the oppressive measures of the southern plantation owners against the Negro masses," wrote Charles Edward Smith in the *Daily Worker*. "It is specifically a folk music. . . . That hot jazz continues to flourish and that at least some of those who produce it are beginning to realize its class content is another indication of the growing class consciousness of the masses." (Never mind that jazz had always been urban, not rural; that it was joyous and affirming rather than tragic; that most musicians, black as well as white, saw playing jazz primarily as a way to make a living.)

Entartete Musik, (Degenerate Music), catalogue of a Munich exhibition organized by the official Nazi cultural watchdog, Dr. Hans Severus Ziegler, in 1937

is said at least once to have threatened to cut Glaser's throat if he ever heard that his manager was pocketing money to which he, Armstrong, was entitled.

But in the end, he told one interviewer, he would always be grateful to Glaser for making it possible for him to focus on what he loved best—his music.

> So all those headaches of keeping a band, keeping musicians, paying them, watching the box office, commissions, paying taxes, picking songs to record—I don't bother with it. Joe just gave me so much every month, and took care of the rest. Maybe I'd be rich now if I'd tried to get the whole hog in one—but I just want to do the things I know how to do. Always looked to me like everybody who made a lot of money didn't do nothing but die and leave it—and rushed themselves into the cemetery. . . . And I'm going to send *everybody* flowers. I come from the old hustling territory, you know. Like the old Creole horn player, [Buddy] Petit, used to say every time we meet a parade or a funeral, "Won't never let this horn kill *me*. I'm going to kill *it*."

In his elliptical memoir, *Music Is My Mistress,* Duke Ellington captured something of the complicated relationship between the two men.

> Louis Armstrong and Joe Glaser; Joe Glaser and Louis Armstrong. Don't put the cart before the horse, they say, and at first glance you might think Louis was the horse doing all the pulling while Glaser was in the driver's seat of the cart. Obviously, a cart is a most convenient place to stash the gold. Then you realize that in spite of how well Joe Glaser did for himself, Louis still ended up a very rich man. . . . Joe Glaser watched over Louis Armstrong like the treasure he was.

SUCH AN AMERICAN THING

Around two-thirty in the afternoon on March 19, 1935, a sixteen-year-old Puerto Rican boy was caught trying to steal a ten-cent pocket knife from the S. H. Kress Five-and-Dime Store at 125th and Lenox Avenue. In the scuffle that followed he bit the hand of a clerk. The police were called and hustled the boy into the basement for questioning. A crowd began to gather. An ambulance arrived. Then, a hearse happened to pass by. Rumors spread, first that the boy was being beaten, then that he had been killed by the store clerks. Protesters began to harangue the police and were arrested. Someone hurled a brick through the Kress window.

Two days of rioting followed. Harlem became "a bedlam of missiles," wrote Alain Locke, "[of] shattered plate glass, whacking night sticks, mounted patrols, police sirens and police bullets." Scores of shop-windows were smashed; store shelves were emptied. One suspected looter was shot dead; one hundred more were injured. Even the Savoy Ballroom was damaged, and had to close briefly for repairs.

In the wake of the riots the editors of the New York *Daily News* sought to foster racial harmony in the city—and sell more news-papers—by sponsoring a Harvest Moon Ball, in which couples of all races from all five of the city's boroughs could compete in the waltz, tango, rhumba, fox-trot—and the lindy hop.

Herbert White—"Whitey" to admirers and enemies alike—was the bouncer at the Savoy. An ex-sergeant in the Hellfighters and the founder of a gang called the Jolly Fellows, whose members prided themselves on both their dancing and their street-fighting skills, he was also a sharp-eyed entrepreneur. The craze for lindy hopping had spread across the city, and Shorty Snowden and Twist Mouth George Ganaway

were already doing a brisk business enter-taining at downtown parties. White wanted a piece of the action, too, and when Snowden and Ganaway rejected his offer to become their manager, he hand-picked six of the Savoy's best young dancers, and began drilling them over and over again for the *Daily News* contest. A well-publicized victory for a group of Savoy dancers whom he controlled could make him a rich man.

Norma Miller and Frankie Manning, both now well known at the Savoy, were

among Whitey's chosen few, and the Harlem semifinals held at the Savoy turned out to be child's play for them. "Chick Webb's band played like they never had before," Norma Miller recalled, and the downtown judges were so dazzled that all three couples were sent on to the finals at Madison Square Garden.

Whitey gave them a pep talk at the Savoy before heading downtown: "We've got to show them what the lindy hop is all about," he said. "That we are the champs. You have

Frankie Manning, at right, urges dancers to perform one of the aerial maneuvers he pioneered at the Savoy.

The people for whom blues music was created in the first place . . . are dance-oriented people. They are dance-beat-oriented people. They refine all movement in the direction of dance-beat elegance. Their work movements become dance movements and so do their play movements; and so, indeed, do all the movements they use every day, including the way they walk, stand, turn, wave, shake hands, reach or make any gesture at all. So, if the overwhelming preponderance of their most talented musicians has been almost exclusively preoccupied with the composition and performance of dance music, it is altogether consistent with their most fundamental conceptions and responses to existence itself.

—Albert Murray

The lindy hop is said to have been born at the Manhattan Casino in 1928, but it reached its peak of perfection at the Savoy Ballroom in Harlem where these photographs were all taken during the 1930s.

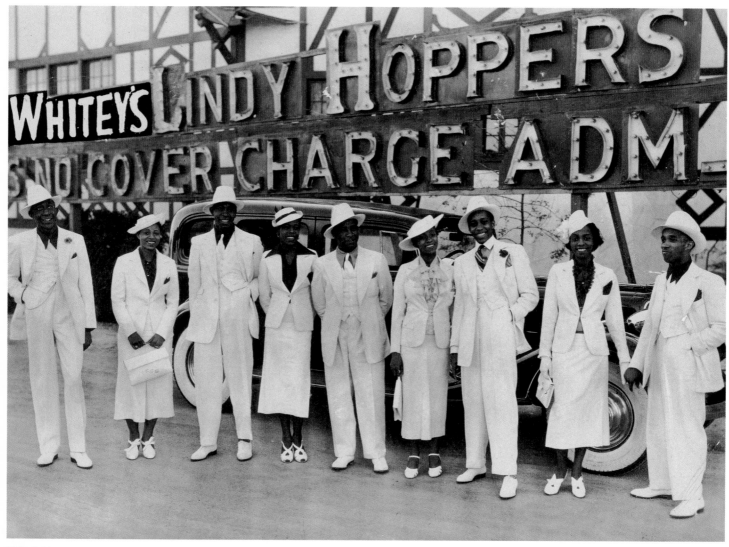

Whitey's Lindy Hoppers. "Whitey"—Herbert White—is the man in the middle; Norma Miller stands to his right. The troupe was performing at the New Cotton Club in Culver City, California while filming *A Day at the Races* with the Marx Brothers in 1937.

got to bring back that Championship. You are the flag-bearers of the Savoy, and you know what we expect. . . . Let the *Daily News* report that we took it all, first, second and third! We want all three. Remember, we don't take out any other prizes. All we got is the lindy hop so you better make sure it belongs to us. Do you dig?"

"We dig!" the dancers answered in unison.

At the Garden, the Abe Lyman Orchestra and the newly reconstituted Fletcher Henderson band were to take turns on the

bandstand. The program began with a Grand March around the dance floor as the big crowd applauded, Norma Miller remembered. "The noise increased as the lindy hoppers, the last in line, entered. We could hear the audience was with us, and we responded to their yells by swinging when we walked. Harlem was on parade."

The more traditional ballroom dancers came first, and Miller couldn't help thinking as she watched them glide past that while the steps they were doing were beautiful they "all had their roots in a foreign

country, but the lindy hop was created in New York. In Harlem. . . . It was an American dance created by Americans. It had soul, and it had swing."

White lindy hoppers from elsewhere in the city went on first. "They seemed clumsy to us," Miller said. "Watching them butcher our dance made our tempers flare, and this made us even more determined to take the crown." Then, as the Henderson band tore into an up-tempo number, the Savoy dancers finally got their chance to take the floor, whirling, leaping, flying into the air—

and bringing the crowd roaring to its feet. When it was over, Norma Miller, Frankie Manning, and their friends had won first *and* second *and* third place, just as Whitey had hoped they would.

As members of Whitey's various traveling troupes—Whitey's Hopping Maniacs, Whitey's Lindy Hoppers, and the Jive-A-Dears—Norma Miller and Frankie Manning would become full-time professional dancers, delighting every kind of audience, appearing in the movies, everywhere spreading the message they had learned at the Savoy. Interviewed together many years later, they reflected on what they had learned on its dance floor.

NORMA MILLER: We lived in a very segregated country. But the most amazing thing about the [Savoy] Ballroom was it was the first building in America, ever in the world, that opened its doors, completely integrated. At the time we didn't understand that. See, the whole time of the years of our dancing, black and white danced together in the Ballroom. It never dawned on us, at least not on *me,* that there was a situation about black and white, 'cause we always had white competitors. We couldn't go to the Roseland [where black dancers were still barred]. But the Roseland could come to our Ballroom. So it was a normal thing for us, any night of the week you would see some of the great white stars come into the Ballroom, all kinds of white musicians. I saw Leopold *Stokowski* in the Savoy Ballroom! So I was raised in an integrated dance world. I didn't know about the other until I went outside the Ballroom. So, my first experience as far as dancing was concerned, was always integrated.

FRANKIE MANNING: Well, I'll tell you, when I was going to the Savoy, I wasn't realizing that white people

and black people were going there. All I could think about was *dancers* were going to the Savoy Ballroom. And whether you were black, green, yellow, or what, if you walked in the Savoy, the only thing we wanted to know is: Can you dance? And if you came in there, it wasn't like a white person walking in, and everybody turn around and look at them. We'd say, "Hey, he can *dance! Right! OK."* You know. But we didn't look up at his face to say he's black, green, yellow or what.

NORMA MILLER: And everybody came to dance. Swing has a marvelous thing of bringing people together.

FRANKIE MANNING: Oh. You said it.

NORMA MILLER: Ah, you *know* it. . . . We had white dancers in the Savoy Ballroom.

FRANKIE MANNING: Oh, yeah.

NORMA MILLER: And I'm telling you they were good.

FRANKIE MANNING: Oh, man, were they ever.

NORMA MILLER: They were so good that you wanted to *hit* 'em. But see, that was such an American thing. We had Italian boys that used to come from the Bronx. You had the Jewish boys that come from Brooklyn, and this melting pot—

FRANKIE MANNING: Oh, man—

NORMA MILLER: —of everybody trying to outdance each other. We didn't know how rich we were in relationships but fifty years ago, when we look back, we realize we had a wonderful thing going with all races and that's what made the Savoy such a wonderful place.

CAN'T YOU BOYS PLAY ANY WALTZES?

"Benny Goodman and his *Let's Dance* band are a great medicine," said *Metronome* in April 1935, "a truly great outfit—fine arrangers and musicians who are together all the time—they phrase together, they bite together, they *swing* together." Things looked bright for Benny Goodman that spring. Thanks to his weekly appearances on network radio and the records his band had begun to make, he was getting a name for himself among young people who loved to dance. And a series of unheralded appearances at the Savoy playing opposite Chick Webb, had, according to Goodman, given his men "a wonderful opportunity to compare our playing with his, to try to match some of the guts he got into the music."

Then, workers at Nabisco went out on strike. All baking stopped. With no biscuits to sell, the company canceled the show.

Goodman had a booking agent now. Willard Alexander, who worked for the Music Corporation of America agency and was himself just out of college, had been willing to gamble that college-age dancers would prefer Goodman's music to that being played by any of the otherwise uniformly sweet dance bands that made up the MCA roster. Alexander hastily arranged an engagement at the Roosevelt Hotel in Manhattan, home of Guy Lombardo. "We wanted to get work for the band," Alexander remembered. "Hell, we would have booked them into the Holland Tunnel." It was a disaster; Lombardo's fans could not abide Goodman's music. The waiters held their fingers in their ears. One indignant customer sent Goodman a scrawled note: "Just by way of *contrast,*" it said, "why not play something sweet and low?" The band was let go after just two weeks.

Meanwhile, determined to keep the Goodman band together, Alexander arranged a cross-country summer tour for the band,

THE VELOCITY OF CELEBRATION

In November of 1935, a young freelance writer from Toronto named Helen Oakley was living in Chicago, where she was disappointed to find very little of the jazz music she loved. She had expected to find the city where King Oliver and Louis Armstrong had first become famous a thriving jazz community. Instead, she remembered, it had become a "musical wilderness" in which jazz musicians were "looked on very poorly—even by their wives." With a friend from the suburbs, Edwin "Squirrel" Ashcraft III, she helped found the Chicago Rhythm Club to keep the music alive through a series of informal jam sessions.

Benny Goodman's weekly Let's Dance *broadcasts in 1934 had meant a great deal to her and her friends; they "lightened our hearts," she*

The Erskine Hawkins orchestra played for Americans of all kinds at the Savoy Ballroom during the late 1930s. Hawkins, always a favorite in Harlem, would eventually replace Chick Webb as the leader of the house band. The secret of his success, one of his veterans said, was that he "kept it simple" and never strayed too far from the blues.

Do you remember what it was like? Maybe you do. Maybe you were there. Maybe you were there in New York two-thirds of the way through the 1930s, when there were so many great bands playing—so many of them at the same time. You could choose your spots—so many spots.

—GEORGE T. SIMON

Midtown Manhattan at the height of the swing era

Charlie Barnet, shown here fronting his band i
an RKO film called *Music in Manhattan*, droppe
out of Yale to play tenor saxophone like his ido
Coleman Hawkins. Lena Horne would be his singe
for a time, and he fought hard to integrate the musi
business. When a fire destroyed all his arrange
ments in 1939, Benny Carter and Duke Ellingto
would ship him new ones to keep the band going

(Below) The Casa Loma Orchestra at the Steel Pie
in Atlantic City, 1931. An offshoot of the Jean Gol
kette Orchestra and named after a Toronto bal
room, the band was a cooperative led by an electe
"president," alto saxophonist Glen Gray (with mous
tache, seventh from the left), and was the first swin
band to have its own commercially sponsored radi
program, the Camel Caravan, beating Benny Good
man to the microphone by nearly two years.

Black bands generally were not signed to the kind of long-term contracts the most popular white orchestras enjoyed, but there were exceptions. The Earl Hines Orchestra (above) presided over the Grand Terrace Ballroom in Chicago for ten years, while the singer-showman Cab Calloway (below, with baton) made New York's Cotton Club his headquarters all through the 1930s. The trumpeter in the foreground is Doc Cheatham.

(Left) A dance at the Knights of Columbus Annex in Gary, Indiana, in 1934. A local band, Rupert Harris and His Black Diamond Orchestra, provided the music.

Clarinetist, saxophonist, and sometime singer Woody Herman and his 1937 "Band That Plays the Blues" (above), the first of a long succession of hard-swinging orchestras he would organize and lead over three decades. Musical tastes changed drastically during that time, and hundreds of musicians passed through his bands, but they always echoed Herman's own infectious love of playing. "My business," he said, "is excitement."

Tommy Dorsey, wearing the light suit (below), was billed as "the Sentimental Gentleman of Swing." His singing tone on the trombone was perfectly suited to the ballads in which his band specialized, but there was nothing sentimental about the man himself. He was combative and tight-fisted, a hard-drinking taskmaster who created his own band mostly because he could no longer bear to play alongside his brother, Jimmy, and took pleasure in publicly berating his men for their mistakes and then could not understand why they didn't like him. But his band was hugely popular and through its ranks moved such stars as Bunny Berigan, Dave Tough, Bud Freeman, Buddy Rich, and a skinny singer from Hoboken, New Jersey, named Frank Sinatra.

Artie Shaw (left) was Benny Goodman's greatest rival—and his own worst enemy. Gifted and articulate, he won an enormous following for his music—and his good looks. But he was "cursed," he said, "with serious-mindedness." He disliked autograph-seekers, disdained jitterbugging, and was made so uneasy by his own success that he repeatedly walked away from the business. "The basic truth," he concluded, "is that popular music has little or nothing to do with musical values at all."

The Glenn Miller Orchestra (below) at the Meadowbrook Ballroom in Cedar Grove, New Jersey, in 1939. Miller, here in the light suit, playing trombone, had no illusions about art. He couldn't understand why he was criticized as a musician. "All I'm interested in is making money," he once told John Hammond. He and his orchestra would turn out a string of hits, including "String of Pearls," "Little Brown Jug," "Moonlight Serenade," and "In the Mood," that would be among swing's most familiar anthems.

theater for a while, but for the first time in his life wherever he went in Kansas City he found himself surrounded by the blues. "Eighteenth Street, at that time, was blazing," he remembered. "I mean, everything was happening there, beautiful . . . you could hear the blues from any window or door. Right away I knew that was for me." The blues would be at the heart of everything he did for the rest of his life, specifically the irresistible Kansas City style of *stomping* the blues that his friend the writer Albert Murray, quoting Duke Ellington, has called "the velocity of celebration." "I really don't know how you would define stomp in strict musical terms," Basie once said. "But it was a real thing. What I would say is if you were on the first floor and the dance hall was upstairs, that was what you would hear, that steady, *rump, rump, rump, rump,* in that medium tempo. It was never fast."

Basie spent several months on the road with Walter Page's Original Blue Devils, but when they began to have trouble finding dates, he returned to Kansas City and went back to working at the Eblon, moving from club to club after it closed, listening and sitting in. At about five o'clock one morning in 1929 he saw a big crowd on Eighteenth Street. "When I asked about them, somebody said that they were the wives and sweethearts and . . . relatives and friends and followers waiting for the Bennie Moten Band that was due back in town from a long tour out in the territory. . . . It was kind of like standing around waiting for the hometown team." Eventually, the band pulled up in two gleaming Chryslers. Bennie Moten and his brother Bus were waving from the first one. "They had a special kind of class," Basie said, "and they also looked like they had it made in some ways, while the Blue Devils were still out there struggling from gig to gig."

Basie wanted to sign on right away, but there was a problem. The band already had a piano player—Bennie Moten himself. It seemed hopeless, Basie recalled. "But I have always been a conniver, and began saying to myself, I got to see how I can connive my way into that band." Basie could read little music but he had plenty of arranging ideas and managed to talk the trombonist, guitarist, and arranger Eddie Durham into working some of them out with him on paper, then passing them along to Moten. Moten liked them, asked for more, and when he went away on a brief business trip, let Basie sit in at the piano. Dancers loved him. After that, Moten played only an opening number or two at each show, then turned the keyboard over to Basie. The Moten band recorded for Victor, and traveled all the way east to New York City where they played at the Savoy and were not disgraced in a battle of the bands with Chick Webb. Playing with Moten's band night after night for five years, Basie said, made him realize that music mattered more to him than show business.

Then, in 1935, after Bennie Moten died on the operating table during a botched tonsillectomy, his band disintegrated and Basie began putting together a nine-piece outfit of his own—"Count Basie and the Barons of Rhythm." Their home base was the Reno Club at Twelfth and Cherry Streets. It was a rough place, with a tiny bandstand. Imported Scotch was fifteen cents a shot, domestic whiskey just a dime. Food came from a hot-dog stand next to the bar. Blue clouds of marijuana smoke hung perpetually above the balcony where the white customers sat, and taxi dancers and their clients climbed constantly up and down a separate staircase that led to bedrooms on

Kansas City's best. The Bennie Moten band at Philadelphia's Pearl Theater during a 1931 foray to the East Coast. The twin keyboards are manned by Count Basie, left, and Bennie Moten. The singer Jimmy Rushing is at the far left.

The Count Basie band as it looked at the Meadowbrook Lounge in Meadowbrook, New Jersey, in 1937. By then, it had been expanded from nine to thirteen men and its rhythm section included the infallible guitarist Freddie Green, behind Basie's piano, between drummer Jo Jones and bassist Walter Page.

the second floor for two dollars a trip. "I liked the atmosphere down there," Basie said. "There was always a lot of action."

The band's nine members would eventually include five fellow veterans of the Blue Devils and Bennie Moten bands: Walter Page, Jo Jones, Buster Smith, Lips Page, Herschel Evans, and Lester Young. But Basie was firmly in charge. "I . . . had some pretty clear ideas about how I wanted the band to sound," he remembered. "I knew how I wanted each section to sound. . . . I had my own way of opening the door for them to let them come in and sit around awhile. Then I would exit them."

"A band can really swing when it swings easy," Basie said, "when it can play along like . . . cutting butter." The rhythm section was the heart of that conception, and Basie's was perhaps the greatest in jazz history. Walter Page's bass provided the powerful "walking" 4/4 pulse that allowed Jo Jones, himself a former tap dancer, to keep time on the high hat and ride cymbals and

abandon the heavy, thumping, insistent emphasis on the bass drum that had characterized much jazz drumming. The result was light and relaxed, fluid and shimmering, less the ticking of a rhythmic clock than a surging wave of percussion, on top of which soloists seemed able to float without apparent effort. "When [Jo Jones] came out with the Basie band," the drummer Louie Bellson said, "it was as if we had been *waiting* for him." And Basie's piano provided the perfect complement. With Page and Jones at work, he had long since given up the steady, four-beats-to-the-bar left hand that the masters of Harlem stride had taught him in favor of spare, witty fills and asides that commented on the music being played and spurred his men to greater effort. Even a single note, Count Basie said, can swing.

His band caught on fast. Soon, a crew from radio station W9XBY was turning up at the Reno Club several times a week to broadcast its music as far east as Chicago.

Like most Kansas City outfits, the Basie band specialized in "head arrangement," worked out informally without sheet music. Buster Smith remembered how one of their favorites came about: "We were fooling around at the club and Basie was playing along in F. That was his favorite key. He hollered that he was going to switch to D-flat and for me to set something from [another tune called 'Six or Seven Times'] on alto. Lips Page jumped in with the trumpet part without any trouble and Dan Minor thought up the trombone part. That was it—a 'head.' "

Basie and his men called the arrangement that resulted "Blue Balls." The band was about to play it with just a few minutes to fill before they went off the air one morning, when the announcer asked Basie for the name of his next tune. Its informal title clearly wouldn't do for the radio audience. He looked up at the studio clock and said, "Call it 'One O'Clock Jump.' " He would play it night after night for the next fifty years.

Swing musicians spent most of their lives on the road. Even for the best-paid bands, like Benny Goodman's and Duke Ellington's, it was wearying. Some bookers insisted that they cover five hundred miles between dates and work seven nights a week until the union finally managed to get it decreased to six nights and four hundred miles. "When I left Duke," one longtime Ellington trumpet player remembered, "I slept almost a whole year." Max Kaminsky played first trumpet for Tommy Dorsey for a time and endured weeks of one-nighters, traveling through the icy winter dark in an unheated bus. "You'd get through playing . . . at one a.m., grab something to eat before riding all night in that frigid torture chamber until anywhere from eight to eleven the next morning, stumble . . . into some ratty little hotel, fall like a corpse onto a bed until it was time to get up and rehearse, and then you'd eat, shave, bathe, put on your band uniform and play again until one a.m. and then repeat the whole routine, week after week, month after month. . . . You'd begin to ask yourself, if you were still on speaking terms with yourself, why in the name of sanity you were doing this."

For those working for less well known outfits, life was a good deal harder. Some bands were too poorly paid to afford even a bus. As many as ten musicians packed into a single touring car and hauled their instruments in a trailer. Sometimes, stranded between engagements, they would simply pull into a roadhouse, begin to play, and hope to raise enough cash to buy dinner by passing the hat.

There were compensations, of course. "To be factual," Rex Stewart remembered, "all of the fellows had little black books crammed with addresses and telephone numbers of fillies from coast to coast," and there seemed always to be women gathered around the bandstand who were, as he said, "ready, willing and eager." "The men didn't have to run after the girls," remembered Myra Taylor, vocalist with a Kansas City–based territory band called Harlan Leonard's Rockets. "The girls ran after the men, and I used to call 'em 'chili bandits.' Because that was about the best that they were going to get was a bowl of chili and a pop, you know. And they would go to the motels and things with these fellows. They played very hard out there on the road, . . . because sometimes they didn't get to see their wives for two months, three months maybe, before they would get back home, so, they had a very nice time."

Black musicians faced obstacles unknown to their white counterparts. Barred from restrooms, white hotels, and restaurants, they had to rely on the black community for help. It was not always forthcoming. "We'd go to some towns," Doc Cheatham remembered, "where they had black restaurants. The minute we'd get there, they'd change the menu, and put the prices up." But in most

places the men received nothing but hospitality. A network of celebrated cooks waited to welcome them. "They cooked for you like they'd cook for their family," one band member remembered. "And they didn't mind filling your plate up." One Atlanta landlady named Mom Sutton served musicians at a table that "looked like a mile long," another man remembered, "everything you could name—sausages, bacon, eggs, biscuits, corn bread, homemade pies—all for just fifty cents." There were black hotels and rooming houses in most big towns, although sleeping on the bus was sometimes preferable. Everyone who checked into the sole black hotel in Macon, Georgia, for example, was issued a baseball bat by the manager. "You might get some rats in your rooms," he said, "and they're often quite big ones, so keep this beside your bed."

Cab Calloway's band, like Duke Ellington's, often traveled from city to city by private Pullman, but when they performed in small southern towns the men had to go by bus. "We'd get in town just in time to get the instruments out and set up the bandstand and go to play," Milt Hinton said.

Hadn't had anything to eat, had no place to stay, or anything. We up there playing and the people crammed in there, and my wife Mona would be the only girl traveling with the band. She would go around to the black neighborhoods and talk to the ladies. She'd say, "One of the musicians is my husband, and we haven't had anything to eat and we haven't any place to stay." And these ladies were always so nice, they would get together and call one another and say, "Well, Miss Jones will take two of them at this house. And Miss Smith, she'll take two." We on the bandstand playing like

The Don Albert Orchestra, led by its trumpet-playing star, at left, traveled all over the southwest and midwest in this brightly painted band bus. According to at least one authority, by billing itself as "America's Greatest Swing Band," Albert's outfit was the first to use the word "swing" in its title.

crazy, and [Mona would] say, "Well, look, they haven't had anything to eat. If I go and get five or six chickens can I pay you to help me fix a little food for them?" By intermission time, Mona would come down to that bandstand with a great big basket of chicken and potato salad and a list of names, "Dizzy you and he are staying over at Mrs. Jones's house, Charlie you and so and so over at Mrs. Smith's house." And this is the way we survived.

Looking back, Andy Kirk, whose Twelve Clouds of Joy played one-nighters for twenty years, had little patience with those who remembered only the bleak side of life on the segregated road. "If it hadn't been for one-nighters," he wrote,

I wouldn't have met Mrs. Mary McLeod Bethune and Dr. George Washington Carver. We couldn't stay in the white hotels. . . . I'm glad now we couldn't. We'd have missed out on a whole country full of folks who put us up in their homes, cooked dinners and breakfasts for us, told us how to get along in Alabama and Mississippi, helped us out in trouble and became our friends for life. . . . If it hadn't been for one-nighters, I wouldn't have known there were other people but rednecks in the South. I wouldn't have found out that not all white southerners wanted to put their foot on me. I wouldn't have found out there were Whites in the South I could talk to person to person, man to man.

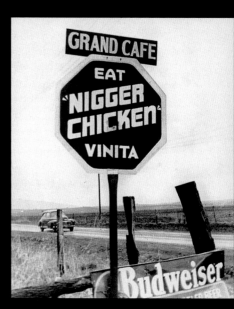

Black musicians, like the members of the Cab Calloway band photographed here by Milt Hinton in 1940, routinely transcended such Jim Crow indignities as (right) the Oklahoma road sign and (top) being forced to enter the Atlanta railroad station through the official "Colored Entrance." (Above) Left to right, Calloway, tenor saxophonist Chu Berry, and trombonist Tyree Glenn bring a taste of the wider world to two awestruck boys in Durham, North Carolina.

Basie himself later claimed he would have been happy enough if he'd stayed in Kansas City forever. But John Hammond's vociferous public enthusiasm for the band made the move east almost inevitable. It seemed to Hammond that the Basie band—blues-based, loose but hard-swinging, with plenty of soloing room—had everything the big commercial bands lacked. "I want to say categorically and without fear of ridicule that Count Bill Basie has by far and away the finest dance orchestra in the country," he wrote in *Down Beat.* "And when I say this I am fully aware of Benny Goodman, Fletcher Henderson, and Chick Webb. . . . He has excellent soloists . . . and a driving rhythm section more exciting than any in American orchestral history."

Enthusiasm like that inevitably attracted the interest of others. Before Hammond could sign Basie for Columbia, Dave Kapp, the brother of Jack Kapp, the head of Decca Records, turned up in Kansas City. Claiming to be Hammond's friend, he talked Basie into agreeing to make twenty-four sides a year for a total of $750—less than union scale and without the promise of so much as a penny for royalties. Joe Glaser came to town, too, and hired away Lips Page—then put him under wraps for a time so that he could not challenge Louis Armstrong's trumpet primacy. Page's replacement in the Basie band was Buck Clayton, a master melodist who had begun life in Kansas but honed his skills in California and in a hotel dance band in Shanghai. Hammond convinced Willard Alexander to book the band but Alexander, in turn, insisted that it be expanded immediately from nine to thirteen men in order to compete with the big swing bands back east.

Duke Ellington happened to be in town on October 31, 1936, the night Basie and his men boarded their secondhand Greyhound bus for the journey east. "Go ahead," Ellington assured Basie. "You can make it." Basie himself was not so sure. As he set off, he knew that his band, which had been

small and tight, was now ragged, unwieldy, and under-rehearsed.

Its first engagement—at the Grand Terrace in Chicago—did not provide much encouragement. The Basie men already played the blues better than anyone else in the country, but management insisted they also master more complicated arrangements to accompany an elaborate floor show. (Basie didn't even attempt the special arrangement of *The Poet and Peasant Overture* he was handed, he remembered; a "lady pianist" had to be called in just to play it.) Only the dancers seemed to like the band: "Why don't you just lay off," one told her boss when he complained about Basie's men. "Take it easy. These are just a nice group of country boys. . . . My God, one of these days you might be trying like hell to get them back in here. Just wait and see." They played a one-nighter in Buffalo on their way to New York, Basie remembered, and Mal Hallett's orchestra—the same outfit that Jean Goldkette's band had so badly intimidated in Massachusetts in 1926—"ran us out of there."

"Basie, who'll be in a New York ballroom by the time this gets into print hasn't been . . . impressive," the critic George T. Simon wrote in *Metronome* that fall. "True, the band does swing, but that sax section is so invariably out of tune. And if you think that sax section is out of tune, catch the brass! And if you think the brass by itself is out of tune, catch the intonation of the band as a whole! Swing is swing, but music is music. Here's hoping the outfit sounds better in person."

The band's first appearance in Manhattan, at Roseland, was little better. Basie's men knew no waltzes, no tangos, few standards. The young clarinetist and bandleader Woody Herman, making his own New York debut at Roseland that week, kindly lent Basie several of his own arrangements. "[Basie] was so green," Helen Oakley recalled. "Lester's saxophone was tied with string. And Basie had his back to the [crowd]. . . . He was afraid of the people."

Humiliated, Basie determined to take hold. He commissioned arrangements of current tunes, replaced some of his men, tightened discipline among the rest, and spent most of the next year and a half on the road, trying to make his orchestra better.

Meanwhile, the Great Depression, which had showed signs of lifting, suddenly deepened instead. The stock market collapsed again. In less than six months, four million more men and women lost their jobs. One-third of the people of Akron, Ohio, were thrown onto the relief rolls. When funds ran out in Cleveland, sixty-five thousand men, women, and children found themselves without any money for food or clothing. Poor Chicago children scavenged for food in garbage cans. Sharecropper families huddled along Missouri roads in makeshift tents, driven from their homes by landlords for daring to talk of organizing. It was called the "Roosevelt Recession," the steepest economic decline in American history. Things got so bad in Basie's native New Jersey that the state began issuing licenses to beg. If ever the country needed the healing power of the kind of blues Basie and his men played it was now—blues born in the dance halls and roadhouses and juke joints of Texas and Oklahoma, Kansas and Missouri; pulsing and stomping and played by men who had honed their skills in cutting contests that sometimes went on all night.

SCARY

On the morning of March 3, 1937, the Benny Goodman orchestra was to begin a two-week run at the Paramount Theater on Times Square. The movie, a dour Pilgrim-era drama called *Maid of Salem,* went on first, and by the time Goodman and his men took their places on the movable orchestra pit and the elevator began its slow rise, every seat in the house was filled. As the band came into view, playing its theme song, "Let's Dance," it was greeted by a roar so loud and so prolonged, Goodman said,

A security man struggles to keep an overexcited New York fan from getting to Benny Goodman in 1939. The trumpet star Harry James looks on warily, just over the intruder's head.

that it seemed "like Times Square on New Year's Eve . . . exciting, but also a little frightening—scary." The applause did not let up for four or five minutes, Goodman remembered. "We looked at them . . . as if they were the show and we were the audience." Soon, the audience *was* the show—or at least a large part of it. As the band resumed playing, and despite efforts by an army of uniformed ushers to stop them, young people leaped from their seats, filled the aisles, even jumped onto the stage to dance. (Much later, a Goodman publicist admitted that the first two dancing couples had been plants, but there was nothing orchestrated in the response of the rest of

the audience, which had started lining up that morning at seven o'clock.)

Until then, Goodman's high school–age fans had had to content themselves with hearing their hero on records. His band had traditionally played hotels and ballrooms, where alcohol was served, prices were high, and the customers were mostly adults. But before noon at the Paramount, anybody with a quarter was welcome. By three that afternoon, 11,500 teenagers had paid their way inside; by closing time that evening the number had risen to 21,000, and the aisles had been alive with dancers all day.

The Paramount appearance set a strange sort of benchmark for Goodman

and his rivals. If they couldn't get their audiences up and dancing no matter where they played, they had failed. "We'd go to another place like Philadelphia or Detroit," Goodman said, "and the manager would say, 'What about the kids dancing in the aisles?' . . . He would be rather disappointed if the whole theater didn't . . . dance, whereas we were always trying to curtail it and avoid it because it did interfere with the actual program that was going on."

Swing music had been growing in popularity for years, but it was adolescents— working-class adolescents, for the most part—who now turned it into a national craze. In spite of the Depression, trumpet sales doubled, while sales of clarinets— Artie Shaw's and Benny Goodman's instrument—tripled. There was an unofficial swing "uniform": boys dressed in sport jackets and slacks, like the ones their heroes wore on the bandstand; girls favored bobby socks and saddle shoes, blouses and sweaters, and pleated skirts that flared when they got onto the dance floor.

Young fans had their own language, too, and Cab Calloway lent his name to a *Hepster's Dictionary* to aid the uninitiated. A hot number was a "killer-diller." "Armstrongs" were musical notes in the upper register. "Swingaroos" or "hep-cats" were divided between "jitterbugs"—who danced —and "ickies"—who didn't, but stayed on the sidelines shouting encouragement to the musicians and clapping, usually just off the beat. Young women showered the best-looking players with letters and telephone numbers and some waited at the stage door, as one Goodman saxophonist fondly remembered, willing to "do anything" to meet their heroes.

Swing inevitably had its critics. When bandleaders began "swinging the classics"—rifling well-known works by everyone from Bach to Stephen Foster in search of familiar airs that could be turned into danceable hits—some radio stations barred the results altogether as artistic desecration. After a Detroit station cut the singer Maxine Sullivan's swing version of the traditional Scottish ballad "Loch Lomond" off the air, Sullivan sent Eleanor Roosevelt the titles of other familiar songs she hoped to record to see if the First Lady was in any way offended. "My dear Miss Sullivan," Mrs. Roosevelt replied from the White House, "I can't imagine what the songs you mention would be like in swing tempo, but there is nothing wrong in doing it. If people like it, and you succeed, you will be doing other things. You cannot please everyone all the time."

The sweet bandleader Blue Barron denounced swing as "nothing but orchestrated sex . . . a phallic symbol set to

sound." The Catholic archbishop of Dubuque called it a "communistic endeavor," a pretext for "cannibalistic rhythmic orgies." To others, it seemed a "mass contagion . . . musical Hitlerism." Dr. A. A. Brill, a Manhattan psychiatrist, went before newsreel cameras to declare that "Swing music represents our regression to the primitive tom-tom-tom, a rhythmic sound that pleases savages and children. . . . It acts as a narcotic and makes them forget reality. They forget the Depression, the loss of their jobs. . . . It is like taking a drug." There was nothing new in any of this. The sight of white youths enthusiastically adopting dances that had been born in the black community had always alarmed their elders. "If they'd been told it was a Balkan folk dance," Duke Ellington said, "they'd think it was wonderful."

Still, even musicians sometimes grew alarmed at the unbridled enthusiasm of their fans. Jerry Jerome, who played tenor with Benny Goodman for a time, remem-

bered what it was like. "They'd scream and yell and dance and carry on and enjoy themselves," he said. "I was shocked when I stood up to take a tenor solo, there was such a scream, and I realized they didn't hear one note of my solo. They were there because someone stood up, 'He's with the band,' you know. 'He's a soloist.' But what he played? They weren't listening."

They *were* listening at the Savoy. It was still Harlem's best-loved ballroom, still home to the most demanding dancers in the country. "The lindy hoppers up there made you watch your p's and q's," Dicky Wells recalled. "The dancers would come and *tell* you if you didn't play. They made the guys play, and they'd stand in front patting their hands until you got the right tempo." Frankie Manning and his dancing partner Frieda Washington had now added "air steps" to the lindy, lifting their partners over their shoulders, sliding them between their legs, hurling them high in the air. And Chick

The Goodman band drives dancers back out into the aisle during a return engagement at the Paramount in 1938.

Webb was still in charge. On the night of May 11, 1937, Benny Goodman himself ventured uptown to challenge him at what was billed as the "Music Battle of the Century."

Webb considered the Savoy his personal territory, to be defended against all invaders, but he also had far bigger dreams. "You know something, man?" he once told Artie Shaw. "Someday I'm gonna be walkin' up the street one way and you gonna be comin' down the other way, and we gonna pass each other and I'm gonna say, 'Hello, best white band in the world' and you gonna say, 'Hello, best colored band in the world.'" Webb had scrimped and sacrificed to keep his men together, sometimes using his rent money to buy arrangements, and he was never able to pay his men enough to fend off job offers from more successful bandleaders. (Whenever he spotted Fletcher Henderson at the Savoy, he would call out, "Well, who do you want this time?")

It was not lost on Webb that Benny Goodman's band had succeeded spectacularly with music that greatly resembled his own. ("Stompin' at the Savoy," and "Don't Be That Way," both big hits for Goodman, had in fact been written and arranged for Webb's band by its alto saxophonist, Edgar Sampson.) Nor had he forgotten those evenings back in 1934 when Goodman had brought his brand-new band up to the Savoy, hoping his men would learn how to play with what Goodman called the same sort of "guts" Webb's men employed. Now he called special afternoon rehearsals. The brass, reed, and rhythm sections each went through its precise paces in a separate room. "Fellas, [this] is my hour," Webb told his men as they took the bandstand. "Anybody misses notes —don't come back to work!"

Four thousand fans had jammed into the ballroom on that May evening, and mounted policemen had to be called to control the crowd of five thousand more who couldn't get in and refused to go home. Among those who managed to squeeze through the door were Norma Miller and

Showdown at the Savoy

Frankie Manning, professional lindy hoppers now, who had been taking on all comers in dance contests across the country. Now, they had come home to the Savoy to see their hero face the best-known band in the country.

FRANKIE MANNING: This was an electrical night. I mean, here's Benny Goodman, the king of swing, and here's . . .

NORMA MILLER: . . . Chick Webb, the king of swing.

FRANKIE MANNING: The king of swing, you know as far as *we* are concerned. We knew about Benny Goodman. A lot of people may not realize that a lot of arrangements that Benny Goodman had, Chick Webb had the same arrangements and when they get on a bandstand, now this is when you can know which band is the best—by listening to them play the same

arrangement. And to me, Chick Webb outswung Benny Goodman that night.

NORMA MILLER: I say the same thing, yeah.

FRANKIE MANNING: That was my feeling. I'm not saying this because . . .

NORMA MILLER: . . . Not being prejudiced.

FRANKIE MANNING: I feel that Chick Webb outswung Benny Goodman that night, you know, because I saw guys on Benny Goodman's bandstand when Chick Webb was playing. I seen guys on there, . . . they just shook their heads.

The Goodman band was routed. Gene Krupa bowed low before the man who had beaten him. Chick Webb, he said later, had "cut me to ribbons." "Nobody," one of Webb's men remembered, "could have taken it away from Chick that night."

Lester Young (above) takes off in front of the Count Basie band. (Below, left) Occupants of some of the higher-priced seats. Nearly twenty-five thousand swing fans were on hand from all five boroughs of New York City as well as Connecticut and New Jersey. (Below, right) Ivie Anderson sings "St. Louis Blues" with the Duke Ellington orchestra.

In January 1938 a young German Jew named Henry Ries, in flight from the Nazis, managed—after two attempts—to reach sanctuary in the United States. Anti-Semitic laws in Germany had barred him from studying music, his first love, but he now hoped to pursue a career as a photographer. On Sunday, May 29, he took his camera out to Randalls Island in the East River. There, Martin Block, a disc jockey for radio station WNEW, was to host twenty-five bands in a daylong Festival of Swing.

Ries had never seen or heard anything quite like it. The music was amazing, he remembered sixty-two years later, but still more amazing to him was the nature of the crowd that gathered to hear it. "It was fully integrated. I can only remember seeing one black person in my life before that day and that was Jesse Owens at the Olympics in Berlin. I was there when Hitler refused to shake his hand." More astonishing still was the fact that when the Duke Ellington band broke into a new number called "Diminuendo and Crescendo in Blue," black dancers first, and then white ones, leapt from their seats and began to dance while the police stood by and watched. "I was fresh from Germany under the Nazis, remember," Ries said, "where you had to ask permission to go the bathroom. That kind of freedom was simply unthinkable. I never forgot it." Ries went on to serve in the U.S. army during the war and then became a well-known New York photographer. These images, shot that day on Randalls Island, have never before been published.

(Top) Ellington's "Diminuendo and Crescendo in Blue" brings dancers out of their seats and onto the field. (Below, left) Ellington in charge. (Below, right) Woody Herman and his band

Helen Oakley, in the light dress, then working for Irving Mills, organized this 1937 jam session at the Brunswick recording studio in New York to help launch the Master and Variety record labels. Chick Webb, Artie Shaw, and Duke Ellington all volunteered their time. Milt Gabler kneels behind Ellington; Oakley's British-born future husband, the jazz historian Stanley Dance, stands against the far wall.

had far less attention than he'd liked since Victor dipensed with his services in 1930. He had moved to Washington, D.C., tried and failed as a fight promoter, taken up with another woman without bothering to tell his wife, gone through all of his money, and had to sell off all his diamonds except the one that glittered from his front tooth. He finally opened a dingy little place variously called The Music Box, The Blue Moon Inn, and The Jungle Club. Only his ego had remained intact. When he heard a radio announcer introduce W. C. Handy as "the Father of the Blues and Jazz," he dashed off an angry letter to *Down Beat* in which *he* claimed to be the creator of jazz. Just to make things perfectly clear he signed it "Very Truly Yours, Jelly Roll Morton, Originator of Jazz and Stomps, Victor Artist, World's Greatest Hot Tune Writer." That

same spring, the folklorist Alan Lomax sought him out and encouraged him to play and reminisce into a wire recorder at the Library of Congress. The heavily edited result, a book called *Mr. Jelly Roll*, constituted a gaudy but priceless record of the music's early days in New Orleans.

Morton was thin and frail by the time Commodore and Blue Note and Victor asked him to record again, but he was just as demanding of other musicians as he had been in the old days. He was soon back on the street again, threatening lawsuits against ASCAP and former managers who he believed had misappropriated his music and fulminating against the younger musicians who ignored him. When he finally died in Los Angeles in 1941, four well-known black bandleaders, including Duke Ellington and Jimmy Lunceford, happened

to be playing nearby. Not one attended his funeral. And the night before he was to be buried, according to one of the few friends who remained loyal to him, someone slipped into the funeral home and chiseled his last diamond from his tooth.

THE RAY

Benny Goodman's band was never quite the same after Carnegie Hall. Gene Krupa would soon leave to form his own orchestra; so would other stars—Teddy Wilson and Harry James and Lionel Hampton—forcing Goodman to rebuild the most popular orchestra in America.

Personnel was never Benny Goodman's strong point. Singer Helen Ward had been one of the band's prime attractions—and she was in love with its leader. When an admirer urged her to leave the band early on, Goodman had assured Ward he planned to marry her. Then, not long after she turned her suitor down, Goodman explained that he had had second thoughts. He was too young to get married, after all. When she finally told him over dinner that she planned to leave the band anyway, he threw his menu in her face.

All through the years, Goodman's musicians would find him distant, preoccupied, so obsessed with making music that he sometimes couldn't even remember their names. Stories about his odd behavior are legion. Offstage, he was simply oblivious. Helen Ward also remembered rehearsing with him at his home on a cold winter's day and complaining that there wasn't enough heat. "You know, you're absolutely right," Goodman said, and went and got himself a sweater. The singer Peggy Lee recalled getting into a taxi with Goodman at a Manhattan stoplight. Goodman was silent, lost in thought. The light changed. He still said nothing. Finally, the driver asked, "Where to?" Startled, Goodman reached for his wallet and asked, "What do I owe you, Pops?"

The tenor saxophonist Zoot Sims played for Goodman in the late 1940s. One day he brought to rehearsal a bright shiny apple and put it on his music stand to eat during a break. "Benny had a habit of grabbing your cigarettes or anything," he remembered, "and I saw him looking at that apple. I said, 'Oh, oh. There goes my apple.' I had a solo coming up. So Benny grabbed my apple. I stood up to take my solo, and it's the longest solo I ever had with Benny Goodman. . . . He kept signaling 'one more,' until he finished the whole apple. Then he said, 'That's enough.'"

On the bandstand, "Benny wanted perfection," Helen Ward remembered, "and he got it." Anything less yielded the disconcerting owlish stare that his sidemen called "the Ray."

Helen Oakley suggested that Goodman simply couldn't help himself.

Benny got such a bad name for himself. But what people didn't realize about Benny was that he had a God-given gift, and he never to his dying day realized that other people didn't have that same gift. He didn't know. He turned the "Ray" on the guys in the band. He didn't know it was the "Ray." But he would simply turn his eyes on you, and look at you as though asking, "Are you real?" "Did you really do that?" "Couldn't you have done better?" And they withered. His guys were terrified. But until he read about it, he didn't even know he did it.

One musician who had spent several unhappy months with the band, trying to figure out just what it was his leader wanted from him and always seeming to fall short, finally stormed into Goodman's dressing room. "That's it, Benny!" he said. "I can't take this anymore. I'm quitting!"

He slammed the door on the way out.

"Who *was* that?" Goodman asked his manager.

In rebuilding his band, Benny Goodman would often have more help than he liked from John Hammond. In 1939, Mary Lou Williams told Hammond about a twenty-three-year-old musician from Oklahoma City who, she said, had figured out how to bring something of Lester Young's light, loping, rhythmically surprising style to the electric guitar. His name was Charlie Christian. He was the son of a blind, itinerant blues singer, and had been a local hero since his school days when he played a homemade instrument and, Ralph Ellison remembered, "No other cigar box ever made such sounds."

Without hearing Christian and without consulting Goodman, Hammond arranged for the young guitarist to board a train for Los Angeles, where Goodman was playing with his band. The next night, when Goodman got to work at the Victor Hugo Restaurant, he found Christian's amplifier already set up onstage and Christian himself waiting in the wings, wearing an outfit of his own design that featured a purple shirt and yellow shoes. "Goodman watched Charlie approach the bandstand," Hammond recalled, "looked around the room until he spotted me, and zapped me with the famous Goodman 'Ray.'"

Goodman's quintet was onstage. He called for "Rose Room." Christian fell right into the tune as if he'd been rehearsing it for days. "All he had to do was hear the melody and chord structure once and he was ready to play twenty-five choruses, each more inventive than the last," Hammond wrote. "Benny would play a chorus or two, Lionel would answer him, and their talent would inspire Charlie to greater improvisations of his own. Before long the crowd was screaming. . . . 'Rose Room' continued for more than three-quarters of an hour."

Goodman hired Christian right away. The Benny Goodman Quintet became a sextet. Before tuberculosis and too many good times cut short his career at twenty-five, Charlie Christian would bring a new, experimental spirit to the Goodman band—and to the guitar. More than anyone else, he would make it a solo instru-

Charlie Christian, wearing dark glasses, says goodbye to Oklahoma City friends and family before setting out for Los Angeles to join Benny Goodman in August of 1939.

YOU'LL GET THROUGH

"Why is it," *Down Beat* once asked, "that outside of a few sepia females the woman musician never was born capable of sending anyone further than the nearest exit? . . . You can forgive them for lacking guts in their playing but even women should be able to play with feeling and expression and they never do it." That kind of complacent chauvinism has characterized jazz since the beginning.

The trumpet player and singer Valaida Snow was the best-known female soloist of the thirties, both at home and in Europe, where she settled in 1936. Billed as "Queen of the Trumpet" and "Little Louis," she was especially admired in Paris and Scandinavia, where, a friend remembered, she was driven around in an "orchid-colored Mercedes Benz, her pet monkey rigged out in an orchid jacket and cap, with the chauffeur in orchid as well."

But with a handful of exceptions like Snow, only female pianists and singers have found a consistent welcome in the jazz world. Still, a number of women's bands—"all-girl orchestras"—did take to the road during the swing era. Ina Ray Hutton and her Melodears were perhaps the best-known. "We played the provinces," their leader remembered. "I guess I saw all the men in America out front. Some of them tried to get backstage—some sent mash notes. But I kept the sex in the saxophones."

The Melodears' success inspired Laurence C. Jones, the principal of a threadbare Mississippi school for poor and orphaned black children, to form his own band, the International Sweethearts of Rhythm, and use it to raise funds. (The band was "International," one band member explained, because "we had Mexican and Chinese" as well as black girls.) The Sweethearts quickly outgrew Piney Woods. Professional musicians, black and white, signed on, and they found themselves playing top ballrooms all over the country. "You could put those girls behind a curtain," one bandleader said, persuaded he was being flattering, "and people would be convinced it was *men* playing."

That kind of attitude was all too familiar to the pianist, composer, and arranger Mary Lou Williams, but she did her best to ignore it. "As for being a woman, I never thought much about that one way or another," she said, looking back over her long career. "I never thought about anything but music." She earned the respect of every man with whom she played.

She was born Mary Scruggs in Atlanta in 1910 and was raised in Pittsburgh. "Jazz is a self-taught art," she remembered, "and I was a loner." A child prodigy, at the age of six she was already helping to support her ten half-

brothers and -sisters by playing piano for parties, and she was playing hopscotch in the backyard when her first offer to play the carnival and tent-show circuit came. It was "a terrible life," she remembered, but she stuck with it, at seventeen married a saxophone player named John Williams, and eventually found work doing double duty as pianist and chauffeur for one of the best of the riff-based territory bands, Andy Kirk's Twelve Clouds of Joy. Between engagements she drove a hearse. When Kirk's band settled in Kansas City in 1928, the Williamses moved there, too. Soon, she was the band's full-time pianist, with a sure touch and a feeling for the blues rarely matched by any pianist, male or female. "Women during that era were not really allowed to be in with a group of men," she remembered. "That made the people scream and carry on because they saw a woman that weighed about ninety pounds—to hear me play so heavy, like a man, that was

something else." Soon, she was being billed—accurately—as "The Lady Who Swings the Band." She was also its top arranger, and by the mid-thirties was writing for other big bands, as well—Louis Armstrong, Earl Hines, Benny Goodman, even Duke Ellington—often working furiously by flashlight at night as the Kirk band bus hurtled down the highway.

Later, she moved to Manhattan and become a musical mentor to younger musicians, including the modernist masters Dizzy Gillespie, Bud Powell, and Thelonious Monk. "You've got to play, that's all," she said. "They don't think of you as a woman if you can really play. . . . No musician ever refused to play with me. No one ever refused to play my music or my arrangements. . . . A woman I know once came to me and said, 'They won't play my arrangement because I'm a woman.' I said, 'Do your work to the best of your ability, and you'll get through.' "

Mary Lou Williams

ment that could hold its own with brass or saxophones. "After I heard him, I could forget about everybody else," one younger guitarist remembered. "Charlie Christian was *it*."

Not long after Hammond surprised Goodman with Charlie Christian, Goodman would surprise Hammond by marrying Hammond's own sister, Alice Hammond Duckworth, the divorced wife of a British member of parliament. Soon, the pseudo-black accent Goodman had developed while still a struggling musician in Chicago was replaced with a new one, "Long Island lockjaw," his old friend James T. Maher would call it, better suited to the new life the boy from Maxwell Street now found himself leading among New York patricians. Being a member of the family did not immunize Goodman against Hammond's hectoring criticism. "Benny is still a great musician," his new brother-in-law wrote not long after the wedding, "but he is no longer an innovator or a musical radical. . . . [I]t is the increasing conservatism of a man who has made his pile and who no longer wishes to buck popular prejudice."

SCENT OF MAGNOLIAS

In 1938, Count Basie had fired Billie Holiday. He later said they'd disagreed over money; she claimed John Hammond had insisted she sing the kind of blues Bessie Smith had sung a decade earlier, she had angrily refused, and Basie had too meekly sided with Hammond.

Then, Artie Shaw asked her to join his band. Black singers with white bands were almost unheard of, although Jimmy Dorsey had featured a singer named June Richmond for a time. Shaw's musicians were delighted. Max Kaminsky, now playing first trumpet in the band, remembered how Holiday "stood up in front of the mike, listening sort of dreamily [and] came sliding in, in the

nick of time, like a lazy ball player starting to lope around the bases but taking his own good time because he knows the ball he just hit is *never* going to stop sailing."

The reaction of dancers and hotel owners was more problematic. In Toronto, one musician's wife recalled, there was no problem about finding Holiday a hotel room. "She took it as she should have taken it, that it was her right." But in her own country, she was often turned away from the hotels in which the other musicians stayed, and in some places she even had to leave the bandstand between numbers.

She hadn't been sure she should accompany the band when it went south, Artie Shaw remembered.

On the way down below the Mason-Dixon line, that mystic line, she said, "You think I should come down?" I said, "Yeah, Billie, I think it's important that you do this." I wasn't thinking in terms of black-white. I was thinking it important that she come and stay with this band. And everything was fine and they loved her until one night she sang a tune and after the tune was over, some redneck in front of the band hollered up, "Have the nigger wench sing another song." She was a pretty hot-tempered girl, and she looked over at him and you could see her flushing under the tan, and calling him a "Motherfucker." So, a little turmoil arose out there and I was prepared for it, and I had a couple of cops in the wings, just in case, and they hustled her off into the bus and drove her away.

Things were almost as bad in New York City, the town Holiday now considered home. When the band appeared twice weekly on network radio, the sponsor, Old Gold cigarettes, insisted that only the band's white singer, Helen Forrest, perform on the air. And when the band played the Hotel Lincoln, Holiday was ordered to use the

freight elevator so that other guests wouldn't assume blacks were staying in the hotel. She spent most of the engagement holed up in her room.

Holiday finally left Shaw. Both he and Basie, she told *Down Beat,* were prisoners of "too many managers, too many guys behind the scenes who told everybody what to do." She returned to the clubs she knew best, vowing never to travel with a dance band again. "She did what she liked," a club owner remembered. "If a man she liked came up, she'd go with him; if a woman, the same thing. If she was handed a drink, she'd drink it. If you had a stick of pot, she'd take a cab ride on her break and smoke it. If you had something stronger, she'd use that. . . . When she told you off, you were damn well told—white, black, rich, poor."

On December 30, 1938, Café Society, a nightclub like no other, opened its doors just off Washington Square in Greenwich Village. It was the creation of an ex–shoe salesman named Barney Josephson, who hoped—with John Hammond's help—to demonstrate that New Yorkers would turn out to hear jazz presented "with dignity and respect" before a genuinely integrated audience. He billed it as "The Wrong Place for the Right People"—and it was a hit, not only with those who shared his liberal politics but even with some of the society people its slogan was meant to lampoon.

Billie Holiday was on the first bill—Hammond had convinced Josephson to hire her—and she stayed for almost nine months, doing three shows a night backed by the trumpeter Frankie Newton's band. In April 1939, a young, leftist high-school teacher named Abel Meeropol turned up at the club to see her. He had written a poem and set it to music, he said. Would she sing it? It was about lynching, and the picture it painted—of innocent victims of southern mob violence hanging from poplar trees, faces distorted in death, blood spattered on the roots—was brutal in its candor:

Billie Holiday records "Strange Fruit" for Commodore Records, April 20, 1939. The guitarist is Jimmy McLin.

walked out. One woman who cried out, "Don't you dare ever sing that song again. Don't you dare," turned out to have witnessed a lynching as a little girl and had found it unbearable to be reminded of it in a nightclub. Even John Hammond, now at Vocalion Records, thought the song too inflammatory for its catalogue, but agreed to allow Holiday to record it for Milt Gabler at Commodore. Backed by "Fine and Mellow," a blues she and Gabler put together, "Strange Fruit" reached number sixteen on the record charts in April of 1939—and transformed Holiday's career. From then on, she would be the musical and emotional focus of every record she made, no longer just another soloist who happened to be singing, not blowing. She never sang another explicitly political song, but she did also gradually alter her repertoire, de-emphasizing the kind of sly upbeat tunes that had won her her first following, in favor of increasingly dolorous songs, such as "Lover Man," "I Cover the Waterfront," her own bitter "God Bless the Child," and "Gloomy Sunday"—subtitled "The Hungarian Suicide Song."

Holiday would consider "Strange Fruit" her own for the rest of her life. "It's my song," she said. "It has a way of separating the straight people from the squares." She sometimes claimed to have written it herself. Once when the folksinger Josh White dared perform it at Café Society, she threatened to slit his throat if he ever tried it there again.

TAKE CARE OF ELLA

When the Count Basie and Chick Webb bands had warred at the Savoy, dancers had been divided about the overall outcome, but there had been no doubt whose band singer they liked best. Billie Holiday had still been Basie's vocalist then, but she lost out three to one to Webb's twenty-one-year-old singer, Ella Fitzgerald, already the favorite singer of Harlem lindy hoppers and

Scent of magnolias, sweet and fresh.
Then the sudden smell of burning flesh.

Holiday called herself "a Race woman," but she was frankly reluctant to try the song at first. It was completely different from anything she'd ever sung before, and it was grim beyond measure. "I was scared people would hate it," she said. "The first time I sang it I thought it was a mistake. . . . There wasn't even a patter of applause when I finished. Then a lone person began clapping nervously. Then suddenly everyone was clapping."

Soon, Barney Josephson recalled, she was singing it at the end of every set.

I made her do it as her last number, and no matter how thunderous the

applause, she had orders from me not to return for even a bow. I wanted the song to sink in. . . . The room was completely blacked out, service stopped—at the bar, everywhere. The waiters were not permitted to take a glass to the table, or even take an order. So everything stopped—and everything was dark except for a little pin spot on her face. That was it. When she sang "Strange Fruit," she never moved. Her hands went down. She didn't even touch the mike. With the little light on her face. The tears never interfered with her voice, but the tears would come and knock everybody in that house out.

The song and Holiday's chilling rendition of it caused a sensation. A few customers

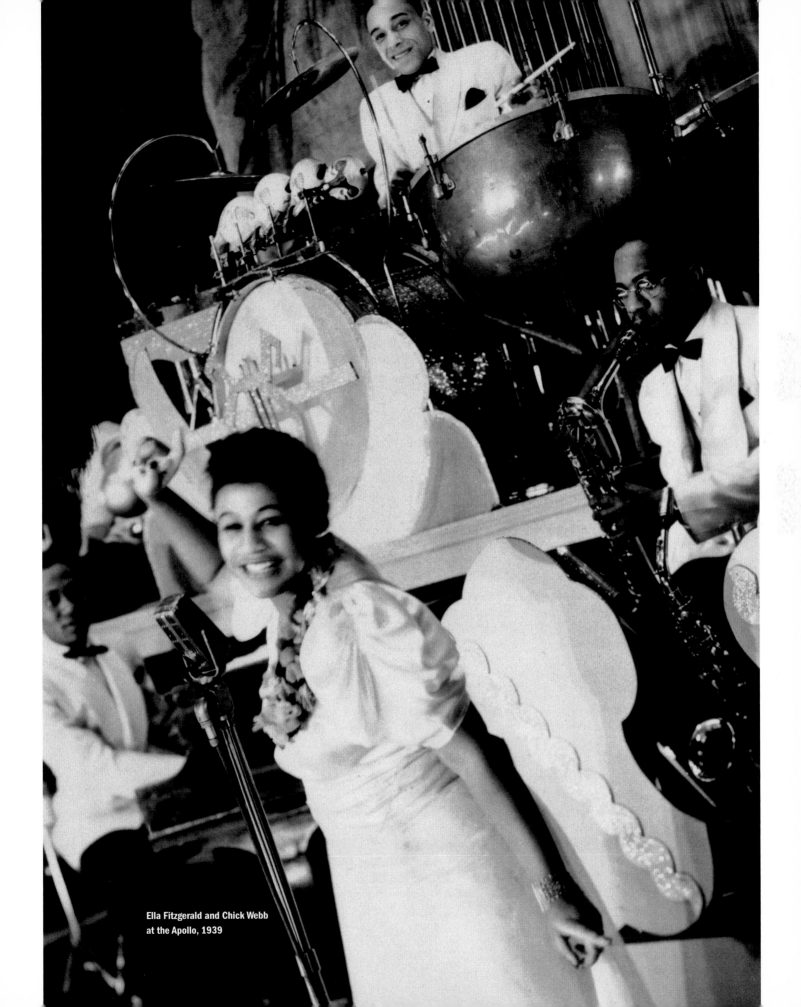

Ella Fitzgerald and Chick Webb
at the Apollo, 1939

soon to become first "the First Lady of Swing," and eventually "the First Lady of Song."

Fitzgerald's childhood had been nearly as bleak and troubled as Holiday's. Her parents never married. Her stepfather abused her. Her mother died when she was fourteen. She dropped out of high school, then ran away from the Colored Orphan Asylum in Riverdale to which the court sent her for truancy. For nearly two years she was homeless, living on the Harlem streets, dancing and singing for tips, sometimes supporting herself as a numbers runner or a lookout for a brothel. Her dream was to be a dancer.

On the evening of Wednesday, November 21, 1934, she was scheduled to dance in an amateur show at the Apollo Theater in Harlem. But when she learned that two already well-known dancing sisters were to close the show, she decided she'd try singing, instead.

She was overweight and awkward, wearing secondhand clothes and men's boots as she stepped into the spotlight. And she was terribly nervous—she knew Apollo audiences could be brutal. Somehow she started by singing off-key. The crowd grew restive. The master of ceremonies stopped her. "Folks, hold on now," he said. "This young lady's got a gift she'd like to share with us tonight. She's just having a little trouble getting it out of its wrapper. Let's give her a second chance."

That was all she needed. Backed by the Benny Carter Orchestra she sang two songs—she and Carter both remembered them as "Judy" and "The Object of My Affection"—and she did so in the style of her favorite singer, Connie Boswell of the Boswell Sisters. Boswell "did things that no one else was doing at the time," Fitzgerald said much later, she phrased like a horn player, shifted rhythms, rearranged melodies. Fitzgerald brought down the house and was awarded the first prize of ten dollars, which was supposed to carry with it a week's salaried work onstage. But the

manager of the Apollo reneged. He didn't think Ella Fitzgerald good-looking enough for show business. She returned to the streets, entering other amateur shows when she could, sometimes singing without pay for local bands.

Meanwhile, Chick Webb, still seeking a way to reach the huge white audience that Benny Goodman and Artie Shaw and other bandleaders now commanded, resolved to find what was then called "a girl singer" or "canary," someone who could sing but also be a decorative addition to his band. His male vocalist, Charles Linton, was assigned the task of scouring the city for likely candidates. Linton brought back Ella Fitzgerald.

Webb was appalled: "You're not putting *that* on my bandstand," he whispered. "No, no, no. Out!" But Linton threatened to quit if she weren't given a chance and Webb relented. It was the best decision he ever made. Fitzgerald's flawless ear and perfect pitch astonished other musicians; her girlish voice and ferocious sense of swing delighted the public. One of their first records together, "Sing Me a Swing Song (and Let Me Dance)" got the Webb band onto the hit parade for the first time in its history. Soon his orchestra—featuring Ella Fitzgerald—was appearing regularly on the radio and in ballrooms all over the country, with hit after hit on the jukebox.

In 1937, still just twenty, she won the Number One Female Vocalist poll in both the country's leading jazz magazines, *Down Beat* and *Metronome*. The following spring, she and Chick Webb recorded an old nursery rhyme, "A-Tisket, A-Tasket," and turned it into a swing anthem. It reached number one and stayed there for seventeen weeks. By autumn, Webb and Fitzgerald had three more novelty tunes on the charts—all at once.

Down Beat now called the Chick Webb orchestra "one of the best known and most popular swing bands in the country." But Webb was paying a price for his new success: the spotlight was on his young singer

now. His band was taking a back seat, its jazz quotient leached away in favor of bouncy commercial swing arrangements of popular songs. "Chick had been totally immersed in the *band,* and the guys stood behind him 100 percent," Helen Oakley recalled. "But after he got Ella it was different." Over the next few months, Webb issued just fourteen instrumentals and more than sixty vocals, almost all of them by Ella Fitzgerald. Billie Holiday, who had faced Ethel Waters's scorn at the beginning of her own career, now showered some of her own on the newcomer. One member of the Orchestra recalled that she came into the Savoy several times wearing a big fur coat, muttered "A great band like that with Ella—that bitch," turned around, and stalked out.

Then, Webb's lifelong physical frailty began to grow worse. His kidneys weakened, complicating his struggle against the spinal tuberculosis that had plagued him since childhood. He collapsed several times after performances and was finally confined to a Baltimore hospital. "Anything happens to me," he told a friend, "take care of Ella." He died on June 16, 1939, not yet thirty. Thousands filed past the casket at his family's church. Gene Krupa sat next to it all day, weeping. Most of the mourners wept during the funeral service when Fitzgerald sang "My Buddy." Webb's band stayed together but changed its name to "Ella Fitzgerald and Her Famous Orchestra." She didn't need anyone to take care of her.

BROWN SUGAR

"When I was a kid," Louis Armstrong once wrote a friend, "my grandmother used to say to me that the only person that makes money sitting on his ass is a shoemaker." During the swing era, Joe Glaser made sure Armstrong was perpetually on the move. Glaser was convinced that Armstrong, already a big star, could be still bigger if he would focus as much of his energy on show-manship as he did on music.

Armstrong needed little urging. He had always seen himself as an all-around performer—his passport listed his profession as "actor and musician"—and his show business hero was Bill "Bojangles" Robinson, who danced and sang and cracked jokes, and did them all superlatively well and without blacking-up. "People love me and my music," Armstrong once said. "The minute I walk on the bandstand . . . they know they're going to get something good. *I see to that.*"

He was playing differently now—there were fewer high-note flights—but his tone was even warmer than it had been before, if anything, and by hewing more closely to the melody, paraphrasing rather than recomposing, he somehow seemed still more magisterial. Asked to record every kind of material, he happily obliged. "There are no bad songs," he once said, and he approached each one as if it could be made into a masterpiece. Nor did the big band craze ever hold any terrors for him. The first records that brought him fame had been made with small New Orleans–style groups but he'd been playing with large orchestras off and on ever since taking his seat with Fletcher Henderson in 1924, and it was he who had first brought the whole notion of "swinging" to New York. He produced spectacular new big-band versions of old favorites like "Struttin' with Some Barbecue," as well as brand-new hits like "I'm in the Mood for Love," "You Are My Lucky Star," "Jubilee," and his own "Swing That Music." He cut two comedy records as "Elder Eatmore," a version of the sticky-fingered preacher he had first impersonated for South Side audiences back in Chicago. On several sides, he thoughtfully softened his playing so as not to overwhelm the Mills Brothers' imitations of musical instruments, and, with an all-white choir, he recorded spirituals, on one of which —"Going to Shout All Over God's Heaven" —he struck a characteristically sly blow

On a Hollywood soundstage tricked up to look like a white set designer's notion of a Harlem street, Louis Armstrong plays a tune called "Public Melody Number One" for a corked-up Martha Raye in the 1937 film, *Artists and Models.*

against the racial expectations of his producers. While the chorus determinedly murmurs a stereotyped "hebbin, hebbin, hebbin" in the background, Armstrong clearly sings out "Heaven, Heaven, Heaven."

Glaser arranged appearances for Armstrong in big-budget Hollywood films, too: *Pennies from Heaven,* with Bing Crosby, *Every Day's a Holiday,* with Mae West, *Going Places* (in which he plays a groom named Gabriel and sings "Jeepers Creepers" to a horse), and *Artists and Models,* in which his trumpet playing drives the blacked-up comedienne Martha Raye to dance so frantically that *Variety* warned her never to do such a thing again. "While Miss Raye is under cork, this intermingling of the

races isn't wise, especially as she lets herself go into the extremest manifestation of Harlemania torso-twisting and gyrations. It may hurt her personally." (It didn't.) All of the roles Armstrong played were stereotypical—such parts were virtually all that 1930s Hollywood offered black performers. In each of them, however, he remains uniquely himself: funny, guileful, supremely gifted, and utterly undisturbed by anything going on around him. Armstrong was written up in *Esquire* and *Vanity Fair* and in 1936 he published a book called *Swing That Music,* a sanitized version of his life that was nonetheless the first jazz autobiography ever to appear anywhere. That same year, he became the first black performer to host his own national sponsored radio program, substituting for Rudy Vallee on *The Fleishmann's Yeast Hour.* And when he was not making movies or records or appearing on the radio, Armstrong was on the road, fronting the big Luis Russell band that included several old friends from New Orleans.

His battered lip continued to plague him from time to time and in 1937 Glaser added Henry "Red" Allen to front the band at each performance until it was time to showcase its star. There were new challengers now, as well. Young Roy Eldridge could play faster and higher than Armstrong could, and most white fans were said to prefer Harry James, who said he felt embarrassed being mentioned in the same sentence with the man he very nearly worshiped. (When James won the *Down Beat* reader's poll for trumpet in 1944, he said, "That's ridiculous, Louis Armstrong is Number One," and to the end of his life, he would preserve a torn fragment of brown paper bag because Armstrong had once scrawled a few encouraging words to him on it.)

The road itself was wearing. As Pops Foster remembered,

It was tough traveling through the South in those days. We had two white guys with us—the bus driver and Joe Glaser. If you had a colored bus driver back then, they'd lock him up in every little country town for "speeding." It was very rough finding a place to sleep in the South. You couldn't get into the hotels for whites, and the colored didn't have any hotels. You rented places in private homes, boarding houses and whore-houses. The food was awful and we tried to find places where we could cook. We carried a bunch of pots and pans around with us.

But for all the problems that afflicted his lip, for all the rival trumpet players now attracting attention, and for all the hardships encountered along the way, Armstrong remained a hero in black neigh-

borhoods all over the country. The bassist Johnny Williams remembered the crowds that gathered to see Armstrong off the morning after every performance. There were usually fifty to sixty people on the street to say good-bye no matter where they were, he said, including old friends as well as complete strangers, "a fellow sitting in a wheelchair, or on crutches, a woman—whatever." As his bus waited, Armstrong would go slowly down the line slapping backs, shaking hands, and giving out cash to anyone with a hard-luck story. "You know, not saying, 'Look, look, look, look, look, I'm giving this.' [He'd just] ball it up, put it in their hand, and say, 'Please take care of yourself.' "

In September 1937, Armstrong and his band were in Savannah, Georgia, when they suddenly came upon Joe Oliver standing by the side of the road, peddling tomatoes and potatoes from a vegetable stand. As Armstrong went from triumph to triumph, his old mentor had gone from bad to worse. His music had long since fallen from fashion. A crooked manager had collected deposits on all the dates he'd set up for one tour, then run off with the money. There were troubles on the road, too, as his saxophone player Paul Barnes noted in his diary.

November 1—having bus trouble. Stay on road all night. Weather cold. Orchestra makes bonfire with bus tire. Get help next morning.

November 7—Bus seized by clothing store, finally redeemed. . . . too late for Orchestra to make date in Cumberland, Kentucky. Woman proprietor of Southern Hotel holds King Oliver's trumpet for rent.

Even Oliver's diet had betrayed him: years of eating slice after slice of bread heaped with sugar caused him to lose all his teeth. He was fitted with dentures but afterwards found it impossible to play for more than a

Louis Armstrong onstage and in command, at the Apollo, 1939. "For me," said Duke Ellington, "he's the epitome of the kind of American who goes beyond the rules."

few minutes at a stretch and had been forced to take the job selling vegetables just to keep going.

"He was standing there in his short-sleeves," Armstrong said. "No tears. Just glad to see us. Just another day. He had that spirit." Armstrong gave him all the cash he had on hand—some $150—and took up a collection among the other New Orleanians in the band. "That night we played at a dance and look over and there's Joe standing in the wings," Armstrong wrote. "He was sharp like the old Joe Oliver of 1915. He'd been to the pawn shop and gotten . . . his suits and all—Stetson hat turned down, high-button shoes, his box-back coat. He looked beautiful and he had a wonderful night."

Armstrong and his men moved on the next morning. Oliver remained stranded in Savannah. "I'm still out of work," he wrote his sister from there three weeks later. "Since the road house close I haven't hit a note. But I've got a lot to thank God for because I eat and sleep. . . . Soon as the weather can fit my clothes I know I can do better in New York."

An old admirer eventually took pity on him and gave him a job.

Dear Sister:

I open the pool rooms at 9 a.m. and close at midnite. If the money was only ¼ as much as the hours I'd be all set. But at that I can thank God for what I am getting. Which I do night after night. . . .

Now Vick . . . I'm going to tell you something but don't be alarmed. I've got high blood pressure. Was taking treatment but had to discontinue . . . because it cost $3.00 per treatment. Now it begins to work on my heart. . . .

Should anything happen to me will you want my body? Let me know because I won't last forever. . . .

Don't think I am afraid because I wrote what I did. I am trying to live near[er] to the Lord than ever before. So I feel like the Good Lord will take care of me. Good night, dear.

Joe

Joe Oliver died on April 10, 1938. The headline of the Savannah *Tribune* read:

"DADDY" JAZZ MUSIC PASSES
KING OLIVER, NOTED BAND LEADER
FOUND DEAD IN BED
WAS THE DISCOVERER OF LOUIS ARMSTRONG

His funeral was held in Harlem, paid for by the Negro Actor's Guild. Louis Armstrong attended, along with a host of Oliver's old friends, and never forgave the presiding clergyman, Adam Clayton Powell Jr., for feeling called upon to draw moral lessons from the fact that Oliver had once had money but had been unable to hold on to it. "Just because the Guild buried him was no reason for rubbing it in," Armstrong said.

————————

Louis Armstrong breaks it up at Connie's Inn, 1936. "When I commenced to put a little showmanship in with the music," he said, "people appreciated me better."

Lucille Wilson as a chorus girl at the Cotton Club where, Louis Armstrong remembered, "I paid strict attention to her . . . looking beautifuler 'n beautifuler every night."

Late in the summer of 1938, Lil Hardin agreed to grant Armstrong a divorce. They had spent most of their fourteen-year marriage apart. A few days later, on tour in Texas, he finally married Alpha Smith, with whom he'd been living off and on for nearly ten years. Lil claimed he had begged her *not* to give him his freedom and that she'd done so only to spite him, knowing that Alpha was threatening a breach of promise suit if he didn't wed her right away. In any case, it was not a happy match. "[Alpha's] mind was on furs, diamonds and other flashy luxuries and not enough on me and my happiness," Armstrong said later of his third wife. "I gave her all the diamonds she thought she wanted, but still she wanted other things. She went through all my money."

That fall, he opened at the new Cotton Club, located on Broadway at Forty-eighth Street, sharing the stage with his old idol, Bill Robinson. There, he spotted Lucille Wilson, a beautiful twenty-four-year-old dancer in the chorus line. "Maybe her color had

something to do with my falling in love with [her]," he wrote later. "Ever since I was old enough to feel a desire for women I've been drawn to those of darker hue. Lucille was the first girl to crack the high yellow color standard used to pick girls for . . . the Cotton Club."

Wilson sold cookies backstage to supplement her income and support her family—she was the daughter of the owner of a taxi fleet who had fallen on hard times—and Armstrong began his pursuit of her by buying up all her cookies, then passing them out to children in Harlem. She did her best to avoid him, nonetheless, until he cornered her backstage one day and said, "See here, little girl. I know all the cats are sharking after you; I just want you to know I'm in the running, too." He began calling her "Brown Sugar," started taking her for long rides in the chauffeured Packard Joe Glaser had bought for him, asked her if she would learn to cook him red beans and rice.

She said she would. "It seemed to me Lucille was the ideal girl for me," he remembered. "Good common sense . . . not particular about showy people." But the future remained cloudy. So long as he kept bringing money home, Alpha showed no signs of leaving him, and Lucille was not interested in a relationship with a married man.

A VERY DIFFERENT WORLD

In March 1939 Duke Ellington and his orchestra set sail a second time for Europe, this time aboard the *Île de France*. The continent was already moving toward war and the ship's hold was filled with parts for French fighter planes. There had recently been great changes in Ellington's life, as well. Both his parents were now gone: his father had died of tuberculosis in 1937. At thirty-nine, he had fallen in love with a beautiful Cotton Club dancer named Evie Ellis. He left Mildred Dixon and moved in

with Ellis. She would remain loyal to him all his life and even sometimes call herself Mrs. Ellington, but he would never agree to divorce his wife in order to marry her. Then, he had abruptly ended his long partnership with Irving Mills. Ellington never revealed the reason for the break. One story suggested that he had examined the books and found that when his mother died Mills had failed to follow his orders to buy her the finest casket in Washington, D.C. But Ellington may also have been reacting to stinging attacks on his closeness to Mills in the black press. A writer for the Pittsburgh *Courier* denounced Ellington for permitting Mills to write the words to his songs when deserving black lyricists were without work, and the Reverend Adam Clayton Powell Jr. had called him "just a musical sharecropper," dependent for his livelihood on "Massa Mills." Ellington's son, Mercer, believed his father's reputation was simply so well established by 1939 that he no longer needed Mills's services. Whatever the reason, the two men parted company.

The European tour had been Mills's idea, but even he could not have foreseen the sort of impact it would have—on European fans or on Ellington himself. The mass popularity of other bandleaders may have temporarily eclipsed him in the United States, but in Europe he remained supreme. Crowds met his ship at Le Havre with "such adoration and genuine joy," Rex Stewart remembered, "that for the first time in my life I had the feeling of being accepted as an artist, a gentleman, and a member of the human race." Everywhere Ellington went, people paid to hear his music played from the concert stage, not the bandstand. A Paris critic declared that Ellington's music was "related to the rhythm of the atom" and revealed "the very secret of the cosmos." Big crowds turned out in Brussels, Antwerp, The Hague, Utrecht, Amsterdam, Copenhagen, Oslo, and fifteen cities in Sweden, where admirers filled the platforms of every station through which Ellington's train passed in

Duke Ellington enjoying himself at the Savoy in the company of two of the finest singers in jazz, Ivie Anderson, left, who sang with his own orchestra, and Ella Fitzgerald, 1939

hopes of getting at least a glimpse of their hero. "The orchestra's refined appearance made a deep impression," wrote a critic for the Stockholm *Dagens Nyheter* on April 17, 1939, "and was a decided contrast to those slovenly, indifferent, clowning orchestras, which belong in the cheap cabarets, and never have anything of musical quality to offer." Ellington was still in Stockholm on April 29, his fortieth birthday. A sixteen-piece local band woke him that morning and admirers filled his hotel room with flowers. That evening, the whole audience rose to sing him happy birthday.

But not even he—with his highly developed skill at refusing to acknowledge unpleasantness—could overlook the evidence of the mounting crisis all around him. The Nazis had barred jazz music and frowned upon black foreigners, and when the train carrying the band across northern Germany was delayed for six hours at Hamburg, uniformed soldiers patrolled the platform. Barney Bigard saw them shove around "like dogs" an elderly Jewish couple who tried to enter the dining car. In Paris, the band performed in a new underground theater, built to withstand the Ger-

man bombs the French feared would soon be falling. And when their train crossed Holland, Bigard remembered, "we could see out of the . . . windows that they were putting machine-gun posts in all the haystacks and in the ditches. It was kind of scary."

As the *Île de France* steamed into New York harbor in May, Bigard said, "I was never so glad to see that old Statue of Liberty." Ellington was happy to be home, too, but he had also once again been energized by the respect given to his music and his musicians abroad. "Europe is a very different world," he told a friend. "You can go anywhere and talk to anybody and do anything you like. It's hard to believe. When you've eaten hot dogs all your life and you're suddenly offered caviar it's hard to believe it's true." He was about to begin one of the greatest creative periods in his career.

STILL THE BOSS

Two months later, with war in Europe just weeks away, Coleman Hawkins, too, came home to New York. Other American musicians had toured overseas; Hawkins had lived there for more than five years. Appreciative audiences in Britain, France, Scandinavia, and Holland treated him more like a concert artist than an entertainer; he sometimes appeared onstage with symphony orchestras, playing rhapsodic chorus after chorus. He had a good time offstage, too. He loved good food and drink but "girls were his hobby," one Dutch fan remembered. "He used to serenade them with his sax."

His return was "like God coming home," Milt Hinton remembered. Hawkins immediately set out to see for himself whether he could still outplay the younger musicians who had risen to prominence while he was away. After listening in all over town, he was reassured. "I'd been over there for so long . . . I thought by the time I came back . . . the musicians here would be further advanced. . . . But it was just like . . . when I *left*. . . . They're not going to cut me playing that."

Above all, he wanted another shot at Lester Young. At around three o'clock one morning, he found his way to Puss Johnson's basement club in Harlem where a jam session was being held, attended by both Young and Billie Holiday. Word spread fast, and soon, Rex Stewart remembered, the club was filled with musicians eager to see what would happen when the two giants of the tenor saxophone faced off again, six years after they had first met in Kansas City.

Coleman Hawkins sipping tea in London. "He was an aristocrat," a young admirer remembered. "I couldn't take my eyes off him."

[Hawkins] strode in, unpacked his sax and joined them. . . . [W]hen Billie finished, she announced to the house that it had been a pleasure to have had the world's greatest tenor saxophonist backing her up—Lester Young!

You could have heard a pin drop after that remark, but the Hawk ignored it . . . [and began to play]. The tempo Hawk set was almost unbelievable, it was so fast. And he had the tune all to himself. Then he sauntered to the bar, had a big drink, and waited to see how the cats would follow his avalanche of virtuosity. For some reason nobody felt like blowing at the moment. So Coleman picked up where he had left off, this time with a ballad, finishing up with an incredible cadenza, to thundering applause.

Lester sat on the sidelines, drinking with Lady Day, and I must say that he kept his cool. I heard [some musicians talking to one another], "Well, that's that. Coleman is still the boss."

But when *Down Beat* reported that Hawkins had been the victor that morning, Holiday indignantly telephoned the editor to object: "Young really cut the Hawk," she said. "Most everyone there who saw them tangle agreed on that."

A few months later, Hawkins went into the studio with a nine-piece group and recorded four sides, including "Body and Soul," a ballad he had been playing for years as "an *encore*," he said, just "something to get off the stage with." Like Louis Armstrong's "West End Blues" eleven years earlier, Coleman Hawkins's "Body and Soul" shook the musical world. It was in three parts: a tender, elliptical two-bar hint of the melody; two surging choruses that build to a thrilling crescendo; a gorgeous falling unaccompanied cadenza. Except for a brief piano introduction and some gentle supportive chords from the rest of the band, it was all Hawkins's huge, warm, all-encompassing sound.

"Body and Soul" sold astonishingly well for a disc by a jazz soloist in which melody played such an insignificant part. Hawkins claimed not to be surprised. "Gracious," he said, "I play like that all the time!" He had approached "Body and Soul" the same way he approached every ballad, he assured the young singer Thelma Carpenter. "First, you have to tell them the story," by which he meant state the melody. "Then, it's like making love. . . . You must romance her." The climax of the solo is "when you're having the orgasm," he said. And the cadenza? "Well, now that's the *satisfaction*." But musicians heard much more than eroticism in "Body and Soul." Hawkins's startling improvisation would help inspire a whole generation of young musicians to become what one saxophonist called "chord conscious," to see if they could take jazz in a different direction.

JAZZ

DEDICATED TO CHAOS

By 1940, the Great Depression had finally ended. The economy had begun to boom again, as the country readied itself for what growing numbers of Americans saw as inevitable—U.S. entry into World War II. But the swing music that had helped keep American spirits up during the lean years still seemed to be everywhere. Bandleaders like Benny Goodman and Artie Shaw and Glenn Miller were earning as much as $20,000 a week. Cab Calloway and Duke Ellington and Count Basie were doing well, too. But most black bands were no longer sharing in the good times. "Are Colored Bands Doomed as Big Money Makers?" asked Down Beat, *and then answered: "Negro Leaders Could Make More Money Running a Rib Joint."*

The old racial stereotyping that had made it difficult for men like Fletcher Henderson to show all that they could do on records at least had

Somewhere in France. The sounds of swing bring G.I.s together, courtesy of a USO entertainer, 1945.

helped reserve for black musicians—who were supposed to have a natural affinity for it—the kind of hard-swinging music Goodman and his rivals now routinely performed. Their success—as Goodman was always careful to concede—was due in part to the behind-the-scenes contributions of black arrangers. Even many of the snappy onstage routines fans of bands like Glenn Miller's most enjoyed—choreographed derby work by the trumpet section; trombones blaring right and left, up and down, in perfect unison; reedmen leaping up and down to solo—had been pioneered by black bands and carefully taught to them by veterans of those outfits, such as Eddie Durham.

Civil rights legislation did not help, at least at first. New public accommodations laws in northern states initially reduced opportunities for black musicians. Many all-black theaters closed. A good many white club and hotel owners, now forbidden to discriminate openly against black customers, kept them out anyway by refusing to hire any more black bands. While the top white bands wintered in New York, Chicago, and other large cities, playing so-called location jobs at the best hotels and promoting themselves on the radio, all but a handful of black orchestras were forced to stay on the road year-round simply to survive. Few complained: "You may have holes in your shoes," Earl Hines (who himself managed to land a long-term stint at the Grand Terrace in Chicago) often told his men, "but don't let people out front know it. Shine the tops."

White bands like Tommy Dorsey's, which could play a broad spectrum of music, were hailed for their versatility. Their black counterparts who sought to do the same were often indirectly accused of trying to get above themselves. Black bandleaders who larded their music with showmanship—such as Louis Armstrong, Cab Calloway, and Lionel Hampton—continued to do well. Those, like Teddy Wilson and Benny Carter, who focused mostly on their music and pol-

ished it to a fine gloss, foundered. *Their* music, Thelma Carpenter remembered hearing on Fifty-second Street, was "too white."

The lyricist Andy Razaf had seen it all coming back in 1932 and, in three verses of doggerel printed in the *Amsterdam News,* had tried to warn his fellow Harlem musicians:

You're a novelty no longer,
They have copied all your tricks;
'Till white bands can pass for colored
With "gut-bucket" blues and "licks."

Once they marveled at your ragtime
And you gladly showed them how,
So they've mastered all your rhythms;
They don't really need you now.

If you want to hold your places
You had better do your stuff;
Keep rehearsing and rehearsing,
You can never learn enough.

For the "ad lib" days are over,
Noise and faking are passé;
If you feel that you are rusty
Get that music book today.

Studying that music book had not been enough. "The truth is," said *Down Beat* in the spring of 1940, "the public will absorb only a very limited number of Negro bands." A new kind of swing was in favor now, said *Variety.* It was "sweet hot" or "swing sweet," a "white man's style of swing, retaining the Negroid bounce but coupling it to more respect for the melody."

Meanwhile, some black bandleaders felt themselves under the threat of still another kind of siege. In October of 1940, Benny Goodman hired away Duke Ellington's trumpet star, Cootie Williams, for an additional twenty-five dollars a week. Ellington was unruffled. He helped Williams negotiate his contract with Goodman. And he replaced Williams the night after he left with another fine trumpet player, Ray Nance, who, Ellington said, "never played a bad note in his life" and also danced, sang, and played the violin. Williams himself saw the move as a great opportunity: Goodman's was the greatest *swing* band he'd ever heard, he said. And Goodman, in his turn, did his best to soften Jim Crow's impact on his new star. Williams's friend and section mate, Jimmy Maxwell, was assigned the task of checking them both in whenever they reached a strange hotel. "It cost me a fortune [to live] with Cootie," Maxwell remembered, "because I wouldn't eat in the dining room if he couldn't, so we both ended up getting room service. When there were black waiters, though, if you ordered a steak, they would bring you three."

After the United States entered World War II in 1941, venues like the Forest Park Ballroom in Marshalltown, Iowa, would find it more and more difficult to keep their doors open.

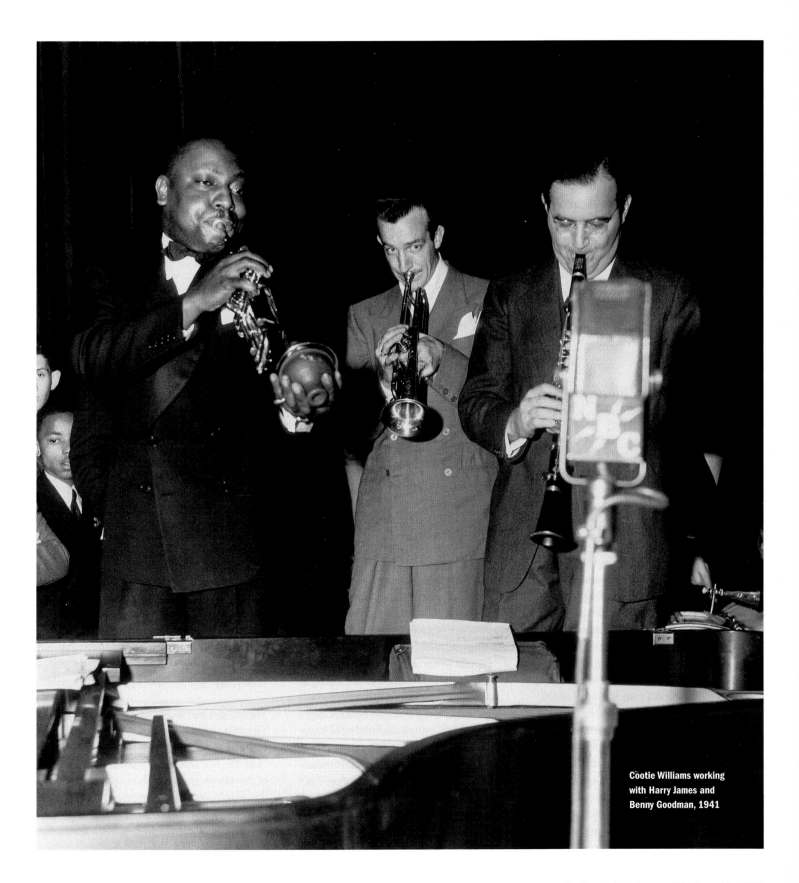

Cootie Williams working
with Harry James and
Benny Goodman, 1941

MEN HAVE DIED FOR THIS MUSIC

Nothing the Nazis could do in occupied Europe could crush the music that propaganda minister Joseph Goebbels called "the art of the subhuman." Jazz stayed stubbornly alive, a bright symbol of resistance. When the Germans barred even the use of the *word* "jazz," the Hot Jazz Club of Belgium renamed itself the "*Rhythmic* Club"— and kept on swinging. And when the Germans banned the performance of all American music in Paris, local musicians simply changed the titles of the tunes they loved: "In the Mood" became "Ambiance"; "Holy Smoke" became "Joyeuse fumée"; and Count Basie's "Jumpin' at the Woodside," turned into "Dansant dans la Clairière." "Swing!" the French jazz enthusiast Charles Delaunay recalled. "This magic word became the watchword for young people everywhere. Swing was on everyone's lips, you swore by it. Everything that was at all original or redolent of American life was baptized 'swing.'"

In 1942, Goebbels changed tactics. Realizing that he could not do away with jazz, he resolved to turn it to the advantage of the Reich, and ordered his ministry to organize its own radio swing band, then aim its broadcasts of familiar American tunes like "Makin' Whoopee" at the Allies with new and poisonous anti-Semitic lyrics added.

> Another war, another profit, another Jewish
>   business trick,
> Another season, another reason for makin'
>   whoopee!
> We throw our German names away,
> We are the kikes of USA.
> You are the goys, folks,
> We are the boys, folks—
> We're makin' whoopee!

In Germany itself, young fans called "swing kids" continued to defy the Gestapo all through the war, to meet in secret, play records, tune in to Allied radio, and dance. The German-born jazz pianist Jutta Hipp later struggled to explain to an American interviewer how important the music had been to her and to her friends during the massive Allied bombing of Germany. "You won't be able to understand this because you were born [in America] but to us jazz is some kind of religion. We really had to fight for it, and I remember nights when we didn't go down to the bomb shelter because we listened to [jazz] records. We just had the feeling that you were not our enemies, and even though the bombs crashed around us . . . we felt safe."

To divert attention from their crimes, the Nazis eventually made a propaganda film intended to demonstrate to the world their supposed "kindness" to the Jews. The infamous Terezin Concentration Camp outside Prague was dressed up as a model "village," and its occupants given new clothes. They were then filmed being "entertained" by inmate musicians, including a jazz band called the Ghetto Swingers. Once the filming was over, the musicians' reward was to be sent to the death camp at Auschwitz, along with hundreds of thousands of other innocent people.

Long after the war, an interviewer asked Dizzy Gillespie if jazz should be considered "serious" music. "Men have died for this music," he said. "You can't get more serious than that."

In a rare frame from a sequence shot for a Nazi propaganda film and now lost, an inmate band called the Ghetto Swingers ostensibly entertains at Terezin concentration camp in 1944. The band's leader, right, is clarinetist Fricek Weiss, who modeled his style on that of Benny Goodman. He and his parents were subsequently gassed at Auschwitz.

notes poured forth with such power and imagination that the great classical guitarist Andrés Segovia is said once to have demanded to know where he could get a copy of the music the gypsy was playing.

"You can't," Reinhardt laughed. "I just made it up."

Reinhardt and Grappelli were in Britain when the war began. Grappelli decided to stay there. Reinhardt returned to Paris and, after the German occupation began, found himself the toast of the city, the best jazz musician in a town starved for jazz. No matter how celebrated he became—and he was a favorite of both French citizens and German officers on leave—he remained a gypsy at heart, wandering off to play billiards while audiences waited in their seats, demanding vast sums before he'd perform, then playing just down the street for free, insisting that restaurateurs serve him gypsy fare like roasted hedgehog, sometimes disappearing altogether for weeks at a time. He managed to avoid ever being made to perform beneath a Nazi flag, and when, in the summer of 1943, he learned that the Germans were planning to send him on a tour of army bases he was determined to escape. He made his way to the border of neutral Switzerland and tried to cross the Alps to safety. A German patrol stopped him before he got very far. He was sure he would be shot or sent to one of the concentration camps to which gypsies less celebrated than he were now routinely condemned. But the officer in command turned out to be a fan, asked for his autograph, and sent him back to Paris.

After France was liberated and the war ended, he toured the United States briefly with Duke Ellington. Reinhardt's playing was wonderful, Ellington remembered, but he had never been certain his guest star would be on hand when the curtain rose. "You had to stay with him every minute because if a chick went by, he'd be behind her, if [he] was coming down the elevator and he saw a sharp chick, oh, man! He'd get in the cab with her. Django was too much!"

Django Reinhardt

The hero of French jazz lovers under the Nazis, the personification of the stubborn individualism that had always been at the heart of the music, was an illiterate and contrary gypsy, to whom politics and patriotism were largely irrelevant. The guitarist Django Reinhardt was born in a horse-drawn wooden caravan in Belgium in 1910, the illegitimate son of a circus clown. His mother, so dark-complected that her nickname was Négros, moved Django and his younger brother back and forth across Western Europe during World War I, trying to keep out of the line of fire of both sides. In 1918, her caravan finally came to rest just outside Paris, where her son began eking out a living playing *muzette,* the music of the French working class. In 1928, he burned his left hand so badly that he lost two digits and the use of the thumb. It took him eighteen months to work out a new and distinctly unorthodox way of fingering. Meanwhile, a friend played him a record of Louis Armstrong's "Dallas Blues." It was the first jazz he had ever heard. He wept at the beauty of it and determined to learn to perform this astonishing music for himself.

By 1934, he and the French violinist Stéphane Grappelli were leading a quintet sponsored by a band of well-to-do jazz enthusiasts who called themselves the Hot Club of France. Their hard-swinging music, influenced by Armstrong and by records they had heard featuring the violin-guitar duo of Joe Venuti and Eddie Lang, caught on quickly all over Europe. Reinhardt's cascades of single

SMOKING PROHIBITED
IN THESE PREMISES

Backstage between sets in New York, Reinhardt watches fellow members of the Duke Ellington band Al Sears, trumpeter Shelton Hemphill, and Lawrence Brown play cards. Bassist Junior Raglin, Harry Carney, and Johnny Hodges also look on from the sidelines.

Music at war. The last known photograph of Glenn Miller (top, left), taken in London just before his plane disappeared over the English Channel, and the cover of the best-selling album made by his Army Air Force Band that was released afterwards. Members of the Count Basie Band (above) surrounded by officers and men at the Tuskegee Army Air Field at Tuskegee, Alabama, in 1943. The musicians visible are, left to right, tenor saxophonist Don Byas, Sweets Edison, Basie, Jimmy Rushing, trumpeter Al Killian (partially obscured), and alto saxophonist Jimmy Powell. The USO staged the servicemen's dance (below) in New York's Central Park. (Opposite) Artie Shaw and his orchestra perform aboard a warship in the South Pacific, 1943.

Members of a U.S. Navy band. President Franklin D. Roosevelt shrank from integrating the armed forces but, he said privately, "there's no reason . . . why we shouldn't have a colored band on some of [our] ships, because they're *darned good at it.*"

is now." But even A. Philip Randolph was unable to persuade President Roosevelt to integrate the armed forces. Black Americans served throughout the war on a strictly segregated basis. Blood supplies for saving the lives of the wounded were carefully separated by race. On one base, a schedule listed separate services for "Catholics, Jews, Protestants, and Negroes." Some commanders forbade black troops to read black newspapers. There were violent confrontations between black and white troops at

military installations. Off-base, American soldiers whose skin did not happen to be white were harassed, beaten, even refused service at restaurants where German prisoners of war were allowed to eat. The Pittsburgh *Courier* mounted a "Double-V" campaign, calling for simultaneous victories over the nation's enemies abroad and discrimination at home. Heavyweight champion Joe Louis got in trouble with his black fans when, after defeating Buddy Baer, he donated his purse to the navy,

when that branch of the armed forces still restricted most African-American sailors to menial tasks.

No one felt more alienated from the war effort than young black musicians. They knew that once drafted they were likely to be sent to the Jim Crow South for basic training, where the relative freedom they had experienced in the North would vanish, and when that ordeal was over, they were less likely than their white counterparts to be offered jobs in military bands.

THESE THINGS CAN'T HAPPEN

Swing had been America's favorite music all through the thirties and no location had been too remote for the radio to reach. The future pianist Dave Brubeck, born in 1920, was a California rancher's son then. His mother wanted him to play classical piano but his rancher father hoped that he would follow in his footsteps, and as a boy Brubeck spent hours on horseback, mending fences and driving cattle. But even as he rode, he had reveries of playing in a swing band. "My dream was that the Benny Goodman Band Bus would want to get through the cattle and I wouldn't let him through unless they let me get on the bus and play with them. In my mind, someday I'd be heard with some band going through there."

Benny Goodman never turned up, but Brubeck's father eventually relented, and he was studying music in college when America entered the war. Graduated in 1942, he joined the army as a rifleman, married a fellow student on a three-day pass, and shipped out to Europe in the summer of 1944, fully expecting to go right into combat with General George Patton's Third Army. Instead, he was picked to lead a band entertaining the men in the field. The United States Army may have been segregated, but Dave Brubeck's Wolf Pack Band was not. The master of ceremonies—named Gil White—was African-American;

so was the trombonist, Jonathan Richard Flowers. The men ate, slept, and lived together, and shared adventures they would never forget. They once played so close to the front lines that German planes swooped down to strafe them—and the whole audience rushed for their weapons to shoot back. During the Battle of the Bulge, Brubeck and his men got lost and found themselves deep in German territory. It was hours before they found their way back to the American lines.

The Wolf Pack Band stayed with Patton's Third Army until the war in Europe finally ended on May 8, 1945. Through it all, the band had remained integrated. But when the men eventually got home the following year, nothing in America seemed to have changed. "When we landed in Texas we all went to the dining room to eat, and they wouldn't serve the black guys," Brubeck remembered. "They had to go around and stand at the kitchen door, and this one guy said he wouldn't eat any of their food and he started to cry and he said, 'What I've been through and the first day I'm back in the United States, I can't even eat with you guys.' He said, 'I wonder why I went through all of this?' "

As the leader of his own quartet, Brubeck would eventually become one of the best-known musicians in

jazz. He refused ever to play anywhere audiences were segregated and once walked off a network television show when he saw that the director planned to shoot his group so that his bassist Gene Wright, who happened to be black, would never appear onscreen. To him, jazz would always represent "the music of freedom." His wartime experiences had something to do with that. So did an experience from his boyhood: "The first black man that I saw," he remembered, "my dad took me to see a friend of his and asked him to 'Open your shirt for Dave.' " More than half a century later, Brubeck's eyes filled with tears at the memory. "There was a *brand* on his chest. And my dad said, 'These things can't happen.' *That's* why I fought for what I fought for."

(Above) Young Dave Brubeck rides the range and (below) performs for the troops with his Wolf Pack band.

Ellington never presented *Black, Brown and Beige* in its entirety again, but he would introduce five more extended works at Carnegie Hall over the next five years: *New World A-Coming, Perfume Suite* (co-composed with Billy Strayhorn), *Deep South Suite, Liberian Suite*, and *The Tattooed Bride*. Neither patronizing critics nor commercial considerations nor the minute-by-minute distractions of life on the road would ever slow his pen. "Ellington always feels that he has found sanctuary when he boards a train," wrote Richard Boyer, who accompanied the band for months in order to write a three-part profile of him for *The New Yorker* in 1944.

He says that then peace descends and that the train's metallic rhythm soothes him. He likes to hear the whistle up ahead, particularly at night when it screeches through the blackness as the train gathers speed. "'Specially in the South," he says. "There the firemen play blues on the engine whistle—big smeary things like a goddam woman singing in the night." . . . Frowning, his hat on the back of his head, swaying from side to side with the motion of the car, occasionally sucking his pencil and trying to write firmly despite the bouncing of the train, humming experimentally, America's latter-day Bach will work through the night.

THAT'S MY HOME

Louis Armstrong was forty when the war began and, like Duke Ellington, too old for the army, but he did what he could, playing army camps and navy training stations, insisting that he be allowed to entertain both black and white units, and visiting military hospitals, where black and white wounded alike begged him to sign their casts "Satchmo."

His courtship of Lucille Wilson remained

Louis Armstrong and friends, somewhere on the road not long before he wed Lucille Wilson in 1942. The woman at the right is Velma Middleton, who would sing with Armstrong's groups for nearly three decades.

stalled so long as he stayed married to his third wife, Alpha. Then, Alpha ran off with Cliff Leeman, the drummer in the Charlie Barnet band. "Thank God," Armstrong wrote a newspaper columnist. "If I could only see him and tell him how much I appreciate what he's done for me by taking that chick away." A Chicago judge granted Armstrong a divorce on October 2, 1942. Ten days later he and Lucille were married. There was no honeymoon; Armstrong began a six-month tour of one-nighters that very evening. Lucille knew enough not to complain—she alone, of all the women he had known, Armstrong said, understood "my horn comes first."

They were still on the road as Christmas approached, and Lucille bought and decorated a small Christmas tree for their hotel room. "I gave him his Christmas present," she remembered, "and we finally went to bed. And Louis was still laying up in bed watching the tree, his eyes just like a baby's eyes." When she reached over to turn off the lights, he stopped her. "No, don't turn

them out. I have to just keep looking at it. You know, that's the first tree I ever had." And when they packed to leave the next day, he insisted she bring the tree along, too. "I kept that tree until way after New Year's," she said, "putting it up every night and taking it down every morning, in a dozen hotels. And then when I did take it down for the last time, Louis wanted me to mail it home."

In fact, there was no home to which to send it. Lucille soon wearied of the road and took the train to New York, determined to find a house in which they both could live. She found a narrow three-story house in a working-class neighborhood in Queens.

When Armstrong's tour ended in March 1943, and his taxi pulled up in the middle of the night to the front door of his new house, he couldn't believe it was his. "*One* look at that big *fine* house and right away I said to the driver, 'Aw, man, quit kidding and take me to the address I'm looking for.' " The cabbie insisted Armstrong was home. "I got up enough courage to get out of the

Armstrong at the Apollo

cab and rang the bell. And sure enough the door opened and who stood in the doorway with a real thin silk nightgown and her hair in curlers? To me [Lucille] looked just like my favorite flower, a red rose."

For the rest of his life, Lucille Wilson Armstrong would provide him with the permanent home for which he'd yearned since his boyhood on the streets of New Orleans. Arvell Shaw, who played with Armstrong for many years, thought he heard something special when his boss sang one of his most frequently requested songs, "That's My Home." "I listened not so much to the timbre of the voice but to the *feeling*," he said, "because it was something that went deep inside. When he would do a tune like 'That's My Home' and sing, 'I'm always welcome back no matter where I roam,//We call it home sweet home,' so help me I'd have to fight back the tears. Now *every night* we'd do that!"

THE STREET

On April 21, 1943, police officers padlocked the doors of the Savoy Ballroom. Both city and military authorities claimed that armed forces personnel had contracted venereal diseases from women they had met there. Angry Harlem residents charged that the real reason was that blacks and whites had not just danced together at the Savoy, but had gone home together afterward. "Hitler has scored a Jim Crow victory in New York," the Reverend Adam Clayton Powell Jr. told his congregation. Closing down the Savoy was "the first step toward segregation" of the city.

There were race riots over jobs and housing all across the North that summer, and in August violence again came to Harlem. Six were killed, seven hundred injured, and nearly fifteen hundred mostly white-owned shops were damaged or destroyed. The old dreams of the Harlem Renaissance were deferred once again. Harlem had already begun to get a repu-

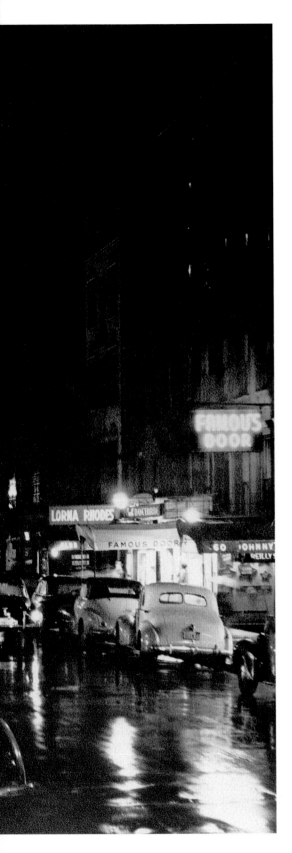

tation among whites as a dangerous place—so dangerous that many jazz fans hesitated to visit it anymore, and the mob-connected men who ran some of its biggest clubs had long since fled downtown to start all over again.

Since the mid-1930s, the living heart of jazz in New York had been two blocks of old brownstones on the West Side—Fifty-second Street, between Fifth and Seventh Avenues. Never, not even in New Orleans at the turn of the century or along the brightly lit Chicago Stroll in the 1920s, had so much great jazz been concentrated in so small a space. Seven jazz clubs still flourished there in the early 1940s. The Spotlite, the Yacht Club, and the Three Deuces were on the south side of the block between Fifth and Sixth; Jimmy Ryan's, the Onyx, and Tondelayo's were right across the street. And there were two more clubs a block further west—Kelly's Stable and the Hickory House.

The Street's unofficial queen was Billie Holiday. It had seemed like "a plantation" to her when she and Teddy Wilson were working there in the mid-1930s, she remembered, but now black musicians were everywhere, black and white customers mingled fairly freely, and the level of musicianship that surrounded her was simply astonishing. Her very first engagement at Kelly's Stables included on the same bill a quartet led by Coleman Hawkins; the hardest-swinging violinist in the history of the music, Stuff Smith (who sometimes fined the members of his quintet ten dollars if they *didn't* come to work high); and at inter-

A rainy night on New York's Fifty-second Street (left), mecca for jazz fans like the rapt duo shown below. Signs for Jimmy Ryan's, Leon & Eddie's, and the Orchid can be seen on the left side of the street facing the marquee for The Famous Door. "Fifty-second Street was total friendship," the songwriter Alec Wilder recalled. "It was the last time that an American street gave you a feeling of security and warmth and the excitement of musical friendship."

Session at Ryan's. On the afternoon of Sunday, February 1, 1942, a New York jazz fan could go and hear this all-star lineup in person: right to left, Al Morgan, Earl Hines, Marty Marsala, Pete Brown, Lips Page, Kenny Hollon, Jack Bland (partly hidden), Red Allen, Zutty Singleton, Max Kaminsky. The identity of the trumpeter at far left is unknown. It all cost just one dollar, and if you missed it there was likely to be another session just as good the following Sunday. Milt Gabler, the man who made it all possible, is at the far left with his finger to his lips.

mission, the pianist Nat "King" Cole and his trio. And competing clubs up and down the Street featured attractions only slightly less stellar.

To a jazz fan like the future impresario George Wein, then a teenager living in Boston, it was an irresistible magnet. "I was just a kid thirteen or fourteen years old and my brother was three or four years older," he remembered, "and we would come down the West Side Highway and we'd get off at Fifty-second Street, and drive. Before we checked into a hotel, we would drive straight across town down Fifty-second Street. . . . It was like being in a candied heaven, and the candy was the jazz that you could grab onto. That night, we would take ten or fifteen dollars that my father had

given us to go out, and I'd go into these bars where I couldn't drink and I would spend a dollar for a ginger ale. We'd go to five clubs. It was just the greatest feeling that one could have, particularly at three o'clock in the morning. I was half-asleep but I wasn't asleep. You were alone, maybe there were three or four couples, and you felt that the musicians were playing for you."

The musicians were playing for one another, too. "We were a brotherhood," one remembered. They moved from club to club to sit in, and crowded the bandstand at Milt Gabler's Sunday-afternoon jam sessions at Ryan's. Sidney Bechet and James P. Johnson and Hot Lips Page and Roy Eldridge and Coleman Hawkins were all regulars. "Eight tenormen could be around at the same

time," a small-time saxophonist named Art Engler remembered.

The courtesy that was shown to each man blowing was unbelievable. If you got a groove going, they'd encourage you, "Take another chorus! Keep going, man!" I remember a session at Ryan's when all the great tenor men in town seemed to be around—Ben Webster, Chu Berry, you name them. I was there, too, and I was scared stiff. But I *had* to play. I forget the tune but suddenly, somebody doubled up the time. And with all these great cats around me, I couldn't hold back. I was so excited, I just started blowing and I blew beyond what I could normally play. I could hear Chu, Ben, and the others urging me on. And soon there were three tenors going like mad, me in the middle, God, you'd come out of a session ten feet off the ground.

When one club owner complained to Jack Teagarden that his nightly habit of picking up his trombone between sets and ambling up or down Fifty-second Street to play somewhere else was cutting into business, Teagarden said he was "just being neigh-borly," and kept right on doing it. "It was beautiful because you'd play all kinds of music," the drummer Shelly Manne said. "It was like a history of jazz on one street. . . . It was really healthy for musicians. . . . I think that was the most creative time in jazz. If you were a jazz historian, you could have gone down there and seen and heard, with your own ears, the evolution of the music, right there on the street, and it all made sense."

In December 1943, something new was added to the rich musical mix on Fifty-second Street. Dizzy Gillespie and Oscar Pettiford brought a quintet into the Onyx. (Gillespie, Billy Eckstine, Charlie Parker, and four other musicians had all recently left Earl Hines rather than undertake another tour of the Jim Crow South. Gillespie had hoped to have Parker with him on Fifty-second Street, but a telegram inviting him to join them was evidently never received.) Nineteen-year-old Max Roach

Members of the Billy Eckstine band onstage in Pittsburgh in 1944: Lucky Thompson, Dizzy Gillespie, Charlie Parker, and Eckstine himself. "I can truthfully say . . . without any type of conceit," its leader remembered, "there was no band that ever swung like that band . . . but we never could get anywhere because [nobody could] hear it."

played drums at the Onyx. Don Byas was on tenor for a time, followed by Budd Johnson. George Wallington played piano.

They were an astonishment. The pace at which they played was often furious. Max Roach's drumming—full-force but filled with subtle changes in pitch and timbre and unexpected shifts between sound and silence—was startling. Even their tunes were different. "We'd take the chord structures of various standard and pop tunes and create new chords, melodies and songs from them," Gillespie wrote. "We . . . added substitute chords to songs like 'Night and Day,' 'How High the Moon?' 'Lover,' 'What Is This Thing Called Love?' . . . We added and substituted so many chords that most people didn't know what song we were really playing. 'How High the Moon?' became 'Ornithology,' 'What Is This Thing Called Love?' was 'Hothouse.' " (If customers were sometimes confused, so was ASCAP, which would otherwise have had to be paid for the use of the original songs when the time eventually came to record.)

Above all, there was the sound of the young Dizzy Gillespie, memorably evoked by *The New Yorker* writer Whitney Balliett: "[He] never merely started a solo, he erupted into it. A good many . . . solos began with four- or eight-bar breaks, and Gillespie . . . would hurl himself into the break after a split second pause, with a couple of hundred notes that corkscrewed through several octaves, sometimes in triple time, and well into the solo itself. . . . Gillespie's style at the time gave the impression —with its sharp, slightly acid tone, its cleavered phrase endings, its efflorescence of notes, and its brandishings about in the upper register—of being constantly on the verge of flying apart. However, his playing was held together by his extraordinary rhythmic sense."

The Onyx engagement "was the thing that put us on the map," Gillespie wrote. It was then, he said, that the new style got its new name. For most tunes, he said, "we just wrote an intro and a first chorus. I'd

say, 'Dee-da-pa-da-n-de-bop.' And we'd go on into it. People, when they'd want to ask for one of those numbers and didn't know the name, would ask for 'bebop.' "

The war years had brought more than musical change to Fifty-second Street. New York was the jumping-off place for thousands of soldiers and sailors about to go overseas, and the Street was a natural gathering place. Music lovers were eventually outnumbered by servicemen and the people who catered to them—strippers, B-girls, pimps.

Servicemen about to ship out found Billie Holiday's languorous, melancholy singing perfectly suited to their mood. "I gave so many going-away parties at the Famous Door, I lost count," she said. "It was always the same: three or four young boys would spend the whole night in the joint; we'd lock up, have a final drink, and they'd walk off. A few weeks later, I'd get a letter from some damn island. . . . Some of the letters would break your heart."

Most of the white soldiers and sailors who crowded the Street during the war were just looking for a good time, but as Gillespie noted, there were also some who'd "come down to the Street to start some shit," and the sight of well-dressed black musicians in close proximity to white women seemed especially to enrage them. Gillespie and Oscar Pettiford were once assaulted simply for walking down the block with the light-skinned, red-haired singer Bricktop. Curses were exchanged. A sailor swung at Pettiford, who swung back. More sailors swarmed the musicians. In the near-riot that followed, Gillespie managed to cover Pettiford's escape by wielding his carpet knife with one hand and swinging his trumpet with the other—being sure to use the valves and not the fragile bell to beat off his attackers. Then he started his own run for the subway, holding his hand over his mouth so that his lip would not be injured. He made it down the steps with the sailors pounding after him, vaulted the

turnstile, then climbed onto a narrow catwalk next to the train tracks and crouched there until his drunken pursuers lost interest and stumbled away.

In the spring of 1944, Charlie Parker and Dizzy Gillespie found themselves together again, back playing one-nighters as part of a brand-new band led by Billy Eckstine. It was a modernist orchestra with distinctly modern attitudes: Gillespie remembered that when the manager of the Plantation Club in St. Louis insisted that the band enter through the back door, "we just walked in with our horns, in front"—and got fired. Its music—much of it arranged by Gillespie— was daring, too. It was a "fantastic" band, its drummer Art Blakey recalled, a nurturing ground for bebop. At various times, Eckstine's band included Sarah Vaughan, trumpeter Fats Navarro, alto saxophonist Sonny Stitt, tenor saxophonists Budd Johnson, Gene Ammons, and Dexter Gordon, and Leo Parker on baritone. But it only made a few instrumental records and they were "sadder than McKinley's funeral," according to Blakey, only a pale reflection of what the men could do in person.

By winter, Parker and Gillespie had left Eckstine and were appearing together frequently as part of a quintet at the Three Deuces on Fifty-second Street. "They played very, very fast," the drummer Stan Levey said. "They had great technique, great ideas. They ran their lines through the chord change differently than anybody else. Prior to them, it was Roy Eldridge, Coleman Hawkins, that type of thing. This was a complete left-hand turn with the music. It was wonderful. When I heard this thing, I said it was for me. I got connected."

"It was the height of the perfection of our music," Dizzy Gillespie remembered, "on fire all the time. Sometimes I couldn't tell whether I was playing or not because the notes were so close together. He was always going in the same direction as me." Nothing quite like it had been seen or heard since Louis Armstrong and King Oliver

Fans line up outside the Classic Theater in Dayton, Ohio, to see Louis Jordan in 1945. Black and white teenagers alike had already begun to shift their allegiance from jazz to rhythm and blues.

had seemed uncannily able to complete one another's musical ideas at the Lincoln Gardens more than twenty years before. Musically, it was a perfect partnership; personally, things were more complicated. Parker was often late and sometimes absent. When Gillespie confronted him about it, Parker denied he was using drugs. Gillespie knew he was lying. There would always be tension between them.

There was tension with some older musicians, too. The drummer Dave Tough, who had learned to play jazz in Chicago during the 1920s but had easily made the transition to big band swing and was always interested in what younger musicians were doing, found Parker and Gillespie intimidating at first. "As we walked in . . . these cats snatched up their horns and blew crazy stuff. One would stop all of a sudden and another would start for no reason at all. We never could tell when a solo was supposed

to begin or end. Then they all quit and walked off the stand. It scared us."

The next summer, Gillespie took an eighteen-piece bebop big band on the road, touring the South as part of "Hep-sations '45," a variety package that featured comedians, acrobats, singers, and the tap-dancing Nicholas Brothers. He had thought they were to be booked into theaters where his music—"geared for people sitting and listening"—might have had a chance of finding an audience. Instead, he recalled, "all we were playing was dances" and southern dancers were unmoved by "Salt Peanuts" and "Shaw 'Nuff," "Bebop" and "Night in Tunisia." They wanted blues and most of the young men in Gillespie's band now considered blues a reminder of the bad old days, a legacy of Jim Crow and even Uncle Tom. "The bebop musicians wanted to show their virtuosity," Gillespie wrote. "They'd play the twelve-bar outline of the

blues but they wouldn't blues it up like the older guys they considered unsophisticated. They busied themselves making changes, a thousand changes in one bar."

Changes didn't interest southern dancers. "They couldn't dance to the music, they said," Gillespie remembered in 1979. "But I could dance my ass off to it. They could have, too, if they had tried. Jazz should be danceable. That's the original idea, and even when it's too fast . . . it should always be rhythmic enough to make you wanna move. When you get away from that movement, you get away from the whole idea. . . . But the unreconstructed blues lovers down south couldn't hear nothing else but the blues. They wouldn't even listen to us. After all these years, I still get mad just talking about it."

The fact was that jazz was no longer the music of choice for young black dancers, north or south. Wartime defense jobs had pulled great numbers of black men and women off the land and into the urban industrial world for the first time. The circumstances of their lives had altered, but their tastes had not. Born and brought up on the blues and with more money to spend than ever before, they constituted a fast-growing market looking for down-home excitement, the kind of music that the singer and alto saxophonist Louis Jordan was now making.

Jordan had worked with Chick Webb when Ella Fitzgerald was with the band. He loved playing jazz with an orchestra, loved singing the blues, too; but he had grown up in show business—his father had led the band for a celebrated vaudeville troupe called the Rabbit Foot Minstrels—and he never lost his delight in entertaining people. He also had a shrewd business sense, and as the popularity of the big bands began to fade, he remembered, "jazzmen played mostly for themselves. . . . I still wanted to play for the people, for millions, not just hep cats." Starting in 1942, he had begun to do just that, exploiting some of the most crowd-pleasing aspects of jazz—an infectious beat, suggestive but good-natured novelty lyrics, and his own bluesy saxophone solos—to produce hit after hit with his Tympany Five: "I'm Gonna Move to the Outskirts of Town," "That Chick's Too Young to Fry," "Choo Choo Ch' Boogie," "Ain't Nobody Here but Us Chickens," "Saturday Night Fish Fry," and "Caldonia (What Makes Your Big Head So Hard?)." "With my little band," Jordan said, "I did everything they did with a big band. I made the blues jump." Other jazzmen, including Lionel Hampton and Cootie Williams, Lucky Millinder and Erskine Hawkins, were now seeking to make the blues jump, too. The result would eventually become known as rhythm and blues.

ONE MAD NIGHTMARE

To Lester Young, the world beyond the sound of his horn had always seemed more or less irrelevant, even unreal. And so, when draft notices began to arrive, he simply ignored them. In August 1944, as he had been preparing to appear in a short film by the photographer Gjon Mili, the FBI caught up with him. Young was "actually crying in that film," according to Jo Jones, "because he didn't want to go into the army."

Young did all he could to stay out, carefully noting on his induction form that he smoked marijuana regularly. The army took him anyway. Since his boyhood encounter with a white mob, he had always tried to avoid the Deep South. Now, he was sent to Fort McClellan in Alabama. The black warrant officer in charge of the regimental band was a former college professor who scorned jazz and refused to permit him to play. Instead, he was ordered to perform endless hours of KP, under a white sergeant from rural Georgia with little patience for a black soldier who lived up North and insisted on speaking a strange language of

Lester Young and Jo Jones, newly captured by the draft, pose for an army cameraman at Fort Ord in California, 1944.

his own. And when the sergeant found a photograph of Young's first wife, who had been white, in his trunk, he evidently saw to it that Young was brought up for court martial for possession of marijuana. An army psychologist diagnosed him as in a "constitutional psychopathic state, manifested by drug addiction, chronic alcoholism and nomadism." He was dishonorably dis-

charged, nonetheless, and sentenced to a year in the stockade. He tried to run away once only to return, he said, when he saw "all those cats with guns." He was permitted to play in the barracks band; later, he would tell Zoot Sims that he had made "those sad motherfuckers swing."

He otherwise rarely talked about his time in the army. "It was a nightmare, man," was all he would say, "one mad nightmare." When he finally got back to the music world, he remained a master of his instrument, as deep an influence on the next generation of saxophonists as his older rival Coleman Hawkins had been on his, and his idiosyncratic sense of humor remained intact. "He'd walk by you while you were sitting in a booth, talking to somebody," the pianist Jimmy Rowles remembered, "and as he went by he'd just kind of brush you with his finger. 'Bob Crosby's in the house.' And keep going. That meant that the fuzz was there and if you had any marijuana, you better watch it. And he was way too slick for any of those guys. He could spot a Bob Crosby anywhere. And the reason why he called them Bob Crosby—sometimes there would be two in a club, he'd say, 'Bing is here, too'—he had [been] arrested one time in Kansas City, or Minneapolis or someplace, by some policeman that looked just like Bob Crosby."

But even before the army took him, his music had begun to change, and afterward, the celebrated silences in his playing grew longer, the whisper-to-a-shout shifts more startling, his sound darker and more anguished. There were fewer jump tunes, too, and more introspective ballads. The effect was world-weary and often extraordinarily moving. Young's personality changed, as well. Always shy and detached, he became wary and reclusive after the war, retreating still further behind his hipster facade, fending off strangers with opaque responses to their unwanted questions—"bells" or "ding-dong." He began to drink too much, also, and over the years, he would grow bitter that younger saxophone players whose styles had clearly grown directly out of his—"the other Ladies," he called them—often seemed to be having more success than he was. "It was pitiful," a friend remembered, "to see him . . . hearing all those young kids playing the ideas he had discarded. . . . You could see him wondering where to turn."

NOW'S THE TIME

On November 26, 1945, at the Savoy recording studios in midtown Manhattan Charlie Parker was at last scheduled to make his first recordings under his own name. He and Gillespie had appeared together on Fifty-second Street that January, and he was now known and admired among musicians. "There was a revolution going on in New York," one saxophone player remembered, "a rebellion against all those blue suits we had to wear in the big swing bands." "It was a cult," another recalled, "a brotherhood." Soon, a third remembered, "there was everybody else and there was Charlie."

But beyond the world of music he was still mostly unknown. At first, the session seemed likely to be a debacle. Bud Powell, the pianist Parker had wanted, had disappeared. Powell's replacement, Sadik Hakim, turned out to be unsure of the chord changes, so Dizzy Gillespie sat in at the piano on the first three tunes, "Billie's Bounce," "Now's the Time," and "Thriving on a Riff." Curley Russell played bass; Max Roach played drums; and nineteen-year-old Miles Davis played trumpet on all three. But the fourth tune was "Ko Ko"—not Duke Ellington's composition but a Parker original, based on the changes of "Cherokee"—and it began with a complex, blistering introduction, which so intimidated Davis that Gillespie stood in for him, then raced back to the keyboard while Parker soloed.

"Ko Ko" would astonish those who heard it for the first time, just as the first records Louis Armstrong made under his own name had astonished people twenty years before. With Max Roach boiling along in the background, Parker and Gillespie leap into their furious eight-bar unison chorus. Then, each plays a dazzling eight-bar arabesque before Parker launches into two ferocious, plunging, note-filled choruses that sound like nothing ever heard before on records. " 'Ko Ko' may seem only a fast-tempo showpiece at first," Martin Williams wrote, "but it is

not. It is a precise linear improvisation of exceptional melodic content. It is also an almost perfect example of virtuosity *and* economy. Following a pause, notes fall over and between this beat and that beat; breaking them asunder, robbing them of any vestige of monotony; rests fall where heavy beats once came, now 'heavy' beats come between beats and on weak beats. . . . [It] shows how basic and brilliant were Parker's rhythmic innovations, not only how much complexity they had, but how much economy they could involve."

Other records had hinted at what was to come, and, thanks in large part to Gillespie's willingness to share his discoveries with anyone who asked about them, big bands like those led by Woody Herman, Boyd Raeburn, and Stan Kenton had already incorporated elements of the new music into their arrangements. But these Savoy sessions were unadulterated bebop—intricate unison themes, dissonant chords, and the most demanding kind of virtuosic solo playing, all driven by bold, assertive drumming that both helped set the ferocious pace and provided a sort of running commentary on everything the soloists were doing. Charlie Parker's secret was out.

"Ko Ko" by Charlie Parker's Ri Bop Boys, the record that let the world know what Parker, Dizzy Gillespie, and their cohorts had been up to during the wartime recording ban

WHITE NOISE AND WHITE KNIGHTS: SOME THOUGHTS ON RACE, JAZZ, AND THE WHITE JAZZ MUSICIAN

GERALD EARLY

REBELS AND RACE

Jazz is the product of the whites. . . . It is the progeny of the blacks.

—Tenor saxophonist Archie Shepp,
Down Beat, December 16, 1965

By 1938, when *Life* magazine published a feature article on jazz and thus conferred middlebrow respectability on a music that fifteen years earlier most mainstream publications considered degenerate, whites dominated the scene. Although not always the music's most original thinkers (and one wouldn't expect it of the majority in any genre) they certainly were its most public personalities.

There was no particular reason in 1938 to think that whites would not always continue to dominate jazz, but this is not quite what happened. After World War II, the critical and historical tides turned strongly toward seeing blacks as the art's major innovators and seeing the music as an expression of certain black aesthetic principles involving the elements of swing and the blues. Doubtless, the civil rights movement had something to do with the change, as African-Americans became an assertive political and moral force in American society and racist attitudes were no longer given social or intellectual credence. Some whites, of course, continued to do very well financially and to receive, at times, considerable public acclaim as players, but it is noteworthy that, of the jazz movements that have sprung up since World War II, the ones most denigrated or dismissed by critics and looked upon with the greatest suspicion by most of the jazz-loving public are the ones most dominated by or identified with whites: cool or progressive or West Coast or third-stream jazz, as well as fusion or jazz-rock, genres generally held in lower esteem than the once-controversial avant-garde of the 1960s. To be sure, a good deal of the music made within these movements hasn't aged well, but a lot of hard bop and soul jazz is just as dated and unlistenable today.

Meanwhile, the critics argued that jazz was always hip, on the cutting edge, with an air of rebellion about it. This certainly seemed to be what jazz audiences believed after World War II,

when the notion was popular enough to become a selling point used by the music industry itself. But however much jazz critics may have exaggerated the extent of this rebellion, it is clear that jazz has generally followed the path of other art forms, where both rebellion and reverence, the anxiety of influence and the need for tradition, exist in a state of continual tension. Tradition is both inspiration and a form of oppression and repression. Rebellion is at once the release of new energy and fresh ideas and an impulse to commit fraud through self-indulgence and novelty for novelty's sake. The traditionalist accuses the rebel of lacking craft and discipline; the rebel accuses the traditionalist of being a reactionary formalist.

It is still true that more whites than blacks play jazz and today black audiences show little interest in it except for the highly commercialized and groove-based "smooth jazz" played by black and white musicians like Kenny G, George Benson, George Duke, Joe Sample, Marcus Miller, and Larry Carlton. Indeed, jazz has become global music, a craft practiced by highly skilled musicians all around the world. But even in this age of diversity and multiculturalism we still seem bedeviled with the question of whether whites can play jazz, whether blacks are more gifted jazz players, whether whites have ever done anything truly innovative in jazz. The legendary Bix Beiderbecke, the only white who could be considered a figure in jazz approaching the stature of Louis Armstrong, Charlie Parker, or Miles Davis, exists not as a paradigm, in the end, but as something of an anomaly. The white player is caught in a curious kind of trap. He is condemned—if he plays something called "white" jazz—for being unable to swing (the music's *sine qua non*), and therefore of being inauthentic. He is equally inauthentic (and a thief, besides) if he plays something called "black" jazz. Within these strictures, therefore, it would seem impossible to be white and play jazz on any terms.

Richard Sudhalter has tried to come to the white musicians' rescue with his recent volume, *Lost Chords: White Musicians and Their Contribution to Jazz, 1915–1945,* a long mess of a book that is neither serviceable nor kind to its reader. There has been a certain amount of unavoidable anger over its publication. Some think that the white jazz musician, after all, has gotten more than his due in the amount of money, publicity, and pop culture legitimacy he has garnered over the years and in the greater number of jobs and venues that were open to him but closed to black musicians. (Some will cynically but rightly say that "Crow Jim," or favoritism for black jazz musicians, came in only when jazz seemed to be dying and there was no place to play it anymore.) To write a book such as Sudhalter's (even, as he protests, in the name of the true multicultural nature of jazz), that is a defense of white people in their whiteness, is, for many, racism trying to disguise itself as an exploration of diversity.

Nonetheless, Sudhalter raises very important points. No one would argue that saxophonists like Lee Konitz, Art Pepper, Paul Desmond, and Bud Shank are as important to the history of jazz as Charlie Parker or John Coltrane or Coleman Hawkins or Lester Young, but are they not as important as Eric Dolphy or Sonny Rollins or Sonny Stitt or Pharoah Sanders or Cannonball Adderley or Dexter Gordon or Jackie McLean? If musical evidence shows that they are, then in any responsible history of the music, these white saxophonists ought to be discussed alongside the black ones. Should we know about Papa Jack Laine, a drummer, who was considered the father of white New Orleans jazz and helped develop such famous white musicians of the early period as Nick LaRocca, Paul Mares, Raymond Lopez, and Leon Roppolo? Is he as important as someone like Art Blakey, who over three decades developed a host of hard-bop black musicians? Sudhalter also brings up the more problematic question of how to define jazz. Are swing and blues the essential elements? Are these the elements that blacks contributed to this music? Is white jazz largely understood as jazz that does not swing and is not blues-based? (I think it is.) Are these divisions accurate at all in characterizing the relationship of race to this music?

The careers of two of the most influential and successful white jazz musicians to appear since 1940, bandleader Stan Kenton and pianist Keith Jarrett, may help us understand better the white musician's perception of himself and how he is perceived by others. The two men are very different: they were reared on opposite coasts (Jarrett on the east and Kenton on the west); each emerged during a distinctly different era of jazz and of American social history (Kenton during the Depression, Jarrett during Vietnam and Watergate); each plays a different style of music; and each approaches the piano in a distinctive way. Even physically, the men are opposites: Kenton was very tall with very long arms; Jarrett is sinewy and short with very muscular hands. Yet there are a number of similarities: both have been accused of arrogance, of musical self-indulgence, of recording too much, of pretentiousness, of lack of originality. Both have intense, cult-like followings that view them as almost superhuman and certainly as compellingly original. But among casual jazz fans and music lovers their music generally goes unrecognized and unheard. Both achieved considerable success for people playing complex instrumental music that is rarely played on the radio today, and both did so with little regard for the fickle desires of the marketplace. And both forcefully articulated principles for playing jazz.

BALBOA AND BEYOND

We were wired, that first summer at Balboa. We were glued in. . . . I was so wrapped up in the music, I didn't even know I was married! We used to follow Stan around. He was like a god to us!

—Bassist Howard Rumsey, in Carol Easton's *Straight Ahead: The Story of Stan Kenton*

Jazz is finished.
—Stan Kenton, *Down Beat,* April 23, 1964

In 1964, Stan Kenton voted for Barry Goldwater for president. In 1968, he voted for George Wallace. It can be assumed that his politics were not simply conservative but far right-wing. It can also be assumed that Kenton did not think much of the civil rights movement. A jazz record producer told me that Kenton's records still have enormous appeal to the members of the NRA. Oddly, toward the end of his life—he died in 1979—he had attracted two very different audiences: old fans who remembered the glory days of progressive jazz and cherished the memory of a band that was loud and aggressive; and young kids, reared on hard rock, who appreciated the Kenton band for precisely the same qualities.

When Kenton read the results of the 1956 *Down Beat* critics' poll, in which guitarist Tal Farlow and clarinetist Benny Goodman were the only white musicians to win in any of the "established talent" categories, he fired off this angry telegram to the editor.

JUST SAW YOUR FOURTH JAZZ CRITICS POLL. IT'S OBVIOUS THAT THERE IS A NEW MINORITY GROUP, 'WHITE JAZZ MUSICIANS.' THE ONLY THING I GAINED FROM STUDYING THE OPINIONS OF YOUR LITERARY GENIUSES OF JAZZ IS COMPLETE AND TOTAL DISGUST.

In an open letter to Kenton, published the following month, jazz critic Leonard Feather responded in kind:

You conveniently ignore the theory, long held among most musicians and jazz authorities . . ., that almost every major development in jazz history has been the work of Negro musicians and that even the few exceptions such as Bix, Benny Goodman, and [Lenny] Tristano admit that they leaned heavily on the inspiration of Negro predecessors.

Doubtless, it came as news to Stan Kenton that for the past twenty years he had been performing a Negro art form. He thought of jazz as simply American, and he said as much in interviews over the years. It must be noted that Feather uses the word "theory," not "fact," in talking about the importance of blacks in the history of the development of jazz. Although he seemed not to realize it, Feather was defending the poll results on political and moral, not musical, grounds by accusing Kenton of racism. "Nobody heard you complain when you were winning," he wrote Kenton, who had received just 10 votes to Count Basie's winning 223. But for all his bitterness, Kenton was right in asking for a musical justification for the selections. If, as he said he always believed, "a man's a man" and the individual counts for everything, and if at least as many whites were playing jazz professionally as blacks, why should blacks so dominate the polls?

"The fact that most of the winners in this critics' poll happened to be coloured," Feather wrote, "had nothing whatever to do with any racial attitude, conscious or unconscious, on the part of the voters." But Feather couldn't possibly know this. If whites had done very well in past polls—and they had dominated them all during the 1930s—why should they now be seen as worse than black players? When did this "theory" arise of blacks as the major innovators in the music, and why had it won the hearts and minds of most critics?

As a result of this controversy, Kenton was seen by some as the last great defender of white jazz, the ultimate white jazz musician. His music became, even more intensely, the embodiment of jazz as the great lost cause of whiteness in American culture. His best biographer, Carol Easton, described the source of Kenton's racial views:

> Stan has periodically been accused . . . of discriminating against black musicians. He has. But in their haste to label him racist, his detractors reveal their own ignorance of the Gestalt that is Stan Kenton.
>
> No man can be expected to be any more or less than the environment that shapes him. Stanley is his mother's son. From early childhood, he was indoctrinated with Stella's philosophy of absolutes: right-wrong, good-evil, black-white, democracy-communism. Scratch the superficial veneer of sophistication and you find, at the core of the man, the provincial, chauvinistic, myopic, unshakable values of the quintessential WASP. . . . Morally, he has no peripheral vision; a social conscience is "that liberal crap."

Kenton did hire black musicians, including Ernie Royal, Karl George, Jesse Price, Jimmy Crawford, Curtis Counce, Kevin Jordan, Jean Turner, Julius Watkins, and Don Byas, a point that comedian Mort Sahl, like other Kenton champions, has made. But blacks never had a real presence in his bands nor any impact on the nature of the music. The *character* of the band was always overwhelmingly white, inasmuch as it is legitimate to describe the character of a band in racial terms. Kenton racialized his music conceptually, or certainly his public thought he did, and many may have found this an appealing aspect of it—which is probably why his defenders like to bring up those blacks who occasionally played with him. (In a March 1958 interview with *Down Beat,* Kenton said this about an important nonwhite music's relationship to jazz, "In the future, Afro-Cuban rhythms are going to loom big in modern jazz; so big that people will stop thinking of them as strictly Afro-Cuban. One day, American music will have swallowed up completely the Cuban rhythms." Leftists see white imperialism in these remarks, while the right sees good old American enterprise and artistic Manifest Destiny.) One finds occasional articles about his band's appearances in the black press of the 1940s and 1950s, but it isn't likely that many blacks joined the Stan Kenton Fan Club in those days; it put "KKK" on all its letters, which stood for "Keep Kenton Kicking."

Unlike Keith Jarrett, who was a child prodigy, Kenton was a tall, ungainly youth with no particular aptitude for anything. But he burned with an adolescent's egotism, a belief that he deserved a better life and that he had something to offer the world. He discovered music as a teenager and made it his mission, his calling. He clung to it for dear life and dear identity, banging heavy-handedly for hours on the piano. He felt that if he did not make a go of it in music there would be nothing for him—there would, in fact, be nothing of him. As he said of his youth:

> I had a very hard time becoming a part of anything. I felt I had no right even to *be* here. I was afraid of people. I was very awkward and clumsy, uncoordinated. I couldn't run or play basketball. I was no good at baseball. Scholastically, I was no great shakes. But I wanted so terribly to *be* somebody, to do something important. Then the music came along, and I went after it desperately, was really *driven* into it, because I was so hungry to identify with *something*. . . . At that particular time, it could have been anything. It just happened to be music.

Kenton's big break came in 1933 when Everett Hoaglund, a leading musician in southern California, hired him to play with his band at the Rendezvous in a town called Balboa, a name that became almost mystically meaningful to him. No matter how far or how much he was traveling, Balboa would become synonymous with Kenton; it was his professional and spiritual home.

Kenton took over saxophonist Vido Musso's orchestra in 1938 and organized his own band two years later. In the summer of 1941 his band was booked into the Rendezvous. There, the Kenton sound was born—unbearably loud, rhythmically overwhelming, made up of ponderous blocks of sound. The young people who heard it went crazy. It seemed like Benny Goodman at the Palomar all over again.

By the mid-1940s, Kenton was playing what he called progressive jazz, filled with dissonance, atonality, and other techniques borrowed from European composers like Milhaud, Stravinsky, and Shostakovich. If you were a white composer or arranger with a yen for twentieth-century European music and a love of big bands, you went, composition paper in hand, to Stan Kenton. His band played places like the Philadelphia Academy of Music and Symphony Hall in Boston that almost never permitted nonclassical performers. Despite the disputes that his music generated—no one was neutral about Kenton; he was either loved or hated—he achieved a great deal of respect as a composer and bandleader among a good many young white musicians, his legion of ecstatic fans, and some critics as

Stan Kenton and college-age fans

well. *Down Beat* and *Metronome* usually wrote about him favorably. He also made a great deal of money with hits like "Eager Beaver," "Peanut Vendor," "Intermission Riff," and a slew of songs whose titles started with "Artistry."

In the late 1940s, Kenton put together a new band, the Innovations Orchestra—forty pieces, including sixteen strings—and performed highly experimental pieces like Bob Graettinger's "City of Glass," which seemed to bewilder and stun audiences. His music grew ever more grandiose. (Bassist Howard Rumsey was onto something when he called Kenton "the Wagner of American jazz," but there was also something about him of Paul Whiteman.) The Innovations Orchestra gave way eventually to his twenty-seven-piece Mellophonium Orchestra (named for the four obscure French hornlike instruments it featured, which the other horn players charged had poor tone and threw them off pitch). It, in turn, was replaced by his Neophonic orchestra (Kenton himself coined the name). His staunch admirers stayed with him through it all, but the general public eventually fell away. In the 1955 film *Blackboard Jungle*, the rebellious students destroy their teacher's Stan Kenton records. Things had changed since 1941.

Kenton's music was white jazz—in some ways the apotheosis of white jazz. Swinging was beside the point. To put it crudely,

in the Kenton worldview, blacks had rhythm but whites had theory. Glenn Miller had put it this way in 1940: "I haven't got a great jazz band and I don't want one. Some of the critics, *Down Beat*'s among them, point their fingers at us and charge us with forsaking real jazz. . . . It's all in what you define as 'real jazz.' It happens that to our ears harmony comes first. A dozen colored bands have a better beat than mine. Our band stresses harmony." Kenton reiterated that notion in 1965: "It's time that we get away from that hackneyed part of the field of jazz music. I have always maintained that a thing doesn't necessarily have to swing all the time to be jazz, because there's a certain way of playing music that came from the jazz conception that can be applied to rubato movement in music or any sort of time, any conception of time. It doesn't have to be always a swing thing."

Kenton had a tempestuous personality—he married three times, talked wildly of becoming a psychiatrist, announced that jazz was "neurotic," then "dead," then reborn. By 1975, illness had forced him to give up the road but he continued to conduct hundreds of clinics at high schools and colleges. He left all his music to North Texas State University. Like so many Americans in the modern age, he believed in the efficacious power of education, that jazz was a sort of creed to be passed on.

Stan Kenton and his orchestra in 1946. Shelly Manne is on the drums.

great white knight of American music, but it is difficult for me to tell at this distance whether he was slaying dragons or simply tilting at windmills.

KUNDALINI

Jazz is one of the least learnable art forms.
—Keith Jarrett, *Jazztimes,* May 1999

Keith Jarrett has been accused many times of making music that is not jazz and that certainly does not, in any conventional sense, swing. He has issued solo improvisations on pipe organ, piano, and clavichord, an early album of pop tunes (an effort best forgotten), and another, called *Spirits,* which sounds like Native American music, and on which Jarrett plays all the instruments, including a variety of flutes and drums. But of all the many records that he has made, and he has been staggeringly prolific, none seems stranger than his 1980 album, *Sacred Hymns,* a recording of music by the spiritualist G. I. Gurdjieff. Jarrett's choice of material seems especially bizarre because the music is uninteresting harmonically, simplistic and lifeless, intended not for listening but as accompaniment to ritual dancing. Its tediousness had to be apparent to Jarrett himself, so the album must have been made for extra-musical, or philosophical, reasons. It exists only as programmatic to a set of ideas that have little to do with music but everything to do with consciousness. To a musician as obsessed with the mythological and romantic significance of bringing music into being as Jarrett is, this is certainly a valid enough reason to record it.

Making such an album reaffirmed certain important self-concepts that have been essential to the Jarrett myth: the primacy of process in the making of music; the refusal in any way to compromise with market taste or with the expectations of his fans, thus intensifying his sense of integrity; the idea, widely held in the sixties when he was making his way as a professional musician, that music is a representation of something spiritual and philosophical. Like John Coltrane, the spiritual and musical hero for many musicians of his generation, Jarrett increasingly saw music as a pervasive force that did more than just accompany or induce certain moods. It was capable of producing both large-scale social change and consciousness-altering personal aware-

Kenton's music may not be listened to much these days, but his reach extends far beyond the people who still buy his records. The white jazz musicians who played with Kenton make an impressive list: Maynard Ferguson, Art Pepper, Laurindo Almeida, Mel Lewis, Charlie Mariano, Anita O'Day, June Christy, Bob Cooper, Shelly Manne, Howard Rumsey, Kai Winding, Shorty Rogers, Lee Konitz, Frank Rossolino, Bud Shank, Stan Getz, Zoot Sims, Pepper Adams, and Sal Salvatore. Among the arrangers who worked with Kenton were Bill Holman, Gerry Mulligan, Bill Russo, Johnny Richards, and Pete Rugolo, all among the most famous of the post–World War II era. When one thinks about all the clinics Kenton held and all the high school and college bands in the country today that play Kenton arrangements, it is easy to see that his impact on American music is very wide. There might, indeed, be less than six degrees of separation between any white jazz musician today and Stan Kenton, perhaps between him and any jazz musician. In this sense, he remains an institution. Unlike Keith Jarrett, who thinks of jazz as something intuitive, Kenton always believed that jazz could be "learned," although he also always feared that it might become "over-intellectualized" and lose its "heart" and "validity."

I saw his band perform at Glassboro State College in New Jersey in 1972. My ears did not stop ringing for two days after the concert; my chest pounded during the performance—whether from excitement or from anxiety I'm not sure. Stan Kenton was the last ness. Having grown up with those ideas, Jarrett extended them so far that he was able to play music that clearly was not jazz without much compromising his standing as a jazz musician among listeners of his own generation.

What brought Jarrett to the attention of thousands of listeners, many of whom had no interest in jazz, was his series of solo piano concerts, long blocks of improvised music—no recognized tunes or songs—performed on a grand piano. Neither the critics, the public, nor Jarrett himself saw it as jazz in the traditional sense. During these performances, which lasted anywhere from sixty to ninety minutes, Jarrett combined snatches of Celtic, Indian, and gospel music, as well as blues and jazz, with moments of haunting lyricism. Somehow, the results never seemed a mere pastiche of effects or influences or whims, but rather were highly conceptualized presentations of real music-making.

Jarrett had three things going for him to make what would seem so unpromising a project a great commercial and critical success. He was unquestionably a virtuoso on his instrument; he produced enough interesting, even challenging music during most of these concerts to overcome the boring, tedious, repetitious, or overly ardent passages; and he played the piano in an energetic manner—his detractors would say it was histrionic and ostentatious—to convey to his audience that he was dramatically seized, possessed by the entire process of music-making, and that what he was doing not only required great inspiration but great physical stamina. (These acrobatics struck the more mystical among his fans as physical reenactments of the drama of Kundalini—the energy that certain Yogis believe lies dormant at the base of the spine until it is activated and channeled through the seven chakras, or spiritual centers of the body.) There was always a sense of uncoiling or unfurling about Jarrett's concert performances, which is what Kundalini—the name under which he published his music for several years—means.

Of course, the gyrations were good showmanship, too, and some came to see him as the Gene Krupa of the keyboard. His playing of classical music (which he was to do with increasing frequency after 1980) did not seem to require them. This made the solo concerts seem to Jarrett's admirers not mere music-making but rather a spiritual event, as if Jarrett were a shaman calling upon the spirits, so shamelessly and vigorously did he demand the favor of his muse. In interviews he said such self-important things about the meaning of these concerts (he had to empty himself of music before he began playing, he said; death surrounded his appearances because he was so vulnerable, so open, when at the keyboard) that they also took on significance as demonstrations of a philosophical proposition about music.

Jarrett's thinking in this regard may have been influenced by Karlheinz Stockhausen, the composer-visionary who argued for what he called, in a 1971 lecture, "intuitive music."

> There are certain abilities required . . . in order to play this sort of music . . . that the traditional musician has never learned. . . . The most profound moments in musical interpretation and composition are those which are not the result of mental processes, are not derived from what we already know, nor are they simply deducible from what has happened in the past. Musicians must learn to become the opposite of egocentric; otherwise you only play yourself, and the self is nothing but a big bag full of stored information. Such people are closed systems. But when you become like what I call a radio receiver, you are no longer satisfied with expressing yourself. . . . You become a medium.

The solo concerts, then, had the appearance of being deep music, while remaining accessible to the large audience they generated, an audience that, by and large, did not care for mainstream jazz. Because Jarrett's highly rhythmic music did not swing, one might say that Jarrett succeeded in apotheosizing white jazz or what most people have come to believe constitutes white jazz. The irony is that during the early 1970s, a good many of Jarrett's listeners thought he was black or biracial, which added a kind of sexiness to white jazz that no one ever thought it could have.

So, this complex set of characteristics, along with the fact that solo piano records were cheap to make—one musician, one instrument—and that Jarrett started these grand piano meditations when most younger jazz musicians were still intrigued by electric or rock-oriented music of the kind that Jarrett himself had played in an early edition of Miles Davis's electric band, helped assure his financial success. The company that recorded him, ECM (Editions of Contemporary Music), first released a three-record set of two solo piano concerts, performed in Bremen and Lausanne, that did very well; then a two-record set of just one concert, in Köln. This became not only Jarrett's most popular record but the most popular solo piano record in the history of American music, probably because it is the most insistently lyrical, the prettiest of all his solo efforts. Finally, in the middle 1970s, came a ten-record set of performances in Japan called *Sun Bear Concerts.* No jazz musician, no musician of any genre, had ever before put out such a massive set of original, totally improvised music. Even this sold well, making the top-ten *Billboard* jazz chart for a time.

As Jarrett's fame grew through the solo concerts, skepticism mounted among some critics: Whitney Balliett was gently dismissive in the *New Yorker,* and Gary Giddins in the *Village Voice* expressed unease with what he called Jarrett's "homesick lyricism." It is hard to say how well the solo concerts will hold up as the years go by but it seems likely that, like Thomas Wolfe's novels, Jarrett's solo concerts go down best with the young. I daresay Jarrett's reputation ultimately will not rest on them. Indeed, had he produced solo concerts alone he probably would have been dismissed by the jazz establishment, especially since they helped to spawn a new genre in popular music: the New Age piano solo—sentimental, simplistic, vaguely tied to nature—played by and sold almost exclusively to whites, seemingly meant only to relieve stress while drinking expresso. (The New Age pianist George Winston has, in fact, replaced Jarrett as the best-selling solo pianist in the United States.)

But Jarrett is also a jazz composer of considerable ability, and during the seventies he wrote music for two quartets, one made up of American musicians, the other of Europeans. The music that Jarrett produced with these groups was simply astonishing, a mix of influences that included Ornette Coleman, John Coltrane, Dave Brubeck, Bill Evans, George Gershwin, the Beatles, and Miles Davis, made richly original through the alchemy of his imagination. At least eight of the albums he made with these groups—*Birth, Death and the Flower, Backhand, Shades, Belonging, My Song, The Survivors' Suite, Personal Mountains*—are among the best jazz records of the 1970s; some are clearly among the best small-group jazz records since World War II. (To my mind, "Blossom," from the album *Belonging,* may be the most moving instrumental jazz ballad ever recorded.)

Since the early 1980s, Jarrett has played and recorded concerts with a trio that performs nothing but standards from the Great American Songbook. This series, too, has produced a number of very fine jazz recordings—especially *The Cure, At the Deer Head Inn,* and *Standards, Vol. 2*—that stand among the best of their era. In addition, Jarrett has recorded classical works by composers ranging from Bach to Shostakovich. Indeed, the solo concerts, even if one thinks of them as absolutely fraudulent as jazz, constitute only a small part of his recorded output. Jarrett deserves to be considered one of the major American musicians of the last thirty years for the astonishing variety and quality of his jazz and classical work. He also deserves credit for being a major force in returning younger jazz musicians to acoustic music, by showing there was an audience for it.

It is difficult to say how much race has affected Jarrett's reputation. Would he be more highly regarded if he were black? Does he enjoy the generally good reputation he does in part because he is white? Would he have been given the opportunity to record

Keith Jarrett, 1968

the same sorts of projects with ECM or any record company had he been black? How much did confusion about his race help him in the early days of his career before it became commonly known that he was of French-Hungarian extraction? How much did he exploit the fact that he had wiry hair puffed like an Afro? Jarrett certainly knew that his racial background was of some interest, as he said in a 1972 interview in *Down Beat.* "All music that is important and valuable comes from exactly the same source. It's just a question of the heredity or ancestry of the people. That's why people have trouble with me, trying to figure out what I am because if you can get to the source of all that music, you can play all that music."

The issue of race was raised more recently in an interview with the *New York Times Magazine.* In it, Jarrett lashes out at Wynton Marsalis, who is unquestionably the most famous jazz musician of our era, with a reputation with the general public that far exceeds Jarrett's own:

For a great black player who talks about the blues—I've never heard Wynton play the blues convincingly, and I'd challenge him to a blues standoff any time.

In the 1960s, the only people who had trouble with my being white were whites. Some kinds of playing, taken to their logical extremes, can be the realm of black players, and others maybe of white players, but the whole situation wasn't so—well, so black and white back then. I played with Miles, and he used to tell me I had to be black in some places. It was so free. It was up to us what we did and who we were, and so much of it happened in private.

One's immediate response to Jarrett's remarks was that he was jealous because Marsalis had achieved the fame Jarrett felt he himself deserved and, worse still, that he believed Marsalis had acquired this acclaim largely because he is black and the public, both black and white, demands a black musician to be the authenticator of jazz. This reduces Jarrett to being the equivalent of a disgruntled white man who is upset because he believes some prominent black is where he is because of affirmative action, not merit. I take him at his word when he said in a subsequent interview: "I don't feel envious of Wynton Marsalis. I feel sorry for him. He was too young to know how to handle what happened." But I think his remarks do reveal a distinct frustration with being a white musician in such a starkly racialized field, in some ways, more repulsively racialized than in the 1920s or 1930s. Jarrett exists in a sort of cul-de-sac without the range of influence or impact that a person of his achievement should have in his field.

His remarks about Marsalis grow from his general disappointment with the current jazz scene, which Marsalis symbolizes more than anyone else and which seems to be producing, to Jarrett's mind, little vital music. It must be remembered that in the 1970s, when Jarrett was at the height of his compositional

powers, he was writing music that was not a recapitulation or a reclamation of the jazz that had gone before but, rather, struck out for his own territory on his own terms. There was little in Jarrett in his early years of success that seemed in any way worshipful of the jazz tradition; he did not even want to be called a jazz musician, and, ironically, it was that attitude, more than anything, that made him most true to the tradition of jazz as freedom and individuality, as attitude and ego, as rebellion and jousting with father figures, than I think he is given credit for. For Jarrett, jazz is not simply a body of music or a set of techniques; it is a psychological stance toward music-making. Therefore it must be seized, confronted, doubted, blasphemed, willed, accepted. But it cannot be learned as a set of rules, as a doctrine, as the unfolding of some predestined historical process. To his mind, to "learn" jazz is, in effect, to put the critics on the bandstand, to make the preoccupations of musicians identical with theirs: interpreting and protecting canons. The British writer T. E. Hulme once said, "There are certain catchwords which, while they embody truth, at the same time kill it." It is perhaps Jarrett's view that current jazz is much like the catchword that is killing the truth it embodies.

What Jarrett says about Marsalis is, in one sense, no worse than what many famous jazz musicians have said about their colleagues in interviews over the years. Jarrett is no harsher than, say, Miles Davis was with Oscar Peterson, whose playing he loathed.

But what is disturbing about Jarrett's remarks is that he makes an issue of both his race and Marsalis's. Marsalis is condemned for being an inauthentic *black* player. Marsalis is "jazzy," Jarrett continued, "the same way someone who drives a BMW is sporty"; in other words, he is a bourgeois black making bourgeois jazz. Jarrett claims that as a white, he can outplay Wynton in a blues contest. The concern is not that this childish boast was made, but that Jarrett made a specific issue of his whiteness as proof that blackness is no authenticator of jazz-playing ability. The point about blackness is well taken; the implicit defense of his whiteness is both gratuitous and irrelevant. Jarrett, thus, wavers between offering a critique and making a racial insult that all arises not over Marsalis's abilities but over Jarrett's self-consciousness about being white. Even in this age of diversity and multiculturalism, the chasm between black and white in jazz remains wide if the work of the most accomplished black musician of his generation is so thoroughly dismissed because he is not "really" black, and if the work of one of the most accomplished white musicians in the history of jazz is not given its proper place in the tradition because he is white.

JAZZ

RISK

The singer Jon Hendricks had served in the wartime army and was on a troopship coming home from Europe when he first encountered the new music that had been developing while he was overseas. "I suddenly heard this song over the ship's radio," he said. "It was frenetic and exciting and fast and furious and brilliant and beautiful and I almost bumped my head jumping off my cot. I ran up to the control room and said to the guy, 'What was that?' He said, 'What?' I said, 'That last song you just played, the one you just played!' He said, 'I don't know.' I said, 'Where is it?' He said, 'It's down there on the floor.' I looked down there on the floor, the floor's covered in records. I said, 'Come on, what color was the label?' He said, 'It's a red label.' So I began to sort them out and I would come across red labels and I would ask him, 'Was it this one?' And he said,

Bassist Tommy Potter, Charlie Parker, Dizzy Gillespie, and a very young John Coltrane at Birdland, the New York club named for Parker. "The first time I heard Bird play," Coltrane recalled, "it hit me right between the eyes."

THE EMBODIMENT OF THE AMERICAN EXPERIENCE
An Interview with Albert Murray

The essayist, novelist, and teacher Albert Murray has been listening to and thinking about America's music since his boyhood in Alabama, where he was born in 1916. Educated at the Tuskegee Institute (where he later taught English), he is a retired major in the U.S. Air Force and the author of nine books—three volumes of essays and three novels as well as Good Morning Blues: The Autobiography of Count Basie *(as told to Albert Murray) and* Stomping the Blues, *a seminal work in the history of jazz, which he prefers to call "blues music." Coproducer Lynn Novick interviewed Albert Murray twice for the Jazz film project. The following was gleaned from those conversations.*

What is jazz?

Jazz is a music played by Americans to get rid of the blues. Once you had a group of people here who defined themselves as Americans, there was going to be an American culture. And the musical synthesis of all of the imported sounds plus the indigenous sounds added up to jazz. This synthesis, ironically, was made possible by the people who came here as captives from Africa. They were slaves but they were also the freest people in America when it came to absorbing all the different elements that were brought over by people from other cultures.

They didn't bring over the music as such but they brought over an emphasis on percussive musical statement because they were dance-beat oriented. Everything they heard they turned into a dance beat. It was as if every instrument became a drum. They were wide open to all the influences that were here—Gregorian chant, Christmas carols, Scotch highlanders' songs, German music, Italian, march music—and they heard it all as *American* music. Everything they made was an American synthesis, a music truly indigenous to American experience. What came out of that was the extension, elaboration, and refinement of a truly vernacular or native culture from a folk level through a pop level to a fine art.

Now, a work of art is a statement which encapsulates the artist's basic attitude toward experience. So if the definitive nature of American culture has to do with freedom, then, if you stylize American attitudes, it would be a stylization of freedom. Nothing embodies that with greater comprehensiveness and wider appeal, or greater profundity and more precision, than jazz.

What's your first memory of the music?

Blues music is so much a part of my experience, it's impossible to know when I first heard it. It was as if I was born knowing the blues. One image which comes to me is hearing the blues from somebody's Victrola in an adjoining neighborhood, hearing Ma Rainey and Bessie

Smith. I knew these were living people. Then there was a guitar player who used to come up out of the railroad bottoms around twilight. Mr. Chaucer—of course people in our neighborhood used to say "there comes old Mr. Choicy"—he'd come strolling up the street by our house and he would be warming up his guitar on the way to some juke joint. I didn't live very far from a place called Soda Waters and there were various honky-tonks down the street in this sawmill and railroad section on the outskirts of Mobile.

When you realize that blues music was basically juke joint music or good-time music, you are right at the core of what the music is about. Now, any church member in the neighborhood that I grew up in would hear sermons against it on Sunday mornings. So a honky-tonk was a sinful ritual. That's why people speak of the Sunday-morning service and the Saturday-night function. The Saturday-night function was for having a good time, but what was so mature about it was that you were having a good time by acknowledging the actualities of life and the contingencies of love. The lyrics were about negative experiences but the whole ambiance of a juke joint was downright aphrodisiac—and that's the opposite of despair.

But it was always secular music, and the communities that I grew up in were as religious as they were secular, so there was a sort of division. The Sunday-morning service had to do with getting down on your knees to propitiate God and to profess your unworthiness and to prepare for life beyond this vale of tears, life in the world to come. Whereas blues music was concerned with coming to terms with the everyday problems of life and creating a basis of continuity.

When did you first hear music you'd call jazz?

As I grew up, I became more interested in instrumental music. There were bands connected with dance hall dances and Mardi Gras. There were local bands, bands from New Orleans, and bands for baseball games. By the 1930s, we began to get jazz not only on records but on the radio. The records that dominated everybody's thinking were the records of Louis Armstrong. We knew those records note for note, everybody's part on every record, all the solos, all the jive talk. By high school, we were listening to the great bands—Fletcher Henderson, Duke Ellington, Jimmie Lunceford, and Earl Hines.

Not only did we hear the music all the time on records, but the bands were very real to us. The great bands were also road bands and so you got a chance to see these people. Cootie Williams was in Ellington's band and he was from Mobile. And Louis Armstrong was little old fat Louis from down in New Orleans and people knew him. It went together with the touring baseball teams. You

would see at some rooming house that there would be [a] bus out front and you knew it was either a baseball tea[m] or a band.

What was the impact of seeing and hearing those great musicians?

Even the guitar players and local honky-tonk players re[p]resented style, elegance, sophistication. And when th[e] big bands came along, as Count Basie used to say, "No[ne] of that ring-around-the collar stuff." Those men alway[s] had to be sharp. They were style setters.

What about Duke Ellington?

Duke Ellington's music represented the musical equiva[ent lent of the American spirit of affirmation in the face [of] adversity. It was constantly creative, it generated res[il]ience that made an experimental attitude possible, an[d] he did it all by dealing with the idiomatic elements tha[t] he knew most about—the blues and popular songs. Th[e] synthesis that Ellington made was American, the intera[c]tion of the learned tradition and the vernacular traditio[n] that adds up to an American form, that qualifies as fi[ne] art. That's what Louis Armstrong represented, too. Ellin[g]ton represented a richer orchestration, but the basis wa[s] already laid by Armstrong. Ellington was Armstrong mul[ti]plied by fifteen. He could use more instruments to say [it] than Armstrong could, but the implications were there.

What did Count Basie mean when he said "Nothing's too[o] fast or too slow to swing."

Nothing is too fast to swing, too big or too small to be el[e]gant. Swinging is the elegant response to chaos. In th[e] music, you know its aesthetic if it's swinging. If you ca[n] make the mood specific enough, what could be mo[re] practical? It's more practical than a checkbook.

The Basie repertory became part of the ambiance [of] my college years. When I graduated, the tempo, the bea[t,] the pulse of the United States that I wanted to be able [to] cope with was "Doggin' Around." Can you solo on "Dogg[in'] Around?" Can you reach the state of resilience, the sta[te] of flexibility, the position that will enable you to be [as] stylish as that music made you feel?

You have a special love for Lester Young.

Lester is the embodiment of the blues idiom as I defi[ne] it. There is an element of melancholy but it's overcome [by] elegance. He's laid back, at the same time here's a g[uy] who has been hurt. Like a combat veteran, he's got [a] sporty limp walk because he's been through somethin[g,] and with those trumpets shouting all around, at all side[s] he's got that parade-ground strut of a guy who's be[en] wounded. I grew up in that context. If you are going to a football player, one of the badges of honor is to come limping into the dining room. People know that you had to pay a price for that. Lester Young's music makes me feel that he's paid the price but he's more elegant as a result. That I take as a human triumph of ultimate proportions.

What about Charlie Parker?
To appreciate Parker it's absolutely essential to remember that he's a Kansas City musician, therefore he's a blues musician. The journalistic approach to music became very abstract in his time, and they started talking about flatted fifths and diminished ninths and then lost track. But just get into a dance hall or into a jam session and start that stuff out and see where it goes and then you get it. Parker's music was based on the simplicity, the stripped-down efficiency that had come from Count Basie. So a very pragmatic way of approaching Charlie Parker is to realize that if you took the straight melody and then listened to Basie play it, it's as if he was subtracting. Then you get to Charlie Parker, and it's as if you had a rococo multiplication on the subtraction. What is getting to you is the emotional impact of blues music hitting you with a new form of elegance.

Talk a little about jazz criticism.
Historically, jazz has been appropriated by various political groups for their own purposes and, unfortunately, much jazz criticism at the beginning had less to do with the music than with what critics were interested in. They were enthusiastic about it but condescending, too. Very few editors seemed to see it as something that required first-rate minds. When they thought of brown-skinned Americans, they wrote about problems and victims, protest and suffering, and although they themselves would have a good time listening to it, the one thing they didn't notice was that the people playing it and in the venues where it was played, got dressed up and were out to have a good time; not to be confused with the awkward abandon of over-enthusiastic visitors out to take off their shoes, undo their hair, and let everything hang out.

American criticism of the arts in the twentieth century has been very much caught up in the idea of avant-gardism and has to do with embracing innovation, the pursuit of something new, something rebellious. But an avant-garde is a military metaphor. It has to do with the advance party, the shock troops, the expendable troops that establish the beachhead in order to bring up the main body. They very seldom get on the beach and of the few that do, maybe half are sent back to the veteran's hospital wounded. Or they retire, shell-shocked, or maybe they're just dead. And when the main body comes up and starts dating the girls, what's left of the avant-garde is

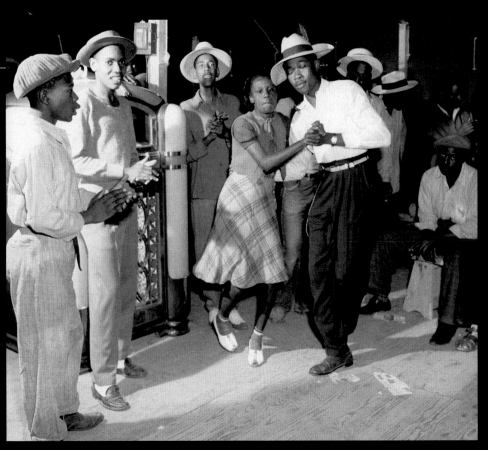

Saturday-night function. Itinerant farm workers shed the blues in a tent near Bridgeton, New Jersey, 1942.

back stateside. American art critics act as if a whole career could be built on that, but an avant-garde not followed by the main body is a lost legion.

Art has to do with security against chaos. What we want are durable forms, things that endure, that go beyond a local situation, a given time, a given circumstance, an approach which addresses itself to humanity, to the whole human proposition. To me there's nothing more boring than the pursuit of novelty.

Ornette Coleman comes up and says, "This is free jazz." But what is freer than jazz? As soon as you *say* jazz, you are talking about freedom of improvisation. The whole thing is about freedom, about American freedom. So why would anybody want to free it from its forms? The whole idea of art is to create a form that is a bulwark against entropy or chaos. Jazz is not meant to be formless and absolutely self-indulgent. That's like embracing the waves in the sea. You cannot embrace entropy. You cannot embrace chaos.

That is where we have come in American jazz criticism. People are praised for being innovative but not for [having] a profound impact. It's simply, "This is new, you should get with it." But true artists are not taken in by that because any really serious artist knows that the creative act itself involves avant-gardism—meaning, to make

that which is out there your own. Giving your own take on it. So each new, creative achievement is, in effect, avant-garde, because if it's powerful enough other people will identify with it. If you make other people want to take something from what you have established, well, that is the *true* avant-garde.

What is it about jazz, after nearly eighty-five years of hearing it, that gives you the most pleasure?
Jazz is the embodiment of the American experience, the American spirit, the American ideal. That's why it means so much to me as a writer to experience people responding to it. They want to move, they want to do something in a certain way, and the best jazz always moves in the direction of elegance, which is the most civilized thing a human being can do. The height of human development is elegance, the ultimate extension, elaboration, and refinement of effort where just *doing* it gives pleasure of itself. That's about as far as we get with life. It's what Ernest Hemingway called the sweat on a wine bottle. If you don't enjoy how those beads of sweat look when you pour the wine out and you taste it and how your partner looks and how the sunlight comes through, well you missed it!

SHOWING YOUR ASS

Most critics remained wary of the new music Charlie Parker and Dizzy Gillespie were making, and the strict traditionalists among them, who had already pronounced swing inauthentic, found bebop still harder to swallow. The *Jazz Record* charged Gillespie with seeking to "pervert or suppress or emasculate jazz." Outnumbered, the youthful champions of modernism, in turn, denounced the opposition as "Moldy Figs." The argument was conducted mostly on the periphery of the music. Ben Webster and Don Byas and other giants of the swing era sought out beboppers with whom to play. Coleman Hawkins recorded with Gillespie and Parker, worked with Howard McGhee, and included Thelonious Monk in one of his groups even when club owners wanted him replaced. Bebop, Hawkins said many years later, was what musicians "*should* have been playing when I came back [to America] in '39."

But there were musicians to whom bebop really did seem little more than noise. When McGhee shared a bill with Kid Ory in Los Angeles, Ory stormed out after one set, saying, "I *will* not play with this kind of music." "We don't flat our fifths," said Eddie Condon, "we drink 'em." Tommy Dorsey denounced Parker and Gillespie as "musical Communists." "Of all the cruelties in the world," said Fletcher Henderson, "bebop is the most phenomenal."

The embattled boppers gave as good as they got. Gil Fuller, who had arranged for Gillespie's big band, said comparing what had gone before with the music he and his

The Dizzy Gillespie All-Stars play New York's Town Hall, May 16, 1945. Gillespie listens as Charlie Parker solos. Harold "Doc" West is on drums. Slam Stewart plays bass. Al Haig (not visible here) played piano that evening and Curley Russell, not Stewart, was on the bass for most of the concert.

associates produced was like equating a "horse and buggy with a jet plane." Gillespie himself once likened earlier jazz to "Mother Goose rhymes. It was all right for its time, but it was a childish time." And the "progressive" bandleader Stan Kenton charged that the trouble with Armstrong and the other members of his generation was that they played without what he called "science."

No one was more offended by remarks like that than Armstrong himself. "These young cats now," he said, "they want to carve everyone because they're full of malice, and all they want to do is show you up, and any way will do as long as it's different from the way you played it before. So you get all them weird chords which don't mean nothing, and first people get curious about it just because it's new, but soon they get tired of it because . . . you got no melody to remember and no beat to dance to. . . . They'll come back to us when all the shouting about bop and science is over, because they can't make up their own tunes, and all they can do is embroider it so much you can't see the design no more. . . . So they're all poor again and nobody is working, and that's what modern malice done for you."

Dizzy Gillespie wanted to bring his audiences what Louis Armstrong called "contentment and pleasure," too. He had helped create the modernist music he called bebop in part to protest against the imperative to entertain with which black musicians had always had to contend. But he had now also encountered audiences that were not just indifferent but openly hostile to it. "Sea to sea," he wrote later, "America in 1945 was as backward a country musically as it was racially. Those of us who tried to push it forward had to suffer." For all his earnestness about his music, he was himself a born entertainer as well as a consummate musician, a product of the swing era who had never lost his love for the power and dynamic range of big bands and who saw no inherent contradiction between demanding

music and a good time being had by all. And he was, as Stan Levey said, "voracious in his drive to succeed."

As soon as Gillespie got back to the East Coast, he began, with help from Billy Shaw of the William Morris Agency, to build himself a new orchestra. "We wanted it to sound like what Dizzy and Bird were doing," said Gil Fuller, "but . . . translated into a big band sound." With arrangements by Fuller, Tadd Dameron, George Russell, John Lewis, and Gillespie himself and tunes like "Ow!" "Oop Bop Sh'bam," "One Bass Hit," and "Things to Come," they succeeded in doing precisely that. Over the next few years, the Dizzy Gillespie band would include an extraordinary number of young musicians who would go on to make names for themselves: Ray Brown, Kenny Clarke, John Coltrane, Kenny Dorham, Paul Gonsalves, Jimmy Heath, Milt Jackson, Yusef Lateef, James Moody, Cecil Payne, and Sonny Stitt.

Few bands in history have matched Gillespie's for sheer excitement. "The power, the rhythm, the harmonies," Kenny Clarke remembered, "were something I'd never heard before. You can't imagine what it was like to play in it." "From the first note to the last note," Milt Jackson agreed, "you could hear that happiness, that togetherness, you can hear it all in that music." The reeds tore through long, intricate lines without so much as a hint of vibrato. "The brass had high notes and lots of 'em," Ray Brown remembered. "Just screaming figures. . . . And after about half an hour of that, you'd look over at the trumpet section, and everybody's lip is hanging down, looking like ground meat." To give the brass section a chance to recover, Jackson and the rhythm section would take over for fifteen minutes or so in mid-performance. (This quartet would later form the first incarnation of the longest-lived combo in jazz history, the Modern Jazz Quartet.)

Gillespie also incorporated something new into the music for his band. Ever since the days when he had played alongside the

Chano Pozo

Cuban-born Mario Bauzá in Cab Calloway's trumpet section, Gillespie had wanted to find a way to bring back into jazz the contagious but complex rhythms of the Caribbean that Jelly Roll Morton had insisted were essential to the music as "seasoning." But Gillespie had something more than spice in mind. He wanted literally to combine the two forms, playing jazz on top of authentic—and authentically complicated —Afro-Cuban polyrhythms. To do it, he needed someone steeped in those rhythms. In 1947, Bauzá told Gillespie of an extraordinary conga player recently arrived from Cuba named Chano Pozo. Pozo spoke virtually no English. "Dizzy no peaky pani," Gillespie claimed he liked to say, "I no peaky engly, but boff peak African." And Pozo was a rough customer—a brawler who carried a bullet lodged too near his spine to be removed, he would soon be murdered by a cocaine dealer with whom he quarreled. But with his help Gillespie produced a series of so-called Cubop recordings that caught on all across the country. The best-known were "Cubana Be–Cubana Bop" and "Manteca" (Spanish for "greasy"), which Gillespie, Pozo, and George Russell put together in December 1947. Both included impassioned drumming, African-style chanting, and trumpet solos by Gillespie based not on chords but on basic scales called modes—an innovation first heard in Duke Ellington's "Tattooed Bride" and that would not be encountered again in jazz for more than a decade.

The impact of these records, Gillespie wrote, "was similar to a nuclear weapon when it burst on the scene. There'd never been a marriage of Cuban music and American music like that before." "Manteca" would remain Gillespie's theme song all his life. Its success helped inspire other bandleaders like Stan Kenton to add Cuban-tinged arrangements to their books, and sent Gillespie and his orchestra on a tour of Scandinavia, Belgium, and France. Everywhere he went in Europe, Gillespie was hailed as a hero. When he borrowed a battered horn to play a Paris concert, young French musicians began distressing their instruments. "They thought they'd get my sound if their horns were beat-up," he said, shaking his head in wonder and delight. "Bebop, the most recent evolution in the history of jazz, has conquered Paris," wrote the poet Boris Vian. "Thanks to Dizzy Gillespie."

Duke Ellington believed that the impact of his own work had been lessened by its having been categorized as "jazz," and he warned Gillespie not to let his music be limited by anyone else's label. But in his eagerness to win a big following and keep his band together, the younger man paid no attention. "If you've got enough money to play for yourself," he said, "you can play anything you want to. But if you want to make a living at music, you've got to sell it." Nobody ever worked harder to sell his music than Gillespie did. He was a dervish onstage, hurtling through breakneck solos

Dizzy Gillespie and his big band at the Orpheum Theater in Los Angeles, 1949. Despite the orchestra's early success, Gillespie wrote, "we were stuck with the old bebop dilemma, whether jazz is primarily a music for dancing or listening."

Bebop as big business. (Above) The opening spread of the 1948 *Life* feature that made Dizzy Gillespie a celebrity—and helped turn his music into a fad; and (below) a Los Angeles appearance at which worshipful dress-alike fans surround their hero

in the highest register, then jitterbugging, singing, swapping jokes with comedians, wearing funny hats. "Comedy is important," he explained many years later. "As a performer, when you're trying to establish audience control, the best thing is to make them laugh if you can. . . . When you get people relaxed, they're more receptive to what you're trying to get them to do. Sometimes, when you're laying on something over their heads, they'll go along with it if they're relaxed." Gillespie did so much to make them laugh during one concert at Carnegie Hall that Louis Armstrong came backstage afterward to tell him he was overdoing it. "You're cutting the fool up there, boy. Showing your ass."

For better or worse, Gillespie allowed himself to become the public face of bebop. The Morris agency billed him as "The Mad Genius of Music" and encouraged the press to write colorful stories about his dark-rimmed glasses and goatee, his berets, the leopard-skin jackets he sometimes wore onstage, the cheeks that puffed alarmingly when he played, and, later, the distinctive upthrust bell of his trumpet, which he said helped him hear himself better—everything except his music. When *Life* planned a big picture story on the new music for the autumn of 1948, Gillespie proved all too willing to play along and even helped persuade the uniformly dignified Benny Carter to cooperate for the camera.

> They made us perform a bebop greeting for them. "Hi-ya, man!" "Bells, man where you been?" Giving the sign of the flatted fifth, a raised open hand.
>
> "Eel-ya-da!" We gave a handshake sign that we were playing triplets, ending with an elaborate handshake. That was supposed to be the bebopper's greeting, but there was no such thing in real life. It was just a bunch of horseplay we went through so they could pretend we were something weird.

Gillespie even pretended to be a convert to Islam, posing in his bedroom with his head bowed toward Mecca because a small but growing number of his contemporaries had become Muslims. He understood the impulse that had made some young black musicians turn eastward—"They've been hurt," he told one writer, with tears in his eyes—and he later bitterly regretted having participated in what he called "blasphemy."

But by 1948, Gillespie's salesmanship seemed to be working. "Dizzy's male fans," wrote *New Yorker* writer Richard Boyer,

> most of whom are in their late teens or early twenties, express their adoration for Gillespie by imitating him. They try to walk with his peculiar loose-jointed, bow-legged floppiness; try to force their laughter up into a soprano squeak; wear blue berets and shell-rimmed spectacles, as he does; smoke meerschaum pipes as he does; and assiduously cultivate on their own lower lips replicas of the tuft of hair that Dizzy wears on his. . . . He knows that his slightest mannerism of action or dress may be reproduced on an international scale. . . . In St. Louis he was photographed with the bottom buttons of his uniform, by chance, unfastened. After the picture appeared in a jazz music magazine, beboppers . . . began leaving their shirts partly unbuttoned.

At one New York club where the Gillespie band played, the owner did a brisk business selling paste-on goatees to female admirers—and to male fans still too young to grow their own.

Like swing music a decade earlier, bebop seemed to be becoming a saleable commodity. "That's right, man!" said a newspaper advertisement for a Chicago tailor, "Bop King Dizzy Gillespie and his great band are another addition to the steadily growing number of top musicians who have made the switch to FOX BROS. for the greatest uniforms and accessories. You dig?" New York's Swing Street had deteriorated steadily since the war—most jazz clubs had been turned into strip joints and Chinese restaurants—but new nightspots, catering primarily to bop fans, now began to open up nearby on Broadway: the Royal Roost, Bop City, the Clique.

The leaders of other big bands, looking for a way to survive in a world increasingly dominated by crooners, thought they saw salvation in Gillespie-style music as well. Woody Herman formed a new band of eager young musicians—his so-called Second Herd—with what he called "the bebop revolution" at its core. Its most memorable recording was Jimmy Giuffre's blistering "Four Brothers," featuring one of the ablest reed sections in jazz history: Stan Getz, Zoot Sims, and Herbie Steward on tenor and Serge Chaloff on baritone. "In the Herman band," bassist Chubby Jackson remembered, "the Marines were coming."

Advertisement (above) for a jam session organized by the jazz disc jockey Symphony Sid Torin; and (below) the marquee of the short-lived Bop City, on Broadway

Ella Fitzgerald enthralls a Manhattan audience that includes Duke Ellington and Benny Goodman, 1948.

Benny Goodman, too, launched a new bop-tinged band that year. It featured Wardell Gray on tenor saxophone, and arrangements by Chico O'Farrill. Bebop "certainly deserves to be encouraged," Goodman said. "They're doing something different, not copying." He especially liked Gillespie and Parker. But "it's nervous music more than exciting music. If some of [the boppers] would just try to simplify their arrangements and solos, they'd come off much better. It seems that they're all trying to outdo and outstartle each other." Still, he said, "I think something good will come out of all of this."

TRYING TO PLAY CLEAN

When Charlie Parker returned to music after his long stay at Camarillo, he was not pleased by the kind of attention Dizzy Gillespie had been getting—or by the eagerness with which Gillespie had seemed to seek it. Parker had brought bebop with him from Kansas City in 1942, he assured one interviewer, implying that no one else had had a hand in its creation. Gillespie's big band was a bad idea, he told another, because it was forcing his old partner to stagnate: "He isn't repeating notes yet, but he is repeating patterns." Parker was still more unhappy with the cultish aura that now surrounded the music. "Some guys said, 'Here's bop.' Wham!" he told another interviewer, shaking his head sadly. "They said, 'Here's something we can make money on.' Wham! 'Here's a comedian.' Wham! 'Here's a guy who talks funny talk.' " The word "bebop" bothered him, precisely as "jazz" had bothered Duke Ellington. "It's just *music*," he said. "It's trying to play clean and looking for the pretty notes."

Parker formed what came to be called his classic quintet, with Max Roach on drums, Tommy Potter on bass, Duke Jordan on piano, and a still-youthful Miles Davis on trumpet. (Later, Davis would be replaced by Kenny Dorham, Al Haig would substitute for Jordan, and Roy Haynes would replace Roach.) Parker played with more assurance and clarity than ever, but he remained perpetually unsatisfied. He was also embarrassed by the acolytes who followed him from bandstand to bandstand, carrying disc recorders, which they turned on whenever he stepped forward to solo and clicked off again the moment he had finished. When someone asked him which three of his records a collector should buy first, Parker told him to save his money.

Meanwhile, young admirers continued to hang on his every note. "When Charlie Parker came on the scene," said Sweets Edison, "he made such an impression on the musicians that if he would play a melody wrong, and if you told one of his disciples that melody was wrong, you might get knocked out."

When the alto saxophonist Art Pepper was introduced by a friend to a recording by Parker, Pepper was as thrilled and thunderstruck as Max Kaminsky had been upon first hearing Louis Armstrong's "West End Blues." "I just got deathly sick," said Pepper. "I couldn't stand any more, and [my friend] was going to play something else [by Parker], and I said, 'No, no, I can't stand it. I can't listen to any more.' "

No one was more eager to follow Parker's lead than a Harlem high school boy and would-be saxophonist named Jackie McLean. He first idolized Lester Young, even bought himself headgear that looked something like Young's trademark porkpie hat. Then he heard Charlie Parker. "As a very young musician," he recalled,

that's how I wanted to play, exactly. I didn't care if someone said I sounded like him. That's what I wanted to do. And that was all I dreamt of doing. I didn't want to be original; I wanted to play like Charlie Parker. This week that he was playing at the Apollo was

perfect for me and the only way I could get to see him would be not to go to school. So, a few of my friends and I would leave home in the morning, and go down in the subway, but instead of going to the Bronx to our school, we would go down to 125th Street and put our books in one of those lockers in the subway and go get in front of the theater and there would be nobody there 'cause it would be so early in the morning like nine, nine-fifteen, something like that. . . . We would sit and watch the movie and then we would wait until it was time for the stage show and then the curtain would come back and there he'd be. And of course, we heard all of this great music that we had heard on these recordings and we would enjoy that show and then we'd get up when the movie came on and dash, sneak out of an exit on the side, so we could see Bird when he came out to get a breath of air and he would just say, "How you guys doing? Aren't you supposed to be in school today?" We'd

The youthful Jackie McLean

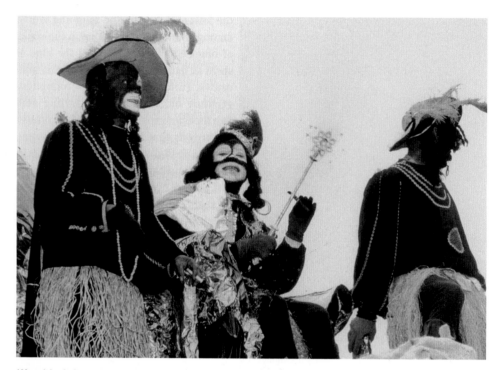

(Above) Louis Armstrong, center, as King of the Zulus during the 1949 Mardi Gras parade in New Orleans; and (below) a collage he created later to commemorate his reign. It includes a roster of all his predecessors as king as well as his lifetime membership card in the Zulu Social Aid and Pleasure Club.

of poverty as great as that encountered by anyone of any color in America, and he had done so without ever putting on airs. He was who he was—"always the same man, offstage or on," according to Barney Bigard —and to have his own people criticize him for remaining true to his New Orleans upbringing seemed hard.

He was especially bitter about one appearance in Dallas where his capacity crowd had been almost entirely white, while just down the street Louis Jordan— "one of them zoot-suit saxophone players playing all that jungle joogie," Armstrong called him privately—had packed another theater with young black fans. When Armstrong said he wanted to play Harlem's Apollo, where he had once been a top attraction, Joe Glaser told him not to bother; it was just another small theater, he said, no longer worth his while. Armstrong had insisted: "Those are my people." But when he finally opened, "he didn't fill the theater," one of his wife's close friends remembered. "And Lucille told me he cried many nights up there, that hurt him so."

Louis Armstrong was now one of the best-known Americans in the world and certainly the best-known African-American, yet the people he had always considered his own were turning their backs on him. It was a wound that would never fully close.

DRASTIC STUFF

In May 1949, a delegation of American musicians landed in Paris for one of the first international jazz festivals ever held anywhere. Sidney Bechet was the best known to French fans, but Charlie Parker had been invited as well. There continued to be dark murmurings in the jazz press that traditional and bebop musicians were mortal enemies. Bechet had told an interviewer that bebop was already "as dead as Abraham Lincoln," and he and Parker had only recently been pitted against each other in a broadcast "Battle of Music," advertised as a "showdown" by its organizer, the writer Rudi Blesh. In fact, they got along fine, once Bechet figured out how to open the dressing-room window to let out Parker's marijuana smoke. Not given to compliments, he nevertheless told Parker how much he admired "those phrases you make," and in the jam session that ended the final day of the festival these two masters—the white-haired New Orleans pioneer and the twenty-nine-year-old architect of bebop—found instant common ground in the blues, the music that was at the heart of everything either man ever played.

Bechet's appearance at the festival marked a triumphant return to the country from which he'd been exiled twenty years before, and he was so well received that he eventually decided to settle in Paris permanently, becoming a revered elder statesman of jazz, known to his legion of admirers as "Sidney Nationale."

To his surprise and pleasure, Charlie Parker, too, found himself a hero to the French, hailed as a worthy successor to Bechet, Armstrong, and Ellington, sought out by Jean-Paul Sartre and other intellectuals, and treated for the first time in his life not as a performer but as an artist. He had already begun to talk of broadening his horizons still further, but when he got back to New York and tried to interest the producer Norman Granz in commissioning works for him to record with a forty-piece orchestra, Granz instead hired dance-band arrangers to produce lush settings for popular standards. The result—an album called *Charlie Parker with Strings*—was disliked by most critics, who found the arrangements bland and unimaginative and accused Parker of selling out, precisely as they'd once scolded Louis Armstrong for abandoning his New Orleans repertoire in favor of popular songs. They failed to see that, as Parker himself said, a performance should be judged "good or bad not because of the kind of music—but because of the quality of the musician." Parker's long, hard-edged, bluesy lines unfurled beautifully above the strings, and

Charlie Parker and Sidney Bechet traveling together to France in 1949, and (below) Bechet striding past the corner of rue Bechet and rue Armstrong in Paris eight years later

Opening night at Birdland, December 15, 1949. The spectacularly eclectic bill included, left to right, Max Kaminsky, Lester Young, Lips Page, Charlie Parker, and Lennie Tristano.

on "Just Friends"—the best-selling of all his recordings—he produced one of the most haunting improvisations of his career. Of all his records, he said, it was the only one he ever really liked.

In December, two weeks after Parker made his first recordings with strings, the refurbished Clique Club on Broadway, renamed Birdland in his honor, opened its bright-red doors for the first time. The opening bill was a smorgasbord of stylists: Max Kaminsky and Hot Lips Page, as well as Lester Young, Charlie Parker, and a little-known singer named Harry Belafonte. "Feelings between the boppers and the traditional jazzmen were strained, to put it gently," Kaminsky wrote. Some of the younger musicians had

been openly disrespectful of Page, and Page had been wounded by their derision. "But Charlie Parker," Kaminsky said, "who was rated the great genius of all that [modern] music, liked my band better than anything else he heard there. We had nothing else in common; I couldn't drink the way he did, and I didn't know his friends and never went out with him on any parties, but musically we became good friends."

Nothing musical was ever alien to Charlie Parker. He often drank at a midtown bar whose jukebox was stocked in part with country music. When one of his acolytes asked why he liked to hear songs they all thought corny, he answered, "Listen. Listen to the stories." A friend remembered leaving him transfixed in a Manhattan

snowstorm late one night, unable to tear himself away from the thump and blare of a Salvation Army band. Another told of driving with him through the countryside when someone remarked idly that livestock loved music. Parker asked the driver to stop, assembled his horn, stalked into a field, and gravely played several choruses to a bewildered cow.

"Jazz has got to go on from here," he had told trumpet player Red Rodney. "We just can't stop with this." And when Rodney asked him who would show the way, he answered, "I'd like to be the one to do that." Like Bix Beiderbecke before him, he began to look to European composers, not American sources, for inspiration. The future, he told one interviewer, lay in finding a way to blend the complex harmonies of modern European music with the emotional color and dynamics of jazz. But, also like Beiderbecke, he knew he lacked the grounding in music theory that would have allowed him to bring about the kind of meeting of musical traditions he had in mind. To rectify that, he sometimes spoke wistfully of returning to France to study composition with Nadia Boulanger, enrolling at the Conservatoire Nationale de Musique, or taking instruction in orchestration from Edgard Varèse. "I only write in one voice," Varèse said Parker told him. "I want to have structure. I want to write orchestra scores."

Parker seemed finally to have found a little domestic peace. His marriage to Doris Sydnor had ended, but he had moved in with a woman named Chan Richardson and adopted her daughter. "He was irresistible," Richardson remembered. "He had a life force, an incredible life force. Bird was a giant. . . . He had a maturity beyond his years. In fact, he said to me one day, 'I'm not one of those boys you're used to.' And I went 'Ooooh!' " They would have two children together, Pree and Baird, and would live for a time on Manhattan's Lower East Side, where Parker led a life that on the surface seemed very like that of his neighbors: breakfasting with the children, strolling to the corner for the morning paper, watching westerns on television.

But with Charlie Parker, nothing was ever quite as it seemed. On the bandstand, he was usually able to discipline his furious talent. But offstage he was all too often out of control. "*This* is my home," he told a friend as he rolled up his sleeve to inject himself. The pianist Hampton Hawes remembered watching in disbelief one evening as Parker, chain-smoking marijuana, first downed eleven shots of whiskey and a handful of Benzedrine capsules, then shot up: "He sweated like a horse for five minutes, got up, put on his suit, and half an hour later was on the stand playing strong and beautiful."

There would still be nights when he'd pull himself together to play strongly and beautifully, but they would grow fewer and further between as the years went by, and the appetites that always gnawed at him would prevent him from seriously following any of the new musical paths of which he'd spoken, precisely as similar hungers had kept Beiderbecke from following his. "Bird tried to kick many times while he was with me," Chan Parker recalled, "sometimes very successfully. But he told me once, you know, you can get it out of your body but you can't get it out of your brain."

"Jazz was born in a whiskey barrel," said Artie Shaw, "grew up on marijuana, and is about to expire on heroin." Alcohol had always been part of the jazz world, helping to relieve the stress of life on the road and the strain of performing every night, and marijuana had been part of it since the twenties. Louis Armstrong continued to smoke it nearly every day. But heroin was different—"drastic stuff," Armstrong called it—and it soon seemed to be everywhere, dumped by organized crime into black big-city neighborhoods, where it found a ready-made market among youthful newcomers from the South who found in it momentary relief from dislocation and disappointment. "Heroin came on the scene like a tidal

Billie Holiday in performance, 1949

wave," Jackie McLean remembered. "I mean, it just appeared after World War II. And I began to notice guys in my neighborhood nodding on the corner, and so we all began to find out that they were nodding because they were taking this thing [we] called 'horse.' " McClean himself would be engulfed by it, and would remain addicted for eighteen years.

One by one, many of the most gifted musicians in jazz would be lost for a time to narcotics, among them Art Blakey, Chet Baker, John Coltrane, Tadd Dameron, Dexter Gordon, Stan Levey, Gerry Mulligan, Fats Navarro, Art Pepper, Max Roach, Sonny Rollins, Sonny Stitt, and eight of the sixteen men in Woody Herman's band. The tenor saxophonist Stan Getz tried to support his habit by holding up a drugstore, spent six months in jail, and returned to drugs and alcohol almost the moment he got out.

Each man's demons are derived differently, of course; no two musicians fell prey to drugs for precisely the same reasons. But there were common threads. To begin with, as Blakey explained, "it makes you feel good. . . . I started it because I liked it. There isn't any other reason." Heroin extended the natural high that playing produced, stretched out the process of winding down after performing. It served to soften the edges of the gritty world in which musicians were forced to earn their living. And, some said, it also seemed to slow things down, made it easier to perform at the accelerated pace the new music often demanded. It didn't help anyone to play better, Blakey said, but it did "make you *hear* better."

Above all, perhaps, there was the example set by Parker, whose genius every aspiring musician envied. Trying to match his dazzling technique, his frantic tempos, his overflowing ideas, worshipful musicians began consciously to emulate his addiction as well as his music, partly in the hope that by sharing it they could somehow share his

genius, too. "Bird was like fire," John Lewis remembered. "You couldn't get too close."

Dope undercut professionalism and served to split the jazz community between users and non-users. "Heroin was our badge," Red Rodney remembered, "the thing that made us different from the rest of the world. It was the thing that said, 'We know. You don't know.' It was the thing that gave us membership in a unique club, and for this membership we gave up everything else in the world. Every ambition. Every desire. Everything. It ruined most of the people."

It would help to ruin Billie Holiday, too. In 1941, she married a sometime marijuana dealer named Jimmy Monroe and began smoking opium. Then she moved in with Joe Guy, a good-looking trumpet player who had once been in Minton's house band. He was addicted to heroin, and soon, she was using it, too. When her mother, Sadie, died suddenly of a stroke at forty-nine, Holiday was devastated. She had often quarreled with her mother but had also relied on her for emotional support. Now she felt abandoned, terrified of being alone. Her casual drug use became complete dependence. She missed dates, fought with accompanists and club owners, and spent virtually all of her income paying for drugs for herself and Joe Guy. Finally, Joe Glaser, now her manager, insisted she have herself hospitalized for six weeks to end her habit. It didn't work.

On May 19, 1947, narcotics agents arrested Holiday and Guy in their New York hotel room and charged them with possession. She pled guilty and was sentenced to a year and a day in the Federal Reformatory for Women at Alderson, West Virginia. At Guy's trial, she refused to say whether or not he had purchased the heroin the agents had seized. He went free. While she was locked up, her New York cabaret card was revoked; she could still give concerts in New York when she got out but was no longer allowed to perform in clubs. Old

friends stopped seeing her. Even Lester Young had drifted away.

Beyond the damage dope did to the lives of the individual musicians who became its victims, it did still more to the jazz world as a whole. Eager always for sensational stories, the press exaggerated the already sordid details until even musicians who had nothing whatsoever to do with narcotics—and the overwhelming majority of musicians did not—came under suspicion. The old link between musicians and the black community was further weakened as well. Before the narcotics plague hit, Dicky Wells remembered, "when word spread that the band was in town, doors flew open." But afterward "they [flew] shut—wham, wham —twice, so they [would] stay closed."

IT REALLY BROKE MY HEART

"BOP IS A FLOP—COMMERCIALLY," *Variety* reported in late 1949. "The musical style is dying almost as fast as it began, according to maestros who employ it, agents who book it and recording companies which grabbed fast a few months ago to corral its exponents." In the end, their brief foray into bebop could not save the big bands. Charlie Barnet broke up his orchestra, admitting that the small crowds who'd turned out to hear him in recent months had "a legitimate beef," because the band's new bop-based arrangements hadn't been "particularly good for dancing." Woody Herman, $175,000 in debt, disbanded his Second Herd. Count Basie temporarily gave up his orchestra in favor of an octet. Benny Goodman surrendered, too, never again to lead a full-time band of his own, and would later blame the new music for his failure. "The damn monotony of it got to me," Goodman remembered. "Bop was mostly publicity and people figuring angles."

Dizzy Gillespie's band had fallen on hard times as well. For all his success, his payroll continued to outpace profits. Music lovers clustered around the bandstand wherever he appeared, but the big crowds of dancers the band needed to stay afloat stubbornly failed to materialize. During one southern tour, even the sight of Gillespie and guest star Ella Fitzgerald doing the lindy together had not been enough to persuade other dancers to join in. "They didn't care whether we played a flatted fifth or a ruptured 129th," Gillespie wrote. "They'd just stand around the bandstand and gawk." Frankie Manning, once one of the best-known professional jitterbuggers at the Savoy Ballroom, admitted to having been stumped by Gillespie's music, too. After five years in the army and off the dance floor, he formed a dance troupe called the Conjurors and tried to go back to doing what he did best.

> I worked with Dizzy's band in Washington, D.C. . . . We went on the stage. I gave him my music, "Jumping at the Woodside"—Count Basie—and he's got this drummer up there, and he's giving me all this "chuck-a-bong pim, chick-a-pim" and I usually hear "chick-a-chu, chick-a-chu, chick-a-chu." When we finished the act and I came off, I said to Dizzy, "What the ———is this you're doing?" It was different from when I used to see kids out there on the floor, *swinging.* Eventually, I got to understand the music, but it was not music for dancing. And that is the thing that I had been used to, music for *dancing.*

Finally, in March 1950, Lorraine Gillespie gave her husband an ultimatum: "You got a hundred musicians or me! Make up your mind." Gillespie reluctantly let all of his men go. "Everybody was sorry about that, man," he said many years later. "Cats were crying. . . . So was I. The fad was finished."

The men in the Duke Ellington band were eventually forced to swap their private Pullman for a bus but the orchestra never left the road. Here, in 1961, more than a decade after most of the big bands had broken up, high-note trumpet star William "Cat" Anderson, an unidentified friend, and Johnny Hodges pass the time playing cards as their bus takes them across America.

EXTREME JAZZ:
THE AVANT-GARDE

GARY GIDDINS

For many jazz lovers, the avant-garde is an inferno that reproaches the musically decorous while derogating mainstream orthodoxy. Though its audience is international, its achievement vast, its influence sweeping, its history fully half as long as that of jazz proper, it is often regarded as a thing apart—a separateness sanctioned by those avant-garde enthusiasts who listen to nothing else. Like much of jazz history, this schism has a precedent in European classical music: the divisive reaction—augured by Shavian critics who championed radical Wagner at the expense of reserved Brahms—to serialism, which begat converts and antagonists but few neutrals.

The avant-garde has been treated as a metaphor rather than as music by proponents and enemies alike. The former have adapted it to suit social and political movements as various as Marxism, mysticism, pacifism, internationalism, black nationalism, and integration, implying at times a revolutionary-cause-du-jour applicability. As a result, the avant-garde is not infrequently characterized as a music of the left. But so is jazz itself—"a people's music," in Sidney Finkelstein's 1940s phrase. Detractors revile avant-gardists as both elitist and barbarous: on the one hand, as insulated academics who hijacked jazz and turned it into a nearly occult pursuit only they can comprehend; on the other, as charlatans who clothe their ineptness in rhetoric and noise. Either way, naysayers invariably insist, the avant-garde alienated the very "people" it hoped to liberate.

I offer two anecdotes to confirm and muddle prejudices in each camp. At a Finnish jazz festival in the early 1980s, two saxophonists from East Berlin, performing outside the wall for the first time, spoke poignantly of jazz's liberating power and then embarked on a fusillade of shrieking high-note blasts. After several minutes of this, a notable American avant-gardist turned to me and said, "Let's go. This stuff is a lot more fun to play than to listen to." At a rehearsal by a New York jazz orchestra a few years later, musicians bitterly groused when it was announced they would be conducted by a famous avant-gardist in a program of his music: "He can't play," "It's a mockery," etc. When the guest conductor arrived and the musicians read his scores, they marveled at his craftsmanship and, having assured themselves of his skill, earnestly embraced the rigors of his music. After the concert, the most outspoken of the early skeptics conceded to me, "He's a brilliant guy. I wish we played more music like that."

If we are to rescue avant-garde jazz from parochialism of any kind, we need to define the term. The dictionary is the place to begin: "n. 1. A group, as of artists and writers, regarded as pre-eminent in the invention and application of new techniques in a given field. 2. The admirers of such a group and critics acting as its spokesmen. adj. 1. Of or relating to the vanguard, as in the arts. 2. Ahead of the times." All these definitions are useful, but quite obviously too general. A distinction must be made between a universal avant-gardism and a school of jazz known as the avant-garde. I emphasize "known," because most innovators resist the pigeonhole; indeed, they vigorously resent a characterization of their music that presumes complexity and mayhem, virtually warning their potential audience to exercise caution.

Jazz has always had a vanguard, performers who propelled the music in new directions, dismaying generations of fans content with what they already knew. Louis Armstrong, Jelly Roll Morton, Duke Ellington, Bix Beiderbecke, Earl Hines, and Coleman Hawkins were among the jazz pioneers of the 1920s, each in his way an avant-garde musician who helped relegate customary jazz, rag, and blues styles to the dead ends of the past. Their innovations were perceived not as assaults on convention, but as the kind of ingenuity that enhances traditions without undermining them. Yet in raising jazz to a new plateau of emotional and technical expression, they precipitated the greatest schism of all, delivering art music from folk music and dividing artists from journeymen. Since we venerate them much more than we do their dimly remembered predecessors, we do not burden them with the stigma of otherness often associated with the avant-garde, but rather honor them as forebears.

Nor do we think of the swing era as avant-garde. The Basies, Goodmans, Shaws, and Luncefords were undeniably "pre-eminent in the invention and application of new techniques," and conservative critics predictably assailed them for enfeebling and commercializing classic jazz, but you can hardly call them "ahead of the times"; they *were* the times. Lester Young may have been considered too far out for New York in 1934, yet two years later countless musicians, and not just tenor saxophonists, were trying to play like him. Staunch anomalies such as Red Norvo's "Dance of the Octopus," Coleman Hawkins's "Queer Notions," or Duke Ellington's "Reminiscing in Tempo," though avant-garde for the day, were too singular to suggest a movement or even a style.

Bebop created a greater divide, splitting the jazz world in two and engendering as much contumely, ridicule, and recrimination as the avant-garde school born in its wake. The methods of Charlie Parker, Dizzy Gillespie, Bud Powell, Thelonious Monk, and dozens of others—a peer group in thrall to a new music and

An evening in Cecil Taylor's Manhattan loft, sometime during the 1980s. The tenor saxophonist is Henry Threadgill; Jerome Cooper plays drums.

a new way of thinking about music—were quintessentially avant-garde, except for one thing. Even as contemptuous pundits poked fun at alleged bebop manners, the musicians supplanted their predecessors almost as completely as Armstrong's generation superseded the raggy beats and polyphony of Dixieland. Armstrong and swing didn't disappear with the advent of bebop, however, but were pressed into a historical frame. Like Bach overlooking Mozart overlooking Beethoven, jazz had now established a history of unceasing revision; it was an expanding and developing art that continued to infuriate the musically complaisant while keeping the adventurous, if not on the dance floor, then certainly on their toes.

Aspects of the avant-garde jazz movement can be traced back to every other kind of jazz. Consider, for example, its reintroduction of polyphony—one of the dominant strengths of the avant-

garde. Bebop evolved from the past with an attitude of determined modernism, setting itself in opposition to the clichés and styles of the past; the avant-garde opposed clichés but not styles, accepting the entire canvas of jazz history as its platform. Still, its direct roots lie in bebop, which raised issues about harmony, melody, rhythm, and instrumentation that succeeding generations could scarcely fail to explore. Charlie Parker said he came alive when he realized he could improvise on the higher intervals of chords. His successors expanded that quest, exploring the limits of chords, then dispensing with them altogether. Even as bop introduced a categorical, tight-knit virtuoso style, it encouraged innovations that challenged its own precepts. Was bop an obstacle course of refined chord changes? George Russell composed a piece for Dizzy Gillespie's orchestra ("Cubana Be/Cubana Bop") that eschewed chords in favor of modes or scales. Were bop's rhythms of such velocity that only cymbals could mark the beat? Gillespie and Parker introduced Afro-Cuban rhythms and Latin percussion instruments. Was bop hot? Miles Davis gave birth to the cool. Were bop variations so cunning they obscured the themes? Monk stressed thematic variations.

Monk was branded a charlatan for his unconventional style as pianist and composer. George Russell's "A Bird in Igor's Yard," which meshed jazz and classical techniques, and Lennie Tristano's "Digression," a "free" group improvisation (without prestated melody, harmonic structure, or tempo), were considered so avant-garde in 1949 that Capitol Records refused to release them. Yet, again, these were isolated performances, and though they heralded jazz schools (third stream, the Tristano cult), they were not the stuff of a movement. That came later, triggered by musicians who came of age during the bop era but were regarded as outcasts by their contemporaries. Considering the number of directions jazz took in the fifties—cool, hard bop, third stream, soul, modal—and the remarkable range of personalities that flourished, a player would have to be fearsome indeed to earn a nearly unanimous disrespect. Happily, a few were.

After three years at the New England Conservatory, Cecil Taylor relocated to New York and was laughed off bandstands until he began to attract like-minded musicians, even disciples. In 1956, at age twenty-seven, he recorded his first album, *Jazz Advance.* Not exactly a salvo, it introduced a startling new voice, that of a pianist who played at and around chords while sidestepping the kind of linear melodies that were the foundation of practically all modern jazz improvisation. His touch was so brisk and percussive, he seemed to be beating drum patterns on the keyboard. On "Rick Kick Shaw," he offered a template for a piano style redolent of diverse jazz and classical influences without quite deferring to any of them. The album was largely ignored or patronized.

At the same time, John Coltrane, an apparently insignificant tenor saxophonist who had worked with Gillespie and Johnny Hodges but was not above playing low-rent bar gigs, experienced a musical and personal rebirth and dedicated himself to the compulsive study of scales. At thirty, he was hired by Miles Davis and revealed a keening high-register sound and a prolix style that crammed so many notes into a chord he left nothing for his accompanists to play. After he recruited a scorching rhythm section—McCoy Tyner, Jimmy Garrison, Elvin Jones—Coltrane developed his music with astonishing fervor, winning and losing audiences along the way. One initially admiring critic described his approach as "sheets of sound," only to dismiss "Chasin' the Trane" as an "airleak" a few years later.

At the same time, in Los Angeles, Ornette Coleman—who, to hear him tell it, was run out of his native Fort Worth for playing alto saxophone in a way that made usually peaceable musicians resort to violence—was attracting followers willing to put their preconceptions on hold, notably Don Cherry, Charlie Haden, and Billy Higgins. Desperate for work, he offered his compositions, singular melodic inventions that could be immensely moving and wittily tumultuous, to Contemporary Records. The label surprised him by signing him to play them. His first album, recorded at age thirty, proffered the exclamatory but reasonable title *Something Else!!!* Its successors were more insurgent: *Tomorrow Is the Question, The Shape of Jazz to Come, Change of the Century.* Coleman's ebullient if raw quarter-tone pitch conveyed the primitivism of rural blues and, at the same time, a shocking modernist mockery.

If Taylor, Coltrane, and Coleman represented the beginnings of a new jazz movement, it was unprecedented in several regards. For one thing, they were making an impact at relatively advanced ages; Louis Armstrong and Charlie Parker effected revolutions at

Pharoah Sanders

twenty-five. For another, they tended to eye each other cautiously, from a distance. Unlike the progenitors of swing or bop, who frequently performed and recorded together, these three offered widely disparate approaches to a new kind of jazz. Coltrane recorded once with Taylor and once with Coleman's band, but never with Coleman, who in turn never recorded with Taylor. Each man was a school unto himself. Their divergent musics reflected uncommonly diverse backgrounds. Parker, Gillespie, and Powell came from different points on the map, but all were spawned by jazz. By contrast, Taylor was classically trained and Coleman apprenticed himself in rhythm and blues; only Coltrane issued directly from jazz.

That they signaled the beginnings of a musical movement did not become clear until the early 1960s, when the attention they garnered encouraged numerous other musicians to join them on the jazz fringe. Unlike musical uprisings of the past, this one did not admit of a generational divide. Eric Dolphy, a late bloomer from California and an accomplished technician by any standard, moved to New York to play with the Charles Mingus Quartet and instantly attached himself to Coltrane and Coleman. Mingus himself, the superb bop bassist who now publicly criticized musicians in his own band for relying on bop's clichés, cast a wary eye at the newcomers but was himself liberated by the spirit of radical adventurism. Jimmy Giuffre, the tenor saxophonist who wrote Woody Herman's "Four Brothers," organized a free-form trio with bassist Steve Swallow and the influential pianist Paul Bley, who had worked with Coleman and was developing his own approach to free or spontaneous improvisation. Sun Ra, born in 1914 and an alumnus of jazz's first great orchestra, Fletcher Henderson's, moved his much recorded but neglected Arkestra to New York in 1960 and emerged as a dynamic mobilizer of the new music.

In 1960, Coleman recorded his double quartet, *Free Jazz,* and gave the movement a name, though ultimately one of limited utility. Free-form improvisations unquestionably accounted for much of the new jazz; they marked an inevitable response to the highly structured patterns of bop. The year before, Miles Davis enjoyed immense success with *Kind of Blue,* one of the most iconic of jazz LPs, popularizing a modal approach to improvisation. "So What" is commonplace in form (AABA, thirty-two bars), but instead of a system of chord changes, the harmony consists of one scale (D minor) for twenty-four bars and another a half step higher for the release. A few weeks later, Coltrane, who played on that session, recorded *Giant Steps,* taking the opposite tack on the title piece, which has two chords to every measure. Davis winnowed bop's harmonies to encourage original improvisations, and Coltrane

maximized them for the same reason. Coleman took the next step: complete freedom from fixed harmonic and, for that matter, rhythmic patterns. He focused on melody, allowing harmonies to emerge serendipitously. His music had a buoyantly swinging rhythmic pulse but abrogated the steady demarcations of a 4/4 beat. You couldn't listen with half a mind, because there were no familiar resolutions; you had to concentrate on the escapade of Coleman's solo and the way the ensemble accompanied it.

The new music took a major leap in 1962, when Cecil Taylor's trio—altoist Jimmy Lyons, drummer Sunny Murray—performed and recorded at Club Montmartre in Copenhagen. In addition to abandoning fixed harmonies once and for all, Taylor pushed further than Coleman had in liberating rhythm. Coleman's beat was rootless, but the pulse was relatively regular. Taylor, with Murray's support, allowed the rhythmic pulse to permutate, moment by moment, as a consequence of whatever he played; the energy of his attack governed the time. Swing was no longer a downbeat you could follow with your foot, but a percussive wailing you followed as closely as you might a melodic variation. Taylor also shared the Club Montmartre bandstand with Albert Ayler, a young tenor and soprano saxophonist, recently discharged from the army, whose ballistic harmonics, sing-song themes, and otherworldly solos were so startling, some thought he had to be kidding.

Meanwhile, Coltrane continued to speed into the stratosphere of musical expressionism. Cynics could deride Ayler and Coleman as fakes, and Taylor and Dolphy as virtuoso aesthetes; Coltrane, however, had come through the ranks. Though one critic branded him "anti-jazz," no one questioned his technical command of jazz harmony and rhythm, the exquisite pitch-perfect beauty of his sound, the emotional resolve of his ballads and blues, or his sincerity. If he chose to play free, committing himself to a new music that alienated so many, he had to be taken seriously.

By 1963, the avant-garde had the verve and brawn of a genuine crusade. A year later, a series of six concerts produced by thirty-nine-year-old trumpeter, composer, and educator Bill Dixon at New York's Cellar Cafe brazenly proclaimed the new order as nothing less than "The October Revolution in Jazz." And a whole generation of players was ready to storm the gates, among them Archie Shepp, Milford Graves, Roswell Rudd, John Tchicai, Marion Brown, and Pharoah Sanders. Two record labels announced their commitment to the new music. The independent ESP-Disk, originally created to promote Esperanto, got off to a heady start with Albert Ayler's *Ghosts,* and introduced new musicians on an almost monthly basis, including a few who considered the avant-garde a musical option, not a religion: pianist Don Pullen, who created one of the major ensembles of the eighties, linking avant-

Lester Bowie

their art had been fatally subverted, and some tried to make common cause with rock, while others accepted private students or joined school faculties, and still others sought studio or pit-band work until the storm abated. The avant-garde players, as always, had an even rougher time. After the novelty value waned, not even the innovators sold enough records to maintain a vivid presence. Many of the most critically admired avant-garde works sold a couple of thousand copies at best.

And yet the influence of the avant-garde was everywhere. Established musicians were responding to its musical challenges and emotional immediacy. They adapted, in their different ways, what they found viable, even if it was nothing more than license to go overboard. I recall musicians in the mid-sixties expressing astonishment at how "inside" Coleman sounded, when only a few years earlier he had seemed impenetrably "outside." Small wonder. In the interim, the avant-garde rubbed off on almost everyone who didn't bolt from jazz entirely. A new genre appeared: the ultramodern album by mainstream-modern musicians to the right of the avant-garde, who could not resist testing its turf. Consider Sonny Rollins's *Our Man in Jazz,* Jackie McLean's *Destination Out,* Charles Mingus's *Black Saint and the Sinner Lady,* Andrew Hill's *Point of Departure,* Stan Getz's *Sweet Rain,* Tony Williams's *Lifetime,* Sam Rivers's *Fuscia Swing Song,* Wayne Shorter's *The All-Seeing Eye,* Roland Kirk's *Rip, Rig and Panic,* Modern Jazz Quartet's *Space,* Jaki Byard's *Sunshine of My Soul,* Miles Davis's *Miles in the Sky,* and Gil Evans's *Blues in Orbit,* among many others, all of which partake of the avant-gardism rife in the 1960s. Rock groups also borrowed licks from the new jazz; by the mid-seventies, the studios were rampant with Coltrane imitators—you heard them on pop records, in TV bands, and in film scores.

Still, with all this going on, the avant-garde appeared to curl up in hibernation. Coleman's label, Atlantic, dropped him in 1961, and he recorded erratically in the years to come, often traveling in the opposite direction of free jazz, with notated works for string quartet, symphony orchestra, rock band, and other ensembles. His unique sound and attack, however, abided. Inexplicably, Ayler, whose finest work was lavishly flamboyant in the best sense, began to record hippie fusion anthems before his tragic death in 1970. Of the major avant-garde figures, Taylor, like Monk before

garde and mainstream techniques; bassist Eddie Gomez, who enjoyed a long association with Bill Evans; and Bob James, the godfather of "jazz lite." The most widely distributed avant-garde label was Impulse, a subsidiary of ABC-Paramount, which signed Coltrane and bannered its gatefold covers with the slogan "The new wave of jazz is on Impulse!"

The movement had a profusion of competing names: free jazz, the new wave, the new music, the New Thing, black music, revolutionary music, fire music, out music. That the term "avant-garde" remained after the rest faded into a miasma of 1960s oratory may be attributed in part to its prevailing, inoffensive meaning. But it also came into play because of the strange circumstances that followed the music's ostensible acceptance, when in spite of its expanding influence, the avant-garde showed signs of corruption and a general languishing.

Avant-garde jazz reflected the turmoil of the 1960s. It was a minority music, expressing euphoria and sadness and daring and resentment and anger and other feelings through styles so extreme as to utterly alienate most of the traditional jazz following—itself a withering minority in the age of rock. The rhetoric for and against was often ugly, as it had been during bop, though now you also heard accusations of racism, tomming, and worse. Most of that passed quickly enough, though a lingering distrust continued to rend the jazz audience. Veteran musicians felt that him, had to wait the longest for acceptance. Between 1962, when he recorded at the Montmartre, and 1973, his only records were two stunning 1966 Blue Note LPs, *Unit Structures* and *Conquistador!,* a concerto written for him in 1968 by twenty-four-year-old Mike Mantler (recorded by his Jazz Composer's Orchestra), and a taped concert from Europe in 1969. Taylor spent a few of those years teaching at colleges in the Midwest.

Coltrane's death in the summer of 1967 had a baleful impact on all of jazz, but it marked the beginning of the Coltrane legend. A church was consecrated in his name in San Francisco, and his record sales—mostly modest during his life—began to soar. His passing symbolized jazz's capitulation to rock in the late sixties, though there was really nothing symbolic about it. ESP-Disk became a reissue operation, as did Impulse, despite a series of ambitious recordings by Archie Shepp and Sam Rivers. Record labels folded, and clubs went dark. The next few years were a rough patch in jazz history.

But jazz came roaring back in the mid-seventies. It was a period in which a slew of not-very-old masters—among them Rollins, Mingus, Dexter Gordon, Sarah Vaughan, Gerry Mulligan,

the Modern Jazz Quartet, James Moody, Hank Jones, Red Rodney, and Phil Woods—tired of their sabbaticals and side trips and returned to action with new energy, helping to refuel the mainstream audience. It was also the period in which a new coterie of avant-garde musicians took much of the jazz world by surprise, thoroughly overturning some of the assumptions generated by their predecessors. They had a broader agenda, and they interpreted the idea of freedom as the capacity to choose between all the realms of jazz, mixing and matching them not only with each other but with old and new pop, R&B and rock, classical music and world music. Lester Bowie recorded an unaccompanied trumpet fantasy called "Jazz Death?" in which he interrupts his purple mosaic of a solo to ask if jazz is indeed dead; at the end, he answers cavalierly, "Well, I guess that all depends on what you know."

These musicians ambushed the national press because they had been honing their music not in New York, where much of the press and the record industry resides, but in points west, especially Chicago, St. Louis, and Los Angeles. Some had toured Europe, and several had recorded for small labels, little more

Performances by members of the Association for the Advancement of Creative Musicians were often accompanied by pageantry. (Right) The group's founder, Muhal Richard Abrams than vanities for the most part, with the noted exception of Chicago's Delmark Records. On that label, one began to hear of a cooperative called the AACM (Association for the Advancement of Creative Music) and to hear the music of its guru, Muhal Richard Abrams, an erstwhile bop pianist, and its younger members, including Bowie, Roscoe Mitchell, Joseph Jarman, Leroy Jenkins, Henry Threadgill, Anthony Braxton, Chico Freeman, Steve McCall, George Lewis, and Leo Smith. Before long, many relocated to New York, where seemingly overnight new venues—in many instances, apartments or lofts (hence the phrase "loft jazz")—opened shop to present their wares.

This was all pretty astounding, sociologically and musically. Instead of lone paladins arriving from different cities, hoping to sit in, win recognition, and make a name, here came gangs of accomplished players, some just getting started, others past forty. In addition to the AACM players, there was the Black Artists Group from St. Louis, including Julius Hemphill, Oliver Lake, Hamiet Bluiett, and Bakaida Carroll. A kind of offshoot of the AACM developed in New Haven, where Yalies Anthony Davis and George Lewis worked with Leo Smith and Fred Anderson. From Los Angeles came a network of players without an acronym but with a history of working together, ranging from John Carter and Bobby Bradford—associates of Coleman long before he came to New York and now in their forties—to Arthur Blythe, a veteran of Horace Tapscott's Los Angeles band, to college students James Newton, Mark Dresser, and David Murray.

It is impossible to overstate the degree to which all these players countered the most meretricious effects of fusion and sparked a renewed hunger for creative jazz, setting the stage for the return of many of the aforementioned mainstream jazz stars. They were a new breed of musician, often doubling as painters and poets and entrepreneurs. They formed small bands that lasted for years, decades, including the trios Revolutionary Ensemble and Air, and the ongoing Art Ensemble of Chicago. They defied expectations; Threadgill's Air played free and used hubcaps for percussion but also cannily interpreted tangos and Scott Joplin. Many musicians harbored big-band ambitions and eventually realized them, energizing orchestral jazz for the first time in a decade. Yet they also performed in any way that was economically feasible, pioneering solo wind concerts and duets. They made it a point of honor to write original music but were not averse to playing standards. Though contentious rhetoric was occasionally heard, it was usually a benign expression of black pride; this music was more often satirical than angry. Arthur Blythe arrived in New York with a nickname given him by friends as a young man, "Black Arthur." One critic attacked him for the moniker alone, assuming him to be a crazed militant. When Blythe played his alto, however, he produced a dynamic, brittle, pear-shaped sound, sweet and sour, that hadn't been heard in jazz since Benny Carter, and that perfectly reflected the man.

Free jazz to these musicians was not a specific, aharmonic way of approaching improvisation, but one style among many. Even when they played free solos, they often couched them in contexts that were scrupulously notated. The more important point is that they were not limited by the artificial boundaries of idiom. Sun Ra, long a Midwesterner, understood this all along, and at his concerts in the 1980s, he typically combined impetuous blowouts with complex arrangements, visual spectacle, blues and tap-dance rhythms, a sermon, a Fletcher Henderson arrangement, and "Hello, Dolly!." It was not uncharacteristic for a pianist like Anthony Davis to play Ellington one season and compose an opera the next; for Muhal Richard Abrams to orchestrate an Ellington piano piece at one concert and employ ripped newspapers as voicings at the next; or for Julius Hemphill to record aggressive unaccompanied sax solos one year and devise a theatrical pageant the next.

Perhaps the most resourceful of the younger players was tenor saxophonist, bass clarinetist, composer, and bandleader David Murray, who at twenty paid homage to Albert Ayler, identifying himself with the avant-garde tradition, and before he was thirty added homages to Hawkins, Young, and Paul Gonsalves. Murray never had one band when he could have several, so you could hear him with a quartet, his widely celebrated octet, his big band, as well as solo and in duos and trios. With Hemphill, Bluiett, and Lake, he created the World Saxophone Quartet, which at first played free because they had nothing written, but soon built up a superb book of original pieces. In the late nineties, Murray played with jazz musicians from every generation, as well as rock, hip-hop, gospel, European, and African musicians.

Wave after wave of avant-garde musicians continue to show up, bringing to bear the influences of whatever musics they know and adapting them into the broadest possible jazz context. In New York, they now appear regularly at places like the Knitting Factory and Tonic. Dozens of labels—the most prominent include the pioneering Black Saint and Soul Note in Italy, DIW in Japan, and the expanding Knitting Factory Records in New York—record them. The names and faces change, but they continue to explore avant-garde traditions. Joe Morris plays Ornette Coleman on guitar, and John Zorn's Masada explores Jewish themes in a context directly related to Coleman's sixties quartet. There is hardly a pianist, no matter how exquisitely trained, whose attack hasn't been affected by the belling cascades of Cecil Taylor. David S.

The World Saxophone Quartet: David Murray, Julius Hemphill, Oliver Lake, Hamiet Bluiett

Ware's quartet, one of the most highly regarded ensembles of the decade, is made up of two Taylor alumni (Ware and the ubiquitous bassist William Parker) and a pianist, Matthew Shipp, who extends Taylor's methods in an entirely personal direction. The Rova Saxophone Quartet transcribed and recorded, note for note, Coltrane's *Ascension,* which thirty years ago was considered the most exhilarating or appalling assault on musical conventions ever played. Several avant-garde players routinely join with mainstream musicians; competence is rarely an issue.

The avant-garde is no longer a jazz school, like swing or bop, and cannot be supplanted. It is rather a kind of parajazz, which has evolved in various directions over the past forty years, blending with every other kind of jazz and every other kind of music, including R&B, klezmer, electronic, country, Bulgarian folk songs, koto, gamelan, Mahler—you name it, you can find it. Though the avant-garde enjoys a predictably narrow following, the audience is constant in the United States and even more so in Europe, where fusions between jazz and classics are more readily assimilated. Most avant-garde jazz is clearly anchored in jazz; some of it is just as clearly anchored alongside. Though no longer an exclusive territory of innovators, gadflies, and prophets, it remains a loose confederation of individualists who take nothing—not even swing or blues—for granted. Like jazz, parajazz offers something for everyone.

JAZZ

THE ADVENTURE

On February 24, 1952, Dizzy Gillespie and Charlie Parker appeared together on a television variety show called Stage Entrance. The kinescope
made that day is all that we have of Parker in
public performance, and the Down Beat awards
ceremony that precedes it provides an excruciat-
ing example of the kind of condescension often
displayed toward jazz and jazz musicians, even
by those who believed themselves boosters. The
critic and composer Leonard Feather delivers a
stiff little speech about brotherhood, then hands
the host, Broadway gossip columnist Earl Wilson,
a pair of wooden plaques to present to Parker and
Gillespie. Wilson greets the musicians, offers up
the plaques—making fun of Gillespie's nickname
as he does so—and then asks, "You boys have anything to say?"

Don Cherry, left, and Ornette Coleman at New York's Five Spot

For once, Gillespie is speechless. Parker, his face without expression, his voice low and icily polite, replies: "They say music speaks louder than words, so we'd rather voice our opinion that way." During that voicing—an abbreviated version of the bop anthem "Hot House"—Parker's face remains impassive, his fierce eyes and the movement of his big fingers on the keys the only outward signs of the effort required to yield such brilliant, jagged cascades of sound, the sound itself the most eloquent possible response to patronization.

The end of the Gillespie big band had been more than a personal disappointment for its leader. It also marked the end of an honorable but doomed effort to build a bridge between the new music and the old jazz audience. Similar efforts by other musicians would be made over the years to come. None would entirely succeed. For better

Pee Wee Ellis and Ron Carter playing for "listeners only" at the Pythod Club in Rochester, New York, 1958

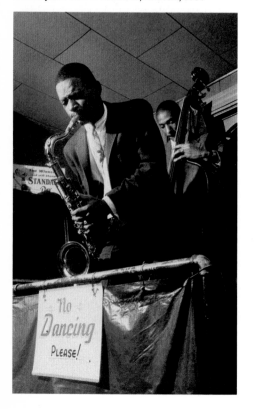

or worse, jazz seemed on its way to becoming an art music, meant for concert halls and nightclubs, not ballrooms—adventurous and demanding; intended for aficionados, not ordinary people; infused with the every-musician-for-himself spirit of the jam session; aligned not with the American mainstream but with the growing counterculture for which commercial success was evidence of corruption, of "selling out." "Our dislikes followed a pattern . . . ," the jazz writer Barry Ulanov once confessed, "which began with our celebration of an unknown musician, singer or band, and ended with our derogation of the same musician, singer or band when he, she, or they had achieved popularity."

No one present at the music's birth in New Orleans could have foreseen that any of this would happen. But then, nothing about the trajectory of jazz had ever been predictable. First, America's most important music had been created by African-Americans, a people from whom little or nothing had been expected by the country's white majority. Then it had been nurtured by the marketplace, which, according to modernist theory, should have been inimical to art. Most of the great figures in jazz's first half century—Buddy Bolden, Jelly Roll Morton, and King Oliver; Louis Armstrong and Duke Ellington; Bix Beiderbecke, Coleman Hawkins, Lester Young, Benny Goodman, and Count Basie—had managed to make unforgettable music while pleasing dancers for a living. "If I hear a sigh of pleasure from the dance floor," Ellington once said, "it becomes part of our music."

"The kind of jazz we [all] played had a functional base," Max Kaminsky remembered. "We . . . played to provide the music for dancing. Before our time, jazz had been played in marching bands, in street parades, at picnics, funerals, weddings. Before that, jazz had been evolved from blues and work songs [and from the churches]. All this was in the music. It came out of the raw stuff of life." But now, Kaminsky continued, everything seemed to be changing.

Jazz, like Dr. Frankenstein, had all unwittingly created a monster in its own image—the jazz addict—who, in becoming all hopped up about . . . its significance as an art form, very nearly snuffed the life out of it. . . . [J]azz no longer belonged to the musicians and the dancers; it was taken over lock, stock, and barrel by the fans, the addicts, the record collectors, the amateur critics, the recording companies, the promoters, the nightclub owners, the A&R men, the lecturers and writers. These were the people who now decided what was jazz and what wasn't, who dictated how it should be played and on what instrument, and specified who could or could not play "real" jazz.

There was more to it than that. Jazz had started out as an exuberant ensemble form, its impact derived in large part from the cooperative spirit of the musicians, their ability simultaneously to play and to listen to one another. A man's reputation then had rested on his individual sound and the imagination and rhythmic sophistication he brought to the two- and four-bar breaks that Jelly Roll Morton said were essential to the music. In the early 1920s, the singular genius of Louis Armstrong had brought the soloist front and center and established once and for all the notion of the improvising jazz musician as romantic hero. But until the early 1940s, even the most celebrated soloists had still been expected to work their magic within a carefully arranged framework. Solos remained relatively brief. A premium was put on telling one's story with economy as well as with emotion and imagination. And the theme on which the improvisation was based was often as familiar to the listener as it was to the musicians.

The music that Parker and Gillespie pioneered was deliberately different. Tunes were either wholly new or consciously disguised. Ensemble passages were almost

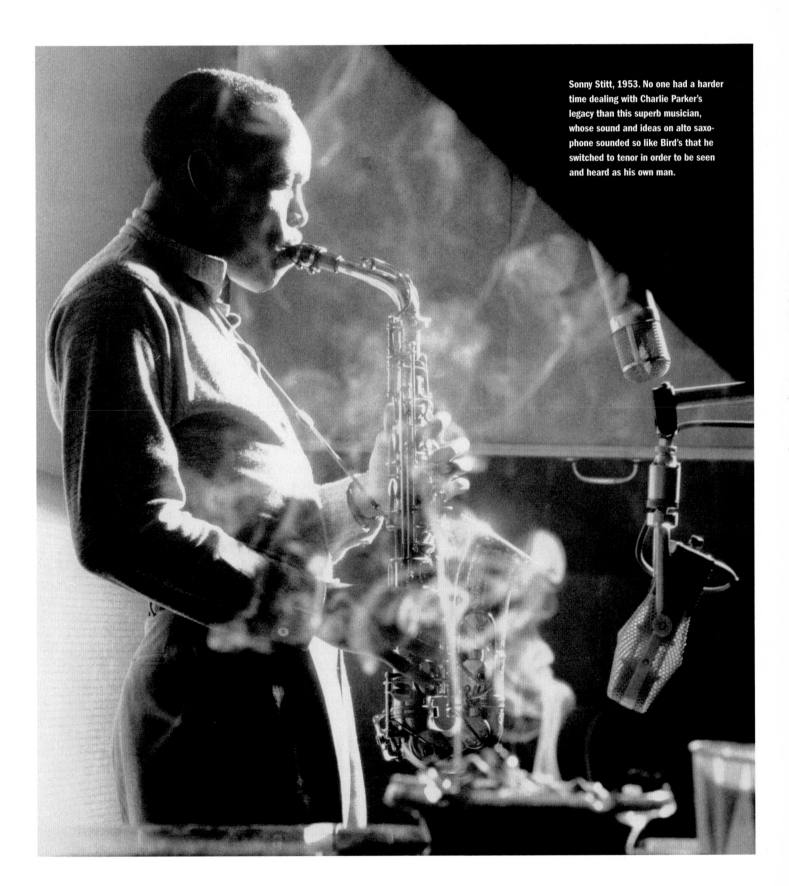

Sonny Stitt, 1953. No one had a harder time dealing with Charlie Parker's legacy than this superb musician, whose sound and ideas on alto saxophone sounded so like Bird's that he switched to tenor in order to be seen and heard as his own man.

beside the point. Everything depended on the energy and ideas of the improvisers. If that energy and those ideas seemed inexhaustible—as they routinely did when bebop's creators were on the bandstand—the sheer momentum and creative power let loose had the potential to thrill anyone willing to listen. But even when Parker and Gillespie were playing, there was always the risk that, by pouring forth so much unrelenting musical complexity, they would eventually inundate even their admirers. (Parker himself understood this. "More than four choruses," he once warned Milt Jackson, "and you're just practicing.") And over a long evening, in the hands of less talented musicians, the standard bebop format—ensemble theme, string of solos, ensemble theme—could exhaust the patience of even the most earnest audience.

"COOL"

"Bird and Diz were great," Miles Davis remembered, but "if you weren't a fast listener you couldn't catch the humor or feeling of their music. Their music wasn't sweet and it didn't have harmonic lines that you could easily hum with your girlfriend trying to get over with a kiss." He would be among the first musicians to begin looking for ways to broaden the music's appeal and restore some balance between the soloist and the ensemble.

In the winter of 1947–48, Davis was part of a steady stream of musicians who filed in and out of an apartment building on East Fifty-fifth Street in Manhattan at all hours of the day and night. The pianist John Lewis often dropped by when he was not on the road with the Gillespie band. So did Max Roach and Kenny Clarke, trumpeter-arranger Johnny Carisi and composer George Russell, trombonist J. J. Johnson, alto saxophonist Lee Konitz, and the lanky, red-haired baritone saxophone player and arranger Gerry Mulligan.

Their goal was the one-room basement home of Gil Evans. Born in Canada of Australian parents in 1912, he had been raised in the American West and learned to love jazz listening to Louis Armstrong and Duke Ellington over the radio. He had for several years been working as an arranger for the Claude Thornhill orchestra, a distinctly unorthodox dance band that featured dreamy, slow-moving arrangements with instrumentation then unusual in jazz: French horns and tuba, flute and piccolo. New York musicians had been mightily impressed by the fresh ways Thornhill had found to apply that sound to bop standards like "Thriving on a Riff," "Yardbird Suite," and Miles Davis's "Donna Lee." Except for the Billy Eckstine band with Charlie Parker, Davis said, Thornhill's was the best band in "these modern times."

But Evans was no longer writing for it. The Thornhill orchestra had gradually become a caricature of itself, he remembered, finally so slow-moving it put even him to sleep, and he was now scuffling, along with most of the musicians who hung out in his apartment, and taking part in a sort of informal round-the-clock music seminar for which his door was always open. Sometime that winter, Evans, Davis, Mulligan, and their friends began to talk of organizing a nine-piece rehearsal band—trumpet, alto saxophone, French horn, tuba, trombone, baritone saxophone, piano, bass, and drums—the smallest number of instruments that could capture the sound and harmonies of the Thornhill orchestra at its best. Evans had hoped Charlie Parker would take part, he recalled, but Parker wasn't willing "to use himself as a voice, as part of an overall picture instead of a straight soloist."

Miles Davis was more than willing. The band would have remained only idle talk if he hadn't been involved. "He took the initiative and put the theories to work," Mulligan remembered. "He called the rehearsals, hired the halls, called the players, and generally cracked the whip." He also talked the Royal Roost into giving the Miles Davis Nonet a two-week run in the summer of 1948—and made sure that the sign outside credited the arrangers by name, something that may never have been done before.

The music of the nonet was carefully organized, supple and smooth whatever the tempo; soloists faded almost imperceptibly in and out of ensemble passages. Count Basie topped the bill at the Royal Roost while the nonet was playing there. It sounded "strange and good," he remembered. "I didn't always know what they were doing, but I listened and I liked it." Walter Rivers, an executive at Capitol Records, liked it, too, and recorded twelve sides. Gerry Mulligan wrote five of the arrangements (John Lewis, Gil Evans, Miles Davis, and Johnny Carisi wrote the others), but there would have been no nonet and no recordings without Miles Davis.

Davis would always want to be in charge. Modernist critics who saw special virtue in newness and record company executives who saw commercial advantage in novelty would insist on portraying him as a great innovator—"the most consistently innovative musician in jazz from the late 1940's through the 1960's," according to *The New Grove Dictionary of Jazz*—and he liked to see himself that way as well. In fact, he was something more complex, more interesting: a master consolidator, able without apparent effort to incorporate other people's discoveries, alter and arrange them to suit his own fierce musical intelligence, and repackage them in ways that made them unmistakably his own. The results were simultaneously admired by other musicians and appealing to a good many listeners who might otherwise have been uninterested in jazz.

He developed his own instantly identifiable trumpet sound by bringing to the complexity of Dizzy Gillespie's music something of the lyricism and simplicity of statement of the trumpet players of an earlier era. Like Duke Ellington, he was a lifelong tal-

Early Miles. (Above) At thirteen, far left, with his sister Dorothy, brother Vernon, and mother Cleota Davis; and (below) the trumpet player farthest from the camera, as a seventeen-year-old member of Eddie Randle's Rhumboogie Orchestra in St. Louis

ent scout, always on the lookout for musicians who sounded "different from everybody else," he said, and then—also like Ellington—capable of creating an altogether fresh collective sound out of those individual differences. Davis's seductive trumpet playing and brooding good looks—"the difference between me and other musicians is that I've got charisma," he once told an interviewer—combined with the peculiarities of his personality and the unique opportunities presented by the changing times through which he lived, allowed him actually to become the sort of musical superstar Parker and Gillespie could only dream of being. But the price of sustaining that success would eventually be the abandonment of the music that made him great.

He was born on May 26, 1926, in Alton, Illinois, and raised in East St. Louis. His full name was Miles Dewey Davis III, but, because he was the son of a well-known dentist and gentleman farmer with the same name, he was known to everyone in town as "Junior." Small and dark and so good-looking that schoolmates called him both "Inky" and "Pretty" just to annoy him, Davis was raised in the kind of cushioned comfort few of his fellow musicians ever knew: a big house in town, as well as a two-hundred-acre farm with a cook, a maid, and a stable of riding horses. He delivered newspapers as a boy, not because he needed the money, but because his parents thought it would be good for him to earn a little on his own. His slight appearance and the relative affluence of his upbringing would eventually embarrass Davis, who wanted above all to be accepted by the street-smart jazz fraternity. To compensate, he would adopt an exaggerated toughness that he never abandoned.

His parents quarreled constantly—they would divorce in 1944—and his father gave him his first trumpet when he was thirteen, Davis said, mostly because his mother wanted him to play the more genteel violin. His first idol was Harry James, whose fat, romantic sound, filled with vibrato, he dreamed of emulating. His trumpet teacher, Elwood Buchanan, worked hard to get him to stop what he called "all that shakin' he's doing. Man, he's gonna shake enough when he gets old." "In high school," Davis told an interviewer many years later, "I was the best in the music class on the trumpet and I knew it, but all the contest prizes went to the boys with the blue eyes. It made me so mad I made up my mind to outdo anybody white on my horn. . . . [P]rejudice and curiosity have been responsible for what I've done in music."

Jazzmen became his heroes: "I was fascinated by the musicians, particularly guys who used to come up from New Orleans and jam all night. I'd sit there and look at them, watch the way they walked and talked, how they fixed their hair, how they'd drink, and of course how they played." One of his idols was a local star, Clark Terry, who would one

day play with Duke Ellington and Count Basie. Davis landed jobs with two local groups, Eddie Randle's Rhumboogie Orchestra and Adam Lambert's Six Brown Cats. Each specialized in small-group swing for dancing, with a heavy emphasis on the blues. When the Billy Eckstine Band came to St. Louis in the summer of 1944 and the third trumpet fell ill, Davis got a chance to sit in for a week. He was a good sight reader and had no trouble with the arrangements, he remembered, but he had barely been able to bring himself to play "because I was listening to what everybody *else* was playing. . . . Bird was unbelievable. . . . [Eckstine's] band changed my life. I decided right then and there that I had to leave St. Louis and live in New York where all these bad musicians were."

He was growing up fast—at eighteen he was already supporting a wife and baby

daughter—but his decision to move to New York to seek out his idols, made a few weeks after sitting in with the Eckstine band, was bitterly opposed by his mother. Like the parents of Bix Beiderbecke, Fletcher Henderson, and Teddy Wilson, she had hoped for a more sedate future for her boy, beginning with a university education at Fisk, and she agreed to his departure only after he promised to attend classes at the Juilliard School of Music.

Though he did develop a lifelong interest in music theory at Juilliard, Davis would spend just one semester there. He found the unrelenting emphasis on the classics wearying; disliked the sort of tone his trumpet teacher insisted upon; was wary of his fellow students, all but a handful of whom were white; and had no faith that any symphony orchestra was going to hire him, no matter how well he played. Instead of attending classes, he spent much of his time and all of his first month's allowance trying to track down Charlie Parker. Eventually, he persuaded his hero to move in with him. Parker's music continued to enthrall him, but he was soon put off by the older man's personality—what he called his "greed." Davis came home from work one evening to find that most of his belongings had disappeared, pawned by Parker to raise money for drugs. Davis was furious, so furious, he said, that he got his knife and went looking for his lodger. When he found him, Parker was on the bandstand, wearing Davis's best suit, though its trousers barely reached his ankles and its sleeves ended inches above his hands. Davis started toward the bandstand, then stood transfixed. "You couldn't believe what he was playing," he remembered. "You couldn't believe what was coming out of his horn. You had to love him."

Davis continued to love Parker, continued to hang around his bandstand wherever he played. "Miles Davis was cocky," Stan Levey recalled. "Always dressed in a Brooks Brothers suit and standing around the Three Deuces when we were

Young Miles Davis, second from the left, in the fastest possible company. Charlie Parker, Allen Eager, and Kai Winding at New York's Royal Roost, 1948

Juliette Greco and Miles Davis in Paris. "Music had been my entire life until I met [her]," Davis recalled. "She taught me what it was to love someone."

there with a matchbook, copying down chord changes." Soon Davis was appearing regularly alongside Parker in clubs and recording studios, doing his best to play in the fleet style of Dizzy Gillespie and his most virtuosic disciple, Fats Navarro.

Then, in the spring of 1949, he traveled to Paris in the same troupe as Parker and Sidney Bechet. Davis had not been prepared to be impressed by the Old World. Still young and unsure of himself, he compensated by trying to appear impervious to everything. But the trip "changed the way I looked at things forever," he remembered. "Paris was where I understood that all white people weren't the same." He met Picasso and Sartre and Albert Camus, and had a brief, heady romance with the singer and actress Juliette Greco. "I had never felt like that in my life," he said. "It was the freedom . . . of being treated like a human being, like someone *important*."

"I was so depressed coming back to this country on the airplane that I couldn't say nothing all the way back," he recalled in his autobiography, and he claimed that his subsequent addiction to drugs had been caused by the stark contrast between the way he had been treated in France and his experience scrounging for jobs back home. "In Paris," he said, "whatever we played . . . , right or wrong, was cheered . . . and we came back over here and couldn't even find . . . work, international stars and couldn't get jobs." But in an earlier interview Davis stated things more starkly. He got hooked, he said then, because "I got bored and was around cats that were hung."

Whatever the truth of the matter, Miles Davis turned to heroin—first snorting it, then injecting it directly into his veins. His marriage ended. To support his habit—"to feed the beast," as he called it—he stole from friends, pawned his horn, even became a pimp. He was briefly jailed for possession in Los Angeles but beat the charge. Then his own father, desperate to make him quit his habit, had him arrested again in the hope that he would commit himself for treatment. Davis refused to sign in, cursed his father, returned to heroin. He was beginning to earn a reputation as difficult, unreliable. Jobs grew still more scarce. "It was bad enough playing the kind of music that we played," he remembered, "but with a habit it was worse. People started looking at me another way, like I was dirty or something. They looked at me with pity and horror, and they hadn't looked at me that way before." Miles Davis then seemed likely to be just one more promising musician devastated by drugs.

JAZZ GOES TO COLLEGE

The twelve sides cut by the Miles Davis Nonet never sold particularly well as singles and when they did finally appear on a twelve-inch LP in 1957, the album was titled *Birth of the Cool* by executives at Capitol Records seeking to cash in on the public's current fascination with what jazz journalists were variously calling "cool" and "West Coast" jazz. In fact, the records didn't represent the birth of anything. There had been cool players since the days of Frankie Trumbauer. Nor did the musicians who played on them ever consider themselves members of any "school." But, like Davis, they were all interested in solving the problems that had inspired them to flock to Gil Evans's apartment in the first place: how best to bring what Evans called the "rhythmic and harmonic revolutions" of bebop to a larger and more receptive audience, and how to bring about a better balance between the soloist and the group.

Gerry Mulligan was among the first to offer a solution. A fine musician, capable of brilliant improvisation in the baritone's rarely heard upper range, he was also a skilled arranger. After working with Davis and Evans, he had moved on to California, where he had shown that even the overbearing Stan Kenton orchestra could *almost* be made to swing if given the right charts. Then, in early 1952, he put together a quartet of his own at the Haig, a small club on Wilshire Boulevard in Los Angeles. On trumpet was Chet Baker, with a pensive sound something like the one Miles Davis had begun to develop. Chico Hamilton was on drums, Bob Whitlock or Carson Smith on bass. There was no piano, but Mulligan didn't seem to need one. The horns played counterpoint. The drums and bass played melodic lines, as well as rhythm, and the rhythm itself shifted effortlessly from Dixieland two-step to 4/4 swing to bop-style polyrhythms and back again. The quartet's sound was rollicking, breezy, and good-humored, inviting to those who found bebop forbidding. It began to build a small but enthusiastic local following. Then, just as had happened to Benny Goodman with such happy results in Chicago in 1936 (and to Parker and Gillespie with such disastrous ones in 1945), a writer for *Time* happened by the club and wrote up the group. Its sound, he said, was "just about unique in

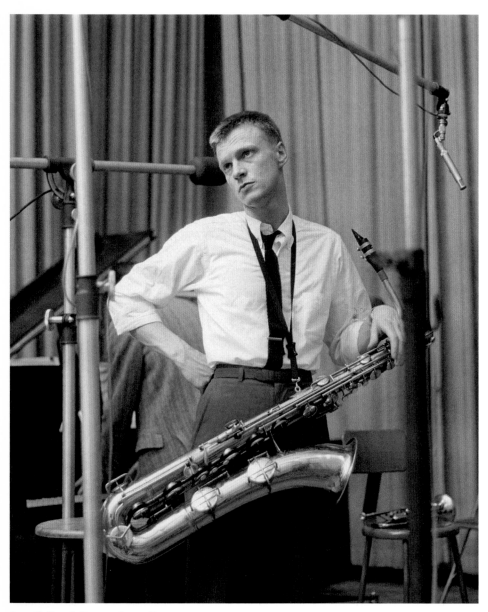

Gerry Mulligan in the recording studio

"What we wanted to do," said the drummer Shelly Manne, "was write some new kind of material for jazz musicians, where the solos and the improvisation became part of the whole, and you couldn't tell where the writing ended and the improvisation began. The spaces were right, it was lighter, maybe a little more 'laid-back.'"

Eastern jazz journalists—and there were virtually no western ones—generally derided West Coast jazz as tepid and derivative, best understood as background music for life in a region where the sun never seemed to stop shining. But a large part of the mostly white record-buying, concert-going public loved it. During the mid-fifties, *Down Beat* readers voted Chet Baker the best trumpet player in the country, ahead of Miles Davis, Louis Armstrong, and Dizzy Gillespie, precisely as their parents had preferred Benny Goodman to Count Basie and Duke Ellington during the late 1930s. Shelly Manne later maintained that *Birth of the Cool* had been the "main influence" on the growth of West Coast jazz. Gillespie disagreed: "Miles wasn't cool . . . like that. . . . Miles is from the part of St. Louis where the blues come from. Just part of his music is played like that, cool. They copped that part—the cool—but let the rest, the blues, go, or they missed it."

The Modern Jazz Quartet's music had all the intricacy and subtle dynamics of the most sophisticated chamber music, but the blues were never out of earshot. Its musical director, John Lewis, another veteran of the *Birth of the Cool* sessions, had always loved Charlie Parker's music but loathed the corrupting influence of Parker's addictions and the terrible damage they had done to the reputation of jazz and the men who played it. And, like Miles Davis and Gerry Mulligan, he saw no reason why the chaos of the jam session should remain the paradigm for small-group jazz. "I think the audience . . . can be strengthened," he once told an interviewer, "if we strengthen our work with structure."

the jazz field. . . . In comparison with the frantic extremes of bop, [Mulligan's] jazz is rich and even orderly, . . . marked by an almost Bach-like counterpoint. As in Bach, each Mulligan man is busily looking for a pause, a hole in the music which he can fill with an answering phrase." Soon there were long lines outside the Haig waiting to get in, and recordings by the quartet—"Line for Lyons," "Bernie's Tune," "My Funny Valentine"—made for a Los Angeles label called Pacific were being heard on the radio. Gerry Mulligan and Chet Baker found themselves stars.

Other California musicians—many of them alumni of the Kenton and Herman orchestras, including clarinet and tenor saxophone player Jimmy Giuffre, flutist and alto saxophonist Bud Shank, and trumpeter Shorty Rogers—were conducting similar experiments, and the jazz press began to write about a new West Coast "cool" school.

The Modern Jazz Quartet grew directly out of the Dizzy Gillespie big band. Lewis, vibraphonist Milt Jackson, bassist Ray Brown, and drummer Kenny Clarke had begun playing together nightly as a sort of entr'acte, mostly to give the winded Gillespie brass section a chance to regroup after one or another of the taxing flag-wavers for which the band was famous. After the orchestra broke up in 1950, they recorded as the Milt Jackson Quartet—the "MJQ." Shortly thereafter, Brown went on the road with his wife, Ella Fitzgerald, and was replaced by another outstanding bassist, Percy Heath. The group recorded again, began to attract some attention, and, since none of the four men wanted to acknowledge any of the others as leader, resolved to stay together as a cooperative renamed the Modern Jazz Quartet in order to retain the initials by which they were already beginning to get known. Connie Kay joined the group after Kenny Clarke moved permanently to Europe in 1955.

John Lewis served for a time as president of the summer music school at Lenox, Massachusetts, headquarters of the "third stream movement," which sought to blend jazz and classical music into something altogether new. He would compose pieces with foreign-sounding names—"Vendome" and *Django,* the "La Ronde Suite" and "Jazz Ostinato"—many of which were filled with fugal passages and counterpoint. And the quartet developed its first following playing concert halls in Europe. But Duke Ellington and Count Basie remained at the heart of Lewis's music. Ellington was his idol—his initial interest in fugues grew out of hearing Ellington's "Fugue-a-ditty" at Carnegie Hall in 1946—and he wanted the quartet to have the same sort of impact Basie's first band had had. Basie, he said, had managed to "integrate ensemble playing which projected—and sounded like—the spontaneous playing of ideas which were the personal expression of every member."

Not since Jelly Roll Morton's Red Hot Peppers thirty years earlier had a small

Members of the so-called cool school got the most critical attention in California during the 1950s but they were never alone on the Pacific Coast, as this souvenir of an all-star jam session at Jimbo's Bop City in San Francisco in 1952 attests. Tenor saxophonists Dexter Gordon and Jimmy Heath are in the left foreground; Heath's brother, Percy, plays bass, Milt Jackson is to his left; Roy Porter is on drums; Hampton Hawes is at the piano; and alto saxophonist Sonny Criss is second from the right. The club owner "Jimbo" Edwards is in the right foreground.

jazz group achieved such an exquisite equilibrium between written and improvised passages, between the soloist and the ensemble, the part and the whole. It was an ideal assemblage of personalities. Lewis's own playing was clear, concise. Milt Jackson, who began his musical life singing in a gospel quartet, was one of the greatest masters of blues feeling in jazz. Percy Heath and Connie Kay played together as if they were joined at the hip; and Kaye was a supremely tasteful drummer, capable of swinging hard using only a set of tiny bells. "Collectively, the group has no peers, past or present," wrote Whitney Balliett. "It exudes tact, understanding, sympathy, and a loyalty that conceals all inward friction, if any. Indeed, its members, having attained a utopian selflessness, listen to each other more than to themselves."

The members of the MJQ wore tuxedoes onstage, did not banter with the crowd, and made it known that they preferred respectful concert hall audiences to raucous night-

clubs—facts that caused writers with short memories to dismiss them as ostentatious and overly solemn. In fact, as Milt Jackson patiently explained, the group's demeanor grew directly out of the prewar African-American jazz tradition: "We wanted to bring back a level of dignity that we all remembered from watching all those great bands in the swing era. That was a very important part of jazz that I think we lost somewhere along the way." "I am an American Negro," John Lewis once said. "I'm proud of it and I want to enhance that position." He and the Modern Jazz Quartet would continue to do precisely that for some forty years.

On Monday evening, March 2, 1953, snow blanketed Tappan Square in downtown Oberlin, Ohio, and the students headed for the big Romanesque-style chapel named for the abolitionist president of Oberlin College, Charles Grandison Finney, were bundled against an icy wind. The Dave Brubeck

Quartet was to appear there that evening, and as the concertgoers filed through the doors, stomping snow from their boots, slipping out of coats and scarves, settling into the yellow-oak pews, neither they nor the musicians nervously waiting backstage were quite sure how the evening would go. Jazz concerts on campuses were still relatively rare in the East, and Brubeck had been told he might find the audience in Finney Chapel especially unresponsive, since it was sure to include music students from the Oberlin Conservatory—*serious* musicians, he was warned, who "don't understand jazz."

No one was more serious about music than the pianist himself, and no one knew better than he how wide the traditional gulf still was between jazz and classical music. When he was an undergraduate at the College of the Pacific before the war, some members of the faculty treated him with open contempt for wanting to play jazz. But afterward, at Mills College, he studied with the French composer Darius Milhaud, who had incorporated elements of jazz into his own music as early as 1923, and whose attitude was very different. When Milhaud asked on the first day of class if there were any jazz musicians in the room, Brubeck was initially afraid to raise his hand. "I'd been so used to being put down for being a jazz musician," he recalled. "Most conservatories in the United States still wouldn't let you play jazz, even in a practice room." He lifted his hand anyway, and

The Modern Jazz Quartet: Percy Heath, Connie Kay, John Lewis, and Milt Jackson. Their music was "tintinabulous," wrote Whitney Balliett. "It shimmers, it sings, it hums. It is airy and clean. Like any great mechanism, its parts are as notable as their sum."

The classic Dave Brubeck Quartet—drummer Joe Morello, bassist Gene Wright, Brubeck, and Paul Desmond—performs at the New York World's Fair in 1964.

so did several others. Milhaud told them that George Gershwin and Duke Ellington were the two most important American composers, and that "if you're going to express America, you've got to have the jazz idiom in your music." Anyone who wanted to write his homework in fugue and counterpoint as jazz was free to do so.

That was all the encouragement Brubeck and his friends needed. They formed an octet in 1946 that employed modernist elements borrowed from European music, including the unusual time signatures that would remain hallmarks of Brubeck's music for half a century. After college, Brubeck formed a trio, then a quartet, and began gathering a following on California campuses. Dance bands had visited colleges since the early days of jazz, but students who wanted to listen rather than dance had been forced to go far afield. Beginning in the 1950s, musicians like Brubeck began to take jazz to them.

Journalists sometimes classified Brubeck with other West Coast musicians because he came from California and enjoyed mak-

ing musical reference to the classics, but there was nothing remotely cool about his playing. He was a fiery, uncompromising improviser—dissonant, unsentimental, rhythmically daring. Some writers dismissed him as ponderous and heavy-handed. "The word 'bombastic' keeps coming up," an exasperated Brubeck once told a friend, "as if it were some trap I keep falling into. Damn it, when I'm bombastic, I have my reasons. I want to be bombastic. Take it or leave it." In any case, his style was perfectly complemented by the playing of alto saxophonist Paul Desmond: light, lyrical, floating, more like Lester Young than Charlie Parker—like the sound, Desmond himself famously said, of a dry martini. "The things I'm looking for musically," Desmond once told an interviewer, "are clarity, emotional communication on a not-too-obvious level, form in a chorus that doesn't hit you over the head but is there if you look for it, humor, and construction that sounds logical in an unexpected way. That, and a good dependable high F-sharp, and I'll be happy."

Each made the other better, and at Oberlin that evening in 1953 they outdid themselves. The audience—including the conservatory students—responded with ovation after ovation. The concert was recorded, and the album that resulted—*Jazz at Oberlin*—helped build enthusiasm for Brubeck. He was signed by Columbia, the nation's biggest label; made another live album, called *Jazz Goes to College;* and soon found himself the leader of the most popular jazz group in the country. Black as well as white fans followed the quartet during the 1950s. It was named the favorite group of the readers of the Pittsburgh *Courier,* and Brubeck never forgot that when Willie the Lion Smith heard one of his records in a blindfold test, Smith had said, "He plays . . . like where the blues was born. . . . He has heavy hands but hits some beautiful chords. . . . You could put this on at anybody's house, and they'd dance all night."

The Dave Brubeck Quartet would introduce hundreds of thousands of young people to jazz over the coming years.

FIFTY-TWO WEEKS
A YEAR

The Oberlin Conservatory students had loved the Brubeck concert, but like other music schools all across the country, the conservatory itself was slow to warm to jazz. When Duke Ellington and his orchestra arrived for a concert on the same Finney Chapel stage three years later, the gleaming grand piano traditionally used by visiting artists was gone, replaced by a smaller, scarred-up instrument. Where was the grand piano? the embarrassed president of the jazz club asked. Back in storage, a custodian explained. The conservatory had a standing rule: jazz musicians were not to play the good pianos; they might hurt them. Ellington, betraying not even a flicker of annoyance, strode onstage, seated himself at the battered piano, and launched into the introduction to "Take the 'A' Train" as if he were seated at the finest instrument on earth.

On Thursday, November 4, 1954, Dave Brubeck was in San Francisco nearing the end of a tour as part of a Norman Granz "Modern Jazz Concert" package that included Gerry Mulligan and Stan Getz, as well as the Duke Ellington Orchestra. No one understood better than Brubeck the debt he owed to earlier generations of black musicians, and he considered Ellington both a good friend and the greatest of all American composers. That morning, Brubeck remembered, "I heard a knock on my hotel room [door] at seven o'clock and it was Duke, and he said, 'Dave, you're on the cover of *Time* magazine.' And my heart sank. . . . I wanted to be on the cover *after* Duke. The worst thing that could have happened to me was that I was there before Duke and he was delivering the magazine to me, saying, 'Here.' "

Ellington, long accustomed to seeing the spotlight trained on other musicians, was characteristically gracious about Brubeck's good fortune and was genuinely fond of him

personally. Toward the end of Ellington's life, after Yale University had given him an honorary degree and set up a fellowship in his name, he would ask his son Mercer to make sure that Brubeck and his onetime drummer Louis Bellson were both made Ellington fellows. "I don't want people to think I only had black friends," he said.

Ellington's creativity had not slowed. The bebop revolution had not directly affected his orchestra, in part because his own music had always been at least as harmonically rich as that of the boppers. Earlier records like "CottonTail" and "Main Stem" had presaged a good many of the changes they had made; but several of his new men, including the trumpet player Clark Terry and the tenor saxophonist Paul Gonsalves, were fully familiar with the style. The long-playing record, introduced by Columbia in 1948, seemed made for Ellington, who could now move beyond the limitations of the three-minute 78. In 1950, he recorded *Masterpieces by Ellington,* concert-length versions of four favorites, including "Mood Indigo." He followed that two years later with *Ellington Uptown in Hi-Fi,* including a definitive thirteen-minute performance of his *Tone Parallel to Harlem,* a richly colored, wonderfully various portrait of the neighborhood he loved, which many believe to have been the finest of his extended works.

But ballrooms continued to close all across the country as Americans turned in ever-growing numbers to television for their entertainment. In February 1950, *Down Beat* presented Ellington with a special award simply for still being in business. By then, every one of the big bands that had appeared in the 1949 readers' poll had left the road but his; even Count Basie had now been forced to give up his orchestra in favor of an octet, before forming what Albert Murray called his "New Testament" band and starting all over again two years later.

The Ellington Orchestra no longer sounded quite the same. Drummer Sonny Greer had left, replaced first by Louis Bellson and eventually by Sam Woodyard. Two

Dave Brubeck on the cover of *Time*

of the most familiar Ellington "voices," Lawrence Brown and Johnny Hodges, also went out on their own for a time. Ellington could no longer afford the sleek private Pullman that had carried his men everywhere —he was frequently working for the same fees he had received twenty years earlier— so he and Harry Carney drove together across the continent in Carney's Cadillac while the rest of the men traveled by bus. Feeling it necessary to scotch persistent rumors that he, too, would be forced to abandon his orchestra, he explained that he was paying his bills with the earnings from his songs. "The . . . reason we're still in it is . . . artistic interest. We're not one of those people who stay in the business only so long as business is good. We stay in it fifty-two weeks a year. . . . The fun of writing and participating in music is the motivating force that keeps us going on and on."

But he was struggling now, as he had not struggled since his early days in the business. Frank Schiffman, proprietor of the Apollo Theatre in Harlem, kept an index card on every artist who ever appeared on his stage, assessing his or her act and detailing how many tickets they had sold. An entry he made in 1954 provided a stark summary of the situation in which Duke Ellington found himself: "Unchanged pattern. Fine personality. Good band. Mediocre draw."

MY NAME IS BIRD

On the night of October 30, 1954, with Dave Brubeck's owlish *Time* cover portrait soon to begin peering out from every newsstand in New York, Charlie Parker appeared at Town Hall. Thelonious Monk was on the bill that evening. So were several of the most promising of Parker's young admirers: tenor saxophonist Sonny Rollins, trumpet player Art Farmer, pianist Horace Silver. But the publicity for the evening had

been poor, more seats were empty than filled, and at intermission the musician's union seized half of Parker's earnings as a penalty for having failed to follow its rules. Several weeks later, the record producer Ross Russell went to see Parker play at an Eighth Avenue spot called Le Club Downbeat. Parker's suit was dirty and unpressed, Russell said, and he was wearing carpet slippers instead of shoes: "His face was bloated and his eyelids so heavy that only half the pupils showed. The first

five minutes of the set were spent in slowly assembling his saxophone while fellow musicians, all of them unknown, stood nervously on the bandstand. When Charlie got around to playing it was evident that he was having trouble getting air through the horn."

Parker was clearly spiraling downward. In March he had been in Hollywood when he received word from Chan in New York that their two-year-old daughter, Pree, was dead of pneumonia. The night he got the

The Charlie Parker Quartet at the Open Door in Greenwich Village, 1953. Left to right, Charles Mingus, Roy Haynes, Thelonious Monk, and Parker

...o more mysterious man ever played jazz than Thelonious Sphere Monk. And few created more memorable music. At first, casual listeners noticed only Monk's eccentricities. He had his own way of dressing and styles of headgear. He went for days without speaking to anyone. He sometimes got up in midperformance to dance in apparent ecstasy and rarely played anyone else's music, he once explained, because he was determined to create a demand for his own. And, though his first label, Blue Note, sought to capitalize on his strangeness by billing him as a "mysterious character . . . a strange person . . . the High Priest of Bebop," he intensely disliked being categorized as part of any "bebop movement." He was always Thelonious Monk, his own man.

Even his distinctive, splay-fingered, stride-based percussive keyboard style caused talk. "Thelonious would wait a minute before he hit a key," recalled Loraine Gordon, whose husband, Max, owned the Village Vanguard where he often played, "and I'd say, 'Oh, my God. Is he going to make it?' . . . And I used to sit there saying, 'Oooh, where's it going to land? Where's it going to?' And it was always right. He always landed on the right note."

In 1951, New York police found narcotics in a parked car in which Monk and his fellow pianist Bud Powell were sitting. The drugs actually belonged to Powell, but when Monk refused to testify against his friend, he was denied a cabaret card and so was forbidden to play anywhere within the city where alcohol was served. Monk refused to consider leaving town. Nor would he take a day job. Instead, for six long years he mostly stayed at home in his crowded apartment, making an occasional date in the suburbs and recording from time to time for Prestige, but otherwise bent over his keyboard, working on the music that was his obsession. His wife, Nellie, supported the family.

Finally, in 1957, Riverside Records issued *Brilliant Corners*, an album on which he played his own compositions with a small group that included the tenor saxophonist Sonny Rollins and the drummer Art Blakey. The jazz writer Nat Hentoff gave it an enthusiastic review in *Down Beat*. Then, with the help of his manager who swore (falsely) that Monk used no drugs, he finally obtained a new cabaret card in time to take a quartet into the Five Spot, then located in Cooper Square in Greenwich Village. Big crowds followed, suddenly eager to hear the man the critics had once scorned. Monk had not changed. He still lapsed into long silences, still broke into dance on the bandstand, still played tunes whose logic was so intricate, the tenor saxophonist John Coltrane remembered, that when his musicians got lost it was "like falling into an empty elevator shaft." It no longer mattered. The jazz public was beginning to learn what musicians had known all along: there was method in his alleged madness, a powerful musi-

...cal logic into which all the sudden stops and starts, the angular rhythms and dissonant passages and unanticipated intervals that had once so alarmed his audiences

...effortlessly fit. "I left I learned from him in every way," John Coltrane recalled. "Working with Monk brought me close to a musical architect of the highest order."

Thelonious Monk, rehearsing in a New York loft with saxophonists Phil Woods and Charlie Rouse, 1959.

DEFINITIVE

Bud Powell

Erroll Garner was the most popular jazz pianist of the period, but Bud Powell was the most influential among other piano players. He, too, was a child prodigy, but there the similarities ended. Powell was the son of a New York stride piano player who saw to it that he had a firm grounding in the classics before he began to play jazz. The fleet, flowing style of Art Tatum was a powerful influence upon his own playing, but Thelonious Monk was his protector when he first began to appear in New York nightclubs as a teenager, already displaying two distinctive characteristics: astonishingly fast right-hand runs—"he almost plays off the end of the piano," another pianist marveled—and strange, sometimes belligerent behavior whenever he swallowed more than a sip of alcohol, an early warning of terrible trouble to come.

During a murky encounter with Philadelphia police in the spring of 1945, Powell was beaten repeatedly over the head. His injuries seem to have intensified his mental problems. He spent ten months in an institution on Long Island, returned to the clubs, then suffered a second breakdown, after which he was locked up for eleven months. Electric shock treatments calmed his outbursts but they also damaged his memory for much more than music. He drew a keyboard on the wall of his cell, ran his fingers silently over it, then asked bewildered visitors how they thought he sounded. He lived and performed in France for several years but was never entirely rational again; he spent time in and out of institutions, sometimes stopped playing for minutes at a time to stare into the audience. He died at forty-two. But Powell was, as Dizzy Gillespie said, "the definitive pianist of the bebop era," and his playing—urgent and acrobatic, elegant and anguished by turns—influenced the way a whole generation of musicians would approach the keyboard.

news, Parker sent four telegrams, each more incoherent than the last.

> MY DARLING. MY DAUGHTER'S DEATH SURPRISED ME MORE THAN IT DID YOU. DON'T FULFILL FUNERAL PROCEEDINGS UNTIL I GET THERE. I SHALL BE THE FIRST ONE TO WALK INTO OUR CHAPEL. FORGIVE ME FOR NOT BEING THERE WITH YOU WHILE YOU ARE AT THE HOSPITAL. YOURS MOST SINCERELY, YOUR HUSBAND,
>
> CHARLIE PARKER.

> MY DARLING, FOR GOD'S SAKE HOLD ON TO YOURSELF.
>
> CHARLES PARKER.

> CHAN, HELP.
>
> CHARLIE PARKER.

> MY DAUGHTER IS DEAD. I KNOW IT. I WILL BE THERE AS QUICK AS I CAN. MY NAME IS BIRD. IT IS VERY NICE TO BE OUT HERE. PEOPLE HAVE BEEN VERY NICE TO ME OUT HERE. I AM COMING IN RIGHT AWAY. TAKE IT EASY. LET ME BE THE FIRST ONE TO APPROACH YOU. I AM YOUR HUSBAND. SINCERELY,
>
> CHARLIE PARKER

He managed to get through the funeral but then seemed unable to hold himself together. An engagement with a string section at Birdland ended in disaster when he drank too much and tried to fire the band. The manager fired him instead. He went home to Chan, quarreled with her—and tried to kill himself by swallowing iodine. Ambulance workers saved him. He twice had himself committed to Bellevue Hospital for psychiatric help, began riding the subways all night, often seemed frightened, suspicious even of his admirers. "They just came out . . . to see the world's most famous junkie," he told a friend.

The man who had hoped to demonstrate that jazz need not be linked to show business had himself become a public spectacle. "No jazzman," wrote Ralph Ellison, "struggled harder to escape the enter-

tainer's role than Charlie Parker. The pathos of Bird's life lies in the ironic reversal through which his struggles to escape what in Armstrong is basically a *make-believe* role of clown—which the irreverent poetry and triumphant sound of his trumpet makes even the squarest of squares aware of—resulted in Parker's becoming something far more 'primitive': a sacrificial figure whose struggles against personal chaos, on stage and off, served as entertainment for a ravenous, sensation-starved, culturally disoriented public which had but the slightest notion of its real significance."

One evening, Parker made his way into a club where Dizzy Gillespie sat listening to a band. Parker was disoriented: "Why don't you save me, Diz?" he said over and over again. "Why don't you save me?" "I didn't know what to do," Gillespie remembered. "I just didn't know what to say." Parker stumbled back out onto the street.

"I ran into him one night about three in the morning," the writer Nat Hentoff recalled. "I was going downstairs into Birdland. Bird was coming up. We didn't [really] know each other. I'd interviewed him a couple of times on radio. And tears were streaming down his face. He said, 'I've got to talk to you, I've got to talk to you.' I said, 'Fine, there's an all-night coffee shop on the corner.' 'No, no. I'll call you tomorrow.' Well, he never called. I could have been anybody, I think."

On Saturday, March 5, 1955, Parker was booked into Birdland again, this time as leader of a quintet that included Art Blakey, the trumpet player Kenny Dorham, bassist Charles Mingus, and the troubled pianist Bud Powell. Parker arrived late, then fled the bandstand when he saw that Powell was so drunk he could barely stay on the piano bench. When Parker came back for the second set and called the first tune, Powell insisted on playing another, then slammed the keyboard shut and walked off while Parker stood at the microphone helplessly calling after him, "Bud Powell," "Bud Powell," over and over again. Finally, Mingus pushed him aside. "Ladies and gentlemen," he told the crowd, "please don't associate me with any of this. This is not jazz. These are sick people."

The night after the Birdland debacle, Parker and a group of friends turned up at the Open Door to hear young Jackie McLean. Ordinarily, McLean would have been thrilled that his hero was showing interest in him. But not this time. "I had rented this horn and used it," he remembered, "and one night I was getting in a cab and I had been drinking a lot and Bird was helping me to get in the cab with some other people, and he said, 'Here, let me take this.' And he took the horn. And of course, about two or three days later, when I saw him, he didn't have the horn. It was in the pawn shop. I was a little angry at him about that, so when he invited to drop me home after the job was over, I said, 'No, that's okay. I'll get a cab.'"

On the evening of March 9, George Wein, now grown up and the owner of a Boston club called Storyville, was expecting Parker to turn up for an engagement that was to begin the following day. "I came into the club about eight o'clock," he recalled, "and Bird was not there. And somebody said, 'Bird's on the telephone.' And I picked up the phone and I dialed the number and a recorded voice said there was a yellow-tipped swallow seen this morning at the Ipswich marshes. It was the Audubon Society. Somebody played a joke on me, you know, to call 'Bird.' . . . And I hung up. I laughed. And Bird never showed up. So far as we were concerned, 'What the hell, Bird goofed again.' But it was his last goof."

Parker had packed his bag that evening, intending to leave New York for Boston. But on the way to Grand Central Station he dropped by the Stanhope Hotel on upper Fifth Avenue to see his friend the Baroness Pannonica de Koenigswarter, a member of the Rothschild family and a generous patron of jazz and jazz musicians. Parker was

Broadway in 1957. The Alvin Hotel, which would one day become the last home of Lester Young, is at the left, just across the street from Birdland.

clearly ill when he got there, and soon began vomiting blood.

Alarmed, the baroness called a doctor. The doctor asked Parker if he drank. "Sometimes," Parker answered, "a sherry before dinner." The doctor urged that he be hospitalized. Parker refused. He'd had enough of hospitals. The baroness and her daughter agreed to do what they could for him.

On Saturday evening, March 12, still at the Stanhope, Parker turned on the television to watch *Stage Show,* the Dorsey brothers' weekly variety program. He had always liked the sound of Jimmy Dorsey's saxophone. The first act was a comedy juggler. Parker laughed, choked, then collapsed. By the time the doctor could get there, he was dead. The official cause was pneumonia, complicated by cirrhosis of the liver. But Parker had simply worn himself out.

"I bought a New York *Post,*" Jackie McLean remembered, "and I sat down on the bus and I rode for several blocks before I opened it, and then when I opened the paper and looked inside, I saw that Bird was dead, that he had passed away at the Baroness's. Of course, I was in tears. I felt especially bad because I had just seen him at the Open Door and, being angry about the horn, I had missed [having] one more moment with him, you know, if I hadn't been over-reacting. Everybody was crushed when Bird died. I didn't go to his funeral. I couldn't, I just couldn't go, couldn't be a part of that."

Although the coroner had estimated Parker's age at between fifty-five and sixty, he was just thirty-four when he died. At thirty-four, Louis Armstrong still had thirty-seven years of music-making ahead of him. At the same age, Duke Ellington had only begun to write the extended works that would help win him his place among America's most important composers. Parker's innovations had been enormously important, but his weaknesses had insured that his dreams of moving jazz in still more new

LIVE!

It seemed to many critics eagerly looking for an heir to Charlie Parker during the late 1950s that Sonny Rollins must be that man. He grew up on the West Side of Manhattan, a neighbor of Thelonious Monk, Bud Powell, and the great Coleman Hawkins, whose huge aggressive tone he would incorporate into his own. Rollins's wellspring of ideas seemed bottomless. He played always with wit and exhilaration and titanic energy and impressed the drummer Art Blakey as being the most determined man he'd ever known. His best-known album from that period was *Saxophone Collossus*—and he seemed the living embodiment of that word. "Every place I went," he remembered, "it was 'Sonny Rollins . . . he's the cat to see.' Which was good, except that I didn't have that feeling within myself. . . . I felt that I disappointed the people."

And so in 1959, he stopped performing for more than two years. At night he would make his way out onto the Williamsburg bridge and play into the wind. "We have to make ourselves as perfect as we can," he said. "I liked to practice there because I could play as loud as I wanted and just go through anything I wanted to do."

When he came back in 1962, to many he seemed more powerful and inventive than ever, pouring forth musical ideas in solos that sometimes stretched on in clubs or onstage for an hour and more. A fearless modernist, Rollins is profoundly old-fashioned in his disdain for recording. Performing before an audience, he said, is "like having sex live"; playing in the sterility of the studio is like "cybersex." And when he is playing, nothing is allowed to get in his way. Once, at an outdoor concert at Saugerties, New York, in the summer of 1985, after playing for nearly fifteen minutes and wanting "to get closer to the people," he jumped off the high stage and shattered his heel. The pain was so great he couldn't get back onto his feet, but he went right on playing from the ground, "not just because the show must go on," he explained, "but because I still was able to blow."

Sonny Rollins

directions would in the end have to be realized by others.

By the time he was buried in Kansas City, admirers had already covered walls in Greenwich Village with the slogan "Bird Lives." For better or worse, he had become the apostle of hipness to some, and his early death only seemed to seal that misapprehension. Beyond his contributions to the music, Ralph Ellison wrote, Parker's "greatest significance was for the educated white middle-class youth whose reaction to the inconsistencies of American life was the stance of casting off its education, language, dress, manners and moral standards: a revolt, apolitical in nature, which finds its most dramatic instance in the figure of the so-called white hipster."

No one loved—or misunderstood—bebop more deeply than the Beat poets. "Jazz," Allen Ginsberg was still saying shortly before he died in 1998, "gives us a way of expressing. It's the spontaneous motions of the heart. The devotions that we feel. The ecstasies that we feel. The transcendence over the material absurdity of mechanized life that everybody's trapped in. It's like a fountain of instantaneous inspiration that's available to everybody. All you've got to do is turn on your radio or put on a record or pick up an ax yourself and blow."

The music of Parker and Gillespie and their peers was complex, sophisticated, exacting—only the most highly skilled musicians were capable of playing it. Yet the Beats insisted it was simple, spur-of-the-moment—*anybody* could do it. They would see themselves as the musician's natural allies, fellow outlaws, kindred spirits in the search for spontaneous expression. In fact, they were simply subscribing to a new version of an old misunderstand-

ing: the same misunderstanding that had made Jim Europe's men hide their music in order to fulfill the white audience's expectation that they were "natural" musicians who simply let their feelings flow through their horns; the same one that suggested that Louis Armstrong's music derived from instinct while Bix Beiderbecke's was drawn from his intellect; the one that led the patrons of the Cotton Club to see Duke Ellington's complicated, worldly compositions as primitive "jungle music"; and the same one that had frequently limited black bands to recording up-tempo tunes for which they were believed to have an inborn gift. Sadly, that misunderstanding would persist through the whole history of the music, and jazz would never entirely shake the reputation for alienation and "weirdness" born out of the era of bebop and the beats.

In the hard-living world of jazz, Clifford Brown stood out. Drugs and alcohol didn't interest him, nor was he temperamental. He routinely arrived an hour early for recording dates to clean his horn and ready his mind. And he always seemed to have time for younger players eager for advice. His only vice was chess.

"Clifford was a profound influence on my personal life," Sonny Rollins remembered. "He showed me that it was possible to live a good, clean life and still be a good jazz musician." As much as his fellow musicians admired Clifford Brown's character, they were awed by the warmth and richness of his tone and the long, melodic, dancing lines that seemed to flow effortlessly from his horn.

Dizzy Gillespie had heard the nineteen-year-old Brown play and began talking him up in New York. In 1954, in California, Brown joined forces with Max Roach. For more than two years their quintet was one of the most widely admired in jazz, and it seemed to many that Clifford Brown was destined to join the ranks of the greatest of all trumpet players: Louis Armstrong, Roy Eldridge, Dizzy Gillespie, Miles Davis.

On the evening of Monday, June 25, 1956, at the end of a rare day off spent with his wife and infant son, Brown took part in a jam session in Philadelphia. He hadn't wanted to be there but, characteristically, was doing a favor for a friend. Now he would be forced to drive through the night to get to his next gig in Chicago. It was after midnight before Brown and the pianist Richie Powell finished playing. They took off in Powell's new car with Powell's wife, Nancy, at the wheel. It began to rain. Suddenly the car skidded out of control, flew over an embankment, and turned over. All three passengers were killed instantly.

Dizzy Gillespie was about to go onstage at the Apollo Theatre in Harlem when he heard the news that Clifford Brown was dead. When the curtain rose, most of the men in his band were in tears. "For his artistry," Gillespie said, "there can be no replacement."

"'ROUND MIDNIGHT"

"I don't go with this bringing 'dignity to jazz,'" Miles Davis once told an interviewer. "The way [the Modern Jazz Quartet] brings 'dignity' . . . in their formal clothes and the way they bow is like [asking Sugar] Ray Robinson [to bring] dignity to boxing by fighting in a tuxedo." The middleweight champion was one of Miles Davis's heroes. He admired Robinson's clothes, his grace and good looks, the beautiful women who clustered around him wherever he went. "But when he was training for a *fight*," Davis remembered, "he didn't have no women around . . . and when he got into the ring . . . he never smiled . . . he was all serious business."

Inspired by Robinson's seriousness about his craft and finally weary of the life his addiction was forcing him to lead, Davis resolved to kick his habit. Characteristically, he determined to do it on his own. He had just finished an engagement with Max Roach in Hollywood. He rode the bus halfway across the continent to his father's farm outside East St. Louis. His father told him he could do nothing for him except offer his love: "The rest of it you got to do for yourself." Davis did. He moved into a two-room apartment on the second floor of the family guest house and locked the door. For seven days, as the craving for drugs raged, he neither ate nor drank, shivering with cold and struggling to keep from screaming with the pain that tortured his joints. Then, he remembered, "one day it was over, just like that. . . . I walked outside into the clean, sweet air over to my father's house and when he saw me he had this big smile on his face and we just hugged each other and cried."

In fact, it wasn't quite over. There would be a good deal of backsliding with heroin and other controlled substances over the years, but when Davis returned to New York in February 1954 he was clean. "All I could think of," he recalled, "was playing music and making records and making up for all the time I had lost." That year alone, he recorded one album for Blue Note and five for Prestige as a leader, using a shifting cast of gifted young musicians. One all-star session that included Kenny Clarke, J. J. Johnson, Horace Silver, and tenor saxophonist Lucky Thompson yielded two of the greatest extended blues performances in jazz history, "Walkin'" and "Blue 'n' Boogie." To the pianist Dick Katz, they constituted "an amazing seminar . . . a sort of summing up of much of what happened musically to the players involved during the preceding ten years. It is as if they all agreed to get together to discuss on their instruments what they had learned and unlearned, what elements of bop they had retained or discarded." If Miles Davis's nonet recordings had suggested to some that the blues might profitably be sacrificed in the interest of broadening the music's appeal, these sessions went a long way toward restoring them to their rightful place.

Davis's own sound was now unmistakable. He had neither the technique nor the temperament for playing in the aggressive Gillespie mode. Instead, he had developed his own spare, introspective style, often employing a stemless Harmon mute to add intensity. It retained the older man's harmonic sophistication but relied more on distillation than on speed or long lines; on playing only what he called "the most important notes." "I always listen to what I can leave out," he once explained. He brought back into the music something of the shrewd, relaxed phrasing of Billie Holiday and Lester Young, and something as well of the emotional dynamism of earlier trumpet players that had been overlooked in the onrushing pyrotechnics of early bebop. He also brought with him an almost androgynous tenderness that, like Ben Webster's breathy intimacy, belied his sometimes belligerent public personality. By 1955, wrote Martin Williams, "one passionate note from Miles Davis seemed to imply a whole complex of expressive sound, and three notes a ravishing melody."

It was becoming fashionable among journalists to see jazz as a sort of musical relay race in which one Great Man handed the baton of innovation on to the next while everyone else faded conveniently into the background. The annual summer jazz festivals held at Newport, Rhode Island, beginning in 1954 should have demonstrated conclusively how misguided this notion was.

Newport was a seaside town of mansions and green sloping lawns, the summer retreat of some of the East Coast's wealthiest old families and about as far from the

places where jazz began as it was possible to get. Two local jazz lovers, Elaine and Louis Lorillard, came up with the idea of the festival, but George Wein made it happen. "I felt that jazz could use a coming together," Wein remembered. "Economically, jazz musicians could not draw large crowds as individuals, not since the big band days. Jazz had become a club music. Jazz musicians needed a festival. By bringing many groups together we could draw many kinds of jazz fans. It became a great source of public relations for the music. People wrote about festivals because they were happenings. They were important events, successful from the start."

Wein insisted that every kind of musician be invited. Jazz should be a family affair, he said. Everyone who played it well should be welcome. Eddie Condon's Chicagoans were asked to come. So was Dizzy Gillespie. Count Basie, Stan Kenton, Dave Brubeck, Louis Armstrong, Pee Wee Russell, and Stan Getz were all going to be there. Roy Eldridge and Coleman Hawkins agreed to appear as well—though Eldridge couldn't resist kidding his old friend about playing under a tent again after nearly forty years on the road.

In 1955, Miles Davis wanted to be invited, too. "I hadn't thought of using Miles," Wein recalled, "because Miles was difficult. You'd call him and he'd say, 'Aw, I don't know if I want to do that.' I knew him. He'd worked in my club and we weren't that friendly, and he treated me like he treated everybody else." But they saw one another in New York that spring and Davis asked, "You gonna have that jazz festival up in Newport?" "Yeah, Miles," Wein replied. "You can't have a jazz festival without me," Davis said.

Wein eventually agreed. Davis would appear on the final night with an all-star group of modernists: Thelonious Monk, Gerry Mulligan, Zoot Sims, Percy Heath, and Connie Kay. "It was a difficult festival because our sound system wasn't very good," Wein recalled. "But Miles put his [muted] horn right in the microphone and

Workin', one of four superb albums Miles Davis made for Prestige in just two days in 1956. It was not released for four years.

the only thing that came through the whole festival was his playing ''Round Midnight.' It was so beautiful that everybody wrote about it. I mean, it changed his whole life. And all I can remember when he came off is that he said to me, 'Tell Monk he plays the wrong changes on "'Round Midnight."' 'Lots of luck,' I said. 'Miles, he wrote the song, what do you want from him?' "

Davis's soft, fragile-sounding solo turned out to be the highlight of the weekend. The crowd stood to cheer him. On the strength of the Newport performance and his recent spate of extraordinary records, he won first place among trumpet players in the annual *Down Beat* Critic's Poll, nosing out Dizzy Gillespie. Davis professed to be surprised at all the fuss: "You'd think I'd been on the moon. What are they talking about? I just played the way I always played."

But George Avakian of Columbia Records had been in the audience that evening, scouting for new talent that would appeal to the same kind of college-educated audience with which Dave Brubeck was now having such success. Not only had Davis played with remarkable lyricism, he noticed, but the crowd had seemed unable to take its eyes off him, even when he was not playing. Columbia offered a contract, and Davis eagerly accepted. "The real money," he said, "was in getting to the mainstream of America," and that was where Miles Davis now wanted to be. Columbia had all the resources to get him there, to make him a jazz star on a scale not seen in jazz since the swing era. But he could not begin officially to record for his new label until he had produced four more albums for Prestige. He was so eager to move on that he managed to make them all in just two daylong sessions. All four—*Cookin', Relaxin', Workin',* and *Steamin'*—were masterpieces.

They also helped to introduce the Miles Davis Quintet, the second group with which Davis would make jazz history. None of its members was well known when Davis found him; each would become a major figure in the music. Bassist Paul Laurence Dunbar Chambers (his middle names given in honor of the turn-of-the century poet) was just twenty, but already possessed of a huge warm sound and a rich melodic imagination. The drummer Philly Joe Jones was so obscure when Davis hired him that he was still sometimes confused with Count Basie's great drummer, Jo Jones, but he played with a rare combination of swing and simplicity, and had an uncanny ability to predict precisely where a soloist was heading and then to be waiting with the perfect support when he got there. Like all the members of the quintet except its leader, Jones was hooked on drugs and sometimes less than reliable. Davis didn't seem to care. "Look," he told one writer, "I wouldn't care if he came up on the bandstand in his BVD's and with one arm, just so he was there. He's got the fire I want. There's nothing more terrible than playing with a dull rhythm section. Jazz has got to have *that thing.*"

Pianist Red Garland was a former boxer—he had once lost to Davis's hero, Sugar Ray Robinson—possessed of an impeccable touch, a distinctive block-chord style, and a willingness to take direction. Dorothy Davis, Miles's older sister, had introduced her brother to the music of Ahmad Jamal, a Pittsburgh-born pianist popular with the public and (in part because of that) unpopular with most jazz

With Percy Heath and Gerry Mulligan, Miles Davis makes musical history at the Newport Jazz Festival in 1955.

His career reborn, Miles Davis takes a break in front of
the Café Bohemia in Manhattan in the autumn of 1955.

writers, who dismissed him as a coy cocktail lounge entertainer rather than a serious musician. But Davis heard something else in the sound of his trio: the power of understatement, a confident willingness to let silence speak—"space breathing through the music," Davis called it—qualities he wanted to adopt for his own group and which Red Garland was able effortlessly to assimilate into his playing.

The most controversial member of the quintet was the tenor saxophonist John Coltrane. A tailor's son, born in Hamlet, North Carolina, in 1926, he was the grandson of ministers, and before he fell under the spell of Charlie Parker and performed in Dizzy Gillespie's big band and with Johnny Hodges, he had made his living playing the blues. The earnest exhortation of the preacher and the intensity of the blues were both evident in everything he ever played. He was unable to stop thinking about music when not onstage; he and his friend and sometime rival Sonny Rollins would phone one another late at night, play a phrase or two into the receiver, then hang up and wait for the other to call back with a musical answer of his own. He was so determined to play every note that crowded into his head that he often did not know when to stop. Once, at the Apollo, he continued to solo for so long that the stage manager ordered the curtain closed; Coltrane kept right on playing. Some jazz writers found his relentlessness off-putting; one compared his onrush of ideas to "epileptic fits of passion." Davis himself sometimes wearied of Coltrane's protracted playing and once asked a friend to find out why he felt it necessary to go on so long. The saxophonist answered a little sheepishly that he simply didn't know how to quit. "Tell him," Davis said, "to try taking the horn out of his mouth." But when other musicians suggested that Davis find a saxophone player better able to edit himself, he remained loyal: "I didn't understand this talk of Coltrane being difficult to understand," Davis said. "What he does is to play

John Coltrane listening to a play-back, 1957

five notes of a chord and then keep changing it around, trying to see how many different ways it can sound. It's like explaining something five different ways."

Davis understood that Coltrane's volubility was the perfect foil for his own lean, laconic approach. The Miles Davis Quintet had everything. It played standards with which most Americans could identify: "If I Were a Bell," "Surrey with the Fringe on Top," "Bye Bye Blackbird," "Some Day My Prince Will Come," "My Funny Valentine." Garland, Chambers, and Jones worked so well together that they became known independently as "The Rhythm Section." Each performance involved a five-man conversation in which each musician listened as well as stated his case. And in the amiable ongoing contest between Miles Davis and John Coltrane, listeners could witness a painter of miniatures pitted against a muralist, rapier against broadsword, haiku versus epic poetry. "All the logic of the bebop group concept had found a kind of resting point, a balance in this band," wrote the critic and pianist Tom Piazza, "a sort of miniature golden age before the assumptions of the music began to be questioned again."

OOFTAH

On the evening of April 3, 1956, a little over a month before Miles first recorded with his new quintet, twenty-one-year-old Elvis Presley was scheduled to perform on the Milton Berle television program. It was not his first television appearance; he had made his debut on the Dorsey Brothers' *Stage Show* (the program Charlie Parker had been watching when he died), performing his own versions of rhythm and blues hits first recorded by the titanic Kansas City blues shouter Joe Turner, "Shake, Rattle, and Roll" and "Flip, Flop and Fly." But the Berle show was the big time. Its star had slipped a little since he was known as "Mr. Television" because of the number of sets people had bought in order to see him, but millions still tuned in each week. This program was to be broadcast live from the deck of the U.S.S. *Hancock,* anchored in San Diego harbor. A septet led by Harry James was also on the bill, and they were openly scornful of Presley when he turned up for rehearsal with his guitar and no arrangements. The drummer Buddy Rich traced the form of a square in the air behind the singer's back and muttered, "This is the worst." James nodded agreement. The audience was filled with sailors' wives and girlfriends, who never stopped shrieking with excitement as Presley performed "Heartbreak Hotel," but after the show, James still assured a friend that this hillbilly had no talent and no future. It was wishful thinking. "Heartbreak Hotel" was already at the top of *Billboard*'s pop, country, *and* rhythm and blues charts; Presley's version of "Blue Suede Shoes" was climbing the same polls fast; his first long-playing album was on its way to becoming RCA Victor's first million-dollar seller; and he had just signed a Hollywood contract. Millions of adolescents, the fortunate beneficiaries of unprecedented American prosperity, with tens of millions of dollars of their own money to spend, were about to transform the music business; every year between

1955 and 1959, American record sales rose 36 percent. The audience for jazz was about to shrink still further. The age of rock 'n' roll had begun.

So had the modern civil rights movement. Just as the 1920s were caricatured as an era of unrelieved hedonism, the fifties have often been misrepresented as a decade of smug tranquility. They were undeniably boom years. The gross national product grew by better than a third between 1950 and 1960. Americans achieved the highest standard of living in the history of the world. The suburbs nearly doubled in size, and by the decade's end, one-quarter of all Americans lived in them.

But black Americans had emerged from the war years with greater expectations for themselves than ever before, just as other Americans had. Racial justice had not been high on the national agenda when the fifties began. Neither the executive nor the legislative branch of government could be made to show much interest, and so, with backing from the NAACP, black citizens took their struggle against segregation into the courts in Texas, Oklahoma, Virginia, Delaware, the District of Columbia, South Carolina, and Kansas, where a Topeka welder and part-time preacher named Oliver Brown and twelve other black parents sued the board of education for forcing their children to travel to distant schools when all-white public schools were closer. On May 17, 1954, the United States Supreme Court ruled in *Brown v. Board of Education* that "in the field of education the doctrine of 'separate but equal' has no place. Separate educational facilities are inherently unequal." When southern legislators urged defiance and southern school boards proved slow to act, the Court issued an order requiring them to make a prompt and reasonable start toward full compliance with "all deliberate speed."

White southerners responded with fury. Nineteen of twenty-two southern senators and eighty-two of 106 southern congress-men signed a "Southern Manifesto" that accused the Supreme Court of "clear abuse of judicial power" and promised to resist implementation of its desegregation order by "all lawful means." Eight black men were lynched in 1955, at least two of them simply for insisting on exercising their right to vote. A young black woman who attempted to enroll at the University of Alabama was manhandled by a mob and then formally "expelled." The Ku Klux Klan experienced a rebirth. Some half a million men and women joined the White Citizen's Councils of America, pledged to maintain segregation at all costs.

Bebop, rhythm and blues, and rock 'n' roll, the head of the North Alabama White Citizen's Council assured his followers, were all part of an NAACP plot to "brainwash" white youth. "Negro music appeals to the base in man," he said, "[and] brings out cannibalism and vulgarity." It was the duty of every white patriot to help stamp it out.

On April 10, 1956, just a week after Elvis Presley appeared on the Milton Berle program, Nat King Cole, the jazz pianist who had transformed himself into one of the most popular crooners in the country, was to perform with the Ted Heath Orchestra on the stage of the Birmingham Municipal Auditorium. There were to be two shows that evening—white fans at eight o'clock, black ones at ten.

As Cole strolled into the spotlight for the first show, singing his latest hit, "Little Girl," five white men leaped onto the stage. All were members of the White Citizen's Council. One hit Cole in the mouth, knocking him back over his piano stool. Another grabbed his foot and began to twist it. Eight police officers, posted in the wings in case of trouble, rushed onstage, flailing at Cole's attackers with their nightsticks. Lee Young, Cole's drummer, shouted to Ted Heath to strike up the national anthem to keep the brawl from getting bigger, but Heath was English and launched into "God Save the Queen" instead of "The Star-Spangled Banner." Cole's assailants were eventually handcuffed and taken to jail. The mayor came to the singer's dressing room to apologize. White fans shouted their regret, and Cole limped back onstage and received a long standing ovation. But he refused to sing again until the black crowd waiting anxiously outside was allowed in at ten o'clock. "Man, I love show business," he told a friend that evening, "but I don't want to die for it."

Such events not only embarrassed people of good will at home, but also grievously damaged the country's reputation overseas. The cold war had become a permanent part of life. The United States saw itself as the leader of "the free world," and Soviet propagandists delighted in spreading news of American shortcomings. Under prodding from Adam Clayton Powell Jr., now a Democratic congressman, the U.S. State Department began to seek out jazz musicians to send abroad in the hope that visits by black and white Americans making music together would help offset the bad press.

First to go was Dizzy Gillespie, who in early 1956 found himself once again in front of a big band, subsidized this time by the State Department, and scheduled to appear before jazz-hungry audiences in South Asia and the Middle East. Gillespie was an ambassador unlike any ever seen before. At an embassy garden party in Ankara, Turkey, he refused to perform until street children peering over the compound wall were allowed inside. "Man," he said when the ambassador protested, "we're not over here to play for any elites!" Everywhere he went, he remembered, reporters "asked us a lot of questions about racism in the United States. But they could see it wasn't as intense [as they'd been told] because *we* had white boys and I was the leader of the band. That was strange to them because they'd heard about blacks being lynched and burned and here I come with half whites and blacks and a girl [trombonist Melba Liston] playing in the band. And everybody seemed to be getting along fine. . . . I didn't try to hide anything, I said,

Beginning in 1944 and continuing for nearly two decades, the California-born promoter Norman Granz led his integrated all-star Jazz at the Philharmonic troupe all over the country and overseas as well. He had two goals in mind: to broaden the audience for the music and to do so without compromising equal treatment for his musicians. He saw his programs as "a variety show of the finest jazz."

Some of the biggest names in the music were part of his package at one time or another: Dizzy Gillespie and Roy Eldridge, Charlie Parker and Benny Carter, Coleman Hawkins and Lester Young. Granz's idea of a good show, Gillespie remembered, was getting musicians "out there to battle one another's brains out onstage." The evening-long, all-star jam sessions—terrific one night, cacophonous the next—always placed a heavy emphasis on stirring up the crowd. The musicians sometimes grumbled, but Granz was unrepentant. "I may give the audience honk-ing," he said, "but it's the best honking there is. . . . Jazz has always been, to me, fundamentally the blues and all the . . . emotions it arouses. . . . My concerts are primarily emotional music."

Granz's deep commitment to ending discrimination was never questioned. "Jazz is America's own," he said. "It is played and listened to by all peoples—in harmony, together. Pigmentation differences have no place. . . . As in genuine democracy, only performance counts." Anywhere Granz's people played, if airlines or hotels or restaurants dared try to discriminate against any of them, he did not hesitate to cancel. "He would just check everybody into the Hilton Hotel," Stan Levey remembered. "We'd all show up in the lobby and [there'd be] a lot of, you know, throat-clearing, and he'd say, 'This is our group. Let's have our rooms.' He was terrific. Norman really broke a lot of barriers. We just showed up: 'Here we are.' "

In October of 1955, only weeks before Rosa Parks refused to give up her seat on a city bus in Montgomery, Alabama, five members of the Dallas, Texas, vice squad slipped backstage at a Jazz at the Philharmonic concert. They were supposedly searching for drugs, but were actually looking for some way to show Norman Granz what they thought of his integrationist principles. They found Dizzy Gillespie and the tenor saxophone star Illinois Jacquet shooting dice in Ella Fitzgerald's dressing room and arrested all three of them. When one officer asked Gillespie his name, he answered, "Louis Armstrong." Another officer headed for the bathroom. Granz hurried after him, sure he was planning to plant narcotics. The policeman pulled his revolver. "I ought to kill you," he told Granz. "They took us down[town]," Fitzgerald remembered, "and then when we got there, they had the nerve to ask for an autograph."

Jazz at the Philharmonic troupe photographed on arrival at the Honolulu airport, 1952. Standing, Ray Brown, pianist Oscar Peterson, guitarist Barney Kessel, Norman Granz, unidentified Hawaiian promoter, Roy Eldridge, pianist Hank Jones, Lester Young. Seated, alto saxophonist Willie Smith, tenor saxophonist Flip Phillips sharing his garland with trumpeter Charley Shavers, Ella Fitzgerald, drummers Buddy Rich and Gene Krupa, and clarinetist Buddy De Franco.

'Yeah, there it is. We have our problems but we're still working on it. I'm the leader of this band, and those white guys are working for me. That's a helluva thing. A hundred years ago, our ancestors were slaves and today we're scuffling with this problem, but I'm sure it's gonna be straightened out someday.' "

Benny Goodman followed in December, fronting a new band for a tour of eight Southeast Asian nations. In Bangkok, he went directly from the airport to the royal palace, where the saxophone-playing king of Thailand was waiting to play duets with him. ("Pretty good player," a tactful Goodman said afterward, "for a king.") Twenty-five thousand Cambodians turned out to hear his band play "Blue Skies." He, too, was asked about the progress of civil rights at home. "I didn't have anything particular to say," he remembered, "other than that we've had colored musicians in the band for twenty-five years."

In the spring of 1956, the State Department turned to Louis Armstrong. He had never been more popular. He'd recently published a second memoir, a vivid account of his early years, *Satchmo: My Life in New Orleans;* he'd made best-selling albums of music by W. C. Handy and Fats Waller; he'd scored a top-40 hit with a buoyant version of "Mack the Knife" (a musical portrait of a fictional pimp and cutthroat who, but for having been born in London instead of Storyville, might have been a figure from Armstrong's own boyhood); and, simply by being himself, he had stolen the movie *High Society* from its ostensible stars, Grace Kelly and Bing Crosby. Wherever he played, as guitarist Danny Barker told jazz historian Jason Berry, his dressing room was filled with people from every part of his remarkable life.

He'd be sitting down in his underwear with a towel around his lap, one around his shoulders and that white handkerchief on his head and he'd put that grease around his lips. Look like a minstrel man, you know . . .

and laughing, you know, natural the way he is. And in the room you see, maybe, two nuns. You see a street walker dressed all up in flaming clothes. You see maybe a guy come out of the penitentiary. You see maybe a blind man sitting there. You see a rabbi, you see a priest, see. Liable to see maybe two policemen or detectives, see. You see a judge. All of 'em different levels of society in the dressing room and he's talking to all of 'em. "Sister So and So, do you know Slick Sam over there? This is Slick Sam, an ole friend of mine." Now the nun's going to meet Slick Sam. Ole Notorious, been in nine penitentiaries. "Slick Sam, meet Rabbi Goldstein over there, he's a friend of mine, rabbi, good man, religious man. Sister Margaret, do you know Rabbi Goldstein? Amelia, this is Rosie, Goodtime Rosie, used to work in a show with me years ago. Good girl, she's a great performer. Never got the breaks." Always a word of encouragement, see. And there'd be some kids there, white and colored. All the diverse people of different social levels . . . and everybody's looking. Got their eyes dead on him, just like they was looking at a diamond.

The State Department asked Armstrong to take his All Stars to the Gold Coast, the first African colony to win its freedom and about to become the republic of Ghana. More than a score of would-be trumpeters met his plane at the Accra airport, blaring a tumultuous version of a local song called "All For You." Seventy tribal chieftains received him at the University of the Gold Coast, each with his own band of drummers and dancers. Later, more than a hundred thousand people turned out to hear the man most of the world now regarded as the living symbol of jazz. And everywhere, he saw people who looked so much like him and the other members of his family that he

came to believe his own ancestors must have come from the Gold Coast. He looked "very wistful," Arvell Shaw remembered. " 'I saw a lady just looked exactly like [my sister] Mama Lucy and somebody like my mother,' he said. 'This is truly where I'm from.' " But a CBS film crew traveling with Armstrong captured something else. When the All Stars played at one large gathering and he invited everyone to dance, no one even tried until Armstrong's wife, Lucille, got up to show them how. They loved seeing Armstrong, and were caught up in the spirit of undiluted joy and celebration he was able to communicate to any audience anywhere, but they also clearly considered the music he was playing *American* music, not their own.

Armstrong now had a new honorary title, "Ambassador Satch," and the following year, when the Soviet Union itself agreed to receive a jazz band, he seemed the logical choice to take America's music behind the Iron Curtain for the first time. But events intervened. As the school year began that September, in open defiance of a federal court order, Governor Orville Faubus of Arkansas sent National Guard troops to block eight black children from entering Little Rock's Central High School. Meanwhile, white mobs jeered at and spat on other African-American children trying to attend schools in Clinton, Tennessee, and Charlotte, North Carolina, and beat a minister in Birmingham, Alabama, to the ground for attempting to enroll his daughter. All of it was covered on television. Washington had so far refused to intervene.

On September 18, Armstrong was on tour in Grand Forks, North Dakota, when a local reporter dropped by his hotel room. Armstrong was shaving—and outraged by what he'd been seeing on the news. President Dwight Eisenhower had "no guts," he told his visitor. Faubus was "an uneducated plowboy." "The way they're treating my people in the South, the government can go to hell," he said. "It's getting so bad a colored man hasn't got any country." He would not go to Russia for the State Department. The reporter asked him if he was willing to be quoted. He said he was.

His road manager was appalled, afraid Armstrong had ruined his career, and hurried to tell the press Armstrong was "sorry he spouted off." When a television newsman with a camera crew caught up with Arm-strong as he was about to board an airplane the next morning, he made it clear that he was not at all sorry. "What are you going to tell the Russians when they ask you about the Little Rock incident?" he was asked. "It all depends what time they send me over there," Armstrong answered, his eyes invisible behind dark glasses, his face without a trace of his usual public smile. "I don't think they should send me now until they straighten that mess down South. And for good. I mean not just to blow over. To cut it out. . . . Because they've been ignoring the Constitution. . . . They're taught it in school, but when they go home their parents tell them different. Say, 'You don't have to abide by it because we've been getting away with it a hundred years. Nobody tells on each

Trummy Young, Louis Armstrong, and Edmond Hall bring America's music to West Africa, 1956.

Louis Armstrong preparing himself to go onstage in Las Vegas, 1960

other. So don't bother with it.' So, if they ask me what's happening if I go now, I can't tell a lie. . . . [That's] the way I feel about it."

Critics, both black and white, attacked him. An old friend from New Orleans took him aside. "Nigger," he said, "you better stop talking about them white people like you did!" Adam Clayton Powell Jr. denounced Armstrong for embarrassing the government. Sammy Davis Jr. said that since Armstrong was still willing to play for segregated audiences, he "did not speak for the Negro people." Station WBKH in Hattiesburg, Mississippi, banned Armstrong's music. The Hearst columnist Jim Bishop called for a boycott of Armstrong's concerts. And not one of the younger musicians who had accused him of Tomming in the past publicly came to his defense.

Armstrong never backed down and in the end lost just one gig—at the University of Arkansas. When Eisenhower did finally send in the 101st Airborne to insure that black children got to and from their school in safety, Armstrong sent the president a congratulatory telegram: "IF YOU DECIDE TO WALK INTO THE SCHOOLS WITH THE LITTLE COLORED KIDS, TAKE ME ALONG DADDY. GOD BLESS YOU."

On January 7, 1959, Armstrong and Dizzy Gillespie would appear side by side on the CBS-TV *Timex All Star Show,* playing and singing a jubilant version of one of Gillespie's favorite numbers, "Umbrella Man." They were near-neighbors now in Queens, their wives were close friends, and it is clear from the fun they had working together onscreen that old arguments had long since been forgotten. Later in the year, when Armstrong suffered a heart attack in Italy, the Gillespies were among the first to hear from him. "Ole Sidney Bechet and Big Sid Catlett [both of whom had recently died]," he wrote, "were trying to get me to come up there with them and hold that 1st chair down on the trumpet. Probably they would have had a little luck if they weren't so damn cheap. Huh—they only wanted to pay me union scale. . . . I got more than that when I first came up North from down in Galilee."

Years later, in his autobiography, *To Be or Not to Bop,* Gillespie explained his change of heart: "If anybody asked me about a certain public image of him, handkerchief over his head, grinning in the face of white racism, I never hesitated to say I didn't like it. I didn't want the white man to expect me to allow the same things Louis did. Hell, I had my own way of 'Tomming.' . . . Later on, I began to recognize what I had considered Pops's grinning in the face of racism was his absolute refusal ever to let any-

thing, even anger about racism, steal the joy from his life. . . . Coming from a younger generation, I misjudged him."

The actor Ossie Davis had a similar conversion experience while working with Armstrong on an otherwise forgettable film, *A Man Called Adam.*

One day at lunch, everybody'd gone out. The set was quiet. As I came back to the set I looked up and there was Louis Armstrong sitting in a chair, the handkerchief tied around his head, looking up with the saddest expression I've ever seen on a man's face. I looked and I was startled and then I started to back away because it seemed such a private moment, but he heard me backing away and he broke out of it right away, "Hey, Pops, looks like these cats are going to starve old Louis to death, hey, man, wow. . . ." And everything you know, I went into it with him but I never forgot that look and it changed my concept of Louis Armstrong. Because I, too, as a boy had objected to a lot of what Louis was doing. I figured all them teeth and that handkerchief— we called it "ooftah," by which we meant you do that to please the white folk. You know, you make them happy and all that stuff, make us look like fools. But it was only then I began to understand something about Louis. He could put on that show, he could do that whole thing, because in that horn of his he had the power to kill. That horn could kill a man. So there was where the truth of Louis Armstrong resided. Whatever he was, the moment he put the trumpet to his lips, a new truth emerged, a new man emerged, a new power emerged and I looked on Louis for what he truly was, after that. You know, he became an angelic presence to me after that moment.

FIRE!

Dizzy Gillespie was not an admirer of West Coast jazz. "There was no guts in that music," he said, "not much rhythm either. . . . This music, jazz, is guts. . . . I guess the idea was not to go 'savage' with it, biting, like we were. But that's jazz to me. Jazz to me is dynamic, a blockbuster."

Jazz was a blockbuster to Art Blakey, too. He wanted to provide a hard-swinging antidote to the cool music then so popular: critics, looking for a label, called the music he and others began to play "hard bop." "Fire! That's what people want," he said. Blakey had begun his career as a pianist and had launched his own big band at fifteen, switched to the drums after being outplayed by the youthful Erroll Garner, and soon developed his own distinctive thunderous, roiling style. He played with Fletcher Henderson, Mary Lou Williams, and Billy Eckstine. "It was like a school to me," he said of his time with Eckstine, "and that's when I realized that we had to have bands for young black musicians—big bands, little bands, a whole lot of bands— because this music is an experience."

He had put himself through every kind of experience, survived every kind of trouble. He was so short—less than five feet— that one critic dismissed him early on as a "pygmy." ("At least she spelled my name right," Blakey said.) A Georgia policeman beat him so badly that he had to have surgery on his skull. His first wife died. Heroin was a frequent companion, and he refused to be apologetic about it. He adopted Islam, renaming himself Abdullah Ibn Buhaina, and traveled to West Africa to learn more about traditional drumming. But jazz, he would always maintain, "is American music. There's nothing like it anywhere on the planet. People are always trying to connect it to something else, to African music, to Latin music. It's not. It's American music. . . . Now, they say, 'Art Blakey, he's black. That makes him an

African.' I'm not. I'm an American and this is American music."

In 1955, Blakey and the pianist and composer Horace Silver established a quintet they called the Jazz Messengers and began to record for Blue Note. "They used fixed arrangements and they brought in gospel influences, blues influences," the record producer Michael Cuscuna remembered, "things that people could relate to who were not deeply into modern jazz. And it caught on very quickly. The message of the group was 'We swing, we're earthy, we play the blues. You can walk away humming it, but we're not going to cheat on the quality of the music or the creativity.' And they found a way to do everything."

"When we're on the stand," Art Blakey said, "and we see that there are people in the audience who aren't patting their feet and who aren't nodding their heads to our music, we know we're doing something wrong. Because when we do get our message across, those heads and feet do move."

When Silver left to form a group of his own, Blakey kept the Messengers name and for forty-five years traveled the world joyfully spreading his message. Two generations of future stars would get their start or hone their skills with Blakey: pianists Joanne Brackeen, John Hicks, Keith Jarrett, Geoff Keezer, Bobby Timmons, Cedar Walton; saxophonists Benny Golson, Branford Marsalis, Jackie McLean, Hank Mobley, Wayne Shorter; trumpet players Donald Byrd, Kenny Dorham, Freddie Hubbard, Brian Lynch, Wynton Marsalis, Lee Morgan, and Woody Shaw.

"The Messengers were the training ground for a lot of great musicians," Wynton Marsalis remembered, "because [Blakey] would put his swing up underneath you so that you could learn how to play, and he would tell you you were sad. And when I first sat in with him, I knew I wasn't playing nothing. He said, 'Man, you sad, but that's all right.' And when you were around him, you were around the essence of jazz music. So he put that in us. 'If you want to

Art Blakey at work. "To me the bandstand is hallowed ground," he said. "You come up here, you're supposed to play. A musician is supposed to play, if he gets up off his deathbed, he's supposed to play."

play this music, you have to play it with soul, with intensity, and every time you touch your horn, you play your horn. You know, this is not a game.' "

Blakey was not a sentimental man. "I'm always kicking them in the ass," he said. "It's as much as anyone can do to keep up with me. . . . I'm not running a post office." "Everybody had to do their job or you were replaced," Jackie McLean remembered. "And in every city that we went to, if there was a star alto player there, Art would invite him to come and play with the band and that was always to keep me on notice that there was always somebody waiting in the wings." On the road, Blakey was indefatigable, the living, laughing symbol of the music's extraordinary resiliency. Even when growing deafness made it hard for him to hear his soloists, he continued to outswing musicians half his age. "Music," he told his audiences nearly every night, "is supposed to wash away the dust of everyday life from your feet."

DIMINUENDO AND CRESCENDO

In the summer of 1955, Duke Ellington was reduced to accompanying ice skaters at a Long Island rink. The following summer he was on the cover of *Time,* his career in high gear again. Newport, which had helped to re-ignite Miles Davis's career the year before, did the same for Ellington.

It was the orchestra's first appearance under the festival's striped tent—Ellington had been asked only to be a master of ceremonies the previous year—and he was anxious to do well. His mood was not improved when he was asked to open the last evening of the festival with the "Star-Spangled Banner" and four of his men failed to turn up on the bandstand. Then, after just two tunes, Ellington was waved off the stage to make way for other performers and had to wait more than three

When Duke Ellington sought to cause a stir at the Newport Jazz Festival on the evening of July 7, 1956, he turned
to "Diminuendo and Crescendo in Blue," the same driving
two-part piece that eighteen years earlier had brought
dancers out of their seats at the Randalls Island Festival of Swing. At Newport, he had important help from two
individuals: tenor saxophone star Paul Gonsalves (opposite), who played twenty-seven furious choruses, and a
woman from New Bedford (opposite, bottom) whose dancing helped whip the normally sedate crowd into a frenzy.
(Below) An exuberant Ellington urges the band to take
its bows.

For a guy's musical development, the same rule applies in jazz as in any other field; you collect facts, and study. . . . You take a riff that Roy Eldridge played, and you play that riff . . . and you figure the alternatives. You say, "Ah, then, you could also go here instead of going there." And when you get that far, finally you'll come up with something different. But it's the same music. It's just progressing all the time.

—DIZZY GILLESPIE

Donald Byrd hones his skills on the subway, en route to a Manhattan date in the 1950s.

Ornette Coleman, 1959. "A lot of people in the mid-fifties were already playing music that had an open concept," Jackie McClean told an interviewer, "what I call the 'big room,' a place where you could cross a threshold and have no barriers, you know, no key signatures, no chord progressions, no particular form, [but it was] Ornette [who] came to New York and stood his ground and made this music really sink in and work. That's the thing I admire about Ornette, not only his writing and playing, but the fact that he stood his ground and stood by his music and took the slings and arrows of all the criticism that came towards him."

Bernstein pronounced Ornette Coleman a genius. John Coltrane came down to play with him between sets. Lionel Hampton asked to sit in. But Roy Eldridge said he'd listened to Coleman drunk and listened to him sober, and couldn't understand him either way. Thelonious Monk said that what Coleman was doing was "bad. . . . Jazz must first tell a story that anyone can understand." Charles Mingus was ambivalent: "He plays right wrong," he said. So was Miles Davis: he liked the fact that Coleman didn't play "clichés," he said, but "psychologically, the man is all screwed up inside." Someone set a car on fire out front; someone else burst into the kitchen between sets and punched Coleman. Most jazz writers were hostile, too, Haden recalled:

> We didn't bother ourselves to take time to even read the criticism of us because we were too busy thinking about making new tunes and improvising and talking about new ways of playing. That's what we were involved in. We couldn't stop to take time to even think about the controversy. Of course, we were disappointed. And we wanted to find some way to bring people closer to what we were doing because people look back on what we were doing now, they hear the early recordings and they're very accessible. They all come from the blues and the thing about our band—the critics labeled it *avant-garde,* you know, what is that?—was that we *swung.* And we felt very strongly about our music.

Coleman saw himself as solidly in the jazz tradition. "Bird would have understood us," he said. "He would have approved of our aspiring to something beyond what we inherited."

"We wanted people to like our music," Charlie Haden said, "we really did. But I really believe that most great musicians are free musicians. If you listen to Coleman Hawkins improvise, if you listen to Thelo-

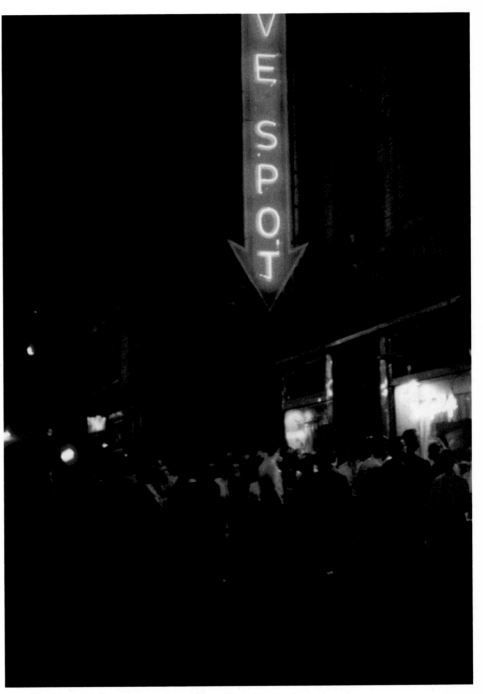

Admirers and adversaries alike line up to see Ornette Coleman at the Five Spot in November, 1959.

nious Monk improvise, if you listen to Bud Powell, they improvised on a level that I call 'beyond category.' You know, it was at this level that's above everyone. Even though they were improvising on a chord structure, they were playing so free and so deeply at

a level . . . I call it with your *life* involved. . . . Being willing to give your life, . . . risking your life, it's almost like being on the front line in a battle. Being able—*wanting*—to give your life for what you're doing."

THE PRESENCE IS ALWAYS THE POINT

STANLEY CROUCH

Within five years of having arrived in New York from California in September 1975, I had the good luck of being able to assess the Manhattan jazz scene from three perspectives—as a drummer; as the booker of a jazz club, the Tin Palace on the Bowery; and as a writer of jazz criticism for the *Village Voice*. When I got to town, Duke Ellington had been dead for over a year, Louis Armstrong had been gone for five, and jazz itself was widely rumored to be on its way out, but the music that had evolved in so many directions during the lives of those two greatest of all jazz musicians had such vitality and presence that thinking back to how it was in those days now seems almost a dream of the way it should have been.

There were still so many fine players of so many different instruments that they created an enormous fugue of individual personalities, interpretations, techniques, and tonal colors. Though they were sometimes demoralized by the position that jazz had been forced into by a largely disinterested media and the notion that actual jazz playing had become a thing of the past, these artists pushed their music into the face of the present with the kind of transcendent coherence that not only improved the quality of their art but bettered the world through what they gave to and inspired in other human beings.

These were, as McCoy Tyner says, "special people." At this point, so many of them are gone that one could start asking if it had all been a dream, a collective wish agreed upon and supported by doctored photographs and unreal images delivered through film and television. Hardly. As with so many of the miracles of American life, those men and women did walk this earth, did take to bandstands and stand at bars and joke in dressing rooms and talk on the telephone and have rehearsals and travel the world, providing the human presence of jazz.

If you were in New York and were able to see and hear jazz for yourself, birth, affirmation, reaffirmation, decline, and death were right there to be had as experiences that would never leave your sensibility. If you lived at 2 East Second Street and felt like walking a couple of blocks west, you could step into Studio Rivbea, the avant-garde stronghold, where it might sound as though the world was ending that very night and where nobody sounded better than its owner, the avant-garde tenor saxophonist Sam Rivers, lean, high brown, and given to nearly knocking his knees together once his music got in complete touch with his nervous system. Or you could walk over to the Cookery at Eighth Street and University Place, where the rediscovered Alberta Hunter, who had been a star in the twenties, and who dressed like a lumberjack during the day, might be singing in a wonderful evening dress, while Barney Josephson, the man responsible for integrating downtown clubs in the thirties, sat and listened, his hair white, his body thin, his glasses held in place on his nose by thick black frames. Were Jo Jones in the house to lead the way, a trip to Gregory's might be necessary, where drummer Sonny Greer, alto saxophonist Russell Procope—both over sixty-five—and pianist Brooks Kerr, nearly blind but youthful and full of drive, were working. Greer and Procope could summon up the sound, or at least the memory, of the entire Ellington band, while Kerr had the whole of jazz piano from the turn of the century to 1940 at his fingertips.

From Gregory's, Jones might take me with him to hear Roy Eldridge at Ryan's in midtown. A small man, like so many jazz giants, Eldridge, with his white hair and mustache, his brown skin and the spirited gait of one who could have been a fast and vicious boxer with class once upon a time, was almost always good for at least one streak of fury through the chords, building, note upon note, a bonfire of intensity, loosing a pugnacious growl from the bell of his horn like the sound of a lion telling the world that he was not about to give up lording it over the jungle that was his bandstand.

Whether talking with his buddies from the good old days or orating about the nature of the world with his clipped enunciation, Jo Jones himself was never less than imperial in his baldness. He seemed indomitable standing there with his newspaper in his pocket, his long johns on if it was winter, his brandy bottle in his coat, a knife hidden somewhere as a testament to his understanding of the nightlife and proof that he was, as he loved to declaim, "a thug." But if one caught him in the aesthetic slaughterhouse that was the West End, a little club across the street from Columbia University way up on Broadway, his position in the hierarchy of the drums was quite evident—the touch, the power, the exultation, the pain, the finesse. It was all still there.

If you went to a concert at New York University presented by Jack Kleinsinger's "Highlights in Jazz," you might witness a miracle of assembly. One after another—at someone else's show—Eubie Blake, Sam Wooding, Earl Hines, and Claude Hopkins sat down to the piano and played alone. Blake was then the oldest man of jazz and told a story of how he had learned a particular seventh chord from a cook when he was just a kid, then illustrated with an original piece from that time. Earl Hines (whom Jo Jones called "Toupee Willie") spoke of how he had been playing the ivory off

V.S.O.P. onstage at the Greek Theater, Berkeley, California, 1977: Herbie Hancock (piano and leader), Ron Carter, Tony Williams, Wayne Shorter, and Freddie Hubbard. The quintet, organized in 1976 at the height of the fusion era, included all the members of the Miles Davis Quintet of the mid-1960s except its leader.

the keys in Pittsburgh one night when Blake—in derby and tuxedo, with cigar and carrying a cane to give more aristocracy to his stroll—warned the younger man that, as much music as he was playing, if "I come back through here and find you in this town I'll wrap this cane around your head." Hopkins, who had led a big band in the thirties, played a soft and beautiful something in which all of the notes and all of the chords sounded as though they were made of feathers and silk.

Part of the reason that a number of jazz musicians were disheartened in those days was that the battle for the future of the music was taking place against a threat that now seems never to have been there at all. The threat had come from a direction so unexpected that when it was first detected around 1970, no one could quite believe what they were starting to see. Major players were abdicating, abandoning jazz in favor of the fusion phenomenon. And the man who showed them the way was Miles Davis himself.

For some, like this one writing, who can still recall how Miles's band with George Coleman, Herbie Hancock, Ron Carter, and Tony Williams looked at an after-hours show sometime in 1964 at the Adams West Theater in Los Angeles, it seemed inconceivable. Then, four grown men had come onstage in dark suits followed by what appeared to be a little boy in a yellow suit with brown shoes who sat down behind the drums. This was the same kid who had been standing next to Ron Carter before the show, drinking a soda and giving off the ready-to-go feeling that ado-

lescents always have. Davis was backstage, having a good time because the trio that came on before him was swinging and he was playing at conducting the band, moving as if in the boxing ring, snapping out his fists in approval, which meant more to those men up there than any kind of review or fat-salaried contract ever could. This little black giant was enjoying them. They had been accepted by one of the masters. His ruffling nickname was "Inky," and he had a house full of night creatures, hustlers and their women mostly—pimps, gamblers, numbers runners, drug dealers, sellers of hot clothes, and females who knew things about men that very few of their sex would want to find out. These were raucous people, given to loud talk and big laughs, too much cologne and too much perfume, their own debased ideas of aristocracy and a kind of distancing that could become intimate through violent confrontations if the wrong word was said or the bitterness resulting from an old grudge forced itself into bloodletting action. But when Miles Davis came onstage, every one of those denizens of the shadows got quiet, each aware that if something out of line took place, the little splendidly dressed prince might turn around and head for the door, no amount of imploring strong enough to bring him back. The genial Inky of backstage was gone when he walked out of the wings. The stern Davis face, a combination of anger and anguish, was in place, and the trumpeter began with a ballad, putting a mood into the air with his tone that seemed to draw something quite gentle out of even these street women, perhaps memories, perhaps dreams. A mist of romance took over and transformed this filled movie theater to a hoop of emotion surrounding the bandstand. Tony Williams, the little boy on the drums, touched them and swiped his cymbals and a sound we had never heard before went out into the theater. When they moved from the ballad tempo into a lightly sailing straight 4//4, a spiritual cheer went up every time the audience felt safe enough to applaud. That was when Miles Davis was at the top of his form, sharp as a tack, clean as a white fish, hipper-seeming and more confident than a man who God had personally guaranteed would be going to heaven when his time came. That musicianship and that ritual then seemed invincible, but Davis proved that it was not and that we can never assume that there is a straight course, even for the greatest among us. Anyone can fall and nearly bring the building down on the way to the dirt.

Given his prominence and power, it is easy to understand how seriously many musicians took Davis when he claimed that his demon for adventure was pushing him "forward" toward fusion. As the bassist Jaymie Merritt said to me one night, "When genius is involved, you have to listen closely." What Davis did in his new guise and with his electronic guile helped set the new trend. Wayne Shorter, one of the most gifted composers and players of his generation, went into Weather Report, which began as a collective many musicians found interesting, but eventually evolved into Joe Zawinul's band, leaving more and more jazz elements behind. Tony Williams led a rock-influenced group called Lifetime, featuring British guitarist John McLaughlin, which seemed intent mostly on setting new levels of volume.

At least for a bit, Herbie Hancock seemed as if he was going to hold up high the flag of jazz truly remaking itself. The Swahili name of his band, Mwandishi, reflected the ethnic pretensions of the time, but that group—with Buster Williams, Billy Hart, Eddie Henderson, Benny Maupin, and Julian Priester—was one of the great ones of that era and perhaps of any. No one had ever heard anything like it, and there were times when no one in the audience seemed to breathe from the first note to the last. The harmonies and the blends of the front line, the shifts in and out of different tempos and rhythms, as well as its sense of adventure, gave the Hancock Sextet that performance glow only the most compelling ensembles have. Had it lasted, a strong alternative to what became known as fusion would have been out there to inspire others to hold on. But Hancock also eventually submitted to the call of the wild cash register, got to the crossroads, and began sinking down.

Jazz was in the process of being redefined as merely a form of instrumental pop music. While the mixture of jazz and rock did create something that had not existed before, it also intro-duced instruments and beats that had nothing to do with swing, the propulsive essence of jazz phrasing. That jazz is a music of adult emotion while rock is focused on adolescent passion created another problem for jazz musicians who tried fusion. They could never get to that teenage feeling of ardent ineptitude and resentment of sophisticated authority because they are not inept and their music is as sophisticated as any performing art that has evolved in the Western world.

But despite everything, evidence began to accumulate even during those dispiriting years that the music could remain true to itself and prosper. In October of 1976, on a very rainy evening in midtown Manhattan where the jazz impresario and pianist George Wein had a nightclub called Storyville, the bebop master Dexter Gordon found himself back in The Apple again. He had been living across the big water since 1962. Long since forgotten was his identity as a founding father of the approach that had so much to do with how Sonny Rollins and John Coltrane played the horn as young men. Or so it seemed before that night. The weather would have been prohibitive in most towns, but the house was packed and the saxophonist was obviously touched that people were so interested in hearing him that they weren't going to be stopped by rain.

Gordon immediately let everyone know that it was worth the wait and the wet. Standing in a cloud of charm at the microphone, his deep voice containing the essence of masculinity and whimsy as well as oblique, ironic humor, the long tall one introduced tunes and sometimes recited a portion of the lyrics of a ballad he and his men were about to perform. He held the saxophone as easily as he might stroke his chin and made the air of the room submit to him, blowing his horn with the magisterial confidence one would expect of a bebop master. At the same time, Gordon didn't seem to be playing bebop. As with any of the masters, the style was secondary to his expression. On that night, the stir began that would not only revitalize Gordon's career but reveal the power and the aesthetic scale of an art that this tenor saxophonist embodied for a moment so radiant it was indispensable.

A few months later Gordon was leading his band at the Village Vanguard for an in-person recording. The Vanguard was packed with musicians and lay listeners night after night, and he was on the way to a level of celebrity that greatly helped turn things around. If we look at it outside of how the business world reacted to it, we might think that the stardom that fell upon Dexter Gordon was some form of magic. It was not. Gordon had one of those unpredictable aces in the hole—Bruce Lundvall, a jazz fan and the president of Columbia Records. Had Clive Davis, the former president—who had fired Ornette Coleman, Keith Jarrett, Bill Evans, and Charles Mingus from the label in one day—still been at the wheel, the course of jazz would surely have been different. Lundvall loved the music and was the only president of a major record label willing to put money behind jazz artists. Tall and always superbly attired, Lundvall was the sole record executive of such high station who often went to clubs or to concerts to listen to his artists. If he signed them, he liked them. If he liked them, he went to hear them.

Gordon's reemergence and all the attention he got due to Columbia's marketing campaign soon sparked interest in straight-ahead swinging jazz and inspired the return of other expatriates. Johnny Griffin, the little giant who had such a fat tone and could play so lickety-split that he seemed actually to grow taller as he blew, came home to play again. Back in the kitchen during his breaks, or at the bar drinking red wine, he would talk of how he, Thelonious Monk, Elmo Hope, and Bud Powell would walk miles through the night on the way to Hope's house far up in the Bronx. Along the way, Powell might suddenly run up to some big guy and slap his face, which meant that Monk, Hope, and Griffin then had to keep this fellow from turning the great genius into mashed potatoes.

With his handlebar mustache and stoic eyes, Art Farmer, visiting from his home in Vienna, was the soul of poise and yearning lyricism. He always seemed somewhere else while on the bandstand, somewhere in the middle of a dream that might be extended as Clifford Jordan, the big, brown-skinned Negro from Chicago who often played tenor saxophone alongside him, unwove his many melancholies. One of Jordan's most remarkable nights came when he played with Harry Edison at Condon's after having been diagnosed with terminal cancer earlier in the day. Featured on "I Should Care," the big saxophonist didn't unburden himself or dirty his music with self-pity. In his own style, he played as Ben Webster might have, announcing that the melody of the life he had lived with both its sweet and bitter harmonies, was all of a lyrical piece, a gift that allowed one to croon or howl or snarl at the moon of a dream as long as there was the strength to do it.

Domestic exiles came home, too, some of them from the temporary sanctuary they had found in academe. All the drummers were there at the Village Vanguard when Max Roach returned to action and taught them, once again, that he was the master, playing with a poetic command of his instrument that has never been equaled, even as he so completely absorbed the free, timeless drumming style that the avant-gardist Rashied Ali, both moping and admiring, said, "Well, Max is playing free now. I guess I'll

Art Farmer

just go home and get my little rubber practice pad and wait for him to get another ten years older."

Roach would go on to perform in duet with Cecil Taylor, to perform with his percussion ensemble M'Boom and with the World Saxophone Quartet at the Cathedral of Saint John the Divine, to do multimedia solo concerts, to create a double quartet—his own pianoless group with a string quartet—and to polish his crown every way he could. But on one of the saddest nights of his life, Roach sat like a kid in Seventh Avenue South, a room now gone, as Jo Jones, who had by then depreciated to being no more than a thin drunk muttering to himself, took over the bandstand and went through a routine that seemed, as Ellington family member Michael James says, "part of the King Lear period."

Trumpeter Woody Shaw's evolution into a bandleader and an individual influence on horn players was very important to the morale of the music in those days because, with Miles Davis and Freddie Hubbard both mired in fusion, there was nobody out there who was making sense of what had happened in the early sixties. On many nights, in his full power, Shaw played as if each note was a finger in the dike holding back the deluge of commercialism.

Betty Carter

There was a way that he went into his stuff. In the Vanguard's no-longer-functioning kitchen, which doubled as a dressing room, he could be cursing someone out or talking about the harmony Charlie Parker played on "Bird at St. Nick's" or recalling some adventure he had had when young and an apprentice member of Horace Silver's or Max Roach's or Art Blakey's band. Then, when it was time to hit, Shaw, who was legally blind but had memorized his way to the bandstand, would walk out of the kitchen, up the narrow hallway into the room, turn right past the front door, make another right behind the chairs, take the couple of steps into the gallery rather casually, move between the tables, and walk out on the stage where he performed a few tai chi moves before playing. This took only a minute or so, and Shaw then commenced to play, almost always something fiery as an opener. If you were close enough, you could see that he had the determined look of a snake about to strike, made even more intense by the vast human intelligence and fire he brought to the music.

Then there was the terrible end. Shaw had been strung out for years. He didn't look good and he was surely blind because I passed him a couple of times, not saying anything since the sight of a man as great as he was looking a few steps from homeless

was depressing. Once I did say something; he turned to me and there, behind the edgy, embittered, and anxious look of those desirous of some dope, were those eyes and that intelligence. I remembered then how much of a jazz musician he was and how, even when he was most successful and winning jazz polls that were thought to have been rigged by his management, Woody would finish off a job at the Vanguard and ride somewhere into Harlem or the Bronx or Brooklyn to sit in with unknown guys he heard were trying to play something.

On a tragic night when Max Roach was at the Vanguard, the drummer arranged for a private car to bring Shaw to hear the band. While Roach was on the bandstand, Shaw got the driver to take him into Brooklyn. The driver had been given instructions not to take Shaw anywhere, but the trumpeter, who could be very aggressive, had apparently convinced him that Max had changed his mind. The next morning Woody either slipped or stumbled down the stairs at a subway station and ended up so near the track that the incoming train cut off his right arm. Max called me after going to see him in the hospital. There Shaw was, he said, his head shaved and a long dark line of stitches down the middle, lying still with his arm shorn away, in a coma from which he would never recover. The sorrow in Max's voice carried the grief he had felt many times for special people who had been removed from the world too early.

In June of 1975, Cecil Taylor, too, came back to New York and performed at the Five Spot. Taylor had never had much of an audience, nor has his music ever been much of an influence on jazz, but that summer Gary Giddins in the *Village Voice* and Robert Palmer in the *New York Times* wrote about Taylor's return as a major event and the club was packed night after night. Audiences, enjoying it or not, sat before the unrelenting fury of Taylor's music, which had created its own category, one in which a vocabulary predominantly influenced by twentieth-century European music was delivered as though the piano was an enemy that had to be beaten into submission by the small brown-skinned man with the knitted cap who took off his glasses before starting and did not stop for an hour or more. The sheer velocity of his articulation, the size of his sound, and the parallel obsession with grandeur and all that either blocked or denied it, made the emotion Taylor projected reflect not so much a jazz feeling as that of a Beethoven without lyricism. Big statements and triumphant pounding delivered with unequaled physical strength arrived as though they could go on forever. Then, never acknowledging the audience, Taylor put his glasses back on and left the stage for the dressing room. There, far more educated and intellectually engaged than 99 percent of jazz musicians, he might be gleeful, full of wit, given to extraordinary leaps of association. Or he might be almost glum. Or, quite easily, he might break into a contemptuous rage leveled at bigotry and critical incompetence, describing the European concert world's aversion to black musicians, the similarities and distances between African dance and ballet, which he loved equally, the historical racial hiring policies that were why he hated the New York Yankees and the Boston Celtics. Taylor knew plenty about plenty. Therefore, whatever he was, and whatever he was playing, those who had heard it knew that he was the only one on the earth who could meet—or even wanted to meet—the challenges he had set for himself. The sheer intelligence of the man, genius actually, gave him a special color in any light, particularly because he had brought together intellectual thought with athletic prowess. While what he played had little to do with jazz, it was still a massive achievement on a human level.

That September, the Art Ensemble of Chicago worked at the same club for two weeks, awakening Manhattan to what would become a migration of midwestern musicians who were members of the Association for the Advancement of Creative Musicians (AACM). They did little of the one-dimensional screeching and honking that characterized the music John Coltrane's talent sank under the burden of embracing in his last years. As Muhal Richard Abrams, one of the AACM's founders often said, they were not interested in playing a style, they wanted to play music.

That was evident at the Five Spot. There on the bandstand were saxophonist Roscoe Mitchell in street clothes, trumpeter Lester Bowie in a white lab coat, saxophonist Joseph Jarman, bassist Malachi Favors, and drummer Don Moye in face paint and African getups. Mitchell and Jarman seemed to have been largely influenced by Ornette Coleman, but Bowie's style owed much to Don Ellis. Ellis had embraced the whole of jazz trumpet, not just what had happened since 1945. His own recordings, such as *New Ideas* and *Essence*, his work on George Russell's *The Outer View*, and his *Down Beat* article, in which he called the New Orleans veteran Red Allen the most avant-garde trumpet player in New York, all make it clear that Ellis had been there first, by a decade. Don Cherry, the greatest mind and heart of all the avant-garde trumpet players, could not have done what Ellis did even if he wanted to, since his command of the horn never went far enough. Bowie was not the trumpet player that Ellis was, either—far from it—but he could play the instrument, which immediately separated him from the one-trick blats and squeals of purported avant-garde trumpet players. New York seemed to be waiting for him and for the Art Ensemble itself.

They had arrived in New York that fall on a big (and old) school bus. Though given to breaking down, it had room for the band, all the saxophones Mitchell and Jarman doubled on, and all the percussion instruments—the "little instruments" that any band member might pick up and use in performance as well as the astonishing array of African instruments at Don Moye's command. Moye had made himself as much a virtuoso at his African battery as any symphonic percussionist surrounded by his array of kettle drums, bells, and xylophones. With Favors and Moye back there, the Art Ensemble could stoke up any kind of ethnic black groove, any kind of beat associated with Afro-American music, while the compositions they played could be as simple as street rhymes or executed with tight, well-rehearsed up-tempo ensemble playing.

It was during that period that Air, featuring saxophonist and flutist Henry Threadgill, bassist Fred Hopkins, and drummer Steve McCall—all of them also AACM members—moved to New York from Chicago. At the time, while living above the Tin Palace, playing drums with my loft mate David Murray, and after a Hamiet Bluiett big band concert we held upstairs drew so many people and got so loud that the police came and told us we were making too much noise, I started booking Sunday-afternoon bands that played for the door. That series presented a lot of musicians new to Manhattan, almost all of them associated with what was considered the vanguard of the time.

On the Sunday afternoon that Air debuted in New York, everybody knew that this was a very special band. Most of the music was written by Threadgill, who went on to form a septet that almost blew the windows out of the Tin Palace.

Musicians who hadn't been heard in New York for a while also came to play at the Tin Palace, like the alto and soprano saxophonist Gary Bartz, who had spent a lot of time messing around in fusion but made it clear that he was one of the great men of his horn. Musicians came to enjoy working that club so much that they started playing an extra fourth set, beginning at two a.m., which meant that the club crowded up again and one might see Dexter Gordon or Art Blakey or Cecil Taylor or Ornette Coleman or Max Roach in there as Clifford Jordan, Barry Harris, Walter Booker, and Vernell Fournier performed opposite Dewey Redman, Freddie Simmons, Mark Helias, and Eddie Moore, who was so black and huge I used to joke with him that Dewey must have mailed a cargo plane ticket to San Francisco so he could fly east in comfort.

Sometimes, as happened during the eighties, a spirit can take over and people will get busy on every level. These were the years when one young musician after another came to New York and seemed intent on doing only one thing—learning how to play jazz while fully aware that it was not the kind of art in which anything lucrative was guaranteed. People such as Wynton Marsalis, Wallace Roney, Geri Allen, Greg Osby, Rene Rosnes, Cyrus Chestnutt, Lewis Nash, Peter Washington, Kenny Washington, Bob Hurst, Reginald Veal, Herlin Riley, Russell Malone, James Williams, Mulgrew Miller, Benny Green, Cassandra Wilson, Vanessa Rubin, Cindy Blackman, Teri Lynne Carrington, Jackie Terrason, Leon Parker, Javon Jackson, Kenny Garrett, Tony Reedus, Jeff Watts, Marvin Smitty Smith, and still more younger players who kept leaving home for The Big Apple, surging up out of the ground, as if the music had its own will to live.

The renaissance of jazz in the eighties was fostered as much by Art Blakey as by anybody else. One Sunday in the middle of the decade there was a Father's Day celebration for Blakey at the Apollo. The theater was filled, and backstage, as the drummer Roy Haynes said, "It looked like some kind of an African king's place." Blakey had many children, grown and toddling, as well as girlfriends, wives, and numbers of musicians who had played in his training school for the art, The Jazz Messengers. He had been the sacrificial hero who played and played, night after night,

while those fledglings stumbled over themselves until they began to swing with enough confidence to take off and begin their own bands. Sitting in the audience that afternoon was the singer Betty Carter, who was now doing exactly the same thing that Blakey had done for years—bringing young musicians into her band and putting them through the rigorous tasks necessary to learn how to swing and to play in many different tempos, from extremely slow to as fast as possible.

They had some help. The reissue boom that had been spearheaded by Orrin Keepnews at Fantasy Records, classic material handsomely packaged and with good liner notes, provided young players with recorded examples of high-quality music that had been unavailable for years. This meant that, perhaps for the very first time, jazz musicians were truly learning how to play in styles that stretched back to the beginnings of the music.

More encouragement came from the stage of Cooper Union, where Abraham Lincoln once spoke. There, the American Jazz Orchestra, conceived by Gary Giddins, gave splendid performances of classic jazz under the leadership of John Lewis. As Loren Schoenberg, who took over after Lewis left, once explained during an especially powerful concert of Ellington music, the repertory movement offered plenty of options. Music could be performed as faithfully to the original recordings as possible, or new improvisations in the styles of the period could be allowed, or different arrangements of a given piece could be brought together, another take on the idea of variations on a theme. The point was that jazz did not have to lose bodies of great music just because those who once played it were no longer in the world.

As the jazz spirit started to rise higher and higher, fine bands came into existence. One of the best was Old and New Dreams, featuring Don Cherry, Dewey Redman, Charlie Haden, and Ed Blackwell, which played a repertoire dominated by the music of Ornette Coleman, and made it clear every night how very different what Coleman had introduced into jazz was from the bulk of the music played by those usually said to be in the jazz vanguard. They swung, they were melody makers, and the whole tradition of jazz flowed through their playing exactly as it did from the best of the musicians who had come forward since the bebop movement of the forties.

There was also the return of the prodigals. Tony Williams began to lead a wonderful band with trumpeter Wallace Roney, saxophonist Billy Pierce, pianist Mulgrew Miller, and—in succession—bassists Charnette Moffett, Bob Hurst, and Ira Coleman. At the Vanguard one night a few weeks after Art Blakey died in 1990, Williams could be heard mixing into his playing signal things that had touched him when he was a kid. Some Max Roach for a bit, then Philly Joe Jones, then Roy Haynes, Elvin Jones, Kenny Clarke—almost an autobiography of his own beginnings. By playing so much less loudly than when he was struggling to blast his way into the fusion world, Williams made the power of his entire conception audible, which included writing that defined him as the most complete drummer-leader of any period. All of the music on that bandstand was his—every note, chord, arrangement. The result was a very serious extension of what the Miles Davis Quintet had been doing in the sixties, the drummer's most glorious period of recognition. No, this didn't mean Williams had gone backwards, as too many of the intellectual clubfeet of jazz writing would automatically assume. By setting aside his apparent dreams of pop stardom, Williams had reached through the recent musical dark ages to a period of illumination, brought forward a flame, and was piling fresh logs on it. At forty-six, Williams was doing what all masters do once they accept the richness of their own perceptions: they come to embody every element of what initially attracted them to music and to their instruments. Williams sometimes jacked himself up chorus by chorus into the sort of swing no young drummer, however gifted, could lay down. For the first time I heard the weight in his sound that only comes of emotion and substantial experience.

But of all the prodigals, the one who returned to the highest point of glory may have been Freddie Hubbard. In almost biblical fashion, the trumpeter had a revelation when he was nearly shocked to death as he was warming up backstage for an outdoor concert and the wire to an electronic gadget he had attached to his trumpet was pulled through some water. Once the fusion ruse was behind him, Hubbard eventually worked at the Blue Note, the largest and best-paying jazz club in the city, the one responsible for presenting people such as Sarah Vaughan, the Modern Jazz Quartet, Oscar Peterson, Billy Eckstine, and Joe Williams in the kind of setting jazz listeners never thought they would experience again.

There, Hubbard did the richest trumpet improvising of the time. Almost gone were the memories of the platform shoes and plaid pants of his fusion days. Handsome and looking more and more like Louis Armstrong, Hubbard now wore exquisitely cut suits, beautiful shirts, and silk ties, and he played with all the accumulated luminosity of a man who has been at his horn for over forty years. His time feeling, which was as witty as it was mock-pugnacious, his melody lines, and his harmonic personalization of what he learned from Coltrane and Rollins were at a point of imposing effortlessness. He was also the ox of his instrument, given to unflagging strength and projection, a clarion authority that recalled Armstrong as much as his looks did. One

Freddie Hubbard

night he picked up the flugelhorn and did a version of "Blue Moon" that included a long, long introduction, a rhythmic rebuilding of the theme, and chorus after chorus of extemporaneous purity, motifs varying from the pinnacle of the horn's reach to the bottom, smears that transformed themselves into melody, harmonic choices that were so surprising they accented themselves, and a longing that heroically emphasized the first word of the tune's title and led his listeners back to the beginnings of the music.

In the end, that this kind of power continues to exhibit itself is far more important than the regret that the music is not appreciated to the degree jazz lovers would like to see. When you get down to it, no matter the style, no matter what anyone says about it, the point is what happened when those musicians were standing there in the flesh, shaping, sweating, and emoting. They displayed the wonders of an extraordinary art through their own talents and their collective victories. If there was truly a paean to the presence of jazz, it was the way they were and what they did.

A MASTER-PIECE BY MIDNIGHT

"Anyone who thinks that it's easy to go onstage every night, three hundred times a year, and create something new, will never get the toll that it takes to be a jazz musician," the record producer Michael Cuscuna has said.

It's incredibly draining to start from ground zero every day and truly create something that's as close as you can humanly get to a masterpiece by midnight. In the creative process of starting from scratch every night and drawing from your heart and from your intellect and making your fingers work your instrument, you have to really lay your soul bare. Because every night you have to put every molecule of your body into creating something. Unlike in other art forms, you don't have private time to tinker with your creation. You're out there. You are in front

Dexter Gordon onstage with bassist Stafford James and drummer Louis Hayes, 1978 of people and you are creating of the moment. And there's no net; there is no safety valve at all. You are out there for all to see, to fail or to succeed. Or to just get by.

No one in jazz worked harder or risked more than Dexter Gordon—"Long Tall Dexter." And few musicians would show the wear and tear more starkly. The son of a Los Angeles doctor who tended Duke Ellington whenever he was in town, Gordon was so tall and so handsome when he was young, an acquaintance remembered, that he could draw a crowd just by putting his tenor saxophone together. He was "an idol around Central Avenue," Art Pepper recalled. "He wore a wide-brimmed hat that made him seem like he was seven feet tall. He had a stoop to his walk and wore long zoot suits, and he carried his tenor in a sack under his arm."

He had an instantly identifiable sound— big and warm and oddly languid even when hurtling through changes—and he had learned his art from the masters. He venerated Lester Young, played with Lionel Hampton and in Louis Armstrong's big band—the arrangements weren't much, he remembered, but he loved hearing Pops play every night—and he had toured with Billy Eckstine's groundbreaking orchestra as well. During visits to New York, he had taken part in the weekly jousts at Minton's that helped produce bebop and afterward was best known for "The Chase," a blistering recorded tenor duel with Wardell Gray—the first of a series of celebrated face-offs that pitted him against other tenor stars, including Sonny Stitt, Teddy Edwards, and Gene Ammons, always with memorable results. He was a born competitor; the struggle to stay on top, he said, consumed "every night, all my life."

As the fifties began Gordon had seemed on the brink of still greater success. But he had also developed a heroin habit that cost him two hundred dollars a day and raged so far out of control that once, after shooting up on a visit to New York, he unpacked his horn at the corner of Eleventh Street and Fifth Avenue and gratefully played for his dealer. In 1952, the law caught up with him. During the next eight years he served time for possession at the Chino, Fort Worth, Lexington, and Folsom federal prisons.

By the time Gordon was back on the street, he found work harder and harder to get. He was not alone. When the English historian and sometime jazz writer Eric Hobsbawm visited the United States for the first time in 1960, he "found the nights too short to listen to everything that could be heard in New York from the Half Note and the Five Spot in the Village to Small's Paradise and the Apollo in Harlem and further west in Chicago and San Francisco." Two years later, he wrote, when he came back eager to hear more music, " 'Bird Lives' could still be seen painted on lonely walls, but the celebrated New York jazz venue named after him, Birdland, had ceased to exist" and "jazz had virtually been knocked out of the ring."

What had happened? The tenor player Johnny Griffin blamed those who had taken jazz "out of Harlem and put it in Carnegie Hall and downtown in those joints where you've got to be quiet. The black people split and went back to Harlem, back to the rhythm and blues, so they could have a good time." Meanwhile, the pianist Hampton Hawes wrote, "white kids were jamming the rock halls and the older people were staying home and watching TV. Maybe they found they couldn't pat their feet to our music anymore." And after 1963, the astonishing global popularity of the Beatles and other British rock groups—their sound initially derived from African-American blues performers, precisely as the music of white American rockers had been a decade earlier—produced a second, still more spectacular surge in the sales of rock music, and a still deeper decline in public enthusiasm for jazz. Even John Hammond now edged away from the music he had always loved most and applied his scouting skills to rock and folk music instead, signing Aretha Franklin, Bob Dylan, and, later, Bruce Springsteen, for Columbia Records.

Desperate jazz musicians took jobs wherever they could find them—in cocktail

The Village Gate, in Greenwich Village, still a jazz stronghold during the 1960s

Louis Armstrong. "Each man has his own music bubbling up inside him," he once told an interviewer, "and—quite naturally—different ones will let it out in various ways. When I blow I think of times and things out of the past that give me an image of the tune. . . . A town, a chick somewhere back down the line, an old man with no name you seen once in a place you don't remember—any of 'em can trigger that image. . . . What you hear from a man's horn is what he is. And a man can be many different things."

On 125th Street in Harlem. By the time this photograph was taken, in the autumn of 1964, stars with jazz roots like Billy Eckstine and Quincy Jones only rarely headlined at the Apollo Theater any more. It did its best business presenting rhythm and blues packages.

lounges, studio orchestras, playing background music for the movies, backing rock 'n' roll performers on records. "You have to eat," said Bud Shank, just one of many West Coast musicians who found themselves forced to find refuge in the Hollywood studios. "You have to survive. When I became a full-time studio musician, I had been unemployed for a long time since jazz music left us in 1962–63. . . . I went into another business. That's what I did . . . using the tools I had, which was playing the flute and the saxophone."

Other musicians abandoned performing altogether. Tenor saxophonist Eddie "Lockjaw" Davis, a veteran of the Count Basie band, became a booking agent for rock groups. Dicky Wells, who had played trombone with Basie, as well as Fletcher Henderson, Benny Carter, and Teddy Hill, took a job as a bank guard on Wall Street, in part, he said, because there were "at least a hundred" other musicians already working in the financial district with whom he could hang out at lunchtime. Still other musicians left for Europe in search of an audience: Chet Baker, Donald Byrd, Don Cherry, Art Farmer, Bud Freeman, Stan Getz, Jimmy Heath, Philly Joe Jones, Oscar Pettiford, Bud Powell, Stuff Smith, Art Taylor, Lucky Thompson, Ben Webster, Randy Weston, Phil Woods.

In 1962, Dexter Gordon joined that exodus. He would stay away for the next fifteen years, living in Paris briefly first and then in Copenhagen, coming home for brief appearances or recording dates when he could get them, then scuttling back overseas again. He reveled in the admiration of European fans, who treated him as an artist, not a drug addict—but he also grew impatient with the local musicians with whom he was sometimes forced to play. They were mostly amateurs, he remembered, doctors, dentists, architects, salesmen. They loved the music, but "all they knew was what they'd learned from the records. And with jazz, you've got to come up by playing with other musicians—older

Dexter Gordon at New York's Royal Roost, 1948

musicians. . . . In the way we all came up in the States." Fewer and fewer young American musicians would be coming up that way in the years to come, and America's music would suffer for it.

The country Gordon left behind was entering an era unlike any it had ever experienced before, a period of selfless struggle and shameless self-indulgence; of unprecedented progress in civil rights and deepening divisions between the races; of calls for collective action and relentless focus on

the individual; and of the mushroom growth of a youth culture powerful enough to begin to dictate America's tastes. Jazz music would struggle to deal with it all, and in the process would increasingly find itself divided into factions, so *many* factions, Duke Ellington said, he didn't see how "such great extremes as now exist can be contained under the one heading." The debate over what was jazz and what was not raged as it never had before, and for a time, the real question would become whether this most American of art forms could survive in America at all.

No book, no shelf of books, could adequately map the course of jazz after 1960, let alone trace the meandering paths of all its proliferating tributaries. No Great Man can be said to have towered over everyone else, as Louis Armstrong and Charlie Parker could be said to have done in their time, but John Coltrane and Miles Davis were surely among the most influential of all post-bebop musicians, and their careers touched upon many of the most important developments in the music, for both good and ill. During Coltrane's too-brief career—he began recording with Miles Davis in 1955 and died in 1967, at the age of forty—his music would first exemplify the idealism that may have been the most admirable quality of the early 1960s, and then prefigure what Cecil Taylor called "the hysteria of the times," the chaos that characterized the decade's end. His truncated life would also further fuel the romantic but dangerous notion, born after Bix Beiderbecke's early death and furthered by Charlie Parker's demise, that the greatest musicians were those who immolated themselves in search of something new. Meanwhile, Davis—who would remain a much admired figure until his death in 1991—developed still another fresh way to work with young musicians, and then, when he saw his own popularity and that of jazz itself declining, would seek to save himself by first denaturing and then deserting altogether the music that had won him fame in the first place.

SOMETHING LIKE HAPPINESS

"The other night I heard a cat on the radio and he was talking about 'modern' jazz," Duke Ellington told an interviewer in the early sixties. "He played a record to illustrate his point, and there were devices in that music I heard cats using in the nineteen-twenties. Those large words like 'modern' don't *mean* anything. Everybody who's

had anything to say in this music—all the way back—has been an individualist. I mean musicians like Sidney Bechet, Louis Armstrong, Coleman Hawkins. Then what happens is that hundreds of other musicians begin to be shaped by that one man. They fall in behind him and you've got what people call a category. But I don't listen to terms like 'modern' jazz. I listen for those individualists."

By 1962, John Coltrane was already one of the music's most influential individualists, and when Bob Thiele of Impulse Records asked Ellington to record with him that year, the older man happily agreed. Before the session, there was some concern that their styles wouldn't blend well, that the generational differences would prove too great between the thirty-six-year-old saxophonist whom many young musicians had already begun to see as the standard-bearer for a new musical revolution, and the sixty-three-year-old elder statesman who had begun recording his own compositions before Coltrane was born. No one need have worried. "Ellington was put into the jazz world to separate the men from the boys," wrote the British saxophonist Benny Green. "His grasp of harmony and instrumental voicing is more advanced than anybody else's in the entire range of jazz, and the reason why many modern fans are unable to accept him is not that they are too modern for Duke, but that Duke is too modern for them." The two men got along famously. Coltrane's scalar improvising didn't scare Ellington—"We're accustomed to . . . adjusting backgrounds to the soloist who's in the foreground," he said, employing the royal "we"—while Coltrane had served a full apprenticeship in jazz and had profound respect for Ellington and his music. The saxophonist's chronic dissatisfaction with his own work might have made the session arduous; he customarily asked record producers to let him try take after take. But Ellington's skill at bending others to his will while seeming to be thinking only of their welfare finessed that prob-

lem. "Don't ask him to do another," he told Thiele after he and Coltrane had finished the first take of their first tune. "He'll end up repeating himself."

John Coltrane was often accused of doing precisely that in the course of improvisations that now sometimes stretched on in live performance for an hour or more.

Eric Dolphy, left, John Coltrane, now playing soprano saxophone, and bassist Reginald Workman reflected in a mirror at the Village Gate, 1961. "When there's something we think could be better," Coltrane said, "we must make an effort to try and make it better. . . . It's the same socially, musically, politically . . . in any departmnent of our lives."

"One man's incantation," wrote Martin Williams, "is another man's monotony." But redundancy was never his intention. Few in the long history of the music ever labored so hard in search of fresh ways to sound. And no one ever had a more exalted sense of the musician's calling. "I would like to bring to people something like happiness,"

Coltrane told an interviewer early in his career. "I would like to discover a method so that if I want it to rain, it will start right away to rain. If one of my friends is ill, I'd like to play a certain song and he will be cured. . . . But what are these pieces and what is the road to travel to attain a knowledge of them? That I don't know." In a less

genuinely modest man such sentiments might have been evidence of megalomania, and some have suggested that Coltrane's behavior did border on madness. He seems clearly to have been an obsessive: so incapable of resisting sweets that he lost most of his teeth by the age of thirty-one; so fanatical about practicing during the day-

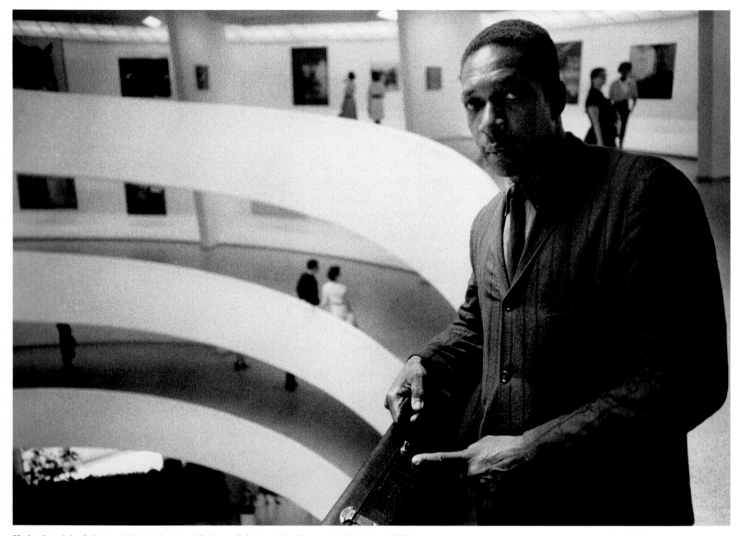

Modernism. John Coltrane at the newly opened Solomon R Guggenheim Museum in Manhattan, 1960

time, his onetime neighbor, the organist Shirley Scott, recalled, that unless his wife was home, he would answer neither the telephone nor the door; so impatient to play at night that when performing in a club he would sometimes complete one lengthy solo, leave the bandstand, go into the men's room and continue blowing while the other members of the group were soloing, then return to play again, repeating the cycle without a break till closing time.

Coltrane's compulsiveness had first taken the form of heroin and alcohol addictions so severe that Miles Davis had had to let him go for a time in 1957. His dismissal

turned out to have been almost literally a blessing. He went home to Philadelphia and there, he wrote later, "I experienced, by the Grace of God, a spiritual awakening which was to lead me to a richer, fuller, more productive life. . . . In gratitude I humbly asked to be given the means and privilege to make others happy through music." For that cause, he gave up drugs and liquor and devoted himself monomaniacally to his craft, more determined than ever to fill his music with more of everything—more notes, more energy, more ideas. He worked with Thelonious Monk for a time, rejoined Miles Davis, then in 1960 struck out on his

own, sometimes performing with the avant-garde reedman Eric Dolphy.

Just as he had once tried to play every note in every chord, Coltrane would be driven by his spiritual and musical quest simultaneously to work his earnest way through nearly every nostrum the sixties had to offer: astrology and vegetarianism, Yoga, the Kabbalah, Kahlil Gibran, Tibetan Buddhism, Hindu mysticism, a book called *Philosophy Made Simple,* and, eventually, LSD. Coltrane listened to North African and Far Eastern music, too, and began to experiment with the drone and scalar playing of Indian ragas. "He was obsessed with learning how to get to what he was hearing," Charlie Haden said. "That's all he thought about. He generated this energy . . . that was almost like the energy of the sun. He lifted everything up when he played."

In 1961, he formed his own extraordinary quartet. Jimmy Garrison brought both ferocity and steadfastness to the bass. McCoy Tyner played the piano; his love for the blues, percussive block chords, and riffs and vamps (brief patterns played over and over to produce something like the drone's effect in Indian music), worked out with Garrison, helped provide the perfect setting for Coltrane's increasingly relentless musings. Elvin Jones played drums—*all* the drums. For him, as Stanley Crouch has written, the trap set was an "ensemble" on which rhythm was not merely played but "orchestrated." "It may sound like a duet or duel," Jones once said of his ruffling, swirling work, filled with cymbal splashes, that sometimes seemed not to back Coltrane so much as engulf the whole group, "but it's still a support I'm lending him, a complementary thing."

In addition to the tenor with which he had first made his mark, Coltrane was now also playing the soprano saxophone, the higher-pitched instrument Sidney Bechet had introduced to jazz. He chose it, he said, because it reminded him of the Eastern and African instruments he had come to love, and he used it to produce his stunning 1961 transformation of the cloying waltz from *The Sound of Music,* "My Favorite Things." It became the first jazz cut since Dave Brubeck's "Take Five" to receive wide play on the radio. It also helped make Coltrane, after Miles Davis, perhaps the best-paid black modern jazz musician in the country.

He barely noticed. By the time his records appeared, he always seemed to have moved on to something else, something he hoped would bring him closer to providing answers to the questions he perpetually asked himself. Now, with "My Favorite Things" still being heard on the radio, Coltrane made a live album at the

Village Vanguard called *Chasin' the Trane.* The title tune, a better-than-sixteen-minute tenor solo covering one whole side of the record—some eighty choruses, nearly three times as many as Paul Gonsalves played at Newport in 1956—was built upon the twelve-bar blues but is otherwise unlike any blues anyone had heard on a record before. Tyner sat this one out, but Jones and Garrison saw to it that it never stopped swinging. Otherwise, it was all Coltrane— swooping, twisting, roaring by turns, his sound filled with yawps and honks, cries and slurs, that he had mastered playing in rhythm and blues bands, and so intense and unrelenting that it battered down his listeners' defenses, leaving them as exhilarated and nearly as drained as he was when he came to the end. That was not actually his intention—"I'm primarily looking into certain sounds, certain scales," he said. "Not that I'm sure what I'm looking for, except that it'll be something that hasn't been played before"—but the impact of his playing was almost palpable and, for those willing to follow wherever he might lead, irresistible. Michael Cuscuna used to hear Coltrane at Birdland. "The energy, the power that came out of that group was just astonishing. In the peanut gallery [a seating area for fans too young to be served alcohol], the tables were very nicely spaced, and I remember we used to just get up and dance to John Coltrane. It was as close to having a religion as I ever got." In an era of steadily heightening racial sensitivity, some young black musicians heard something more—a new, profoundly expressive way to play, derived from African-American rather than European sources, that was the mirror opposite of cool.

The men with whom Coltrane played shared his almost visionary belief in the importance of what they were doing. "Many years later," the tenor saxophonist Branford Marsalis recalled, "a lot of younger musicians were hanging around with Elvin Jones, and they were talking about, 'Man, you know, you guys had an intensity when

you were playing with Coltrane. I mean, what was that like? How do you play with that kind of intensity?' And Elvin looks at him and says, 'You gotta be willing to die with the motherfucker.' They started laughing like kids do, waiting for the punch line, and then they realized he was serious. How many people do you know that are willing to die—period? Die with anybody! And when you listen to those records, that's exactly what they sound like. I mean, that they would die for each other."

On December 9, 1964, the Coltrane quartet made one of the best-selling and best-loved jazz albums of all time, a four-part devotional suite called *A Love*

Elvin Jones. Dubbed ""Emperor Jones," by the great Max Roach, he insisted that the drum set should be played as a single instrument, not an assembly. "You can't isolate the different parts of the set," he said, "any more than you can isolate your left leg from the rest of your body. We live in a world where everything is categorized and locked up into little bitty compartments. But I have to insist that the drum set is one."

BEATING THE BEATLES

Cover of a long-playing album that included Louis Armstrong's hit single

In February 1964, the Beatles landed in America. Their music had preceded them—Beatle records topped the charts, adolescent American girls were as frenzied to see and hear them as were their British counterparts—and theirs was only the first foothold of what came to be called the British invasion. Jazz musicians receded still further into the background—with one notable exception: Louis Armstrong and the All-Stars. "We were playing a club in Chicago called The Chez Paree," Arvell Shaw remembered,

> and our off day was Sunday. We got a call from Joe Glaser, saying, "I want you to go into New York on your off day to make a recording." So we flew into New York on Sunday, we got to the studio, and they gave Louis the sheet music and Louis looked at it and said, "You mean to tell me you called me out here to do this?" He hated it, you know? But we made the record, and then we went back to Chicago and finished out the engagement. Three or four months later we were out on the road doing one-nighters in Nebraska and Iowa—way out. And every night we'd hear from the audience, "Hello Dolly, Hello Dolly." So, the first couple of nights Louis ignored it, and it got louder, "Hello Dolly." So Louis looked at me. He said, "What the hell is 'Hello Dolly?'" I said, "Well you remember that date we did a few months ago in New York? One of the tunes was called 'Hello Dolly'; it's from a Broadway show." We had to call and get the music and learn it and put it in the concert, and the first time we put it in the concert, pandemonium broke out.

Two months after the Beatles landed, Louis Armstrong's "Hello Dolly" became the number one song in America. When Armstrong got back to New York and played a one-night stand at the Metropole, he was greeted by a sign above a musicians' hangout across Forty-eighth Street called the Copper Rail that read, "You Beat the Beatles." Inside waiting to cheer him was a host of musicians who had learned from him over the years: Eddie Condon and Bud Freeman, middle-aged men now, who had been among the youthful acolytes haunting his bandstand on Chicago's South Side; Duke Ellington, who had first heard Armstrong when he came to New York to join Fletcher Henderson; Lionel Hampton, who had played with him in California in 1930; Ben Webster and Buck Clayton and many others. It was a sweet victory, but short-lived. Within a few weeks, rock had recaptured the airwaves.

There would be other jazz and jazz-tinged hits during the 1960s. The tenor saxophonist Stan Getz ushered in a brief flurry of excitement over the Brazilian bossa nova. And Cannonball Adderley would have a big success with a soulful tune called "Mercy, Mercy, Mercy," though he was not fooled by it: "The jazz we knew and loved in the thirties, forties, fifties, yes, even the sixties . . . is gone. The audience for it is gradually fading away. We enjoy a great deal of success playing what we do, because people don't get enough of a chance to hear it. . . . But there aren't that many playing."

Supreme. For Coltrane, music and religion had now become one: "My music is the spiritual expression of what I am—my faith, my knowledge, my being. . . . When you begin to see the possibilities of music, you desire to do something really good for people, to help humanity free itself from its hangups. . . . I want to speak to their souls." Divided into four sections—"Acknowledgment," "Resolution," "Pursuance," and "Psalm"—it is a personal affirmation of Coltrane's faith in a Creator, and during the fevered sixties its air of meditative serenity struck a chord with hundreds of thousands of young people. It continues to be a favorite among young musicians to this day. "I think that record is one of the purest jazz records ever," said the tenor saxophonist Joshua Redman. "The intent is so pure and the feeling is so pure, you just feel that John Coltrane is laying his soul out there, you know. That's one of the first records I

ever heard and I hope it's the last record I ever hear."

His fellow tenor player Branford Marsalis agreed.

> The first time I heard *A Love Supreme* was in college. And it's one of those records I couldn't put down. I listened to it for like six months straight. I just kept listening to it. You know, I would put on *A Love Supreme* in the morning for breakfast. Then I'd put it on at lunch, and I'd put it on when I went to bed at night. I would put it on when I was watching television. It was just on all the time. I couldn't believe that kind of sustained intensity. Everybody talked about the physical challenge of it, but as I spent more time listening to it and as I got older I realized that once you put yourself in a certain intellectual frame of mind, I

mean, what is physical? He had put himself in such a place mentally that the physical wasn't a problem for him because it was almost as though he had transcended the body when he started playing.

The early sixties had not been a good time for John Coltrane's former employer, Miles Davis. He was snorting cocaine and often ill. His second marriage fell apart. He worked with a series of sidemen rather than a full-time group. He was still a celebrity, but men who had played with him in the past—Art Blakey, Horace Silver, Sonny Rollins, John Coltrane, Cannonball Adderley—were now getting serious attention, and he was resentful that while his own music had once been on the "cutting edge," as he called it, "critics—white critics—[had] started supporting the free thing, pushing that over what most everybody else was doing."

Davis had initially been less than impressed with free jazz. "You don't have to think to play weird," he'd said after jamming with Ornette Coleman in 1959. He was for "freedom," he said, "but *controlled* freedom," and when he did finally manage to organize a new quintet in late 1964, it would exemplify that principle. Wayne Shorter—thirty years old and a veteran of Art Blakey's Jazz Messengers but still so respectful of his new leader that he addressed him as "Mr. Davis"—composed for the group and played tenor and soprano saxophone. The rhythm section was Ron Carter, a graduate of the Eastman School of Music, on bass; the pianist Herbie Hancock, who had begun his career at the age of eleven, performing a D major piano concerto by Mozart with the Chicago Symphony; and the drummer Tony Williams, already a masterful percussionist at seventeen but too young to be allowed to play in most clubs. Davis said he himself provided "the inspiration and wisdom" for his new group, but that Williams was the "fire, the creative spark," Carter and Hancock were "the anchors," and Wayne Shorter "the idea person, the conceptualizer of a whole lot of the musical ideas we did." If the musical rules "didn't work," Davis continued, Shorter "broke them but . . . he [also] understood that freedom in music was the ability to know the rules in order to bend them to your satisfaction and taste."

The first of the six albums Davis's new group made together was aptly titled *E.S.P.*—it seemed to many of those who heard it that only extrasensory perception could account for the apparently effortless interchange of musical ideas. The music was more dense, more free-floating, than anything Miles Davis had done before; it encompassed sudden spontaneous shifts in tempo and other elements heard in the music of far freer players, but all still linked to the blues-based music he had always played. "It's really hard to describe what we were doing, because we didn't talk in detail about it," Herbie Hancock remembered. "Things would kind of just happen and you just had

Miles Davis and Wayne Shorter, 1968. Davis, Shorter remembered, "was the only bandleader who paid his personnel not to practice at home, so as to avoid the polish that makes some improvised music sound boring. He always wanted it fresh."

to keep your ears open, keep your eyes open, and keep your heart open."

"I don't know if there's ever been a group of five musicians who communicated spontaneously with each other as well as those five," said Joshua Redman. "They could do anything with any form, with any tune, because they knew each other so well as musicians. Their music will always sound cutting edge and always sound modern of showed up at the age of twenty and started doing that and saying that they were playing. I mean, it was more like a good hustle, to me. Because if you had grabbed Coltrane and said, "Play some blues," he could have played it. You ask these other cats to play some blues, play some Sidney Bechet, play some traditional songs—they can't. I can't consider a guy a jazz musician if he doesn't really understand the entire legacy of the music. I just can't do it.

MY PEOPLE

When, sometime during the 1960s, a young reporter asked Duke Ellington whether he subscribed to the new slogan Black Is Beautiful, he snapped, "I wrote 'Black Beauty' in 1928," and called for the next question. He had little patience with the people who now sometimes charged him with having remained too circumspect about civil rights. "People who think that of me haven't been listening to our music," he said. "For the past twenty-five years, social protest and pride in the history of the Negro have been the most significant themes in what we've done." Even when touring the South in the early thirties—"without the benefit of a federal court order," he added—"we've never let ourselves be put into a position of being treated with disrespect." He had begun his career as a Race man, but now, as some young black musicians declared their separateness, he had moved far beyond it, determined, as always, to avoid being categorized. "You've been quoted as saying that you write the music of your 'people,' " asked a television interviewer. "Now, would you like to expound on that?"

Let's see. My people. Now, which of my people? I mean, you know, I'm in several groups, you know, I'm, I'm in . . . let's see. I'm in the group of the piano players; I'm in the group of the listeners; I'm in the groups of people who have general appreciation of music; I'm in the group of those who aspire to be dilettantes; I'm in the group of those who attempt to produce something fit for the plateau; I'm in the group of what? . . . Now, oh yeah—those who appreciate Beaujolais. Well, and then of course . . . I've had such a strong influence by the music of the people, the people. That's the better word—*the* people, rather than *my* people, because the people are my people.

Ellington stayed on the road all through the 1960s, traveling the world—Europe, Asia, Africa, South America—and writing music inspired by everything he saw, including *The Far East Suite, Latin American Suite,* and *La Plus Belle Africaine.* He also wrote some 230 songs, as well as a sort of musical pageant called *My People,* commemorating a century of Emancipation; incidental music for Shakespeare's *Timon of Athens* and T. S. Eliot's *Murder in the Cathedral;* and, with Billy Strayhorn, new arrangements of Tchaikovsky's *Nutcracker Suite* and Grieg's *Peer Gynt Suite* for jazz orchestra. But he also found the time to play high school proms and college dances, state fairs and Elks Clubs, just as he always had.

In 1965, all three members of the jury for the Pulitzer Prize for Music recommended that Ellington be given a special prize for his life's work. The advisory board turned them down; no such award had ever been given before. Two of the three judges resigned in protest. The sixty-six-year-old Ellington professed to be unperturbed. "Fate is being kind to me," he told a reporter. "Fate doesn't want me to be too famous too young." Privately, he was less circumspect. "I'm hardly surprised that my kind of music is still without, let us say, official honor at home," he told a friend later that year. "Most Americans still take it for granted that European music—classical music, if you will—is the only really respectable kind. What we do, what other black musicians do, has always been like the kind of man you wouldn't want your daughter to associate with."

Duke Ellington's schedule for a month in 1966 includes appearances at big-city ballrooms and nightclubs, an honorary degree ceremony, the taping of a national television program—and an Elks Club dance in North Platte, Nebraska.

Duke Ellington in the studio, 1961. Jimmy Hamilton is at the right. "It's a matter of whether you want to play music or make money," Ellington said. "I like to keep a band so that I can write and hear the music the next day. The only way to do it is to pay the band and keep it on tap. . . . A musical profit can put you way ahead of a financial loss."

Ellington was performing on the road in Reno, Nevada, on May 31, 1967, when he got a telephone call from New York. Billy Strayhorn, his close friend, creative partner, and co-composer for nearly thirty years, was dead of cancer. His death had been expected; Strayhorn had been terminally ill for several years. Ellington fell silent. Someone asked him if he was going to be all right. "No, I'm not going to be all right," he snapped. "*Nothing* is all right now." He was nearly as devastated as he had been when his mother died, and just as he had done thirty-two years earlier, he vanquished his grief by focusing on music, recording an album of Strayhorn's compositions, *And His Mother Called Him Bill.*

On April 29, 1969, Ellington turned seventy. At the suggestion of the Voice of America disc jockey Willis Conover and Leonard Garment, a White House lawyer who had once played saxophone with Woody Herman, President Richard Nixon paid official tribute to Ellington at the White House with the nation's highest civilian honor, the Presidential Medal of Freedom. "In the royalty of American music," the President said, "no man swings more or stands higher than the Duke."

Ellington responded with his customary courtly eloquence. "There is no place I would rather be tonight than in my mother's arms," he said.

Thank you very much, Mr. President. Thank you, ladies and gentlemen. This is the Presidential Medal of Freedom. The word "freedom" is one coincidentally that we are using at the moment in our *Sacred Concert.* And of course we speak of freedom of expression, we speak of freedom generally as something sweet and fat . . . but at the end we get down to the payoff, what we actually say is that we would like very much to mention the four major freedoms that my friend and writing and arranging composer Billy Strayhorn lived by and

MINGUS

The turbulent age had no more turbulent musical symbol than the composer and bassist Charles Mingus. Born in Nogales, Arizona, in 1922 and raised in the Watts neighborhood of Los Angeles, he studied trombone and cello before turning to the bass. He played with—and learned from—everyone from Louis Armstrong and Lionel Hampton to Duke Ellington and Charlie Parker, and his complex, gospel-tinged compositions were filled with witty allusions to all of them: one of his most memorable pieces was called "If Charlie Parker Was a Gunslinger, There'd Be a Whole Lot of Dead Copycats."

Mingus established two different short-lived labels rather than allow record executives to dictate to him. When he recorded "Fables of Faubus," a scathing 1959 attack on the segregationist governor of Arkansas, and Columbia Records refused to allow him to include the uncompromising lyrics on the album, he put out the full version on another smaller label called Candid. The following year, he and Max Roach led an "anti-festival" at Newport to protest what they charged was the growing commercialism of the original. And then, with Roach and Jo Jones, he established the Jazz Artists Guild. It didn't last long, but it set a precedent for subsequent attempts by musicians to wrest control from businessmen.

Mingus was as hot-tempered as he was uncompromising and musically gifted, and stories of his combativeness—often based on fact and given further credence by his own sensational autobiography, *Beneath the Underdog*—were too often allowed to overshadow his extraordinary music. His various "Jazz Workshops" served as training grounds for musicians like Jimmy Knepper, Booker Ervin, John Handy, and Eric Dolphy. No one but Jelly Roll Morton and Duke Ellington ever managed to incorporate more of American life into his work, and only Ellington outstripped him in the range of emotions it expressed: Mingus's music routinely shifted from raucousness to tenderness, intimacy to glorious cacophony.

Charles Mingus

enjoyed, and that was freedom from hate, unconditionally; freedom from self-pity; freedom from fear of possibly doing something that may help someone else more than it would him; and freedom from the kind of pride that can make a man feel that he is better than his brother.

The President played "Happy Birthday" on the piano in the key of G, and then settled into his seat to listen to a jam session that included Earl Hines, Gerry Mulligan, Billy Taylor, J. J. Johnson, and Clark Terry. "When we did 'Squeeze Me,'" Terry remembered, "I got out the plunger mute—the plumber's friend—and [Nixon] was nudging his wife, pointing at it and saying, 'Look at that! Look, it's a toilet plunger! Look at that!' I guess he hadn't seen a whole lot of jazz bands."

JAZZ IS DEAD

By 1969, George Wein remembered, even the Newport Jazz Festival was in trouble. "It was slipping in the eyes of the press because at that time, if you were over forty, you were finished. This was when corporations were hiring twenty-two-year-old kids to tell them about what the youth market was." Rock had taken over so completely that Wein finally decided he had to include it on the program and called friends to find out which rock musicians could actually play. "Well," they told him, "Jethro Tull plays the flute and Frank Zappa plays good guitar, and Jimmy Page with Led Zeppelin plays good blues." "So I hired all these groups. I had a rock festival, but I also had some good jazz. On the last night I had poor Stephane Grappelli playing with the World's Greatest Jazz Band with Yank Lawson, and right after them, I had Sly and the Family Stone, so you can see what a mess it was."

Miles Davis and his quintet were there, too, Wein recalled:

Miles had more people than had ever seen him in concert. We drew something like eighty thousand people in four days, where normally we would draw forty or fifty thousand. The kids were all over town. Miles, who normally didn't appear until he was due on the stage and left afterwards as fast as he could get out of town, stayed the entire four days. He watched the reaction of that crowd and he saw those kids. It changed his life forever. And when we rode back on the plane from Providence, he said to me, "George, what should I do? I don't know which way to go." And so I said to him—with infinite wisdom—I said, "Play the melody," because I remembered those great songs, you know, "Bye Bye Blackbird." He didn't listen to one word I said, naturally, because he was much more concerned with reaching out to youth, which wasn't concerned with melody.

Davis was forty-three years old that summer—and concerned that he was no longer playing to the sellout crowds that had once flocked to hear him. Columbia Records was worried, too. The company had sold 150,000 copies of his albums just a few years earlier; now it was lucky to sell 50,000, and it had advanced him large sums of money that seemed unlikely ever to be paid back. Earlier that year, Miles had called Columbia's new president, Clive Davis, to complain. "He was tired of low sales and angry about it," the executive remembered. "Blood, Sweat & Tears and Chicago had borrowed enormously from him—and sold millions. These young *white* artists . . . were cashing in while he was struggling from advance to advance. 'If you stop calling me a *jazz*man,' he said at one point, 'and just sell me alongside these other people, I'll sell more.'"

"In part, I agreed with him," Clive Davis recalled, and he suggested that if Miles really wanted to reach more people, he ought to try playing places like the country's most celebrated rock palace, the Fillmore Auditorium in San Francisco. The trumpet player slammed down the telephone: he wasn't going to play for "those fucking long-haired white kids," he said; he'd leave Columbia first. But he did not leave.

The astonishing popularity of rock and funk had not been lost on other jazz musicians, especially on the more youthful among them, who had grown up dancing to rock and R&B rather than listening to swing and bebop. In 1967, saxophonist Charles Lloyd had started what would become something like a stampede of jazz musicians eager to find a way of getting in on the action. With a quartet that included the drummer Jack DeJohnette and the pianist Keith Jarrett, he was a hit at the Fillmore. *Time* heralded "the arrival of the first psychedelic rock group," and Lloyd seemed to fill the bill. "I play love vibrations," he said. "Love, totality—like bringing everyone together in a joyous dance." His band soon dissolved, and for a time Lloyd became a teacher of transcendental meditation. But other musicians had been watching. "I wanted a wider audience," said the alto saxophonist John Handy. "I was a little tired of playing for those who sit all night saying, 'yeah, yeah, yeah,' all thirty-five of them. I wanted to know what it was like to play for a stadium full of people. I wanted to see black women in the audience."

Miles Davis had been watching, too, and he was listening to the funk music of James Brown, Jimi Hendrix, and Sly Stone, with its overwhelming backbeat, its heavy use of vamps and electronic instruments. His music had already begun to reflect what he'd been hearing. The electric guitarists George Benson and Joe Beck made appearances on his records. His group's harmonies no longer shifted as they once had. The beat grew ever more dominant. Herbie Hancock began playing electric piano, and was joined by other keyboardists, including Chick Corea, Keith Jarrett, and Joe Zawinul; and two Britons, Fender bassist Dave Holland, and electric guitarist John McLaughlin. Davis had realized, he remembered, "that most rock musicians didn't know anything about music. . . . But they were popular because they were giving the public a certain sound, what they wanted to hear. So I figured that if they could do it—reach all those people and sell all those records without really knowing what they were doing—then I could do it, too, only better. . . . I wasn't prepared to be a memory yet."

On August 16, 1969, a little over a month after the Newport festival, some four hundred thousand young people gathered in a cow pasture near Woodstock, New York, willing to endure hours of rain and mud and discomfort just to be together in the presence of their rock idols. Three days later, Miles Davis made his bid to become one of those idols and began recording the curious mélange of jazz and rock he called *Bitches Brew*. Even before it was released, Davis agreed to appear at the Fillmore East, the New York equivalent of the San Francisco venue he'd turned down as beneath him just a few months before. He would be the opening act for Laura Nyro, a rock singer less than half his age.

Bitches Brew, the best-selling 1969 Miles Davis album that pointed the way toward fusion

Late Miles. Flaunting the trappings of rock stardom (above) and (right) onstage with members of his 1973 band. Left to right, Michael Henderson (electric bass), Cedric Lawson (electronic keyboards), Davie Liebman (tenor saxophone), Reggie Lucas (electric guitar), Badal Roy (tabla), and James Mtume Foreman (congas).

Bitches Brew was a commercial triumph. It sold 400,000 copies in its first year, more than any Miles Davis record ever had sold before. During the next six years he would make thirteen more albums, each one less like jazz than the last. "We're not going to play the blues anymore," he'd told Herbie Hancock even before making *Bitches Brew.* "Let the white folks have the blues. They got 'em, so they can keep 'em. Play something else." His willingness to alter his music so dramatically—and the money he made by doing so—sent a powerful message.

During the 1970s, fusion albums like these all but overwhelmed mainstream jazz.

"Miles led the way for a lot of people," the saxophonist Jimmy Heath said, "because he was one of the ones who got through. He had the fine clothes, the expensive cars, the big house, all the magazine articles and the pretty girls chasing him. He seemed like he was on top of *everything*. Then you had all of this rock getting all of the press and it was like Elvis Presley all over again. Miles stepped out here and decided he was going to get himself some of that money, and a lot of musicians followed his lead. It was as if Miles had led the pack for so long they didn't know how to stop following him, even if the music wasn't any good."

The writer Leonard Feather asked Davis's old friend and mentor Clark Terry what he thought young people heard in his new music. "What they hear in it is less significant than what they *don't* hear," Terry answered. "What they don't hear, because it is not there, is the real balls of jazz, the chord progressions, the structures. . . . [Young people] are not musically mature enough to cope with this, and Miles is smart enough to put something where they can reach it on their own level. . . . If they're not hip enough to know what's happening—say, the way Bird was playing years ago, with

swinging groups—they're going to grasp whatever is simple enough for them to cop. And the simple thing for them to cop happens to be that one-chord modal bag that is so fashionable. . . . To me, jazz has to stimulate, and this is not . . . stimulating."

The trumpet player Lester Bowie was more diplomatic: "I appreciate rock and roll music. I like all kinds of music. I can't think of any music that I dislike, but rock and roll is entry-level music. I mean, a rock and roll gig is the first gig you get. You're supposed to continue development beyond that. To us as hard-core musicians, we always considered [fusion] a little bit lightweight. It was nice. I liked the groups; they sounded good, but they were kind of on the lightweight edge of music."

Fusion—the hybrid music Davis had helped to launch—had set out in part to reunite the worlds of jazz and dance, to rebuild the following that jazz had lost to rock. Early fusion yielded some memorable music, much of it made by bands—Herbie Hancock's Headhunters, Tony Williams's Lifetime, Chick Corea's Return to Forever, John McLaughlin's Mahavishnu Orchestra—formed by musicians who had played in one

or another of Davis's groups over the years. It introduced young people to some of the elements of jazz as well, and it incorporated music and musicians from every corner of the world. Perhaps the most widely admired fusion group was Weather Report, established by two of the men who had played on the *Bitches Brew* album, Wayne Shorter and Joe Zawinul. "Weather Report's music always sounds raw and on the edge and real," the tenor saxophonist Joshua Redman said. "And I think that isn't true of a lot of other fusion music, especially some of the fusion that came later."

"Big business had come into jazz," Michael Cuscuna remembered.

And fusion had become a part of pop music. And with it came a lot of pressures, and a lot of demands that really shouldn't have been applied to the art. Art Blakey used to like to tell the story about [the trumpet player] Donald Byrd [who had crossed over into fusion] coming up to him backstage at some concert and saying, "Man, the pressure of coming up with another record that's going to sell as much as my last one. I'm not sure which direction to go." Art was always a firm believer in sticking to the aesthetics that you've always loved and developing from there. And he said, "I looked at Donald and he had a lot of money, but he had this big potbelly and he looked stressed and he didn't look healthy and I said, "Donald, I never saw an armored car following a hearse."

In 1975, Miles Davis would abruptly put down his trumpet. He was "spiritually tired," he remembered, "without anything more to say musically." He stayed away from the recording studio for six years, struggling with chronic ill health and a continuing problem with drugs, and when he finally came back, even he did not claim to be playing jazz anymore. Jazz was "dead," he said, "the music of the museum." "When

THE DIVINE ONE

Sarah Vaughan at a 1950 recording date

In the era when light-skinned, fine-featured Lena Horne set the standard for black female entertainers, Sarah Vaughan, like Ella Fitzgerald, was at first thought too plain and too dark for show business. Earl Hines, who gave her her first job as a singer in 1942, did so although he said she "looked like home-made sin." But he and other musicians came to love her for her perfect pitch and rhythmic sense, her sophisticated ear for chord changes, and her astonishing voice—she could sing everything from soprano to baritone. They liked her devil-may-care spirit, too, and eventually dubbed her "Sassy," the nickname she would carry until, during her final days as a diva, she became known to her admirers as "the Divine One."

Born in Newark, New Jersey, in 1924 and introduced to music as a singer and substitute organist for the First Mount Zion Baptist Church, she remained an able piano player and, like Billie Holiday, saw herself as a musician before she was a vocalist. "Sassy," Dizzy Gillespie once said, "can sing notes other people can't even hear," and when she closed her eyes onstage, she said, she could see—and sing—lines that might have been improvised on the piano. She was Ella Fitzgerald's most important rival as the most admired vocalist in jazz, but Columbia in the late 1940s set out to make her a pop performer. She hated most of the material she was given to sing and when she moved to another record company in 1954, she satisfied its need for hits by asking for two contracts—one for recording frankly commercial tunes and the other for the jazz she loved. "My contract with Mercury is for pops," she told a friend, "and my contract with [Mercury's jazz subsidiary] Emarcy is for me." She recorded everything from Beatles tunes to the Lord's Prayer. Stephen Sondheim's "Send in the Clowns" became her signature tune in the years before her death in 1990. Hers, wrote the jazz critic Gary Giddins, was "the ageless voice of modern jazz—of giddy postwar virtuosity, biting wit, and fearless caprice . . . a voice that happens once in a lifetime, perhaps once in several lifetimes."

I last heard Miles Davis," Martin Williams wrote three years before the trumpeter's death in 1991, "he was stalking around a stage in what looked like a leftover Halloween fright suit, emitting a scant handful of plaintive notes."

Over the years, much of fusion's remaining jazz content would be worn away. To play jazz well, as Dexter Gordon said, it had always been necessary for young musicians to play with and learn from older ones. Many youthful players had now never had that opportunity. Their music grew closer and closer to instrumental pop—meant for easy listening, and not much else.

"Jazz music," said Jelly Roll Morton, "is a *style,* not compositions. Any kind of music may be played in jazz, if one has the knowledge." Great musicians like Louis Armstrong and Benny Goodman had found ingenious ways to turn the most banal pop material into jazz, but swinging was at the heart of that conception. "When that swing starts to happen," Charlie Haden said, "it's like being on a wave if you're a surfer. Or it's like taking a pebble and skipping it about eight times over a lake that's real still. It's that groove that happens. It's the power that a 747 has when it's taking off. It's a momentum that starts and builds and allows you to stop thinking. Because the creative process, the thought process, stops in the midst of creation. There's just the moment that you're in, you know. There's no yesterday, there's no tomorrow. There's just right now."

By definition rock does not swing; its beat remains the same; that is a large part of its appeal to young dancers. "Jazz has always been able to meet, absorb, and put to its own purposes almost everything in popular prospect," wrote Martin Williams, looking back. "Nevertheless, I don't think fusion worked very well . . . the beat in jazz moves forward; it is played to contribute to the all but irresistible momentum of the music: jazz *goes* somewhere. The beat in most rock bobs and bounces away in one place. . . . Rock *stays* somewhere."

GIVING IT BACK

Louis Armstrong had seen it all: New Orleans before jazz began to spread across the country; the first days of recording, when he had revolutionized first instrumental music and then American singing. He had witnessed the swing era and endured the bebop years—and he was still on the road, as celebrated abroad as he was at home, even behind the Iron Curtain. Arvell Shaw remembered a visit to divided Germany:

All the action was in West Berlin, and we were in East Berlin. So one night we had a few wines, and Louis said, "Man, let's go to West Berlin." The promoter said, "You can't. You got to get permission." Louis said, "The hell with it. You get in the bus." We get in the bus. We went to Checkpoint Charlie and the East German guards stopped us, came on the bus with these loaded machine guns. They said, "Where are your passes? Where are your passes?" And then one of them said, "Louis Armstrong!" They said, "Oh, Mr. Armstrong! Go right on through." And then we got to the American side and they said, "Where are your passes?" The guys came through. "Hey, Pops!" one of the soldiers said, "Pops, go on," and we went through. Every night we used to go from East Berlin to West Berlin and hang out all night and we'd go through every night without a pass, *stoned,* you know?

Between dates, Armstrong came back to Lucille and the modest home in Queens that she had found for them when they were first married. He never saw any need for anything fancier. "He loved every room," the Armstrongs' close friend Victoria Joseph remembered. "That was his home." And when his wife suggested from time to time that they move to a grander place in a more exclusive neighborhood, he wouldn't hear

Mr. and Mrs. Louis Armstrong, photographed on a rare night out in New York sometime during the late 1960s. Armstrong rarely ventured far from his home in Queens during his last years because of the horde of autograph-seekers that descended on him as soon as he was spotted.

of it. "He said, 'What for? We know everybody here, and we'd get lost in the bigger house. I'd be looking for you half the time.'" "If Louis came home to the neighborhood," Phoebe Jacobs remembered, "very often the neighbors would have banners out, 'Welcome Home Pops.' If the weather permitted, he'd sit on the front steps of his house and buy kids Good Humors. And he'd ask them, 'Was your homework good? Were you a good boy?'"

In the fall of 1968, decades of hard living caught up with him. He suffered acute heart failure and spent seven months off and on in Manhattan's Beth Israel Hospital. "Louis used to call his sickness 'an intermission,'" Jacobs remembered. "He'd be lying in the hospital with a couple of tubes in him and you'd say something to him and he'd say, 'This is intermission.'" While he was in the hospital, Joe Glaser also suffered a heart attack, then fell into a coma from which he never recovered. Armstrong was crushed. He poured out his feelings in a long, rambling memoir in which he again expressed his gratitude to the Karnofsky

family, who had befriended him as a small boy and who, like Glaser, had been Jewish, and he let out some of the bitterness he continued to feel toward those members of his own community who he felt had abandoned him: "The other White Nationalities kept the Jewish people with fear constantly [in New Orleans but] I will always remember how the Jewish people living in the Negro neighborhood advanced and did so much, right under their noses. Boy—if the Negroes could stick together half that much. But I doubt that it would ever happen. Hmm look where we would be today. Too much malice and hate among us."

When he was released from the hospital in the spring of 1969, he was forbidden to play his horn. The strain, his doctors said, would prove too much for his heart. "He felt so bad not being able to play his trumpet," said Joseph, "but he would walk from room to room with his trumpet under his arm, in his hand, sit it on his desk. He always had the trumpet. He'd be fingering it. And when he'd be interviewed, he'd have his trumpet with him, always. Always."

In May of 1970, Bob Thiele brought Armstrong into his New York studio to make an album called *Louis Armstrong and His Friends.* An impromptu assembly of musicians turned out to pay him tribute. Old friends and admirers like Eddie Condon and the cornetists Bobby Hackett and Ruby Braff were there, but so were Ornette Coleman and Miles Davis, who said, "You can't play anything on a horn that Louis hasn't played—I mean even modern." They all joined together as a chorus while Armstrong sang, "We Shall Overcome." At the same three-day session he recorded a set of brand-new lyrics to the tune of "When the Saints Go Marching In." It was called "The Boy from New Orleans" and offered a sentimental overview of Armstrong's career from his birth in black Storyville to his celebrity as the ambassador of jazz. The lyrics were saccharine, and the record was made worse by a cumbersome overdubbed big band arrangement, but Armstrong managed—as he had so many times in the past—to infuse it with warmth and life, and it became part of his standard stage show.

A few weeks later, on July 11, George Wein staged a celebration at Newport for Armstrong's putative seventieth birthday. Many of the musicians with whom he'd played over the years came back to be with him. Dizzy Gillespie was there, too. "Without him," he said, "no me." Wein, wanting both to surprise the audience and to spare Armstrong any extra effort, suggested that he simply walk onstage unannounced, rather than sing his theme song, "Sleepy Time Down South." Armstrong wouldn't hear of it. His fans expected it, and he never wanted to disappoint them. "As long as I live," he said, " 'Sleepy Time Down South' will be my lifelong number because it lives with me."

"When he dressed up for that evening," Wein recalled, "he had on a nice brown suit and there was a glow on his face and there was a glow in his eyes. There was a glow in his skin." It was raining, and he came onstage earlier than planned because he didn't want his fans to get wet. Usually people left their seats to find shelter during a downpour, but for Louis Armstrong they stayed put. "And he just sang so beauti-

Louis Armstrong at home. "Just think," he wrote in 1970, "through the . . . years we've been living in this house we have seen just about [three] generations come up. . . . Lots of them have grown, married, [and] had children. Their children still come to visit Aunt Lucille and Uncle Louis. . . . Now that [Pops] has recuperated—feel good—blowing his horn every evening before supper with his doctor's permission, the whole neighborhood rejoices at hearing his horn every day."

In the realm of music only the funeral of Louis Armstrong could have brought together Guy Lombardo and Dizzy Gillespie; seated in the pew behind them are Gene Krupa and Arvell Shaw. The young mourners below are Little League ballplayers from Armstrong's neighborhood.

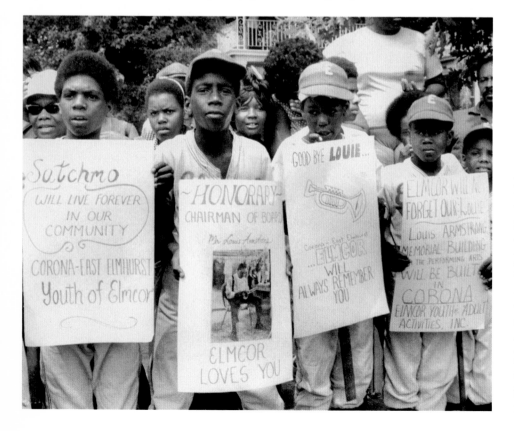

fully," Wein remembered. "It was like, 'Hey, I'm here again.' You know, 'I'm still here. I'm still Louis Armstrong, and I'm still going to give you a great evening of music and entertainment.' " Soon, he was playing trumpet again.

In the spring of 1971, Armstrong accepted a two-week engagement at the Waldorf-Astoria in Manhattan. Arvell Shaw was with him for that last engagement and almost thirty years later still had difficulty recounting it: "He had so much music in him till there's no way he could have lived and not played. The doctor told him, 'Louis, don't do it. You can't do it.' Louis said, 'Well, I got a contract, I got to do it [for] my fans.' And they had to help him. . . ." Shaw's eyes filled with tears and his voice broke. "They had to help him on and off." Victoria Joseph and her husband were in the wings on Armstrong's closing night. "The last song he sang," she remembered, "was 'The Boy from New Orleans,' and he had to stop. He was crying, tears just coming down his face, and when he finished it, you could hear a pin drop in there. For about ten seconds, there wasn't a sound and then, thunderous applause. *Thunderous.* And my husband and I were standing on either side of him, and as he came down the steps, he said, 'That's my last show, Vickie.' He knew it. That was his last show. Yes, he knew."

He was hospitalized again, survived two more heart attacks, finally insisted on being taken home. Joseph was there for dinner on the evening of July 5, the day after what he believed had been his seventy-first birthday. "He was in good spirits," she remembered.

> He said, "Vickie, the doctor gave me the OK to go back to work. I can start playing my trumpet again. The first place we'll be going will be the Black Sea, in Russia." Lucille was cooking in the kitchen for him, which he liked for her to do. And just my husband and I were sitting in the dining room with him at the table. He stood up and he grabbed the edges of the table. I think Death hit him. And he didn't say a word, he just held on tight to the table, and my husband stood up and I stayed in my seat, but we kept our eyes on him and then he straightened. I was scared to death, really. And he shrugged and sat back down and kept on talking. So I said to myself, "Now, shall I say something to Lucille and upset her or just let it go?" I never told her. I didn't. And then I could have beat myself the next day. Maybe they could have saved him; maybe they couldn't have. He came out on his stoop as we left at about eleven-thirty, quarter to twelve, saying he'd be up to see us Wednesday.

He had called for a rehearsal with the All Stars for the following day, but at about four-thirty that morning he died in his sleep. Some weeks earlier, Victoria Joseph had been helping him with his mail. There were hundreds of letters from all over the world. Every one of them was affectionate. "Pops," she had asked him then, "what do you do with all that love?"

"It gets heavy," he answered, "but I give it right back."

SO MUCH TO DO

"I loved and respected Louis Armstrong," Duke Ellington said when he heard of his death. "He was born poor, died rich, and never hurt anyone on the way." The following spring, Ellington himself was diagnosed with lung cancer. No one knows how much he was told of his prospects; his physician and close friend, Dr. Arthur Logan, would die before he did. But he rarely mentioned his deteriorating condition, even when he became too weak to conduct rehearsals without sitting down. "The music kept him going," his granddaughter Mercedes Ellington recalled. "This is what made him go through all the pain, the suffering of the last part of the sickness, of being out on the road. It was the driving force for him. It was something he had to do, every day."

Religious music had begun to interest him long before the onset of his illness. He had always been privately religious, wearing the gold cross around his neck given to him after his mother died, reading the Bible through at least seven times, but now he seemed consumed with the need to spell out his religious beliefs in music. He was "God's messenger," he said, and one member of the band thought he intended "to play his way into heaven." "You can jive with secular music," Ellington told someone who'd asked why he seemed so especially demanding about how his religious works were played, "but you can't jive with the Almighty."

He had already written two *Sacred Concerts*—ambitious works, performed in churches and cathedrals, where his orchestra was augmented by choirs, vocal soloists, dancers. Now he hurled himself into a third, which he hoped to premiere at Westminster Abbey on United Nations Day, October 24, 1973. "He knew it was his last shot," Mercer Ellington said, "and he wanted it to be good." On the day of the concert, Ellington looked frail and thin and was uncharacteristically curt with the press, objecting to the presence of TV cameras at rehearsal, unwilling to answer more than a few questions. The music was all that mattered. "Every man prays to God in his own language," he told the audience before the concert began, "and there is no language which God does not understand."

In the end, the *Third Sacred Concert* went reasonably well, though Ellington himself nearly collapsed halfway through it. George Wein flew with him the following day to Denmark.

> Duke was wiped out. . . . I was with him in the cabin. He had to take a wheelchair to the plane. And when he got to Denmark, he took a wheelchair again. I'd never seen him use a wheelchair before. He was very, very tired and much sicker than anybody realized. We took the ferry from Copenhagen to Malmö, and on the ferry, in the sea air, he sat and had Danish shrimp, the little ones that he loved. And he sat there, and you could just see him coming back. And that night he played a concert; he was so into the music that when the concert was over, he didn't want to stop. The band had left the stage and Duke came back with the people cheering and yelling and sat down at the piano and started to play. And the bass player came back and the drummer came back and one or two of the horns came back, and nobody else came back. The band just didn't respond. He played for about twenty, twenty-five minutes in a little jam session, and you could just feel he was young again for a moment. But this was his last hurrah.

Duke Ellington in Paris. "The music is that . . . very elusive medium that goes around you, over you, under you," he once told an interviewer. "You first get to know it by hearing it and you're attracted to it. It's a very delightful acquaintance and you spend all the rest of your life chasing this melody around. You think you've got it and you reach out . . . and all you get is a little piece of the tail. Other people hear it and they say, 'Yes, that's the end.' Well, you know it is the end in one way, but it isn't the total. So you continue because you want to get more of this thing. So you continue pursuing the melody. You eat with it, sleep with it, that's it. You're always in pursuit." (Opposite) Duke Ellington and vocal chorus at Westminster Abbey, rehearsing for his third Sacred Concert, October 25, 1973. Tenor saxophonist Harold Ashby warms up in the foreground.

Ellington kept on performing, regardless. He arrived home from Europe on December 4 and was back onstage in Pittsburgh the following night. When the band got to Sturgis, Michigan, on March 22, he was so weak his men begged him not to go on. He played two shows anyway, in what his son remembered as "an old firehouse," and then collapsed. It was his final public performance. He was flown back to New York the next morning and entered Columbia Presbyterian Hospital, where he immediately asked to have his electric piano brought to him so that he could keep working. He made improvements to the *Third Sacred Concert,* worked on a comic opera to be called *Queenie Pie,* and finished up *The Three Black Kings,* a new score for Alvin Ailey's dance troupe. When his eyesight began to fail, he simply wrote larger, using the backs of some of the hundreds of get-well cards that flooded his room. "I have so much to do," he said, "so much more I have to do."

He died at 3:10 in the morning, May 24, 1974. Sixty-five thousand people filed past his coffin in the funeral home. Ten thousand mourners filled the huge Cathedral of St. John the Divine for his funeral, and two thousand more stood silently outside, many weeping openly, as Ella Fitzgerald sang "Solitude" and one of the hymns most often played at New Orleans funerals in the earliest days of jazz, "Just a Closer Walk with Thee." Ellington was buried in Woodlawn Cemetery next to his mother, who had been the first to tell him he was "blessed."

TOTALLY LOST

The city of New Orleans had torn down the house in which Louis Armstrong was born to make way for a police station in 1964. By then, the Lincoln Gardens on the South Side of Chicago, where Armstrong had played with King Oliver, had long since been razed for a housing project. Law and order had come to Kansas City, and most of the wide-open clubs in which Lester Young and Count Basie and Charlie Parker played had vanished. The Cotton Club in Manhattan, where Duke Ellington first broadcast his "jungle music," was gone. So was the Savoy Ballroom, where Chick Webb once took on all comers and Ella Fitzgerald first became a star. Birdland, the club named for Charlie Parker, abandoned jazz for rhythm and blues. In 1968, the Hickory House, the last club on Fifty-second Street, finally closed its doors. Even the Five Spot, where Cecil Taylor, Ornette Coleman, and John Coltrane performed their demanding music, eventually went out of business.

During the late 1930s, according to one estimate, swing music had provided some 70 percent of the profits in the recording industry. By the mid-1970s, jazz would yield less than 3 percent. Things became so desperate that a group of black New York musicians who called themselves the Jazz and People's Movement disrupted network television programs to protest their lack of work. On October 13, 1970, the British actor Trevor Howard was a guest on Dick Cavett's television talk show. Cavett asked

HOME COOKIN'

Black big-city musicians of the bebop era had generally shunned too-vivid reminders of the lives most black people down South had been forced to lead: even the blues fell from favor for a time. But with the growth of the civil rights movement a transformation took place and among a good many young people the down-home aspects of black culture came to be seen as a source of pride, not embarassment. Those feelings were soon mirrored in music. Ray Charles showed the way, combining the blues with the organlike piano playing and call-and-response patterns of the church. Soon he and those who followed his lead began to be seen as "soul" artists. "Black musicians were saying," the writer Gerald Early remembered, "'We're going to invent a musical style and form that white people can't copy. . . . It's going to be so ethnicized that they really can't copy it without absolutely looking like a minstrel show.'"

That same kind of musical style and form took root in jazz, as well, and nobody was more important to its success than "Incredible" Jimmy Smith, the master of the Hammond B-3 organ who began recording for Blue Note Records in 1957. There had been other organists before him, pianists like Wild Bill Davis and Milt Bruckner, who had simply switched keyboards without mastering the instrument's full potential. Smith was different. The photographer Francis Wolf recalled seeing him for the first time at Small's Paradise in Harlem: "A man in convulsions, face contorted, crouched over in apparent agony, his fingers flying, his foot dancing over the pedals. The air was filled with waves of sound I had never heard before."

Even the titles of the tunes Smith and his cohorts recorded celebrated the African-American world from which they came—"Home Cookin,'" "The Sermon," "The Preacher," "Cornbread," "Grits 'n Gravy," "Back at the Chicken Shack." It was all good-time music, and it worked for a time. According to one survey, five Dave Brubeck albums reached the top-40 charts during the 1960s; Jimmy Smith had ten. Others did almost as well: Cannonball Adderley, Ramsey Lewis, Les McCann, Lee Morgan, Horace Silver, Bobby Timmons. And bars featuring organ-tenor trios became fixtures in big-city black neighborhoods all across the country. Then, an arsenal of other electric instruments took over—electric basses, electric keyboards, synthesizers, and the rest, and Jimmy Smith and his Hammond B-3—along with most other jazz musicians—found themselves drowned out by rock and funk and the new amalgam called fusion.

Jimmy Smith

GREAT BLACK MUSIC

Members of the Art Ensemble of Chicago performing at New York's Bottom Line, 1977

Beginning in the mid-1960s, all across the country young musicians—both black and white—tried to gain control over their music by forming cooperatives. The best-known and longest-lasting was the Association for the Advancement of Creative Musicians (AACM), based in Chicago. Its prime mover was the pianist and composer Muhal Richard Abrams, but one of its most eloquent spokesmen was the trumpet player Lester Bowie. "The AACM was formed," Bowie remembered, "so that we would have a venue, a mode, a way we could express the music we were actually feeling, our original music. Because there was nowhere in town to do it. The club owners in the South Side didn't want to hear anything about any intellectual music; they wanted to have something that sold drinks."

The AACM, in turn, yielded a number of important groups—Air, the Revolutionary Ensemble, and the Art Ensemble of Chicago. Formed in 1965 by Bowie, Roscoe Mitchell, Malachi Favors, and Joseph Jarman (later joined by drummer Don Moye), the ACM created exuberant music that drew upon everything from waltzes and funeral marches to free jazz and rhythm and blues. They called what they played "Great Black

Music," not jazz, Lester Bowie said, because "The name 'jazz' had a lot of negative connotations—whorehouse music, nigger music, bullshit music, devil's music. So, we came up with the term 'Great Black Music.' We wanted to distinguish ourselves from a normal jazz [group] that played taverns. The music was an art form, and we wanted to present it as such. But there was no place to do this, and there was no one to help us, no one was supporting the arts or thinking about the musicians. So, we said, 'We've got to take care of this ourselves.'"

For the first time since the days of Black Swan Records in the 1920s, African-American musicians were fully in charge of every aspect of their art—from booking and recording to promotion and distribution. But nothing the Art Ensemble of Chicago—or any other group of free musicians—could think to do seemed able to win back the black audience, which was now devoted to the sounds of Motown. The Art Ensemble once found itself playing to just three people in its own hometown, and it attracted its largest following among white college students—in France.

him, "What is it about New York that has changed?" Howard innocently replied that there was no longer any place to hear jazz. At that, members of the audience stood up, blowing whistles and wooden flutes. Two months earlier, led by the multi-instrumentalist Rahsaan Roland Kirk and the trumpet player Lee Morgan, the same group had disrupted the Merv Griffin show; five months later they threatened Johnny Carson with the same thing and were given half an hour with network executives to talk over their grievances. Eventually, Kirk, along with Charles Mingus and Archie Shepp, got himself invited to play on the Ed Sullivan show on CBS. Off-camera, Kirk asked Sullivan why he had never presented the late John Coltrane on his show. Sullivan, genuinely bewildered, asked, "Does John Coltrane have any records out?"

At the Newport Jazz Festival the following summer—while Dionne Warwick sang "What the World Needs Now Is Love, Sweet Love" onstage—thousands of young people, chanting that all music should be free, tore down the chain-link fence and rioted. The festival had to be canceled. "Everybody just felt totally lost," George Wein remembered, "because something that meant something to them had been destroyed by stupid kids that couldn't have cared less about the music that was being played."

The 1960s had been a period "when everyone was up and the music was hot and burning," the New Thing drummer Milford Graves remembered. "But the 1970s is like everyone went to sleep. Everyone got split up." Graves himself joined the faculty of Bennington College. Less fortunate avant-garde musicians found themselves playing mostly for one another, their friends and families, and a small but stubbornly devoted band of followers in lofts and private apartments. Clubs continued to close. There were many reasons, but in a mid-seventies conversation with the drummer Art Taylor, Eddie "Lockjaw" Davis, the tenor-playing veteran of the Basie band, placed the blame squarely on the avant-garde.

There was a different atmosphere about jazz years ago. The players themselves projected lighthearted feelings. There was a margin of humor in playing; there was a happier atmosphere. Today, the jazz musician comes to the bandstand with a grim outlook; he's too serious. . . . The whole joint looks like a graveyard. . . . Jazz was never meant to be that way. . . . You're not supposed to go with a pencil and pad and figure out what they're playing. . . . The only way you can get your wages is from the people who support the club. The people are going to support the club only if they enjoy what they hear. If a person comes to a club and does not understand or enjoy what the musicians are playing, he's not coming back. Therefore, there's no business, you don't get your wages, there's no more entertainment. This is why there are no clubs to speak of today. There's one here and there, and I assure you there are no freedom musicians working in them.

HOMECOMING

Dexter Gordon had been away from America for nearly fifteen years when he came home in 1976, and when he opened in New York, first at George Wein's Storyville and then at the indestructible Village Vanguard, he wasn't sure how he would be received. He still played straight-ahead jazz, without the synthesizers and electric bass and drum machines of fusion, and within the boundaries of swing, lyricism, and blues feeling that had been at the heart of the music he'd played since boyhood but that many avant-garde players had discarded. The crowds stood to cheer him after every tune. "It was just amazing to feel the impact of his sound and his presence on that stage," the tenor saxophonist Joe Lovano remembered. "To be in a room with him, at that time, for

me—I was twenty-three years old at the time—it just hit me like a ton of bricks. Just his *sound,* the power of his tone."

Columbia offered Gordon a contract, and the two-record live album he made at the Vanguard called *Homecoming* sold surprisingly well when it appeared the following year. There still seemed to be an audience for music that was wholly fresh and richly inventive but that also flowed directly from Louis Armstrong and Lester Young and Charlie Parker. "Dexter *is* jazz," said the youthful pianist George Cables, who appeared with him for three years after his return. "Playing with him really brought me back to the acoustic piano, [but] the thing I learned mostly from him was the history of the music. The roots."

Gordon's success was fresh evidence that a revival of interest in mainstream jazz might be in the offing. It had never died completely, of course. Norman Granz's Pablo label, featuring artists like Count Basie, Duke Ellington, Dizzy Gillespie, and the Canadian-born pianist Oscar Peterson, had done well all through the years of drought, and other record companies had begun to discover that there was money to be made reissuing long-dormant titles from their catalogues. The music of earlier jazz giants was becoming widely available for the first time in years. The death of Duke Ellington in 1974, and the thought that his work might never be heard live again, helped inspire the creation of jazz repertory companies at the Smithsonian Institution and elsewhere. In 1976, the writer Albert Murray published *Stomping the Blues,* an elegant reaffirmation of the music's African-American origins and the centrality of the blues to its history. In 1977, the same year that Dexter Gordon's *Homecoming* appeared on the record charts, a young saxophone player named Scott Hamilton caused a stir by improvising not in the bop or Coltrane styles but in the manner of the masters he most loved, Ben Webster and Coleman Hawkins.

Three years after Gordon's triumphant comeback, Art Blakey was in New York, auditioning young musicians for his Jazz Messengers, just as he had been doing for three decades. Michael Cuscuna happened to be on hand.

This young kid sat in on trumpet, and he was astonishing. His ideas were fresh and different, very concise and clear. And at the end of the set, I asked Art, "Who the hell is that?" And he said, "That's Ellis Marsalis's kid." And Ellis Marsalis is a wonderful New Orleans pianist who was little known outside New Orleans, but a favorite musician of a lot of us. And he introduced me to him, and later on he said, "He's in his first year at Juilliard and, of course, you know, I couldn't do that to Ellis. I just couldn't pull him out of school and offer him a job, so I can't give him the gig." About two sets later, about four in the morning, we were all hanging out at the club, and I said, "So, Art did you decide on any new members?" He said, "Um, just one—Wynton Marsalis."

Dexter Gordon's triumph, 1977

No musician in jazz history has ever risen so far so fast as Wynton Marsalis: signed by Columbia Records at twenty, winner of Grammys in jazz *and* classical music at twenty-two, cofounder of Jazz at Lincoln Center at twenty-six and its creative director at thirty-one, winner at thirty-five of the first Pulitzer Prize ever awarded to a jazz composer, for his oratorio *Blood on the Fields.* Because his climb seemed so meteoric, because he was born in New Orleans and was the son of one jazz musician and the brother of three more, and because for many people he would become the symbol of the rebirth of mainstream jazz, his success seems to have been almost preordained.

But the world into which he was born in 1961 had had little use for the music his father played. Even in the city of his birth, jazz had lost most of its audience. None of his boyhood friends ever listened to it. "Jazz was for old people," he remembered, and if anybody had heard of Louis Armstrong or Duke Ellington, "they thought they were Uncle Toms." Funk was the music of choice: James Brown; Stevie Wonder; Earth, Wind and Fire; Tower of Power. When, during the early seventies, Wynton and his older brother Branford were in high school and performing with a funk band called the Creators, they sometimes played to crowds of better than two thousand and brought home a hundred dollars a night; their father's audiences were rarely larger than one-tenth that size, and he was often paid only half as much.

But at the age of twelve, Wynton Marsalis had also begun to listen to records from his father's collection: John Coltrane's *My Favorite Things* (initially just because he liked the blue and red cover) and then *Giant Steps.* "I listened to the music," he remembered. "I didn't know I could participate in it. I thought it was something really for my father and them, but I knew that I loved it. And I knew it was what we needed. There was just something in the sound of it. When I would listen to Trane,

Wynton, right, and Branford Marsalis, at home in Kenner, Louisiana, about 1964

it was as if he was talking to me. And he was just telling me that it was going to be all right. There was a certain engagement in it. And just the soul and the cry in the sound of it. It's just so soulful and warm."

During his early years, Marsalis experienced all manner of of music, from marching in a children's church band led by the guitarist Danny Barker to performing the Haydn Trumpet Concerto with the New Orleans Civic Orchestra at age fourteen, and he eventually resolved to become a professional musician. But when he arrived at Juilliard, he was still not sure whether he would end up playing classical or jazz music. Even when he was on the road with the Blakey band, then with Herbie Hancock, and finally with his own group, attracting attention for his big, warm tone, his astonishing facility, and the richness of his rhythmic imagination, he later admitted ruefully that he knew almost nothing about the music before the era of Miles Davis. At first, it didn't seem to matter. His first record sold more than a hundred thousand copies—then virtually unheard of for an acoustic jazz album—and

record companies scrambled to sign up young players of their own. "Wynton was the first new acoustic jazz player with something to say," Michael Cuscuna recalled. "And fortunately, thereafter, with his brother Branford and a lot of people that Wynton knew, the floodgates opened and suddenly in the eighties there were a lot of new players that pumped new blood into jazz. Which was very much of a saving grace."

But Marsalis wasn't satisfied. His father sent him a tape of Louis Armstrong soloing on a tune called "Jubilee," and when he found, in trying to play the solo himself, that he didn't have the endurance to make it all the way through, he began to realize that there had been much more to Armstrong than his genial grin. Soon, with help from Albert Murray and Stanley Crouch, he began to soak up all the jazz history he could.

George Wein first heard Marsalis at a jazz festival in Chicago.

I listened to him play and I started to cry. I couldn't believe it, because I never thought I'd hear a young black musician play that way. Because they were all influenced by the bebop scene or the Coltrane scene. Wynton could play it all, but I could hear that he had been listening to Louis Armstrong. And that meant so much to me because the only musicians, the *young* musicians, that paid attention to Louis Armstrong were white musicians. Young African-American musicians did not pay attention to Louis Armstrong.

"All jazz," Marsalis came to believe, "is modern. The only thing that makes it old is when nobody plays it." Soon, he was playing it all—from Thelonious Monk to Jelly Roll Morton, Louis Armstrong to Miles Davis—and making it all his own. He did something else as well: he took on the critics. "In my generation it was easiest for me to be the person to do that," he said, "because I don't have to deal with the same type of overwhelming racism and worry about working that the older musicians did." He insisted that neither most fusion nor much of the avant-garde should ever have been considered jazz, since they didn't swing and lacked blues feeling. He denounced the cult of the "new," scoffed at the notion that change necessarily means progress, that one kind of jazz is ever an "advance" over another. "Is Charlie Parker *better* than Sidney Bechet?" he asked. "No, just different." Some critics and other musicians fought back in a battle that has continued now for nearly twenty years. "The debate around jazz is always heated and strong because jazz music deals with the soul of our nation," Marsalis said. "And through this music, we can see a lot about what it means to be American. And everybody wants to own it. And you can't own it. I can't own it. I can do my best to define it the way I think it is. But that is all I can do."

The writer Gary Giddins once asked the pianist Cedar Walton where he thought the music was going. "It'll go wherever we take it" was the answer. "We're the musicians." By the very nature of the music, no individual artist has ever been the sole focus of jazz in America. A host of survivors who made it through the fusion era are still at work, and there are dozens of talented younger musicians now feeding the music's many tributaries as well, so many that anyone's list of favorites is necessarily arbitrary: bassist Christian McBride; drummer Lewis Nash; pianists Geri Allen, Bill Charlap, Eric Reed, Marcus Roberts, Jacky Terrasson, Gonzalo Rubalcaba; saxophonists James Carter, Steve Coleman, Branford Marsalis, Chris Potter, and Joshua Redman; trombonist Wycliffe Gordon; trumpet players Nicholas Payton and Roy Hargrove; violinist Regina Carter; singers Dianne Reeves and Cassandra Wilson. "There's plenty of us out here," said Wynton Marsalis. "We're still swinging and we ain't going nowhere."

Each musician has a distinctly individual voice but, as Stanley Crouch has said, they all have one quality in common: courage. "Courage is something you can't buy. And when somebody actually takes a real risk, like these young people do who go into jazz knowing that they're never going to be 'Puff Daddy' Combs, or Madonna, or any of those people—that assertion among young people of real courage, real aesthetic belief, can only beget good."

The number of Americans who listen to and love jazz music is still minuscule compared to what it once was. The African-American community remains largely estranged from the music to which it gave birth. There are too few places where young musicians can get a chance to play. And the jazz world continues to be divided into mutually antagonistic camps. But despite it all, the musical journey that began in the dance halls and saloons and street parades of New Orleans in the early years of the twentieth century continues into the twenty-first—and shows no sign of slowing down. Jazz remains gloriously inclusive, a proudly mongrel American music, filled with brilliant echoes of the past but still brand-new every night.

Above all, as Wynton Marsalis has said, jazz offers Americans hope: "That's the thing in jazz that got Bix Beiderbecke up out of his bed at two o'clock in the morning to pick that cornet up and practice with it into the pillow for another two or three hours. Or that would make Louis Armstrong travel around the world for fifty years nonstop, just get up out of his sickbed, crawl up on the bandstand, and play. The thing that would make Duke Ellington, Thelonious Monk, Miles Davis, Charlie Parker—any of these people that we've heard about, all these wonderful people—give their lives. And they did give their lives for it, because it gives us a glimpse into what America is going to be when it becomes itself. And this music tells you that it *will* become itself. And when you get a taste of that, there's just nothing else you're going to taste that's this sweet. That's a sweet taste, man."

At a grade school in Mississippi Wynton Marsalis meets some eager representatives of the future.

Joe Lovano, playing a custom-made straight tenor
saxophone, and pianist Gonzalo Rubalcaba

ACKNOWLEDGMENTS

This book grew out of a ten-part documentary-film series on the history of jazz—a project that began back in 1995 and continued unabated for five years. So many people contributed their extraordinary talents to that film, and to this book, that it will be impossible to thank all of them here. Throughout, we have been inspired by the wisdom, sophistication, and enthusiasm of Wynton Marsalis, who taught all of us so much about this music and what it says to us about America: "The real power of jazz and the innovation of jazz," he tells us at the beginning of our film, "is that a group of people can come together and create art. Improvised art. And can negotiate their agendas with each other. And that negotiation is the art."

We like to think that the team of gifted individuals who contributed to this massive undertaking was in many ways similar to a jazz orchestra, with each individual making his or her own unique contribution, but always with the selfless goal of making our film and book as good as they could be.

We cannot imagine how this project could have gone forward without the important contribution made by our writer, Geoffrey C. Ward. Not only did he bring his customary eloquence and subtlety to bear in his crafting of the script for the series, but he also infused it with his own deep and abiding love for jazz music, helped us to comprehend the impossibly vast whole, and shaped a meaningful and propulsive narrative. For all of that we are more grateful than we can say.

Our team of dedicated producers, each of whom contributed to the project above and beyond the call of duty, was also essential to our efforts. With the utmost dedication, coproducers Peter Miller and Victoria Gohl managed to find, order, and obtain clearances for the hundreds of hours of motion picture footage and the thousands of still photographs we needed to create our film. They were ably assisted by our wonderfully talented associate producers, Natalie Bullock Brown and Shola Lynch, who enthusiastically hurled themselves into every new and daunting task we threw their way. Together, they managed to research and keep track of all the photographs and stock footage that we required, organized our film shoots, researched historical issues, and in general kept our ship afloat. Associate producer Sarah Botstein found the music for this film and seemed to be everywhere at once, bringing her inexhaustible energy to every aspect of the production. Madison Davis Lacy, our consulting producer, helped us a great deal in the early stages of the project and conducted some of our best interviews.

Like all of our previous films, this series was truly created in the editing room. Without our terrific staff of editors, assistant editors, apprentices, and interns, there would be no *Jazz* series. Our team was led by the exceptionally gifted Paul Barnes, our supervising film editor. Not only did he edit our first episode, but he also oversaw the editing of all the others, insuring that they all shared the same cohesion and energy. Lewis Erskine brought a fine intelligence and an abiding love for jazz to his work, infusing his episodes with enormous respect for the artists who created the music. Sandra Christie, who knew almost nothing about jazz when she began the project, brought to her work a relentless drive and dedication that kept her at her editing table late into the night, unwilling to settle for anything less than perfection. The incomparable Tricia Reidy brought a determination to push the boundaries of the documentary form, and an unbridled enthusiasm for making the most challenging music accessible to everyone. Editors Sarah Hill and Shannon Robards worked closely with Tricia to make our film better than we could ever have dreamed possible. Erik Ewers, who never ceases to astound us, took charge of two complex episodes and made them soar. Aaron Vega, who began the project as an assistant editor, took charge of an entire episode and turned it into one of our best, while editor Craig Mellish kept our complicated operation running smoothly and at the same time managed to edit some of the most compelling scenes in the whole series. Our able staff of assistant editors, Barnard Jaffier, Dave Faulker, Dave Mast, Matt McGrail, Dave McMahon, Kevin Mercier, Thor Neureiter, and Meg Schindler, all contributed in ways large and small while our army of dedicated interns somehow kept the hundreds of hours of film footage organized and our logs and databases up to date. Tim Clark had the difficult task of dealing with hundreds of hours of narration, while Kara Mickley kept the photo department together.

Not a day goes by that we do not think about how thankful we are to have been able to convince the fine actor Keith David to serve as narrator for the series. His humanity, his intelligence, his extraordinary voice, and his professionalism never cease to amaze us. He spent hour upon hour in the studio, reading take after take, never complaining, always giving us his absolute best, infusing our series with warmth, elegance, and soul. We were also terribly fortunate to enlist a group of extraordinary actors to read first-person voices for the series: Philip Bosco, Matthew Broderick, Kevin Conway, Bruce Davison, Charles Durning, Samuel L. Jackson, Eriq La Salle, Delroy Lindo, Anthony LaPaglia, Courtney B. Vance, and many others added immeasurably to our attempts to breath life into the past.

We were fortunate, too, to have an inordinately talented crew of sound editors—Jennifer Dunnington, Marlena Grzaslewicz, Bruce Kitzmeyer, Dan Korintus, Jacob Ribicoff, Ira Spiegel—and to have worked with the greatest sound mixers in America—the incomparable Lee Dichter and Dominick Tavella—who made the music literally jump off the screen and, in the process, made our film truly come alive.

The exquisite cinematography of Buddy Squires, who shot most of the film, as well as of Allen Moore and Stephen McCarthy, infused our film with pure unadulterated beauty, while the animation photography of Ed Joyce and Ed Searles at the Frame Shop brought a new life to the still photographs in the series. Without the magnificent work of our colorist, John Dowdell, our film would not have the luminance and visual clarity we know it has.

All along, we relied heavily on the dedication of Pam Baucom, Susan Butler, Brenda Heath, and Patty Lawlor, who kept our office running smoothly, kept track of a thousand details, made sure that our budgets added up—and that we paid our bills.

Throughout the project, we also relied heavily on the wisdom of our esteemed panel of advisors. First and foremost, we want to thank Dan Morgenstern, our beloved senior advisor, who answered every question, read every script, and guided us on matters large and small, from the very beginning of the project to the last day of editing. In addition, we received enormously helpful input from Michael Chertok, James Lincoln Collier, Stanley Crouch, Michael Cuscuna, Dayton Duncan, Julie Dunfey, Gerald Early, Tom Evered, Gary Giddins, Matt Glaser, Joanna Groning, Eric Hobsbawm, Robin D. G. Kelley, Charlie Lourie, Allen Lowe, Albert Murray, Daniel Okrent, Bruce Boyd Raeburn, Loren Schoenberg, Gunther Schuller, and Margaret Washington.

Undertaking this project would have been impossible without the assistance we received from the following organizations and individuals: the Institute for Jazz Studies, the Hogan Jazz Archive, the Louis Armstrong Archives, Blue Note and Mosaic Records, the Collections of Charles Peterson and Bob Parent, the Prints and Photographs Division at the Library of Congress, the Louisiana State Museum, the Jazz Record Center, archivists Michael Cogswell, Jan Grenci, and Ken Vail, photographer Paul Christensen, historian Richard Sudhalter, and photo collectors Frank Driggs and Duncan Scheidt. They answered a thousand questions, provided us with priceless information, advice, music, photographs, and guidance.

An extraordinary group of the finest jazz art photographers in the country also generously lent their pictures to us for the film and the book: Anthony Barboza, Bill Gottlieb, William Claxton, Enid Farber, Lee Friedlander, Milt Hinton, Paul Hoeffler, Don Hunstein, Jimmy Katz, Herman Leonard, Bruce Polansky, Herb Snitzer, Chuck Stewart, Lee Tanner, and Francis Wolf.

Without the magnificent talents of our designer, Wendy Byrne, this book would not embody the spirit of jazz music as beautifully as it does, and we are equally grateful to the wonderful people at Alfred A. Knopf for making it possible for us to put this book together: Sonny Mehta, Ashbel Green, Kathy Hourigan, Asya Muchnick, Carol Devine Carson, Pat Johnson, Andy Hughes, Kevin Bourke, and Bette Graber.

We are also grateful to our good friends at Columbia / Legacy and the Verve Music Group: Jeff Jones, Seth Rothstein, Adam Block, Steve Berkowitz, Don Iener, Kristin Kozusko, Ron Goldstein, Ben Young, Richard Seidel, Mike Charlash, Robert Silverberg, Nate Herr, and Jeffrey Peisch.

Neither this book nor our film would have been possible without the generous support of the General Motors Corporation—and we would like to especially thank Phil Guarascio, Luanna Floccuzio, Peg Holmes, Denny Bolen, Judy Hu, and last but certainly not least, Skip Roberts, for their unwavering commitment to the project. We also received financial support from the Public Broadcasting Service, the Corporation for Public Broadcasting, the Park Foundation, the PEW Charitable Trusts, the Louisiana Department of Culture, Recreation, and Tourism, the Doris Duke Charitable Foundation, the National Endowment for the Humanities, the Arthur Vining Davis Foundations, the National Endowment for the Arts, the John D. and Catherine T. MacArthur Foundation, the Reva and David Logan Foundation, and Helen and Peter Bing.

Our partners at WETA-TV in Washington, D.C., have also been with us every step of the way, and in particular we want to thank Sharon Rockefeller, David Thompson, Craig Impink, and Karen Kenton for their indefatigable assistance. We are also grateful to Dan Klores and his talented colleagues: especially Joe DePlasco, Allyson Felix, and Susan Makarichev, for their tireless efforts to promote the film.

As is the case in any effort of this scope, there are scores of other people who contributed to the project—archivists, collectors, historians, music producers, researchers, production assistants, technicians, and many others—and we deeply regret that we lack the space to thank each of them individually for the work they have done to help us bring to millions of people the message and the healing power of jazz.

KEN BURNS
LYNN NOVICK

———————————

As the author of this book's text, I'd like to express my personal thanks to several people who helped make possible what was for me a labor of love:

My friend Ken Burns, with whom I've been working for some eighteen years and who continues to astonish me by his willingness to take on important subjects and turn them into important films;

Victoria Gohl, who devoted all of her extraordinary energy and intelligence to finding and researching the illustrations that fill this volume;

Wendy Byrne, whose unerring eye and infinite patience with last-minute changes of heart and mind remain a source of wonder;

Adrienne Sockwell, who tirelessly searched out materials for me all over the city;

Dan Morgenstern, who brought his encyclopedic knowledge and profound love for the music to his reading of the manuscript and in the process saved me from countless errors;

and Wynton Marsalis, whose friendship and insights, encouragement and candor, meant more to me in writing this history than I have words to express.

GEOFFREY C. WARD

SELECTED BIBLIOGRAPHY

AUTHOR'S NOTE: Because bibliographies give each title equal weight, they are inevitably misleading. I learned something from every one of the books listed below, but some were obviously far more useful than others. No one can ever write about Buddy Bolden without drawing heavily upon Donald M. Marquis, for example, or understand James Reese Europe without reading Reid Badger's comprehensive biography; the late Philip Evans's books lay out most of the material needed to write about Bix Beiderbecke and Frank Trumbauer; and it is hard to see how anyone can ever write a more rewarding and insightful book about early jazz in Chicago than William Howard Kenney's or a more elegantly written study of the bebop era than Scott Deveaux's. I owe them and a good many more authors an enormous debt of gratitude.

I'd also like to express my personal thanks to Peter Pullman and Richard Sudhalter, who kindly lent me important materials; my old friend Richard Meryman, who gave me access to the unedited transcripts from which his classic interview with Louis Armstrong was drawn; Bruce Raeburn, whose omniscience about New Orleans music and patience with foolish questions are both matters of wonder; and Lawrence Gushee, whose irreplaceable articles on early jazz remain unaccountably uncollected.

Albertson, Chris. *Bessie.* New York, 1972.

Alkyer, Frank. *Down Beat: 60 Years of Jazz.* Milwaukee, 1995.

Armstrong, Louis. *Louis Armstrong in His Own Words: Selected Writings.* New York, 1999.

———. *Satchmo: My Life in New Orleans.* New York, 1986.

———. *Swing That Music.* New York, 1993.

Arnaud, Gerald, and Jacques Chesnel. *Masters of Jazz.* Edinburgh, 1991.

Asbury, Herbert. *The French Quarter.* New York, 1936.

Badger, Reid. *A Life in Ragtime: A Biography of James Reese Europe.* New York, 1995.

Baker, David N., ed. *New Perspectives on Jazz.* Washington, D.C., 1986.

Balliett, Whitney. *American Musicians II: Seventy-one Portraits in Jazz.* New York, 1996.

———. *American Singers.* New York, 1979.

———. *Barney, Bradley and Max: Sixteen Portraits in Jazz.* New York, 1989.

———. *Goodbyes and Other Messages: A Journal of Jazz 1981–1990.* New York, 1991.

———. *Jelly Roll, Jabbo and Fats.* New York, 1983.

———. *New York Notes.* New York, 1976.

———. *The Sound of Surprise.* New York, 1961.

Barker, Danny. *Buddy Bolden and the Last Days of Storyville.* London, 1998.

———. *A Life in Jazz.* New York, 1986.

Barnet, Charlie, with Stanley Dance. *Those Swing Years: The Autobiography of Charlie Barnet.* New York, 1992.

Bayles, Martha. *Hole in Our Soul: The Loss of Beauty and Meaning in American Popular Music.* Chicago, 1994.

Bechet, Sidney. *Treat It Gentle.* New York, 1960.

Berendt, Joachim E. *The Jazz Book: From Ragtime to Fusion and Beyond.* New York, 1992.

———. *The Story of Jazz.* Englewood Cliffs, N.J., 1978.

Berger, Morroe, and James Patrick. *Benny Carter: A Life in American Music.* Newark, 1982.

Bergmeier, Horst J.P., and Rainer E. Lotz. *Hitler's Airwaves.* New Haven, 1997.

Bergreen, Laurence. *Louis Armstrong: An Extravagant Life.* New York, 1997.

Berrett, Joshua. *The Louis Armstrong Companion: Eight Decades of Commentary.* New York, 1999.

Berton, Ralph. *Remembering Bix: A Memoir of the Jazz Age.* New York, 1974.

Bigard, Barney. *With Louis and the Duke: The Autobiography of a Jazz Clarinetist.* New York, 1980.

Blesh, Rudi. *Shining Trumpets.* New York, 1980.

Borchert, James. *Alley Life in Washington: Family, Community, Religion and Folklife in the City 1850–1970.* Chicago, 1980.

Brandt, Nat. *Harlem at War: The Black Experience in WWII.* Syracuse, N.Y., 1996.

Britt, Stan. *Dexter Gordon: A Musical Biography.* New York, 1989.

Brown, Claude. *Manchild in the Promised Land.* New York, 1965.

Brown, Letitia Woods. *Free Negroes in the District of Columbia 1790–1846.* New York, 1972.

Brown, Sanford. *Louis Armstrong: Swinging, Singing Satchmo.* New York, 1993.

Brunn, H. O. *The Story of the Original Dixieland Jazz Band.* Baton Rouge, 1960.

Bryant, Clora, et al. *Central Avenue Sounds: Jazz in Los Angeles.* Berkeley, 1998.

Büchman-Møller, Frank. *You Just Fight for Your Life: The Story of Lester Young.* New York, 1990.

Buckner, Reginald T., and Steven Weiland, eds. *Jazz in Mind.* Detroit, 1991.

Budds, Michael J. *Jazz in the Sixties: The Expansion of Musical Resources and Techniques.* Iowa City, 1990.

Bultman, Bethany Ewald. *New Orleans.* New York, 1996.

Bushell, Garvin, and Mark Tucker. *Jazz from the Beginning.* New York, 1998.

Callahan, John F., ed. *The Collected Essays of Ralph Ellison.* New York, 1995.

Carmichael, Hoagy. *The Stardust Road & Sometimes I Wonder: The Autobiographies of Hoagy Carmichael.* New York, 1999.

Carner, Gary. *The Miles Davis Companion: Four Decades of Commentary.* New York, 1996.

Cassandra Wilson

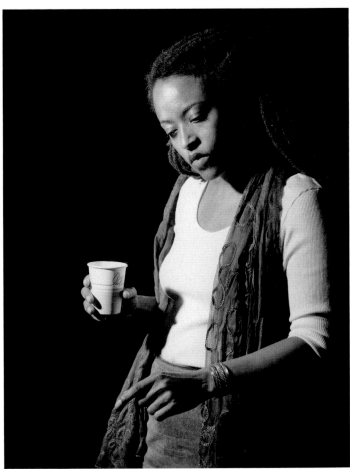

Carr, Ian. *Keith Jarrett: The Man and His Music.* New York, 1992.

———. *Miles Davis: The Definitive Biography.* New York, 1998.

Carr, Ian, and Digby Fairweather. *Jazz: The Rough Guide.* London, 1995.

Carruth, Hayden. *Sitting In: Selected Writings on Jazz, Blues and Related Topics.* Iowa City, 1993.

Carver, Reginald, and Lenny Bernstein. *Jazz Profiles: The Spirit of the Nineties.* New York, 1998.

Chamberlain, Dorothy, and Robert Wilson, eds. *In the Spirit of Jazz: The Otis Ferguson Reader.* New York, 1997.

Chambers, Jack. *Milestones: The Music and Times of Miles Davis.* New York, 1998.

Charters, Samuel B., and Leonard Kunstadt. *Jazz: A History of the New York Scene.* New York, 1984.

Cheatham, Aldolphus. *I Guess I'll Get the Papers and Go Home: The Life of Doc Cheatham.* London, 1995.

Chilton, John. *Billie's Blues: The Billie Holiday Story 1933–1959.* New York, 1975.

———. *Let the Good Times Roll: The Story of Louis Jordan and His Music.* Ann Arbor, 1997.

———. *Ride, Red, Ride: The Life of Henry "Red" Allen.* London, 1999.

———. *Sidney Bechet: The Wizard of Jazz.* New York, 1996.

———. *The Song of the Hawk: The Life and Recordings of Coleman Hawkins.* Ann Arbor, 1990.

———. *Stomp Off, Let's Go.* London, 1983.

———. *Who's Who of Jazz: Storyville to Swing Street.* Philadelphia, 1978.

Clarke, Donald. *Wishing on the Moon: The Life and Times of Billie Holiday.* New York, 1994.

Cole, Bill. *Miles Davis: The Early Years.* New York, 1994.

Coleman, Bill. *Trumpet Story.* London, 1990.

Coleman, Janet, and Al Young. *Mingus/Mingus: Two Memoirs.* New York, 1994.

Collier, James Lincoln. *Benny Goodman and the Swing Era.* New York, 1989.

———. *Duke Ellington.* New York, 1987.

———. *Jazz: the American Theme Song.* New York, 1995.

———. *Louis Armstrong: An American Genius.* New York, 1983.

———. *The Making of Jazz.* Boston, 1978.

Collier-Thomas, Bettye, and V. P. Franklin. *My Soul Is a Witness: A Chronology of the Civil Rights Era, 1954–1965.* New York, 1999.

Collins, R. *New Orleans Jazz: A Revised History: The Development of American Music from the Origins to the Big Bands.* New York, 1996.

Condon, Eddie. *We Called It Music: A Generation of Jazz.* New York, 1992.

Condon, Eddie, and Richard Gehman, eds. *Eddie Condon's Treasury of Jazz.* New York, 1956.

Condon, Eddie, and Hank O'Neal. *The Eddie Condon Scrapbook of Jazz.* New York, 1973.

Cook, Richard, and Brian Norton. *The Penguin Guide to Jazz on Compact Disc.* London, 1996.

Cooke, Mervyn. *The Chronicle of Jazz.* New York, 1997.

———. *Jazz.* New York, 1999.

Crouch, Stanley. *The All-American Skin Game, or, The Decoy of Race.* New York, 1995.

———. *Always in Pursuit: Fresh American Perspectives, 1995–1997.* New York, 1998.

———. *Notes of a Hanging Judge: Essays and Reviews 1979–1989.* New York, 1990.

Crow, Bill. *From Birdland to Broadway: Scenes from a Jazz Life.* New York, 1992.

———. *Jazz Anecdotes.* New York, 1990.

Cusic, Don. *The Sound of Light: A History of Gospel Music.* Bowling Green, Ohio, 1990.

Dahl, Linda. *Stormy Weather: The Music and Lives of a Century of Jazz Women.* New York, 1992.

Dance, Stanley. *The World of Count Basie.* New York, 1980.

———. *The World of Duke Ellington.* New York, 1970.

———. *The World of Earl Hines.* New York, 1977.

———. *The World of Swing.* New York, 1979.

Davis, Allen, and Mary Lynn McCree. *Eighty Years at Hull House.* Chicago, 1969.

Davis, Clive, with James Wilwerth. *Clive: Inside the Record Business.* New York, 1975.

Davis, Francis. *The History of the Blues: The Roots, the Music, the People: From Charley Patton to Robert Cray.* New York, 1995.

———. *In the Moment: Jazz in the 1980s.* New York, 1996.

———. *Outcats: Jazz Composers, Instrumentalists and Singers.* New York, 1990.

Davis, Miles, with Quincy Troupe. *Miles: The Autobiography.* New York, 1989.

DeCarava, Roy. *The Sound I Saw: The Jazz Photographs of Roy DeCarava.* New York, 1983.

Deffaa, Chip. *Swing Legacy.* Newark, 1989.

———. *Voices of the Jazz Age.* Champaign, Ill., 1992.

Delannoy, Luc. *Pres: The Story of Lester Young.* Fayetteville, Ark., 1993.

Delaunay, Charles. *Django Reinhardt.* New York, 1961.

DeLong, Thomas A. *Pops: Paul Whiteman, King of Jazz.* Piscataway, N.J., 1983.

Deveaux, Scott. *The Birth of Bebop: A Social and Music History.* Berkeley, 1997.

———. *Jazz in America: Who's Listening?* National Endowment for the Arts Research Report #31, Carson, Calif., 1995.

Dupuis, Robert. *Bunny Berigan: Elusive Legend of Jazz.* Baton Rouge, 1993.

Dyer, Geoff. *But Beautiful: A Book About Jazz.* New York, 1996.

Early, Gerald. *The Culture of Bruising: Essays on Prizefighting, Literature and Modern American Culture.* Hopewell, N.J., 1994.

———. *One Nation Under a Groove: Motown and American Culture.* Hopewell, N.J., 1995.

———. *Tuxedo Junction: Essays on American Culture.* Hopewell, N.J., 1989.

Ellington, Edward Kennedy. *Music Is My Mistress.* New York, 1975.

Ellington, Mercer, with Stanley Dance. *Duke Ellington in Person: An Intimate Memoir.* New York, 1979.

Emerson, Ken. *Doo-dah! Stephen Foster and the Rise of American Popular Culture.* New York, 1997.

Epstein, Daniel Mark. *Nat King Cole.* New York, 1999.

Erenberg, Lewis. *Steppin' Out: New York Nightlife and the Transformation of American Culture, 1890–1930.* Chicago, 1981.

———. *Swingin' the Dream: Big Band Jazz and the Rebirth of American Culture.* Chicago, 1998.

Erlewine, Michael, and Vladimir Bogdanov. *All Music Guide to Jazz.* San Francisco, 1996.

Evans, Philip R., and Larry F. Kiner. *Tram: The Frank Trumbauer Story.* Rutgers, N.Y., 1994.

Evans, Philip R., and Linda K. Evans. *Bix: The Leon Bix Beiderbecke Story.* Bakersfield, Calif., 1998.

Feather, Leonard. *The Book of Jazz.* New York, 1959.

———. *The Encyclopedia of Jazz.* New York, 1955.

———. *The Encyclopedia of Jazz in the Sixties.* New York, 1966.

———. *From Satchmo to Miles.* New York, 1984.

———. *The Jazz Years: Earwitness to an Era.* New York, 1987.

Feather, Leonard, and Ira Gitler. *The Biographical Encyclopedia of Jazz.* New York, 1999.

Feather, Leonard, and Jack Tracy. *Laughter from the Hip: The Lighter Side of Jazz.* New York, 1979.

Finkelstein, Sidney. *Jazz: A People's Music.* New York, 1948.

Firestone, Ross. *Swing, Swing, Swing: The Life & Times of Benny Goodman.* New York, 1993.

Fitterling, Thomas. *Thelonious Monk: His Life and Music.* Berkeley, 1997.

Floyd, Samuel A., Jr. *The Power of Black Music: Interpreting Its History from Africa to the United States.* New York, 1995.

Foster, Pops, with Tom Stoddard. *Pops Foster: The Autobiography of a New Orleans Jazzman.* Berkeley, 1971.

Fox, Ted. *Showtime at the Apollo.* New York, 1993.

Freeman, Bud. *Crazeology: The Autobiography of a Chicago Jazzman.* Urbana, Ill., 1989.

———. *You Don't Look Like a Musician.* Detroit, 1974.

Friedlander, Paul. *A Social History of Rock and Roll.* Boulder, Colo., 1996.

Friedwald, Will. *Jazz Singing: America's Great Voices from Bessie Smith to Bebop and Beyond.* New York, 1996.

———. *Sinatra! This Song Is You.* New York, 1995.

Gabbard, Krin. *Jammin' at the Margins: Jazz and the American Cinema.* Chicago, 1996.

———, ed. *Jazz Among the Discourses.* Durham, N.C., 1995.

———, ed. *Representing Jazz.* Durham, N.C., 1995.

Gammond, Peter, ed. *Duke Ellington: His Life and Music.* New York, 1977.

Gara, Larry. *The Baby Dodds Story.* Baton Rouge, 1992.

Gennari, John Remo. *The Politics of Culture and Identity in American Jazz Criticism.* Ph.D. thesis. Ann Arbor, 1993.

George, Don. *Sweet Man: The Real Duke Ellington.* New York, 1981.

Giddins, Gary. *Celebrating Bird: The Triumph of Charlie Parker.* New York, 1987.

———. *Faces in the Crowd: Players and Writers.* New York, 1992.

———. *Rhythm-A-Ning: Jazz Tradition and Innovation in the 80's.* New York, 1985.

———. *Riding on a Blue Note.* New York, 1981.

———. *Satchmo.* New York, 1988.

———. *Visions of Jazz: The First Century.* New York, 1998.

Gill, James. *Lords of Misrule: Mardi Gras and the Politics of Race in New Orleans.* Oxford, Miss., 1998.

Gillespie, Dizzy, with Al Fraser. *To Be or Not to Bop: Memoirs of Dizzy Gillespie.* New York, 1979.

Gillet, Charlie. *The Sound of the City: The Rise of Rock and Roll.* New York, 1996.

Gillis, Frank J., and John Miner, eds. *Oh Didn't He Ramble: The Life Story of Lee Collins.* Chicago, 1989.

Gioia, Ted. *The History of Jazz.* New York, 1997.

———. *The Imperfect Art: Reflections on Jazz and Modern Culture.* New York, 1988.

———. *West Coast Jazz: Modern Jazz in California, 1945–1960.* New York, 1992.

Gitler, Ira. *Jazz Masters of the Forties.* New York, 1983.

———. *Swing to Bop.* New York, 1985.

Godbolt, Jim. *A History of Jazz in Britain 1919–50.* London, 1984.

Goldberg, Joe. *Jazz Masters of the Fifties.* New York, 1965.

Goodman, Benny, and Irving Kolodin. *The Kingdom of Swing.* New York, 1939.

Gordon, Max. *Live at the Village Vanguard.* New York, 1980.

Gottlieb, Robert, ed. *Reading Jazz: A Gathering of Autobiography, Reportage, and Criticism from 1919 to Now.* New York, 1996.

Gottlieb, William P. *The Golden Age of Jazz.* San Francisco, 1995.

Gourse, Leslie. *The Billie Holiday Companion: Seven Decades of Commentary.* New York, 1997.

———. *The Ella Fitzgerald Companion: Seven Decades of Commentary.* New York, 1998.

———. *Every Day: The Story of Joe Williams.* New York, 1995.

———. *Madame Jazz: Contemporary Women Instrumentalists.* New York, 1995.

———. *Sassy: The Life of Sarah Vaughan.* New York, 1994.

———. *Straight, No Chaser: The Life and Genius of Thelonious Monk.* New York, 1997.

———. *Unforgettable: The Life and Mystique of Nat King Cole.* New York, 1991.

———. *Wynton Marsalis: Skain's Domain: A Biography.* New York, 1999.

Graham, Charles. *The Great Jazz Day.* Emeryville, Calif., 1999.

Green, Benny. *The Reluctant Art: Five Studies in the Growth of Jazz.* New York, 1991.

Green, Constance McLaughlin. *Secret City: A History of Race Relations in the Nation's Capital.* Princeton, N.J., 1967.

Gridley, Mark C. *Jazz Styles: History and Analysis.* Upper Saddle River, N.J., 2000.

Groves, Alan, and Alyn Shipton. *The Glass Enclosure: The Life of Bud Powell.* Oxford, 1993.

Guralnick, Paul. *Last Train to Memphis: The Rise of Elvis Presley.* Boston, 1994.

Hadlock, Richard. *Jazz Masters of the Twenties.* New York, 1988.

Hair, William Ivy. *Carnival of Fury: Robert Charles and the New Orleans Race Riot of 1900.* Baton Rouge, 1976.

Hajdu, David. *Lush Life: A Biography of Billy Strayhorn.* New York, 1996.

Hall, Fred M. *It's About Time: The Dave Brubeck Story.* Fayetteville, Ark., 1996.

Hamill, Pete. *Why Sinatra Matters.* Boston, 1998.

Hammond, John. *John Hammond on Record: An Autobiography.* New York, 1981.

Hampton, Lionel, with James Haskins. *Hamp: An Autobiography.* New York, 1989.

Handy, D. Antoinette. *Jazz Man's Journey: A Biography of Ellis Louis Marsalis, Jr.* Lanham, Md., 1999.

Handy, W. C. *Father of the Blues: An Autobiography.* New York, 1969.

Harker, Brian Cameron. *The Early Musical Development of Louis Armstrong, 1901–1928.* Ph.D. dissertation, Columbia University, 1997.

Harris, Michael W. *The Rise of Gospel and Blues.* New York, 1992.

Harrison, Daphne Duval. *Black Pearls: Blues Queens of the 1920s.* New Brunswick, N.J., 1990.

Haskins, James, and Kathleen Benson. *Nat King Cole.* Chelsea, Mich., 1984.

Haskins, Jim. *The Cotton Club.* New York, 1977.

Hasse, John Edward. *Beyond Category: The Life and Genius of Duke Ellington.* New York, 1993.

Hennessey, Mike. *Klook: The Story of Kenny Clarke.* Pittsburgh, 1994.

Hentoff, Nat. *Jazz Is.* New York, 1992.

———. *The Jazz Life.* New York, 1975.

Hentoff, Nat, and Albert J. McCarthy. *Jazz.* New York, 1959.

———, eds. *Jazz: New Perspectives on the History of Jazz by Twelve of the World's Foremost Jazz Critics and Scholars.* New York, 1959.

Herman, Woody, and Stuart Troop. *The Woodchopper's Ball: The Autobiography of Woody Herman.* New York, 1994.

Hilbert, Robert. *Pee Wee Russell: The Life of a Jazzman.* New York, 1993.

Hillman, Christopher. *Bunk Johnson: His Life and Times.* New York, 1988.

Hinton, Milt, and David G. Berger. *Bass Line: The Stories and Photographs of Milt Hinton.* Temple University Press, 1988.

Hobsbawm, Eric. *The Jazz Scene.* New York, 1993.

Hodes, Art, and Chadwick Hansen. *Hot Man: The Life of Art Hodes.* Urbana, Ill., 1992.

Holiday, Billie, with William Duffy. *Lady Sings the Blues.* New York, 1965.

Holtje, Steve, and Nancy Ann Lee. *Music Hound Jazz: The Essential Album Guide.* Detroit, 1998.

Horricks, Raymond. *Gerry Mulligan.* London, 1986.

Huggins, Nathan Irvin. *Harlem Renaissance.* New York, 1979.

Hutlin, Randi. *Born Under the Sign of Jazz.* New York, 1998.

Jasen, David A., and Gene Jones. *Spreadin' Rhythm Round: Black Popular Songwriters 1880–1930.* New York, 1998.

Jewell, Derek. *Duke: A Portrait of Duke Ellington.* New York, 1977.

Johnson, James Weldon. *The Autobiography of an Ex-Colored Man.* New York, 1990.

Johnston, Allan. *Surviving Freedom: The Black Community of Washington D.C. 1860–1880.* New York, 1993.

Jones, Gene, and Robert R. Darch. *The Original Dixieland Jass Band.* Alexandria Bay, N.Y., 1993.

Jones, Leroi. *Black Music.* New York, 1968.

———. *Blues People: Negro Music in White America.* New York, 1963.

Jones, Max, and John Chilton. *Louis: The Louis Armstrong Story 1900–1971.* New York, 1971.

Jonnes, Jill. *Hep-Cats, Narcs, and Pipe Dreams.* Baltimore, 1999.

Jost, Ekkehard. *Free Jazz.* New York, 1994.

Kamin, Ira, and Jimmy Lyons. *Dizzy, Duke, the Count and Me.* San Francisco, 1978.

Kaminsky, Max. *My Life in Jazz.* London, 1965.

Kater, Michael H. *Different Drummers: Jazz in the Culture of Nazi Germany.* New York, 1992.

Keepnews, Orrin. *The View from Within.* New York, 1988.

Keepnews, Orrin, and Bill Grauer Jr. *A Pictorial History of Jazz.* New York, 1955.

Kennedy, Rick. *Jelly Roll, Biz and Hoagy: Gennett Studios and the Birth of Recorded Jazz.* Bloomington, Ind., 1994.

Jackie Terrason

Kenney, William Howard. *Chicago Jazz; A Cultural History, 1904–1930*. New York, 1993.

Kernfeld, Barry. *What to Listen for in Jazz*. New Haven, 1995.

King, Jonny. *An Insider's Guide to Understanding and Listening to Jazz*. New York, 1997.

Kirchner, Bill, ed. *A Miles Davis Reader*. Washington, D.C., 1997.

Kirk, Andy, and Amy Lee. *Twenty Years on Wheels*. Ann Arbor, Mich., 1989.

Kliment, Bud. *Ella Fitzgerald*. New York, 1988.

Klinker, Philip A., with Rogers M. Smith. *The Unsteady March: The Rise and Decline of Racial Equality in America*. Chicago, 1999.

Kmen, Henry A. *Music in New Orleans*. Baton Rouge, 1966.

Korall, Burt. *Drummin' Men: The Heartbeat of Jazz, The Swing Years*. New York, 1990.

Lange, Art, and Nathaniel Mackey, eds. *Moment's Notice: Jazz in Poetry and Prose*. Minneapolis, 1993.

Larkin, Philip. *All What Jazz*. New York, 1985.

Lees, Gene. *Cats of Any Color: Jazz, Black and White*. New York, 1995.

———. *Leader of the Band: The Life of Woody Herman*. New York, 1995.

———. *Meet Me at Jim and Andy's: Jazz Musicians and Their World*. New York, 1988.

———. *Oscar Peterson: The Will to Swing*. Rocklin, Calif., 1990.

———. *Singers and the Song II*. New York, 1998.

———. *Waiting for Dizzy*. New York, 1991.

Leonard, Neil. *Jazz and the White Americans*. Chicago, 1962.

Lester, James. *Too Marvelous for Words: The Life and Genius of Art Tatum*. New York, 1994.

Levine, Lawrence W. *Black Culture and Black Consciousness*. New York, 1977.

———. *Highbrow/Lowbrow: The Emergence of Cultural Hierarchy in America*. Cambridge, 1988.

Lewis, David Levering. *When Harlem Was in Vogue*. New York, 1979.

Lichtenstein, Grace, and Laura Danker. *Musical Gumbo: The Music of New Orleans*. New York, 1993.

Lindemeyer, Paul. *Celebrating the Saxophone*. New York, 1996.

Litweiler, John. *The Freedom Principle: Jazz After 1958*. New York, 1984.

———. *Ornette Coleman: A Harmolodic Life*. New York, 1994.

Locke, Alain, ed. *The New Negro*. New York, 1992.

Lomax, Alan. *Mister Jelly Roll*. New York, 1950.

Lowe, Allen. *American Pop: From Minstrel to Mojo: On Record 1983–1956*. New York, 1997.

Lyons, Len. *The Great Jazz Pianists: Speaking of Their Lives and Music*. New York, 1983.

Lyons, Len, and Don Perlo. *Jazz Portraits: The Lives and Music of the Jazz Masters*. New York, 1989.

Magee, Jeffrey. *The Music of Fletcher Henderson and His Orchestra in the 1920's*. Ph.D. dissertation. University of Michigan, 1992.

Maggin, Donald L. *Stan Getz: A Life in Jazz*. New York, 1996.

Mandel, Howard. *Future Jazz*. New York, 1999.

Marquis, Donald M. *In Search of Buddy Bolden: First Man of Jazz*. Baton Rouge, 1978.

Marsalis, Wynton. *Marsalis on Music*. New York, 1995.

Marsalis, Wynton, and Frank Stewart. *Sweet Swing Blues on the Road*. New York, 1994.

Martin, Donna. *Kansas City . . . And All That's Jazz*. Kansas City, Mo., 1999.

Mattingly, Rick. *The Drummer's Time: Conversations with the Great Drummers of Jazz*. Cedar Grove, N.J., 1998.

Mayer, Harold M., and Richard C. Wade. *Chicago: Growth of a Metropolis*. Chicago, 1969.

McCue, George. *Music in American Society 1776–1976*. New Brunswick, N.J., 1977.

McKee, Margaret, and Fred Chisenhall. *Beale Black & Blue: Life and Music on Black America's Main Street*. Baton Rouge, 1981.

McRae, Barry. *The Jazz Cataclysm*. New York, 1985.

Megill, Donald D., and Richard S. Demory. *Introduction to Jazz History*. Upper Saddle River, N.J., 1996.

Meier, August. *Negro Thought in America 1880–1915*. Ann Arbor, Mich., 1966.

Melnick, Jeffrey. *A Right to Sing the Blues: African-Americans, Jews, and American Popular Song*. Cambridge, 1999.

Meltzer, David, ed. *Reading Jazz*. San Francisco, 1993.

Mezzrow, Mezz, and Barry Wolfe. *Really the Blues*. New York, 1990.

Miller, Marc H., ed. *Louis Armstrong: A Cultural Legacy*. Seattle, 1994.

Miller, Norma, and Evette Jensen. *Swingin' at the Savoy: The Memoir of a Jazz Dancer*. Philadelphia, 1996.

Mingus, Charles. *Beneath the Underdog*. New York, 1991.

Moody, Bill. *The Jazz Exiles: American Musicians Abroad*. Las Vegas, 1993.

Morgan, Thomas L., and William Barlow. *From Cakewalks to Concert Halls: An Illustrated History of African American Popular Music from 1895 to 1930*. Washington, D.C., 1992.

Morgenstern, Dan, and Ole Brask. *Jazz People*. New York, 1993.

Murray, Albert. *The Blue Devils of Nada*. New York, 1996.

———. *Good Morning Blues: The Autobiography of Count Basie*. New York, 1985.

———. *The Hero and the Blues*. New York, 1995.

———. *The Omni-Americans: Some Alternatives to the Folklore of White Supremacy*. New York, 1970.

———. *Stomping the Blues*. New York, 1976.

Nicholson, Stuart. *Billie Holiday*. Boston, 1995.

———. *Ella Fitzgerald: A Biography of the First Lady of Jazz*. New York, 1995.

———. *Jazz: The 1980s Resurgence*. New York, 1995.

———. *Reminiscing in Tempo: A Portrait of Duke Ellington*. Boston, 1999.

Nisenson, Eric. *Ascension: John Coltrane and His Quest.* New York, 1993.

———. *Blue: The Murder of Jazz.* New York, 1997.

O'Day, Anita, with George Eels. *High Times Hard Times.* New York, 1989.

Ogren, Kathy J. *The Jazz Revolution: Twenties America and the Meaning of Jazz.* New York, 1989.

Oliphant, Dave. *Texan Jazz.* Austin, 1996.

Oliver, Paul, and Max Harrison. *Gospel, Blues and Jazz.* London, 1980.

O'Meally, Robert G., ed. *The Jazz Cadence of American Culture.* New York, 1998.

Osofsky, Gilbert. *Harlem: The Making of a Ghetto 1890–1930.* New York, 1966.

Owens, Thomas. *Bebop: The Music and Its Players.* New York, 1995.

Panassie, Hughes. *Louis Armstrong.* New York, 1971.

Patterson, James T. *Grand Expectations: The United States, 1945–1974.* New York, 1996.

Pearson, Nathan W., Jr. *Goin' to Kansas City.* Urbana, Ill., 1994.

Pepper, Art, and Laurie Pepper. *Straight Life: The Story of Art Pepper.* New York, 1994.

Peretti, Burton W. *The Creation of Jazz: Music, Race, and Culture in Urban America.* Urbana, Ill., 1992.

———. *Jazz in American Culture.* Chicago, 1997.

Perhonis, John Paul. *The Bix Beiderbecke Story: The Jazz Musician in Legend, Fiction, and Fact. A Study of the Images of Jazz in the National Culture: 1930–the Present.* Ph.D. dissertation, University of Minnesota, 1978.

Perlo, Don, and Len Lyons. *Jazz Portraits: The Lives and Music of the Jazz Masters.* New York, 1989.

Perry, David. *Jazz Greats.* London, 1996.

Pettinger, Peter. *Bill Evans: How My Heart Sings.* New Haven, 1998.

Piazza, Tom. *Blues and Trouble: Twelve Stories.* New York, 1996.

———. *Blues Up and Down: Jazz in Our Time.* New York, 1997.

———. *The Guide to Classic Recorded Jazz.* Iowa City, 1995.

———, ed. *Setting the Tempo: Fifty Years of Great Jazz Liner Notes.* New York, 1996.

Pinfold, Mike. *Louis Armstrong.* New York, 1987.

Placksin, Sally. *American Women in Jazz: 1900 to the Present, Their Words, Lives, and Music.* New York, 1982.

Plater, Alan. *The Beiderbecke Affair.* London, 1985.

Porter, Lewis. *John Coltrane: His Life and Music.* Ann Arbor, Mich., 1998.

———. *Lester Young.* Boston, 1985.

———, ed. *A Lester Young Reader.* Washington, D.C., 1991.

Porter, Lewis, and Michael Ullman. *Jazz: From Its Origins to the Present.* Englewood Cliffs, N.J., 1993.

Porter, Roy, with David Keller. *There and Back.* Oxford, 1991.

Priestly, Brian. *Mingus: A Critical Biography.* New York, 1983.

Raeburn, Bruce Boyd. *New Orleans Style: The Awakening of American Scholarship and Its Cultural Implications.* Ph.D. dissertation, Tulane University, 1991.

Ramsey, Doug. *Jazz Matters.* Fayetteville, Ark., 1989.

Ramsey, Frederick Jr., and Charles Edward Smith. *Jazzmen: The Story of Hot Jazz Told in the Lives of the Men Who Created It.* New York, 1939.

Reisner, Robert, ed. *Bird: The Legend of Charlie Parker.* New York, 1975.

Rich, Alan. *The Simon and Schuster Listener's Guide to Jazz.* New York, 1980.

Riis, Thomas. *Just Before Jazz: Black Musical Theater in New York 1890 to 1915.* Washington, D.C., 1989.

Rivelli, Pauline, and Robert Levin. *Giants of Black Music.* New York, 1979.

Roberts, John Storm. *Black Music of Two Worlds.* New York, 1972.

Rose, Al. *I Remember Jazz: Six Decades Among the Great Jazz Men.* Baton Rouge, 1987.

———. *Storyville, New Orleans.* Tuscaloosa, Ala., 1974.

Rosenthal, David H. *Hard Bop: Jazz and Black Music, 1955–1965.* New York, 1992.

Rowland, Mark, and Tony Sherman, eds. *The Jazz Musician.* New York, 1994.

Royal, Marshal, with Claire P. Gordon. *Marshal Royal: Jazz Survivor.* London, 1996.

Russell, Ross. *Jazz Style in Kansas City and in the Southwest.* New York, 1997.

Sales, Grover. *Jazz: America's Classical Music.* New York, 1992.

Sanford, Herb. *Tommy and Jimmy: The Dorsey Years.* New York, 1972.

Schaefer, William John. *Brass Bands and New Orleans Jazz.* Baton Rouge, 1977.

Schuller, Gunther, *Early Jazz: Its Roots and Musical Development.* New York, 1986.

———. *The Swing Era.* New York, 1989.

Shadwick, Keith. *Gramophone Jazz Good CD Guide.* Middlesex, England, 1997.

Shapiro, Nat, and Nat Hentoff. *Hear Me Talkin' to Ya: The Story of Jazz as Told by the Men Who Made It.* New York, 1966.

———, eds. *The Jazz Makers.* New York, 1957.

Shaw, Arnold. *52nd Street: The Street of Jazz.* New York, 1971.

———. *Honkers and Shouters.* New York, 1978.

———. *The Jazz Age: Popular Music in the 1920s.* New York, 1987.

Shaw, Artie. *The Trouble with Cinderella: An Outline of Identity.* Santa Barbara, Calif., 1992.

Shipton, Alyn. *Groovin' High: The Life of Dizzy Gillespie.* New York, 1999.

Short, Bobby, with Robert Mackintosh. *Bobby Short: The Life and Times of a Saloon Singer.* New York, 1995.

Sidran, Ben. *Talking Jazz: An Oral History.* New York, 1995.

Silvester, Peter J. *A Left Hand Like God: A History of Boogie-Woogie Piano.* New York, 1988.

Simon, George T. *The Big Bands.* New York, 1981.

Simone, Nina. *I Put a Spell on You: The Autobiography of Nina Simone.* New York, 1993.

Siskind, Aaron. *Harlem Documents: Photographs 1932–1940.* Providence, R.I., 1981.

Škvorecký, Josef. *The Bass Saxophone.* New York, 1994.

Smith, Jay D., and Len Guttridge. *Jack Teagarden: The Story of a Jazz Maverick.* New York, 1988.

Smith, Willie the Lion. *Music on My Mind: The Memoirs of an American Pianist.* London, 1966.

Southern, Eileen. *The Music of Black Americans: A History.* New York, 1983.

Spellman, A. B. *Four Lives in the Bebop Business.* New York, 1966.

Starr, S. Frederick. *Red and Hot: The Fate of Jazz in the Soviet Union.* New York, 1994.

Stearns, Marshall. *The Story of Jazz.* London, 1982.

Stearns, Marshall, and Jean Stearns. *Jazz Dance: The Story of American Vernacular Dance.* New York, 1994.

Steed, Janna Tull. *Duke Ellington: A Spiritual Biography.* New York, 1999.

Stewart, Rex. *Boy Meets Horn.* Ann Arbor, Mich., 1994.

———. *Jazz Masters of the Thirties.* New York, 1972.

Stoddard, Tom. *Jazz on the Barbary Coast.* Berkeley, 1998.

Stokes, W. Royal. *The Jazz Scene: An Informal History from New Orleans to 1990.* New York, 1991.

———. *Swing Era New York: The Photographs of Charles Preston.* Philadelphia, 1994.

Storb, Ilse. *Louis Armstrong: The Definitive Biography.* New York, 1989.

Stovall, Tyler. *Paris Noir: African Americans in the City of Light.* New York, 1996.

Stowe, *David W. Swing Changes: Big Band Jazz in New Deal America.* Cambridge, 1994.

Stroff, Stephen M. *Discovering Great Jazz.* New York, 1993.

Sudhalter, Richard M. *Lost Chords: White Musicians and Their Contribution to Jazz, 1915–1945.* New York, 1999.

Sudhalter, Richard M., and Philip R. Evans. *Bix: Man and Legend.* New Rochelle, N.Y., 1974.

Swed, John F. *Space Is the Place: The Lives and Times of Sun Ra.* New York, 1997.

Tanenhaus, Sam. *Louis Armstrong.* Los Angeles, 1988.

Taylor, Arthur. *Notes and Tones.* New York, 1982.

Taylor, Frank C., and Gerald Cook. *Alberta Hunter: A Celebration in Blues.* New York, 1987.

Taylor, Jeffrey. *Earl Hines and Black Jazz Piano in Chicago, 1923–28.* Ph.D. dissertation, City University of New York, 1997.

Tibbetts, John C., ed. *Dvorak in America.* Portland, Ore., 1993.

Tinker, Edward Larocque. *Creole City: Its Past and Its People.* New York, 1953.

Tirro, Frank. *Jazz: A History.* New York, 1977.

Tucker, Mark. *Ellington: The Early Years.* Urbana, Ill., 1991.

———, ed. *The Duke Ellington Reader.* New York, 1993.

Turner, Frederick. *Remembering Song: Encounters with the New Orleans Jazz Tradition.* New York, 1982.

Ulanov, Barry. *Duke Ellington.* New York, 1975.

———. *A History of Jazz in America.* New York, 1952.

Vail, Ken. *Bird's Diary: The Life of Charlie Parker 1945–1955.* Surrey, Eng., 1996.

Van Rijn, Guido. *Roosevelt's Blues: African-American Blues and Gospel Songs on FDR.* Oxford, Miss., 1997.

Wade, Richard C., ed. *Hull House Maps and Papers: Residents of Hull House—A Presentation of Nationalities and Wages in a Congested District of Chicago.* New York, 1970.

Waldo, Terry. *This Is Ragtime.* New York, 1991.

Walker, Leo. *The Wonderful Era of the Great Dance Bands.* New York, 1990.

Walser, Robert, ed. *Keeping Time: Readings in Jazz History.* New York, 1999.

Watkins, Mel. *On the Real Side: Laughing, Lying and Signifying.* New York, 1994.

Weinstein, Norman C. *A Night in Tunisia: Imaginings of Africa in Jazz.* New York, 1992.

Wells, Dicky, and Stanley Dance. *The Night People: The Jazz Life of Dicky Wells.* Washington, D.C., 1991.

Whiteman, Paul, and Mary Margaret McBride. *Jazz.* New York, 1926.

Williams, Martin. *Jazz Changes.* New York, 1992.

———. *Jazz Heritage.* New York, 1985.

———. *Jazz in Its Time.* New York, 1989.

———. *Jazz Masters in Transition 1957–1969.* New York, 1970.

———. *Jazz Masters of New Orleans.* New York, 1967.

———. *The Jazz Tradition.* New York, 1993.

———, ed. *The Art of Jazz.* New York, 1980.

Wilmer, Valerie. *As Serious As Your Life: The Story of the New Jazz.* New York, 1992.

———. *Jazz People.* New York, 1977.

Wilson, Samuel, Jr. *Benjamin Henry Latrobe: Impressions Respecting New Orleans—Diary and Sketches 1818–1820.* New York, 1951.

Wilson, Teddy, with Arie Ligthart and Humphrey van Loo. *Teddy Wilson Talks Jazz.* London, 1996.

Woideck, Carl. *The Charlie Parker Companion: Six Decades of Commentary.* New York, 1998.

———. *Charlie Parker: His Music and Life.* Ann Arbor, Mich., 1996.

———. *The John Coltrane Companion: Five Decades of Commentary.* New York, 1998.

Zenfell, Martha Ellen. *New Orleans.* Boston, 1995.

Christian McBride

Lewis Nash

Geri Allen

Joshua Redman

Nicholas Payton

Marcus Roberts

Steve Coleman

TEXT PERMISSIONS

Louis Armstrong materials are reprinted here by kind permission of Oscar Cohen, President, Associated Booking Corporation, New York, N.Y., Sole and Exclusive Representative for
Louis Armstrong Educational Foundation, Inc.: David Gold, Phoebe Jacobs, Oscar Cohen
Louis Armstrong House and Archives: Michael Cogswell, Director
Louis Armstrong Estate

Grateful acknowledgment is made to the following for permission to reprint previously published material:

Amsterdam News: Column by Dan Burley (*Amsterdam News*, Nov. 23, 1940). Reprinted by permission of the *Amsterdam News.*

Jason Berry: Jason Berry interview with Danny Barker as found in *Louis Armstrong: An American Genius* by James Lincoln Collier, Oxford, 1983. Louis Armstrong Oral History Project, William Ransom Hogan Jazz Archive, Tulane University, New Orleans, LA. Reprinted by permission of Jason Berry.

Citadel Press: Excerpts from *Really the Blues* by Mezz Mezzrow and Bernard Wolfe (published by Citadel Press, an imprint of Kensington Publishing Corp.), copyright © 1946 by Mezz Mezzrow and Bernard Wolfe. Reprinted by permission of Citadel Press.

Condé Nast Publications, Inc.: Excerpts from "The Hot Bach" by Richard O. Boyer (*The New Yorker*, 6/24/1944 & 7/1/1944), copyright © 1944 by The New Yorker Magazine, Inc. All rights reserved. Reprinted by permission of Condé Nast Publications, Inc.

Doubleday: Excerpts from *To Be or Not to Bop* by Dizzy Gillespie, copyright © 1979 by John Birks Gillespie and Wilmot Alfred Fraser. Reprinted by permission of Doubleday, a division of Random House, Inc.

Doubleday and CMG Worldwide: Excerpts from *Music Is My Mistress* by Duke Ellington, copyright © 1973 by Duke Ellington, Inc. UK and British Commonwealth rights by TM Estate of Duke Ellington under license by CMG Worldwide, Inc. Reprinted by permission of Doubleday, a division of Random House, Inc., and TM Estate of Duke Ellington under license by CMG Worldwide, Inc.

The Estate of John Hammond: Excerpts from *John Hammond on Record* by John Hammond (Ridge Press, 1977; Penguin Books, 1981), copyright © Estate of John

ILLUSTRATION CREDITS

Hammond. Reprinted by permission of the Estate of John Hammond.

Frank Music Corp.: Excerpt from "Poor Man's Blues" by Bessie Smith, copyright © 1930, copyright renewed 1958 by Frank Music Corp. Reprinted by permission of Frank Music Corp., administered by Hal Leonard Corporation.

Hill and Wang and Mark Paterson and Associates: Excerpts from *Treat It Gentle* by Sidney Bechet, copyright © 1960 by Twayne Publishers and Cassell & Company, Ltd. Reprinted by permission of Hill and Wang, a division of Farrar, Straus and Giroux, LLC and Mark Paterson and Associates on behalf of the Estate of Sidney Bechet.

Alan Lomax: Excerpts from *Mister Jelly Roll: The Fortunes of Jelly Roll Morton, New Orleans Creole and Inventor of Jazz* by Alan Lomax (Revised and updated paperback edition forthcoming from University of California Press, Berkeley, CA, in 2001). Reprinted by permission of Alan Lomax.

McIntosh & Otis, Inc.: Excerpts from *We Called It Music* by Eddie Condon (Holt, Rinehart and Winston, 1947), copyright © 1947 by Eddie Condon. Reprinted by permission of McIntosh & Otis, Inc.

Macmillan Press Ltd.: Excerpts from *A Life in Jazz* by Danny Barker, edited by Alyn Shipton. Reprinted courtesy of Macmillan Press Ltd., Basingstoke.

The New York Times: Excerpt from "Review of Louis Armstrong" by Irving Kolodin (*New York Times*, Feb. 1, 1933), copyright © 1933 by the New York Times Co. Reprinted by permission by *The New York Times*.

Random House, Inc.: Excerpt from *Sleepless Nights* by Elizabeth Hardwick, copyright © 1979 by Elizabeth Hardwick. Reprinted by permission of Random House, Inc.

Random House, Inc., and William Morris Agency, Inc.: Excerpts from *Shadow and Act* by Ralph Ellison, copyright © 1953, 1964, copyright renewed 1981, 1992 by Ralph Ellison. Rights in the British Commonwealth from *The Collected Essays of Ralph Ellison* (Modern Library, 1995). Reprinted by permission of Random House, Inc., and William Morris Agency, Inc. on behalf of the author.

Razaf Music: Four-stanza verse by Andy Razaf (published in the *New York Amsterdam News*, 1932). All rights reserved. Reprinted by permission of Razaf Music, care of The Songwriters Guild of America.

Scribner: Excerpts from *Jazz Masters of the Thirties* by Rex Stewart, copyright © 1972 by the Estate of Rex W. Stewart. Reprinted by permission of Scribner, a division of Simon & Schuster.

Simon & Schuster: Excerpts from *Miles: The Autobiography* by Miles Davis and Quincy Troupe, copyright © 1989 by Miles Davis. Reprinted by permission of Simon & Schuster.

Smithsonian Institution Press: Excerpts from *The Night People* by Dickey Wells as told to Stanley Dance, published by the Smithsonian Institution Press, Washington, D.C.; copyright © 1991. Reprinted by permission of the Smithsonian Institution Press.

Stackpole Books: Excerpts from *The Kingdom of Swing* by Benny Goodman with Irving Kolodin (Stackpole & Sons, New York, 1939). Reprinted courtesy of Stackpole Books.

University of California Press: Excerpts from *Pops Foster: The Autobiography of a New Orleans Jazzman as Told to Tom Stoddard* by George Foster, copyright © 1971 by the Regents of the University of California. Reprinted by permission of the University of California Press.

University of South Carolina Press: Four telegrams from Charlie Parker to Chan Parker taken from *My Life in E-Flat* by Chan Parker, copyright © 1999 by the University of South Carolina. Reprinted by permission of the University of South Carolina Press.

The Wylie Agency, Inc.: Excerpts from *Stomping the Blues* by Albert Murray, copyright © 1976 by Albert Murray. Reprinted by permission of The Wylie Agency, Inc.

The Yale Law Journal: Excerpt from "My World with Louis Armstrong" by Charles L. Black (originally published in the *Yale Review, 1969*, reprinted in *The Yale Law Journal,* Vol. 95, pp. 1595–1600, 1986). Reprinted by permission of The Yale Law Journal Company and William S. Hein Company.

Yale University Press: Excerpts from *Latrobe's View of America* by Edward C. Carter II, et al., editors. Copyright © 1985 by Yale University. Reprinted by permission of Yale University Press.

Each credit lists source, negative number (where one exists), and photographer/artist (where one is known). When there is more than one credit for a page the images will be listed clockwise from top left.

PHOTOGRAPHER & INSTITUTION ABBREVIATIONS

ABC	Anthony Barboza Collection
AP	Archive Photos
BP	Photograph by Bob Parent
CI	Corbis Images, Inc.
CP	Photograph by Charles Peterson
CS	Photograph by Chuck Stewart
DSC	Duncan P. Schiedt Collection
FDC	Frank Driggs Collection
HJA	Hogan Jazz Archive, Tulane University
HL	Photograph by Herman Leonard
HNC	Historic New Orleans Collection
IJS	Institute of Jazz Studies
KS	Photograph by Kathy Sloane
KWC	Ken Whitten Collection
LAH	Louis Armstrong House and Archives
LOC	Prints and Photographs Division, The Library of Congress
LSM	Louisiana State Museum
LT	Photograph by Lee Tanner
MI	Mosaic Images; Photograph by Francis Wolff
MJH	Photography by Milton J. Hinton
NMA	Archives Center, National Museum of American History, Smithsonian Institution
NYPL-H	Humanities and Social Science Library, The New York Public Library
NYPL-P	Performing Arts Library, The New York Public Library
NYPL-S	Schomberg Center for Research in Black Culture, The New York Public Library
PH	Photograph by Paul J. Hoeffler
SM	SONY Music Archives; Photograph by Don Huntstein
WC	William Claxton
WG	Photograph by William Gottlieb

Archival set-up photography by Paul H. Christensen and Chris Leary

Jazz film picture research by Shola Lynch

Picture coordination by Kara Mickley.

ENDPAPERS: WG **FRONTMATTER:** i NMA ii–iii: BP iv: BP vi: FDC viii: FDC xi: Bill Trumbauer xii: CS xiii: HL xiv: HL xv: HL xvi–xvii: HL xviii: FDC xix: CP xx–xxi: CP

CHAPTER ONE: GUMBO xxii–P 1: LSM 2: LSM #372 Photograph by George Francois Mugnier 3: LSM Rowles 1979.120.244 4–5: HNC 6: Yale–Beinecke Rare Book Library UNCAT–JWJ #13MS.59; Courtesy Eugene Groves 7: LSM Photograph by George Francois Mugnier 8: Museum of the City of New York 32.483 ab; Museum of the City of New York Theater Collection #32.340.36 9: The Brown Brothers–TH95 10: CI#PG8587 11: IJS; FDC 12–13: HJA 14: © Joshua Mann Pailet, A Gallery for Fine Photography; LSM Photograph by George Francois Mugnier 15: FDC 17: LSM 1978.118(B)991 18: HJA; HJA 19: LSM #1978.118(B)5733; FDC 20: FDC 21: HJA 23: LSM #1978.118(B)532 24: NYPL-S #SC-CN-80-0094; FDC; David A. Jasen Archive; David A. Jasen Archive 25: FDC 26: HNC 27: LSM #1978.118(B)886 29: LSM #1978.118(B)883 30: FDC 31: FDC 32–33: HJA 35: LSM #1978.118(B)533

CHAPTER TWO: THE GIFT 36–37: FDC 38: HJA 39: FDC 40: Courtesy Mollyne Karnofsky 41: FDC 42: HJA 43: HJA 44–45: LSM#1978.118(B)675 46: HNC 47: FDC 49: NYPL-S #SC-CN-98-0172; FDC; NMA 50: Historical Society of Washington, DC #HSW 5878 51: Historical Society of Washington, DC #CHS 5718A 52–53: LSM #1978.118(B)958 54: FDC; FDC 56: FDC 57: Ladies Home Journal 12/1914 © Meredith Publishing Group 58–59:

Maryland Historical Society MS2800 Box 72 59: FDC 60–61: FDC; HJA

CHAPTER THREE: THE JAZZ AGE
62–63: CI # U174082INP>2 64: The RCA Records Label of BMG Entertainment 65: FDC; Yale–Music Library, Dance Collection Bands-M 66: Moorland-Spingarn Research Center, Reid Badger Collection. 67: Maryland Historical Society #Z24.1575 68: National Archives III-SC 20417 69: National Archives #38760 WW1 box 284 71: FDC; FDC 72: DSC #H-4630 73: FDC 74–75: LSM #1979.1(2)77: FDC; Iowa State Historical Society #PA 183—Crane Collection 78: FDC 80: FDC 81: FDC 82: DSC #H-2579 83: FDC 84: UMI / The Chicago Defender Newspaper 85: FDC 86: FDC 87: FDC 88: DSC #H-1001 89: Courtesy Chris Albertson; ABC 90: IJS; Universal Music Enterprises/Brunswick; NYPL–H #XMG-767-393 91: FDC; Culver Pictures, Inc. #PH0001CP001141 92: Courtesy Chris Albertson 93: FDC 94: IJS/Melrose Publishing 95: DSC #H595; Collection of Franz Jantzen 96–97: FDC 97: DSC #RI-34 98: DSC #H-6 99: FDC 100: FDC 102–103: DSC #H2580 104: Phil Pospychala; DSC 105: FDC 107: IJS 108: FDC; IJS 109: FDC; David A. Jasen Archive 110–111: AP 113: FDC 114: FDC; DSC #H-600 115: FDC

INTERVIEW WITH WYNTON MARSALIS Photographs by Frank Stewart

CHAPTER FOUR: OUR LANGUAGE
122–123: FDC 124: DSC 125: DSC #H2818; DSC #H2818A 126–127: FDC 128: FDC 129: FDC 130: FDC 131: LSM #T5. 1996.80 132: Chicago Historical Society #ICHi 01436 133: FDC; Chicago Historical Society #894 134: University of Illinois JAMC #894 135: DSC #H-3878 137: LSM #1978.118(B).542; The RCA Records Label of BMG Entertainment 138: FDC 139: FDC 140: FDC 142: FDC 143: FDC 145: CI 146–147: FDC 148: FDC; DSC #H3640 149: FDC 150–151: FDC 152: FDC 153: Courtesy Chris Albertson 154: DSC 155: DSC #H345 156: Poster Photo Archives, Posters Please Inc., NY; Roger-Viollet 157: FDC 158: LAH 159: FDC 160: Chicago Historical Society #ICHi-14428; Yale Music Library 161: IJS 162: Courtesy Artie Shaw 163: DSC 164–5: FDC 166: LSM 167: FDC 168: David A. Jasen Archive 169: Courtesy Chris Albertson 170: UMI/Davenport Daily Democrat 170–171: FDC

CHAPTER FIVE: HARD, HARD TIMES
172–173: DSC #H3226 174: NYPL–S FSA Collection–Louisiana 175: FDC 176: Courtesy Dorothy Miller 177: Elizabeth Campbell Rollins, Map by E. Simms Campbell; FDC 178: FDC; FDC 179: NYPL–S #SC-CN-81-0009 180: DSC# H-465 181: FDC 183: FDC 184: FDC 185: LAH 186: FDC; LAH; FDC 187: HNC; FDC; LSM 188: FDC 189: FDC 191: FDC 193: FDC 194: Kansas City Museum #PC35:435 195: FDC; DSC 196: Special Collections Department, Kansas City, Missouri Public Library 197: Kansas City Museum Association 199: FDC 200: FDC; FDC 201: FDC 203: DSC #W-31; DSC #W-28 204: DSC #H-3158 206: FDC 207: FDC 208–209: Courtesy James T. Maher 210: Courtesy James T. Maher 211: NMA Ruth Ellington Collection 415 Box 9 Folder 1 212: LAH #photo 1-1/49 213: FDC 214: FDC 215: LAH 216: Miles Educational Film Productions 217: Photograph by Cornell Capa 218: NYPL–S #SC-CN-98-0040; NYPL–P Music #166a(c4010) Photograph by Otto Hess; NYPL–P Music #166C(c4012) Photograph by Otto Hess 219: Photograph by Cornell Capa 220: IJS 222–223: FDC

ESSAY BY DAN MORGENSTERN 225: WG 226: WG 229: DSC 231: WG

CHAPTER SIX:THE VELOCITY OF CELEBRATION 232–233: NYPL–S #SC-CNN-98-0041 By Otto Hess 234: CI #U1036094INP>5 235: FDC 236: NYPL–P Music #2a B1780 By Otto Hess 237: FDC 238–239: AP 241: FDC 242: FDC; DSC 243: DSC; DSC #H-1448a; FDC 244: DSC #H-3982; FDC; FDC 245: FDC; CP 246: FDC 248: American Jazz Museum #12.42.OP10 249: FDC 250: FDC 251: MJH; MJH; LOC #USZ62-120259 253: The New York Daily News 254: CI # U833074INP>8 255: FDC 256: FDC 258: KWC 259: FDC 260–261: All photos by Henry Ries 262: FDC 264: CP 265: CP 266: CP 267: FDC 268: CS 270: CP 271: FDC 273: FDC 274–275: LAH: photo# 3 9/45 276 LAH photo# 3 9/50; LAH photo# 3 9/48; LAH photo# 3 9/49 277: LAH 278: KWC 279: FDC

CHAPTER SEVEN: DEDICATED TO CHAOS 280–281: National Archives III-SC-191838 282: LOC #USF34-29475-D 283: FDC 285: CP 286: HL 287: HL 288–89: FDC 290: FDC 292:

HL 292: FDC 293: Courtesy of Jeanie Bryson 294: MJH 295: Courtesy of Patricia Willard 297: University of Missouri, Dave E. Dexter Collection 298: "That's Jazz" Exhibition Catalogue 1988 Darmstadt Germany Pg. 390 299: WG; WG 300: FDC; FDC; RCA Records Label of BMG Entertainment; AP 301: FDC 302: National Archives #NWDNS-208-NP-8T-2 303: (both): Dave Brubeck Collection, Holt-Atherton Special Collections, The University of the Pacific, Stockton, CA. 304: CI #U726565ACME>1 306: FDC 307: FDC 309: NYPL–S #SC-CN-98-0244 310: NYPL–P Music #19c [D1745] Photo by Otto Hess 311: IJS 312–313: LOC #LC-USW-3-23967-D Photo by Gordon Parks 314: LAH Photo #5–15/12 315: LAH 316–317: FDC 317: The New York Daily News 318: CP 319: FDC 321: Courtesy Marvin Christian Collection #N-3-334 Photo by William Preston Mayfield 322: FDC 323: Savoy Records

ESSAY BY GERALD EARLY 327: WG 328: FDC 330–331: LT

CHAPTER EIGHT: RISK 332–333: FDC 334:Warner Special Products/Musicraft Records 335: WG 337: LAH Scrapbook #4 across from #873; LAH Snaps #3 3/68; LAH Snaps 3 3/33 338: HNC 339: CP 340: WG 341: FDC 343: LOC LC-USF-34-52589-D Photo by Marion Post Wolcott 344: FDC 345: HL 346: FDC 348: Life Magazine © Time Inc.Photographs by Allan Grant 348: Michael Ochs Archives 349: FDC; HL 350: HL 351: MI 352–353: HL 354: LSM #1978.118(B)179 354: LAH 355: FDC 355: Photograph by Ralph Ginzburg 356: DSC #H-3780 357: HL 359: Photograph by Herb Snitzer

ESSAY BY GARY GIDDINS 361: ABC 362: Photograph by Enid Farber 364: Photograph by Enid Farber 365: KS; KS 367: ABC

CHAPTER NINE: THE ADVENTURE 368–369: BP 370: PH 371: HL 373: ABC; FDC 374: HL 375: FDC 376: CS 377: FDC 378: FDC 379: BP 380: © 1954 Time Inc. 381: BP 382: Photograph by W. Eugene Smith 383: MI 384–385: MI 386: HL 387: HL 388: Fantasy Records/Prestige 389: HL 390: SM 391: MI 393: AP 395: LAH 396: HL 398–399: BP 399: MI; HL; HL 400: PH; BP; PH 401: PH; PH 402: WC 404: BP 405: SM #1169C3#22 406: Courtesy

Val Wilmer Collection. Photograph by Daniel Filipacchi 407: SM #1464 C1 #23A 408: SM #1675 C2 #11; SONY Music/Columbia Records #CL 1041; SONY Music/ Columbia Records #CL 466312 409: WC 410–411: WC 412: HL 413: Universal Music Enterprises/Verve MGV 4013 414: KS 415: WC 416: WC 417: BP

ESSAY BY STANLEY CROUCH 419: KS 421: Photograph by Carol Friedman 422: Photograph by Carol Friedman 425: ABC

CHAPTER TEN: A MASTERPIECE BY MIDNIGHT 426–427: Photograph by Bruce Polonsky 428: FDC 429: Life Magazine © Time Inc. Photograph by John Loengard 430: CI #U1436829A>8 431: HL 432–433: LT 434: WC 435: CS 436: Universal Music Enterprises/Kapp Records 437: LT 438: SMA Photograph by Vernon Smith 438: Candid Records 79002 439: CS 440: Universal Music Enterprises/Impulse Records A-9124 440: Universal Music Enterprises/Impulse Records A-42 441: Photograph by Bengt H. Malmqvist 442: NMA #301 Box #6 Folder 2 443: Photograph by Herb Snitzer 444: KS 445: SONY Music/Columbia Records #GP 26 446: ABC 446–447: SMA Photograph by Urve Kuusik C11025 6/73 448: SONY Music/Columbia Records #468209 448: SONY Music/ Columbia Records #31067 449: HL 450: DSC 451: LAH 452: CI #U1709660>1 452: The New York Daily News #5 by00k6m.jpg 454: AP 455: NMA Ruth Ellington Collection 456: MI 457: ABC 458: SONY Music/ Columbia Records #C2K46824 459: Ellis & Dolores Marsalis 460–461: Photograph by Nubar Alexanian

Backmatter 462–487: Photographs by Jimmy Katz

Permission granted by The Estate of Duke Ellington under License by CMG Worldwide Inc.

Louis Armstrong materials are reprinted here by kind permission of Oscar Cohen, President, Associated Booking Corporation, New York, N.Y., Sole and Exclusive Representative for

Louis Armstrong Educational Foundation, Inc.: David Gold, Phoebe Jacobs, Oscar Cohen

Louis Armstrong House and Archives: Michael Cogswell, Director

Louis Armstrong Estate

FILM CREDITS

A Film By
KEN BURNS
Directed By
KEN BURNS
Written By
GEOFFREY C. WARD
Produced By
KEN BURNS
LYNN NOVICK
Co-Producers
PETER MILLER
VICTORIA GOHL
Supervising Film Editor
PAUL BARNES
Episode Editors
PAUL BARNES
SANDRA MARIE CHRISTIE
LEWIS ERSKINE
ERIK EWERS
SARAH E. HILL
CRAIG MELLISH
SHANNON ROBARDS
TRICIA REIDY
AARON VEGA
Narrated By
KEITH DAVID
Cinematography
BUDDY SQUIRES
KEN BURNS
Associate Producers
SARAH BOTSTEIN
NATALIE BULLOCK BROWN
SHOLA LYNCH
Consulting Producer
MADISON DAVIS LACY
Senior Creative Consultant
WYNTON MARSALIS
Senior Advisor
DAN MORGENSTERN
Board of Advisors
MICHAEL CHERTOK
JAMES LINCOLN COLLIER
STANLEY CROUCH
MICHAEL CUSCUNA
DAYTON DUNCAN
JULIE DUNFEY
GERALD EARLY
TOM EVERED
GARY GIDDINS

MATT GLASER
JOANNA GRONING
ERIC HOBSBAWM
ROBIN D. G. KELLEY
CHARLIE LOURIE
ALLEN LOWE
ALBERT MURRAY
DANIEL OKRENT
BRUCE BOYD RAEBURN
LOREN SCHOENBERG
GUNTHER SCHULLER
MARGARET WASHINGTON
Voices
ADAM ARKIN
VERNEL BAGNERIS
PHILIP BOSCO
TOM BOWER
MATTHEW BRODERICK
HODDING CARTER III
KEVIN CONWAY
HARRY CONNICK, JR.
BRUCE DAVISON
ANN DUQUESNAY
CHARLES DURNING
KEITH LEE GRANT
ERIC GEORGE
DEREK JACOBI
SAMUEL L. JACKSON
CHERRY JONES
ANTHONY LAPAGLIA
ERIQ LASALLE
DELROY LINDO
AMY MADIGAN
WENDY MAKKENA
JOE MORTON
JAMES NAUGHTON
KEVIN RAMSEY
STUDS TERKEL
COURTNEY B. VANCE
Post-Production Coordinators
CRAIG MELLISH
AARON VEGA
Associate Editors
BARNARD D. JAFFIER
DAVE MAST
Assistant Editors
DAVID CHRISTIAN FAULKNER
MATTHEW L. McGRAIL
KEVIN J. MERCIER

DAVID McMAHON
THOR K. NEURIETER
MEG ANNE SCHINDLER
Editing Assistant in Charge of Narration
TIM CLARK
Production Associate
KARA E. MICKLEY
Additional Cinematography
STEPHEN McCARTHY
ALLEN MOORE
Assistant Camera
SCOTT D. CARRITHERS
ELIZABETH DORY
ANNE MARIE FENDRICK
DAVID A. FORD
ANNE GWYNN
ROGER HAYDOCK
MARK HERSHFELD
JUDY HOFFMAN
ANTONIO ROSSI
ANTHONY SAVINI
FOREST THURMAN
WADE WHITLEY
ANDREW YARME
Sound Recording
MARC DICHTER
ERIK EWERS
CHARLES B. FITZPATRICK
JEFF KENTON
STACEY COHEN MAITRE
BRUCE PERLMAN
RICHARD POOLER
MARK ROY
WILLIAM SAROKIN
GEORGE SHAFNACKER
BARRY SPILLMAN
JOHN ZECCA
Chief Financial Officer
BRENDA HEATH
Coordinating Producer
PAM TUBRIDY BAUCOM
Administrative Assistants
SUSAN YEATON BUTLER
PATTY LAWLOR
Supervising Sound Editor
IRA SPIEGEL

Dialogue Editors
MARLENA GRZASLEWICZ
DAN KORINTUS
Effects Editor
BRUCE KITZMEYER
Music Editors
JENNIFER DUNNINGTON
JACOB RIBICOFF
Assistant Sound Editors
MARIUSZ GLABINSKI
CONOR GUY
Re-Recording Mixers
LEE DICHTER
DOMINICK TAVELLA
SOUND ONE
Additional Music
WYNTON MARSALIS
VICTOR GOINES
WYCLIFFE GORDON
DELFEAYO MARSALIS
HERLIN RILEY
DON VAPPIE
RODNEY WHITTAKER
TEESE GOHL
THE 2ND SOUTH CAROLINA
   STRING BAND
THE OLD TOWNE BRASS BAND
Animation Stand Photography
THE FRAME SHOP
Edward Joyce and
   Edward Searles
Archival Still Photography
PAUL H. CHRISTENSEN
Digital Image Restoration
CHRIS LEARY
Voice-Over Recording
A&J RECORDING STUDIOS
Lou Verrico
Negative Matching
NOELLE PENRAAT
Title Design
CHURCH & MAIN, INC.
JAMES MADDEN
Color
DUART FILM LABS
Video Post-Production
THE TAPE HOUSE/NEW YORK

Spirit Data Cine Film Transfer
JOHN J. DOWDELL III
Archival Film Transfers
RICK PAGLIAROLI
On-Line Editors
JOE SALLERES
GEORGE T. BUNCE
Film Editing Equipment
THE BOSTON CONNECTION
Dwight Cody
Legal Services
ROBERT N. GOLD
THOMAS R. LEVY
National Publicity
DAN KLORES ASSOCIATES

A Production of Florentine
Films and WETA, TV
in Association with BBC

A General Motors Mark of
Excellence Presentation

Funding Provided by
General Motors
PBS
Park Foundation
The Corporation for Public
   Broadcasting
The Pew Charitable Trusts
The Doris Duke Charitable
   Foundation
Louisiana Department of Cul-
   ture, Recreation and
   Tourism
The National Endowment for
   the Humanities
The Arthur Vining Davis
   Foundations
The John D. and Catherine T.
   MacArthur Foundation
The Reva and David Logan
   Foundation
The National Endowment for
   the Arts
Helen and Peter Bing

A NOTE ABOUT THE AUTHORS

GEOFFREY C. WARD, historian, screen-writer, and former editor of *American Heritage,* is the coauthor of *Not for Our-selves Alone, The Civil War,* and *Base-ball* and principal writer of the television series on which they were based. He is also the author of *The West* and prin-cipal writer of the script for that series, and has written seven other books, in-cluding *A First-Class Temperament: The Emergence of Franklin Roosevelt,* which won the 1989 National Book Critics Cir-cle Award for biography and the 1990 Francis Parkman Prize from the Soci-ety of American Historians. He is cur-rently at work on a new book, *A Disposition to Be Rich.*

KEN BURNS, director and producer of *Jazz,* has been making award-winning documentary films for more than twenty years. He was director of the landmark PBS series *The Civil War* and *Baseball* and executive producer of *The West.* His other films include the Academy Award–nominated *Brooklyn Bridge; The Shakers; The Statue of Liberty* (also nominated for an Oscar); *Huey Long; Thomas Hart Benton; The Congress; Empire of the Air; Jefferson; Lewis & Clark; Frank Lloyd Wright;* and, most recently, the acclaimed *Not for Ourselves Alone: The Story of Elizabeth Cady Stanton and Susan B. Anthony.* He is currently working on a film biography of Mark Twain.

A NOTE ON THE TYPE

This book was set in Centennial, designed by Adrian Frutiger on com-mission from the Linotype company to mark its one hundredth anniversary in 1986.

Adrian Frutiger was born in Inter-laken, Switzerland, in 1928 and stud-ied type design there and at the Kunstgewerbeschule in Zurich. In 1953 he moved to Paris, where he joined Deberny et Peignot as a member of the design staff. Frutiger has designed numerous typefaces of world renown, most notably the phenomenally suc-cessful Univers.

Composed by North Market Street Graphics, Lancaster, Pennsylvania

Printed and bound by R. R. Donnelley & Sons, Willard, Ohio

Designed by Wendy Byrne